VANCOUVER BEST PLACES®

The most discriminating guide to
Vancouver's restaurants, shops, hotels,
nightlife, arts, sights, and outings

Edited by Kasey Wilson

SASQUATCH BOOKS
SEATTLE

RAINCOAST BOOKS
Vancouver

Printed in the United States
Distributed in the United States by Sasquatch Books
Distributed in Canada by Raincoast Book Distribution Ltd.

Second edition published in 1997.

Library of Congress Cataloging in Publication Data

Vancouver best places : the most discriminating guide to Vancouver's restaurants,
   shops, hotels, nightlife, sights, and outings / edited by Kasey Wilson.
                      p.   cm. — (The best places destination guides)
            Includes index.
            ISBN 1-57061-091-6
            1. Vancouver (B.C.) —Guidebooks. I. Wilson, Kasey, 1944- .
      II. Series.
      F1089.5.V22V355 1997
      917.11'33044—dc21   96-53855
                                                           CIP

Canadian Cataloguing in Publication Data

Wilson, Kasey, 1944-
      Vancouver best places
      (Best places)
      ISBN 1-55192-052-2
      1. Vancouver (B.C.)--Guidebooks. I. Irving, Stephanie, 1962-
      II. Title. III. Series.
      FC3847.18.W56 1997   917.11'33044   C96-910567-3
      F1089.5.V22W56 1997

Cover illustration by Nick Gaetano
Cover design by Karen Schober
Interior illustrations by Jerry Nelson
Interior design by Lynne Faulk
Map by David Berger
Composition by Kate Basart

The Best Places® guidebooks have been published continuously since 1975. Our evaluations are based on numerous reports from locals and travelling inspectors. Final judgements are made by the editor. Readers are advised that places listed in previous editions may have closed or changed management, or are no longer recommended by this series. Reviews in this edition are based on information available at press time and are subject to change. The editors welcome information conveyed by users of this book, as long as they have no financial connection with the establishment concerned. A report form is provided at the end of the book.

Published in the United States by:
Sasquatch Books, 615 Second Avenue, Suite 260, Seattle, WA 98104, (206) 467-4300
e-mail: books@sasquatchbooks.com   http://www.sasquatchbooks.com
Published in Canada by:
Raincoast Books, 8680 Cambie Street, Vancouver, BC V6P 6M9, (604) 323-7100
e-mail: info@raincoast.com

CONTENTS

Acknowledgements

The real people behind *Vancouver Best Places* are not only the lucky contributors who eat, shop, and travel—but also our readers who have alerted us to their favorite Vancouver finds. True, Best Places® inspectors (who always review anonymously, and who never accept any freebies) are the ones who decide what is best about our city, but not before taking into consideration comments from myriad regional spies and sources. As the most discriminating and evaluative guide to British Columbia's most vibrant metropolis heads to the printer, we'd like to thank everyone who ever wrote, called, faxed or e-mailed us a suggestion.

In particular, we'd like to give an extra star to the intrepid reviewers who scoured Vancouver from top to bottom, ferreting out the best places for you to dine, sleep, shop, dance, hike, explore, or just sip some tea with a good friend: Scott Barratt, Pat Fraser, Anthony Gismondi, Liz Grant, Sandra Hainle, Jason Jones, Deanna Krushinsky, Mark Laba, Martin Laba, Susan MacDonald, Lynne McNamara, Kerry McPhedran, Bob Mackin, Stevie Mitchell, Ray Müller, Angela Murrills, Tim Pawsey, Kim Parish, Eve Rockett, Shannon Rupp, Joanne Sasvari, Steven Threndyle, Elizabeth Wilson, and Stephen Wong. In addition, a special thanks for the expertise and fearless pen of poet/artist Mark Laba.

But a book is not made by writers alone. Another round of applause is due for all the dedicated people who worked in the trenches: assistant editor extraordinaire Meghan Heffernan, copy editor Carolyn Bateman, and proofreader Joanne Richardson. Finally, I want to thank the publishers on both sides of the border, Sasquatch Books in Seattle and Raincoast Books in Vancouver: an author never had better friends.

—*Kasey Wilson*

Introduction

Vancouver is a city of magical contradictions. From rough-and-tumble Hastings Street, where timeworn brickwork still exudes a wild, beer-for-a-dime seaport-town atmosphere, to trendy Robson Street, with Japanese noodle houses that look like something out of *Blade Runner*. Lotus land, la-la land, supernatural, astrological, New Age, old age, every age—it all culminates in this city nestled between mountains and ocean.

Vancouver is the end of the road. People come here to warm up and chill out. With the mild climate, there's always something to do out-of-doors: skiing, golfing—we enjoy raising hackles by bragging about doing both in the same day—hiking, whale watching, windsurfing. Where else will you see senior citizens in their Gore-Tex warrior-wear zipping by on Rollerblades and mountain bikes? Leisure is where our real living goes on.

When we're not zipping around, you'll find our bums in seats. Along with an excellent opera company, symphony, ballet and theatre, you'll also find music, dance, art, performance, and film in uniquely Vancouver guises: the Recital Society, bringing in soon-to-be stars; the Kiss Project, featuring new and innovative local dance; the unpretentious artist-run galleries, committed to pushing the boundaries of art and promoting local talent; or the Folk Music Festival, when world music calls Vancouver home for one blissful weekend every year.

Hardly anybody is from Vancouver, and that fact is reflected in its lively neighbourhoods. A walk through Chinatown, the second-largest in North America, transports you across the Pacific. And that's merely the beginning. A huge influx from all points east (or west, to Vancouverites), has created outposts of Thai, Vietnamese, Malaysian and East Indian cultures that dot the city. You can take a virtual gastronomic tour through the Orient without leaving town. Fragments of Europe remain, too. Board the #20 bus up to Commercial Drive, fondly called "The Drive", where *Details* magazine meets Little Italy and the ultra-hip exist side-by-side with the old European in a surreal smorgasbord of punk and pasta.

Simple pleasures and a relaxed frame of mind are the status quo. We love to eat—and especially to eat out—and we can afford to be choosy. Our culinary standards are high, but we're not stuffy. Here, you can go upscale and dine on cutting-edge Pacific Rim cuisine, or you can kick back with a fresh-caught barbecued salmon and locally-brewed beer. In either case, a tie is not compulsory.

What's the secret ingredient to this place? Maybe it's that we don't take ourselves too seriously. Most of us use phrases like "world class" only in verbal quotation marks. Maybe it's those big mountains that form our horizons. Here, in one of the oldest human habitations in North America, what we create is still less impressive than what nature has given us. And the myths of the Raven, the Bear and the Whale—the stories the Native peoples have always told—are still woven into the landscape. In Vancouver, mystery, like magic, abounds.

—*Kasey Wilson*
Vancouver

How to Use This Book

This is a rare city guidebook, as candid and frank as it is informative and trustworthy. It is written by and for locals, but visitors will find it just as valuable. Best Places® reviewers do not identify themselves when they review an establishment, and they accept no free meals, accommodations, or any other services. These books have no sponsors or advertisers.

Star Rating System We rate restaurants and lodgings on a scale of zero-to-four stars (with half stars in between), based on uniqueness, enjoyability, loyalty of local clientele, excellence of cooking, performance measured against the place's goals, cleanliness, and professionalism of service. *All listings are recommended, even those with no stars.*

★★★★ The very best in the region

★★★ Distinguished, many outstanding features

★★ Some wonderful qualities

★ A good place

[no stars] Worth knowing about, if nearby

[unrated] New or undergoing major changes

Price Range When prices range between two categories (for example, moderate to expensive), the lower one is given. Call ahead to verify, as prices are subject to change. All prices are in Canadian dollars.

$$$ Expensive (more than $90 for dinner for two; more than $150 for lodgings for two)

$$ Moderate (between expensive and inexpensive)

$ Inexpensive (less than $35 for dinner for two; less than $65 for lodgings for two)

Cheques and Credit Cards Most establishments that accept cheques require a major credit card for identification. American Express is abbreviated as AE, Diners Club as DC, Discover as DIS, Enroute as E, Japanese Credit Card as JCV, MasterCard as MC, Visa as V.

Addresses All listings are in Vancouver unless indicated otherwise. If an establishment has two Vancouver-area locations, we list both addresses; if there are more than two, we list the original, downtown, or recommended branch, followed by the words "and branches". Website and e-mail addresses are indicated in a few listings where we felt they would be particularly useful.

Phone Numbers All calls are local from Vancouver (area code 604), except where indicated. In October 1996, a new area code, 250, was introduced; it affects Vancouver Island and many of the smaller islands as well as areas well north of Vancouver. Telephone numbers preceded by this area code are long distance from Vancouver.

Map Indicators The letter-and-number code listed with the basic facts for many of the establishments in the book (usually after each phone number) refers to the coordinates on the fold-out map included in this book. Letters A—M refer to the Greater Vancouver map while letters N—Z refer to the downtown Vancouver map. If an establishment does not have this code listed, it means that its location falls beyond the boundaries of these maps.

Restaurants Our reviews are based on information that was accurate at press time. In the inconstant restaurant business, chefs and serving staff may move from one establishment to another. A restaurant's menu may alter, reflecting the season's bounty, the latest dining trend, or a change in chef or ownership. These variables (for better or worse) may affect quality and consistency.

Lodgings Many hotels and other lodgings fill up quickly due to the influx of tourists (in summer) and business-folk (year-round). It is wise to make reservations as far in advance as possible. Some B&Bs have two-night minimum-stay requirements and particular cancellation policies. Some do not welcome children or smokers. Most prefer that you leave your pets at home. Ask before making your reservations.

Kids and Free We have provided **[KIDS]** and **[FREE]** labels throughout the book to indicate attractions and events that are especially suited to children or that are free of charge.

Reader Reports At the end of the book is a report form. We receive hundreds of reports from readers suggesting new places or agreeing or disagreeing with our assessments. They greatly help in our research and help inform our evaluations. We encourage and appreciate your response.

Money-Back Guarantee Please see page 344.

RESTAURANTS

Restaurant Indexes

STAR RATING

★★★★
Bishop's
Chartwell (The Four Seasons)
Le Crocodile
Tojo's

★★★¹/₂
Beach Side Cafe
Grand King Seafood Restaurant
The William Tell (The
  Georgian Court Hotel)

★★★
Allegro Cafe
Bacchus Ristorante (The
  Wedgewood Hotel)
The Beach House at
  Dundarave Pier
Beetnix Pasta Bar and Grill
Caffe de Medici
CinCin
The Fish House at Stanley Park
Five Sails (Pan Pacific Hotel)
Fleuri (Sutton Place Hotel)
Gianni Restaurant and
  Norcineria
Il Giardino di Umberto
Kirin Mandarin Restaurant
Kirin Seafood Restaurant
Landmark Hot Pot House
Le Gavroche
Lola's Restaurant
Lumière
Mangiamo!
Montri's Thai Restaurant
Phnom Penh Restaurant
Piccolo Mondo
Quattro on Fourth
Seasons in the Park
Shanghai Lo Ching Hing
  Restaurant
Sun Sui Wah Seafood
  Restaurant
Villa del Lupo

★★¹/₂
Herons (Waterfront Centre
  Hotel)
Horizons on Burnaby Mountain
Joe Fortes
Zeppo's Trattoria

★★
Anderson's
Arirang House
Ashiana Tandoori
The Avenue Grill
Bandi's
Bianco Nero
Bridges

Cafe de Paris
Cafe Norté Mexican Restaurant
Capers
Century Grill
Chili Club Thai Restaurant
Chiyoda
Cipriano's Ristorante & Pizzeria
Corsi Trattoria
Da Pasta Bar
Dario's La Piazza Ristorante
Earl's
Farrago
Favorito Pasta Trattoria
Fiasco
Floata Seafood Restaurant
Fortune House
Giraffe
Griffins (Hotel Vancouver)
The Hermitage
Imperial Chinese Seafood
  Restaurant
Kalamata Greek Taverna
Kamei Sushi
Koji Japanese Restaurant
La Belle Auberge
La Cucina Italiana
La Toque Blanche
Le Grec
Maple Garden Restaurant
Meinhardt Fine Foods
Mescalero
Nat's New York Pizzeria
Ouzeri
Paradiso
The Pink Pearl
Planet Veg
The Prow
Raku Kushiyaki
The Red Onion
Romano's Macaroni Grill
Rubina Tandoori
The Salmon House on the Hill
Shanghai Chinese Bistro
Shanghai Garden Restaurant
Shijo Japanese Restaurant
Shiro
Sophie's Cosmic Cafe
Spumante's Cafe Ristorante
Star Anise
Szechuan Chongqing
  Restaurant
Szechuan Chongqing Seafood
  Restaurant
The Teahouse at Ferguson
  Point
Top Gun Chinese Seafood
  Restaurant
Uncle Herbert's Fish & Chip
  Shop

Vassilis Taverna
Victoria Chinese Restaurant
Vij's
Vivace!
Vong's Kitchen
Wonton King

★¹/₂
La Villetta
Shabusen Yakiniku House
Water Street Cafe
Wonton Noodle Restaurant

★
Accord
Aki
Al Ritrovo
Annapurna Vegetarian Cuisine
  of India
Bodai Vegetarian Restaurant
Bo-Jik Vegetarian Restaurant
The Bread Garden
Casa Sleigh
Delilah's
El Caravan
English Bay Boathouse
Flying Wedge
Hon's Wun Tun House
Isadora's
Kilimanjaro
Kitto Japanese Restaurant
Las Margaritas
Liliget Feast House
Lok's Chinese Restaurant
Milestone's
Moutai Mandarin Restaurant
Mui Garden Restaurant
Nazarre BBQ Chicken
New Grand View Restaurant
New Japanese Deli House
Noor Mahal
O-Tooz The Energie Bar
Olympia Seafood Market and
  Grill
Park Lock Seafood Restaurant
Pho Hoang
Pho Pasteur Vietnamese
  Restaurant
President Chinese Restaurant
Settebello
Shil-La Korean Restaurant
Singapore Restaurant
Stepho's Souvlakia
Steveston Seafood House
Subeez
Sun Wong Kee
Surat Sweet
Tang's Noodle House
Tio Pepe

The Tomahawk
Tomato Fresh Food Cafe
Tropika Malaysian Cuisine
Won More Szechuan Cuisine

[no stars]
Boss Bakery and Restaurant
Ezogiku Noodle Cafe
Hamburger Mary's
Ikea
J J's Dining Room
Kam Gok Yuen
Major the Gourmet

Musashi Japanese Restaurant
Naam
Natraj
On Lock
The Only Seafood Cafe
Picasso Café
Umberto Al Porto
White Spot

[unrated]
Aqua Riva
Cafe Centro
The Cannery

Diva at the Met
   (Metropolitan Hotel)
L'Arena
Monterey Lounge & Grill
   (Pacific Palisades Hotel)
900 West (Hotel Vancouver)
Planet Hollywood
Raincity Grill
Raintree at the Landing
Starfish

LOCATION

Burnaby
The Bread Garden
Earl's
Horizons on Burnaby Mountain
Kamei Sushi
Milestone's
Szechuan Chongqing Seafood
   Restaurant
White Spot

Chinatown
Boss Bakery and Restaurant
Floata Seafood Restaurant
Hon's Wun Tun House
Kam Gok Yuen
New Japanese Deli House
Park Lock Seafood Restaurant
Phnom Penh Restaurant
Pho Hoang
Pho Pasteur Vietnamese
   Restaurant

Downtown
Aki
Allegro Cafe
Anderson's
Aqua Riva
Bacchus Ristorante (The
   Wedgewood Hotel)
Bandi's
Bianco Nero
Cafe de Paris
Caffe de Medici
Century Grill
Chartwell (The Four Seasons)
Chili Club Thai Restaurant
Chiyoda
CinCin
Da Pasta Bar
Delilah's
Diva at the Met (Metropolitan
   Hotel)
Earl's
El Caravan
English Bay Boathouse
Ezogiku Noodle Cafe
Farrago
The Fish House at Stanley Park
Five Sails (Pan Pacific Hotel)
Fleuri (Sutton Place Hotel)
Flying Wedge

Griffins (Hotel Vancouver)
Hamburger Mary's
The Hermitage
Herons (Waterfront Centre
   Hotel)
Il Giardino di Umberto
Imperial Chinese Seafood
   Restaurant
J J's Dining Room
Joe Fortes
Kamei Sushi
Kirin Mandarin Restaurant
Kirin Seafood Restaurant
Kitto Japanese Restaurant
Koji Japanese Restaurant
L'Arena
Le Crocodile
Le Gavroche
Liliget Feast House
Lola's Restaurant
Mangiamo!
Mescalero
Milestone's
Monterey Lounge & Grill
   (Pacific Palisades Hotel)
Moutai Mandarin Restaurant
Musashi Japanese Restaurant
900 West (Hotel Vancouver)
O–Tooz The Energie Bar
Olympia Seafood Market and
   Grill
Paradiso
Piccolo Mondo
Planet Hollywood
The Prow
Raincity Grill
Romano's Macaroni Grill
Settebello
Shabusen Yakiniku House
Shanghai Chinese Bistro
Starfish
Stepho's Souvlakia
Subeez
The Teahouse at Ferguson
   Point
Tropika Malaysian Cuisine
Victoria Chinese Restaurant
Villa del Lupo
White Spot
The William Tell (The

Georgian Court Hotel)
Won More Szechuan Cuisine
Wonton King

East Vancouver
Accord
Al Ritrovo
Arirang House
Ashiana Tandoori
Bodai Vegetarian Restaurant
The Cannery
Cipriano's Ristorante & Pizzeria
Dario's La Piazza Ristorante
La Villetta
Le Grec
Lok's Chinese Restaurant
Mui Garden Restaurant
Natraj
Nazarre BBQ Chicken
Noor Mahal
On Lock
The Only Seafood Cafe
Pho Hoang
The Pink Pearl
Rubina Tandoori
Shanghai Garden Restaurant
Shil-La Korean Restaurant
Spumante's Cafe Ristorante
Sun Sui Wah Seafood
   Restaurant
Sun Wong Kee
Szechuan Chongqing
   Restaurant
Tio Pepe
Vong's Kitchen
Wonton Noodle Restaurant
White Spot

Gastown
Kilimanjaro
Raintree at the Landing
Umberto Al Porto
Water Street Cafe

Granville Island
Bridges
Isadora's

Ladner
La Belle Auberge
Uncle Herbert's Fish & Chip
   Shop

North Shore

The Beach House at
  Dundarave Pier
Beach Side Cafe
Cafe Norté Mexican Restaurant
Capers
Corsi Trattoria
Earl's
La Cucina Italiana
La Toque Blanche
The Salmon House on the Hill
The Tomahawk
Vivace!
White Spot

Richmond

Casa Sleigh
Floata Seafood Restaurant
Ikea
Kamei Sushi
Maple Garden Restaurant
President Chinese Restaurant
Shanghai Lo Ching Hing
  Restaurant
Steveston Seafood House
Sun Sui Wah Seafood
  Restaurant
Top Gun Chinese Seafood
  Restaurant
Tropika Malaysian Cuisine

Surrey

Earl's
White Spot

West Side

Annapurna Vegetarian Cuisine
  of India
The Avenue Grill
Beetnix Pasta Bar and Grill
Bishop's
Bo-Jik Vegetarian Restaurant
The Bread Garden
Cafe Centro
Earl's
Favorito Pasta Trattoria
Fiasco
Flying Wedge
Fortune House
Gianni Restaurant and
  Norcineria
Grand King Seafood Restaurant
Kalamata Greek Taverna
Kamei Sushi
Kirin Seafood Restaurant
Landmark Hot Pot House
Las Margaritas
Lumière
Major The Gourmet
Meinhardt Fine Foods
Montri's Thai Restaurant
Naam
Nat's New York Pizzeria
New Grand View Restaurant

Ouzeri
Paradiso
Phnom Penh Restaurant
Picasso Café
Planet Veg
Quattro on Fourth
Raku Kushiyaki
The Red Onion
Seasons in the Park
Shabusen Yakiniku House
Shijo Japanese Restaurant
Shiro
Singapore Restaurant
Sophie's Cosmic Cafe
Star Anise
Surat Sweet
Szechuan Chongqing Seafood
  Restaurant
Tang's Noodle House
Tojo's
Tomato Fresh Food Cafe
Tropika Malaysian Cuisine
Vassilis Taverna
Vij's
White Spot
Won More Szechuan Cuisine
Wonton Noodle Restaurant
Zeppo's Trattoria

White Rock

Earl's
Giraffe
White Spot

FOOD AND OTHER FEATURES

African

Kilimanjaro

All Night

The Bread Garden
Naam

Breakfast

The Avenue Grill
Bacchus Ristorante (The
  Wedgewood Hotel)
The Bread Garden
Capers
Diva at the Met (Metropolitan
  Hotel)
Griffins (Hotel Vancouver)
Hamburger Mary's
Herons (Waterfront Centre
  Hotel)
Isadora's
Monterey Lounge & Grill
  (Pacific Palisades Hotel)
Picasso Café
The Red Onion
Tomato Fresh Food Cafe
White Spot
The William Tell (The
  Georgian Coast Hotel)

Breakfast, All Day

Subeez
The Tomahawk
White Spot

Brunch

Anderson's
Aqua Riva
The Avenue Grill
Bacchus Ristorante (The
  Wedgewood Hotel)
Beach Side Cafe
Bridges
Diva at the Met (Metropolitan
  Hotel)
The Fish House at Stanley Park
Giraffe
Griffins (Hotel Vancouver)
Herons (Waterfront Centre
  Hotel)
Horizons on Burnaby Mountain
Isadora's
Joe Fortes
Lumière
Mescalero
Milestone's
Paradiso
The Prow
The Salmon House on the Hill
Seasons in the Park

Sophie's Cosmic Cafe
Subeez
The Teahouse at Ferguson
  Point
Tomato Fresh Food Cafe

Buffet Offered

Arirang House
English Bay Boathouse
Fleuri (Sutton Place Hotel)
Fiasco
Griffin's (Hotel Vancouver)
Herons (Waterfront Centre
  Hotel)
Imperial Chinese Seafood
  Restaurant
J J's Dining Room
Kamei Sushi
Romano's Macaroni Grill
The William Tell (Georgian
  Court Hotel)

Burgers

The Avenue Grill
Earl's
Griffins (Hotel Vancouver)
Hamburger Mary's
Milestone's
Planet Hollywood
Planet Veg

The Red Onion
Sophie's Cosmic Cafe
Subeez
The Tomahawk
White Spot

California Cuisine
The Avenue Grill
Beetnix Pasta Bar & Grill
Giraffe
Monterey Lounge & Grill
  (Pacific Palisades Hotel)

Cambodian
Phnom Penh Restaurant

Caterers
Aqua Riva
Ashiana Tandoori
The Avenue Grill
Beach Side Cafe
Bodai Vegetarian
The Bread Garden
Bridges
Cafe Norté Mexican Restaurant
Casa Sleigh
Chili Club Thai Restaurant
El Caravan
English Bay Boathouse
The Fish House at Stanley Park
Giraffe
Grand King Seafood Restaurant
The Hermitage
Hon's Wun Tun House
Imperial Chinese Seafood
  Restaurant
Isadora's
Kilimanjaro
Kirin Mandarin Restaurant
Kirin Seafood Restaurant
Koji Japanese Restaurant
La Toque Blanche
Le Gavroche
Liliget Feast House
Major the Gourmet
Mescalero
Monterey Lounge & Grill
  (Pacific Palisades Hotel)
Montri's Thai Restaurant
Moutai Mandarin Restaurant
New Grand View Restaurant
On Lok
Picasso Café
The Pink Pearl
Raintree at the Landing
Raku Kushiyaki
The Red Onion
Rubina Tandoori
Shijo Japanese Restaurant
Shiro
Singapore Restaurant
Star Anise
Subeez
Surat Sweet
Tang's Noodle House
Tojo's
Tomato Fresh Food Cafe

Top Gun Chinese Seafood
  Restaurant
Umberto Al Porto
Vong's Kitchen
Water Street Cafe
The William Tell (Georgian
  Court Hotel)

Children's Menu
Bridges
Cafe Norté Mexican Restaurant
Chartwell (The Four Seasons)
The Fish House at Stanley Park
Griffins (Hotel Vancouver)
Herons (Waterfront Centre
  Hotel)
Isadora's
Kalamata Greek Taverna
Las Margaritas
Monterey Lounge & Grill
  (Pacific Palisades Hotel)
Naam
The Prow
The Red Onion
Romano's Macaroni Grill
Singapore Restaurant
Sophie's Cosmic Cafe
Tio Pepe
The Tomahawk
Tomato Fresh Food Cafe
White Spot

Chinese
Accord
Floata Seafood Restaurant
Fortune House
Grand King Seafood Restaurant
Hon's Wun Tun House
Imperial Chinese Seafood
  Restaurant
Kam Gok Yuen
Kirin Mandarin Restaurant
Kirin Seafood Restaurant
Landmark Hot Pot House
Lok's Chinese Restaurant
Maple Garden Restaurant
Moutai Mandarin Restaurant
Mui Garden Restaurant
New Grand View Restaurant
On Lock
Park Lock Seafood Restaurant
The Pink Pearl
Shanghai Garden Restaurant
Shanghai Lo Ching Hing
  Restaurant
Sun Sui Wah Seafood
  Restaurant
Sun Wong Kee
Szechuan Chongqing
  Restaurant
Szechuan Chongqing Seafood
  Restaurant
Tang's Noodle House
Top Gun Chinese Seafood
  Restaurant
Vong's Kitchen

Won More Szechuan Cuisine
Wonton King
Wonton Noodle Restaurant

Chinese Fine Dining
Fortune House
Grand King Seafood Restaurant
Imperial Chinese Seafood
  Restaurant
President Chinese Restaurant
Shanghai Chinese Bistro
Victoria Chinese Restaurant

Continental
The Beach House at
  Dundarave Pier
Chartwell (The Four Seasons)
Delilah's
The Prow
The William Tell (Georgian
  Court Hotel)

Delivery
The Avenue Grill
Beetnix Pasta Bar and Grill
Flying Wedge
Giraffe
The Hermitage
Kilimanjaro
Meinhardt Fine Foods
Nat's New York Pizza
New Grand View Restaurant
O–Tooz The Energie Bar
The Only Seafood Cafe
Romano's Macaroni Grill
Rubina Tandoori
White Spot

Desserts:Excellent
Allegro Cafe
Aqua Riva
Bacchus Ristorante (The
  Wedgewood Hotel)
The Beach House at
  Dundarave Pier
Beach Side Cafe
Beetnix Pasta Bar and Grill
Bishop's
The Bread Garden
Chartwell (The Four Seasons)
CinCin
Diva at the Met (Metropolitan
  Hotel)
Farrago
Gianni Restaurant and
  Norcineria
Giraffe
Le Crocodile
Lola's Restaurant
Lumière
Mangiamo!
900 West (Hotel Vancouver)
Piccolo Mondo
Quattro on Fourth
Raintree at the Landing
The Red Onion
Romano's Macaroni Grill

Star Anise
Starfish
The William Tell (The
  Georgian Court Hotel)

Dim Sum
Floata Seafood Restaurant
Fortune House
Grand King Seafood Restaurant
Hon's Wun Tun House
Imperial Chinese Seafood
  Restaurant
Kirin Mandarin Restaurant
Maple Garden Restaurant
Park Lock Seafood Restaurant
The Pink Pearl
Shanghai Chinese Bistro
Sun Sui Wah Seafood
  Restaurant
Szechuan Chongqing
  Restaurant
Szechuan Chongqing Seafood
  Restaurant
Top Gun Chinese Seafood
  Restaurant

Entertainment
Al Ritrovo
Anderson's
Bacchus Ristorante (The
  Wedgewood Hotel)
Fleuri (Sutton Place Hotel)
Cipriano's Ristorante & Pizzeria
El Caravan
Floata Seafood Restaurant
Herons (Waterfront Centre
  Hotel)
Joe Fortes
Monterey Lounge & Grill
  (Pacific Palisades Hotel)
Naam
Romano's Macaroni Grill
The Salmon House on the Hill
Zeppo's Trattoria

Fireplace
Bacchus Ristorante (The
  Wedgewood Hotel)
Bandi's
The Beach House at
  Dundarave Pier
Cafe Norté Mexican Restaurant
English Bay Boathouse
The Cannery
Chartwell (The Four Seasons)
El Caravan
The Fish House at Stanley Park
The Hermitage
Herons (Waterfront Centre
  Hotel)
La Toque Blanche
Le Gavroche
Monterey Lounge & Grill
  (Pacific Palisades Hotel)
Naam
Raintree at the Landing
Romano's Macaroni Grill
Seasons in the Park

The Teahouse at Ferguson
  Point
Villa del Lupo
Water Street Cafe

Fish 'n' Chips
Olympia Seafood Market and
  Grill
The Only Seafood Cafe
Uncle Herbert's Fish & Chip
  Shop

French
Cafe de Paris
The Hermitage
Le Crocodile
Le Gavroche
Lumière

Fusion
Diva at the Met (Metropolitan
  Hotel)
Grand King Seafood Restaurant
Herons (Waterfront Centre
  Hotel)
Raku Kushiyaki
Star Anise
Tojo's

Greek
Kalamata Greek Taverna
Le Grec
Ouzeri
Stepho's Souvlakia
Vassilis Taverna

Health-Conscious
Isadora's
Mescalero
O–Tooz The Energie Bar
Planet Veg
Raintree at the Landing
Tomato Fresh Food Cafe

Hungarian
Bandi's

Indian
Annapurna Vegetarian Cuisine
  of India
Ashiana Tandoori
Natraj
Noor Mahal
Rubina Tandoori
Surat Sweet
Vij's

Italian
Al Ritrovo
Bacchus Ristorante (The
  Wedgewood Hotel)
Bianco Nero
Caffe de Medici
CinCin
Cipriano's Ristorante & Pizzeria
Corsi Trattoria
Da Pasta Bar
Dario's La Piazza Ristorante
Fiasco
Favorito Pasta Trattoria

Gianni Restaurant and
  Norcineria
Il Giardino di Umberto
La Villetta
Mangiamo!
Paradiso
Piccolo Mondo
Quattro on Fourth
Romano's Macaroni Grill
Settebello
Spumante's Cafe Ristorante
Umberto Al Porto
Villa del Lupo
Vivace!
Zeppo's Trattoria

Japanese
Aki
Chiyoda
Ezogiku Noodle Cafe
New Japanese Deli House
Kamei Sushi
Kitto Japanese Restaurant
Koji Japanese Restaurant
Musashi Japanese Restaurant
Raku Kushiyaki
Shabusen Yakiniku House
Shijo Japanese Restaurant
Shiro
Tojo's

Korean
Arirang House
Shil-La Korean Restaurant

Late Night
Accord
The Bread Garden
CinCin
Earl's
Fiasco
Hamburger Mary's
Hon's Wun Tun House
Kitto Japanese Restaurant
Landmark Hot Pot House
Lok's Chinese Restaurant
Mescalero
Naam
Ouzeri
Shanghai Chinese Bistro

Lebanese
El Caravan

Malaysian
Singapore Restaurant
Tropika Malaysian Cuisine

Mexican
Cafe Centro
Cafe Norté Mexican Restaurant
Las Margaritas
Mescalero
Nazarre BBQ Chicken
Tio Pepe

Native Peoples
Liliget Feast House

Outdoor Dining

Bandi's
The Beach House at
  Dundarave Pier
Beach Side Cafe
The Bread Garden
Bridges
Cafe Norté Mexican Restaurant
Caffe de Medici
The Cannery
Capers
Casa Sleigh
Chili Club Thai Restaurant
CinCin
Da Pasta Bar
Earl's
English Bay Boathouse
Farrago
Fiasco
The Fish House at Stanley Park
Five Sails (Pan Pacific Hotel)
Flying Wedge
Giraffe
Hamburger Mary's
Horizons on Burnaby Mountain
Il Giardino di Umberto
Isadora's
Kamei Sushi
Kilimanjaro
La Belle Auberge
La Cucina Italiana
La Villetta
Las Margaritas
Le Crocodile
Le Gavroche
Le Grec
Mangiamo!
Mescalero
Milestone's
Monterey Lounge & Grill
  (Pacific Palisades Hotel)
Naam
O-Tooz The Energie Bar
Ouzeri
Picasso Café
The Prow
Raincity Grill
Raintree at the Landing
Romano's Macaroni Grill
The Salmon House on the Hill
Seasons in the Park
Settebello
Sophie's Cosmic Cafe
Subeez
The Teahouse at Ferguson
  Point
Tojo's
Tomato Fresh Food Cafe
Umberto Al Porto
Vassilis Taverna
Vivace!
Water Street Cafe
White Spot
The William Tell (The
  Georgian Court Hotel)
Zeppo's Trattoria

Pizza

CinCin
Cipriano's Ristorante & Pizzeria
Diva at the Met (Metropolitan
  Hotel)
Earl's
Fiasco
Flying Wedge
900 West (Hotel Vancouver)
Nat's New York Pizza
Settebello

Post-Theatre Menus

Bacchus Ristorante (The
  Wedgewood Hotel)
The Bread Garden
CinCin
El Caravan
Hamburger Mary's
The Hermitage
Hon's Wun Tun House
Le Gavroche
Mescalero
Milestone's
Naam
Subeez
Villa del Lupo
The William Tell (The
  Georgian Court Hotel)
Zeppo's Trattoria

Private Rooms and Parties

Aqua Riva
Arirang House
Ashiana Tandoori
Bacchus Ristorante (The
  Wedgewood Hotel)
The Beach House at
  Dundarave Pier
Beach Side Cafe
Beetnix Pasta Bar and Grill
The Bread Garden
Bridges
Cafe Centro
Cafe de Paris
Caffe de Medici
The Cannery
Chartwell (The Four Seasons)
Chili Club Thai Restaurant
CinCin
Cipriano's Ristorante & Pizzeria
English Bay Boathouse
Farrago
Fiasco
The Fish House at Stanley Park
Five Sails (Pan Pacific Hotel)
Floata Seafood Restaurant
Fortune House
Giraffe
Grand King Seafood Restaurant
The Hermitage
Herons (Waterfront Centre
  Hotel)
Horizons on Burnaby Mountain
Il Giardino di Umberto

Imperial Chinese Seafood
  Restaurant
Isadora's
Joe Fortes
Kalamata Greek Taverna
Kamei Sushi
Kirin Mandarin Restaurant
Kirin Seafood Restaurant
Koji Japanese Restaurant
La Belle Auberge
La Cucina Italiana
Landmark Hot Pot House
Le Gavroche
Lola's Restaurant
Lumière
Mangiamo!
Maple Garden Restaurant
Mescalero
Milestone's
Monterey Lounge & Grill
  (Pacific Palisades Hotel)
Moutai Mandarin Restaurant
New Grand View Restaurant
Picasso Café
The Pink Pearl
The Prow
Raintree at the Landing
Raku Kushiyaki
Romano's Macaroni Grill
Rubina Tandoori
Seasons in the Park
Settebello
Shabusen Yakiniku House
Shanghai Chinese Bistro
Shanghai Garden Restaurant
Shijo Japanese Restaurant
Shil-La Korean Restaurant
Sophie's Cosmic Cafe
Steveston Seafood House
Sun Sui Wah Seafood
  Restaurant
Surat Sweet
Szechuan Chongqing
  Restaurant
Szechuan Chongqing Seafood
  Restaurant
The Teahouse at Ferguson
  Point
Umberto Al Porto
Uncle Herbert's Fish & Chip
  Shop
Vivace!
Villa del Lupo
Vong's Kitchen
Water Street Cafe
The William Tell (Georgian
  Court Hotel)
Zeppo's Trattoria

Romantic

Allegro Cafe
Anderson's
Aqua Riva
Bacchus Ristorante (The
  Wedgewood Hotel)

Bandi's
Bishop's
The Beach House at
  Dundarave Pier
Bridges
Cafe Centro
Cafe de Paris
Cafe Norté Mexican Restaurant
Caffe de Medici
The Cannery
Chartwell (The Four Seasons)
CinCin
Delilah's
Diva at the Met (Metropolitan
  Hotel)
English Bay Boathouse
Farrago
The Fish House at Stanley Park
Five Sails (Pacific Hotel)
Fleuri (Sutton Place Hotel)
Gianni Restaurant and
  Norcineria
Giraffe
Il Giardino di Umberto
Imperial Chinese Seafood
  Restaurant
La Belle Auberge
La Cucina Italiana
La Villetta
Le Crocodile
Le Gavroche
Lola's Restaurant
Lumière
Mangiamo!
Mescalero
Monterey Lounge & Grill
  (Pacific Palisades Hotel)
Montri's Thai Restaurant
900 West (Hotel Vancouver)
The Prow
Raintree at the Landing
The Salmon House on the Hill
Seasons in the Park
Star Anise
The Teahouse at Ferguson
  Point
Umberto Al Porto
Villa del Lupo
The William Tell (Georgian
  Court Hotel)
Zeppo's Trattoria

Seafood
(See also Fish 'n' Chips)
Accord
Anderson's
The Beach House at
  Dundarave Pier
Bishop's
Bridges
The Cannery
CinCin
Diva at the Met (Metropolitan
  Hotel)
English Bay Boathouse
The Fish House at Stanley Park
Five Sails (Pan Pacific Hotel)

Floata Seafood Restaurant
Gianni Restaurant and
  Norcineria
Grand King Seafood Restaurant
Griffins (Hotel Vancouver)
Il Giardino di Umberto
Imperial Chinese Seafood
  Restaurant
Joe Fortes
Le Gavroche
Liliget Feast House
Lola's Restaurant
Lumière
Mangiamo!
900 West (Hotel Vancouver)
Park Lock Seafood Restaurant
Piccolo Mondo
Quattro on Fourth
Raintree at the Landing
The Salmon House on the Hill
Shanghai Chinese Bistro
Starfish
Steveston Seafood House
Subeez
Sun Sui Wah Seafood
  Restaurant
Szechuan Chongqing Seafood
  Restaurant
Tojo's
Victoria Chinese Restaurant

Singaporean
Singapore Restaurant

Soup/Salad/Sandwich
The Bread Garden
Bridges
Earl's
Meinhardt's Fine Foods
Milestone's
Monterey Lounge & Grill
  (Pacific Palisades Hotel)
The Red Onion
Sophie's Cosmic Cafe
Tomato Fresh Food Cafe

Southwestern
Mescalero

Spanish
Casa Sleigh

Sushi
Aki
Ezogiku Noodle Cafe
Kamei Sushi
Kitto Japanese Restaurant
Koji Japanese Restaurant
Musashi Japanese Restaurant
New Japanese Deli House
Raku Kushiyaki
Shiro
Tojo's

Swedish
Ikea

Swiss/French
The William Tell (The
  Georgian Court Hotel)

Takeout
The Avenue Grill
The Beach House at
  Dundarave Pier
Beetnix Pasta Bar and Grill
Bodai Vegetarian Restaurant
The Bread Garden
Cafe Norté Mexican Restaurant
Casa Sleigh
Cipriano's Ristorante & Pizzeria
Earl's
Fleuri (Sutton Place Hotel)
Flying Wedge
Giraffe
Hermitage
Kilimanjaro
Major the Gourmet
Meinhardt Fine Foods
Montri's Thai Restaurant
Nat's New York Pizza
Nazarre BBQ Chicken
New Grand View Restaurant
O–Tooz The Energie Bar
The Only Seafood Cafe
The Pink Pearl
The Red Onion
Romano's Macaroni Grill
Rubina Tandoori
Sophie's Cosmic Cafe
Tio Pepe
Tojo's
Tomato Fresh Food Cafe
Uncle Herbert's Fish & Chip
  Shop
Vassilis Taverna
Vong's Kitchen
White Spot

Tapas
Casa Sleigh
Mescalero

Thai
Chili Club Thai Restaurant
Montri's Thai Restaurant

Valet Parking
Bacchus Ristorante (The
  Wedgewood Hotel)
The Beach House at
  Dundarave Pier
English Bay Boathouse
Chartwell (The Four Seasons)
CinCin
Diva at the Met (Metropolitan
  Hotel)
Five Sails (Pan Pacific Hotel)
Fleuri (Sutton Place Hotel)
Giraffe
Griffins (Hotel Vancouver)
Imperial Chinese Seafood
  Restaurant
Joe Fortes
Le Crocodile
Lola's Restaurant
Mangiamo!
900 West (Hotel Vancouver)
Raincity Grill

Seasons in the Park
Villa del Lupo
The William Tell (Georgian
    Court Hotel)

Vegetarian
Annapurna Vegetarian Cuisine
    of India
Bodai Vegetarian Restaurant
Bo-Jik Vegetarian Restaurant
Capers
Isadora's
Naam
New Grand View Restaurant
O–Tooz The Energie Bar
Surat Sweet

Vietnamese
Phnom Penh Restaurant
Pho Hoang
Pho Pasteur

View
Anderson's
The Beach House at
    Dundarave Pier
Beach Side Cafe
Bridges
The Cannery
Chili Club Thai Restaurant
English Bay Boathouse
The Fish House at Stanley Park
Five Sails (Pan Pacific Hotel)
Giraffe
Herons (Waterfront Centre
    Hotel)
Horizons on Burnaby Mountain
Imperial Chinese Seafood
    Restaurant
La Toque Blanche
Milestone's
The Prow
Raincity Grill
Raintree at the Landing
The Salmon House on the Hill
Seasons in the Park
The Teahouse at Ferguson
    Point
Vivace!

West Coast Cuisine
The Beach House at
    Dundarave Pier
Beach Side Cafe
Bishop's
Capers
Chartwell (The Four Seasons)
Delilah's
English Bay Boathouse

The Fish House at Stanley Park
Five Sails (Pan Pacific Hotel)
Griffins (Hotel Vancouver)
Horizons on Burnaby Mountain
Joe Fortes
Monterey Lounge & Grill
    (Pacific Palisades Hotel)
Raincity Grill
Seasons in the Park
Star Anise
The Teahouse at Ferguson
    Point

Wheelchair Accessible
Bacchus Ristorante (The
    Wedgewood Hotel)
The Beach House at
    Dundarave Pier
Beach Side Cafe
The Bread Garden
Bridges
Cafe Centro
Cafe Norté Mexican Restaurant
Caffe de Medici
Chartwell (The Four Seasons)
Chili Club Thai Restaurant
Chiyoda
Corsi Trattoria
Delilah's
English Bay Boathouse
The Fish House at Stanley Park
Five Sails (Pan Pacific Hotel)
Fleuri (Sutton Place Hotel)
Floata Seafood Restaurant
Flying Wedge
Griffins (Hotel Vancouver)
Ikea
Isadora's
Kamei Sushi
Kirin Mandarin Restaurant
Kirin Seafood Restaurant
Koji Japanese Restaurant
La Cucina Italiana
La Toque Blanche
Landmark Hot Pot House
Le Crocodile
Mescalero
Monterey Lounge & Grill
    (Pacific Palisades Hotel)
Montri's Thai Restaurant
Moutai Mandarin Restaurant
Naam
900 West (Hotel Vancouver)
Ouzeri
The Pink Pearl
Raincity Grill
Raintree at the Landing

The Red Onion
Romano's Macaroni Grill
Seasons in the Park
Shijo Japanese Restaurant
Sophie's Cosmic Cafe
Stepho's Souvlakia
Subeez
The Teahouse at Ferguson
    Point
Tio Pepe
Tojo's
Top Gun Chinese Seafood
    Restaurant
Vassilis Taverna
Vij's
The William Tell (The
    Georgian Court Hotel)

Wine Savvy Restaurants
The Beach House at
    Dundarave Pier
Beach Side Cafe
Bianco Nero
Bishop's
Century Grill
Chartwell (Four Seasons Hotel)
CinCin
Dario's La Piazza Ristorante
Diva at the Met (Metropolitan
    Hotel)
The Fish House at Stanley Park
Five Sails (Pan Pacific Hotel)
Fleuri (Sutton Place Hotel)
The Hermitage
Il Giardino di Umberto
Joe Fortes
La Cucina Italiana
Le Crocodile
Le Gavroche
Mangiamo!
Monterey Lounge & Grill
    (Pacific Palisades Hotel)
Montri's Thai Restaurant
900 West (Hotel Vancouver)
Piccolo Mondo
The Prow
Quattro on Fourth
Raincity Grill
The Salmon House on the Hill
Star Anise
Umberto Al Porto
Villa del Lupo
Vivace!
Water Street Cafe

Restaurants

Accord ★ Behind white venetian blinds, this restaurant serves excellent Cantonese seafood. Try the live spot prawns steamed in the shell and brought to the table with a serrano soy-based dipping sauce, or the beef tenderloin with pickled vegetables. The menu also includes a handful of Chiu Chow specialties. Open till the wee hours—perfect for those late evenings when only Chinese food will do. Ask for the midnight snack menu, now available in English. Sixty-eight half-sized dishes ranging between $5 and $8 each, including deep-fried spicy baby octopus, Chinese smoked pork with gailan, clams with black bean sauce, and a wonderful beef with satay sauce. ■ *4298 Main St; 876-6110; map:E3; $$; wine & beer; MC, V; no cheques; dinner, midnight snacks every day.*

Aki ★ A few steps from Vancouver's own Japantown (which centres on Oppenheimer Park) is the small, unpretentious Aki. With its screened rooms and tatami mats, this intimate Japanese restaurant was the place where more than a few locals were introduced in the '70s to the then-dubious joys of sushi and sashimi. Sophisticates that we are now, we still go back—for the same reasons we went in our student days: the food is good and the bill won't make a major dent in your pocketbook. The menu embraces all the favourites: teriyaki, sunumono, and those uniquely Japanese udon noodle dishes that manage to be both light and robust. A crisp and fragile batter lifts the tempura here far above the usual. Sushi choices let you stay with the tried and true or experiment with sea urchin or flying-fish roe. Service is concerned and consistently charming. ■ *374 Powell St; 682-4032; map:W3; $$; full bar; AE, MC, V; no cheques; lunch Mon–Fri, dinner every day.*

Allegro Cafe ★★★ If a restaurant can be called a flirt, this is it. Tucked away in the courtyard of a businesslike office tower across from the Law Courts, Allegro beckons with a warm, intimate appeal. All decked out in curvy, dark green velvet banquettes, warm lighting, and red, green, and gold draperies, this restaurant has become a hot spot for the young urban set. Partly it's the great '60s modern decor, but mostly it's the excellent food at more-than-reasonable prices. Mike Mitton from Il Barino has hooked up with chef Barbara Reese (of the Reese peanut butter cup family) to offer Mediterranean dishes with a West Coast panache: flavourful soups (try the roasted garlic), creative pastas (capelli with grilled scallops, leeks, Roma tomatoes, and tarragon in a mascarpone cream sauce with salmon caviar), and seafood and meat cooked to perfection. Reese knows when to go all out with flavour—and when to approach a dish with finesse. For instance, a charbroiled veal chop with gorgonzola and grainy mustard cream sauce could have been a disastrous cacophony of flavours but instead was a symphony of subtlety. The only drawback is the place is so popular you may wait quite a while for your table. Pull up a stool at the bar, order an excellent martini, and settle in for some serious people-watching. Yes, there's a peanut butter pie for dessert. ■ *1G-888 Nelson St; 683-8485; map:R4; $$; full bar; AE, DC, MC, V; no cheques; lunch Mon–Fri, dinner Mon–Sat.*

▼

Top 175 Restaurants

▲

Al Ritrovo ★ The family-owned Al Ritrovo is warm and inviting, the kind of place where you can relax over a glass of Chianti, eat heartily and watch the colourfully mixed crowd. With its backlit paintings of moonlit piazzas; the odd string of fairy lights; Italian classics played on the accordion, guitar, and bass (on weekends); and couples of all ages taking to the floor, the ambience seems to come straight from the cover of a romance novel. The mainstream Italian menu occasionally plays second fiddle to the dancing, with service scheduled around the sambas and tangos. Expect solid Italian cuisine like Mamma used to make. Servings of lasagna or tagliatelle alla boscaiola—pasta laden with bacon, mushrooms, and cream—are robust. A flavourful veal saltimbocca is aromatic with fresh sage. For lovers of old-time dancing, Al Ritrovo is heaven. Pizzas after 10pm. Minimum of $15 per person after 9pm. When the urge to dance strikes you in Vancouver, this is the spot. Go with a group. ■ *2010 Franklin St; 255-0916; $$; full bar; AE, MC, V; local cheques only; lunch Tues–Fri, dinner Fri–Sun (closed in Aug).*

Anderson's ★★ The great sweep of windows overlooking False Creek ensures that this waterside eatery is visited as much for its scenic as for its culinary pleasures. It's fascinating by day, as pleasure craft and ferryboats provide a constantly changing picture; and it is dazzling at night, as lights flicker like fireflies across the water. It's the place Vancouverites take out-of-towners bent on business or pleasure to show off their scenery—as well as their seafood: delicate sole paupiette rolled with prawns and blanketed in a lobster sauce, prawns briskly sautéed with tomatoes and shallots and finished with garlic butter. Local salmon is served in the best way possible: simply cooked and drizzled with lemon butter. The fresh sheet offers the best of the fresh fish available, such trans-Pacific fusions as shellfish in black bean sauce, seaweed-wrapped fillets of halibut, or salmon served with a decidedly Asian cilantro and ginger chile butter. Sunday brunch boasts live jazz and prime rib. ■ *1661 Granville St; 684-3777; map:Q6; $$$; full bar; AE, DC, JCB, MC, V; no cheques; lunch Mon–Fri, dinner Mon–Sat, brunch Sun.*

Annapurna Vegetarian Cuisine of India ★ The Annapurna was the first restaurant in the Lower Mainland to tap into the most highly developed vegetarian cuisine in the world. Every vegetarian who's opened a menu at an Indian restaurant to see the same standard meatless dishes just one too many times is going to like Annapurna a lot. There are unfamiliar dishes to try, and some of them—like the lentil dumplings soaked in yogurt with chickpeas and chutney—are especially good. The service, however, is long on grand gestures and short on noticing when your water glass needs to be filled. And the small dining room, its ceiling covered with lanterns, has a ringside view of a busy intersection. ■ *1812 W 4th Ave; 736-5959; map:O7; $; full bar; MC, V; no cheques; lunch, dinner every day.*

Aqua Riva [unrated] Like its siblings Salmon House on the Hill and Horizons on Burnaby Mountain, the Toseki Group's latest addition, Aqua Riva, boasts an outstanding view. Executive chef Deb Connors, formerly of Horizons, is rattling the pots and pans and manning the wood-fired oven and rotisserie in this sparkling restaurant near Canada Place. Prices are reasonable for lamb sausage penne, spit-roasted pizza, and fried noodle cake with emerald curry sauce. So far, service is unfailingly friendly, and the stunning decor is especially soothing when you're settled into a booth with Dana Irving's art decor wraparound mural above you. Very popular with the lunch crowd who inhabit the office tower atop Aqua Riva, but it's waiting to be discovered in the evening. ■ *30-200 Granville St; 683-5599; map:T3; $$; full bar; AE, MC, V; lunch, dinner every day; brunch Sun.*

Arirang House ★★ Located at the south end of the Cambie Street Bridge, Arirang House, one of the city's first Korean restaurants, continues to be a popular venue for those who consider garlic a major food group. In the evenings, the restaurant serves a dish revealingly called Jumuluck Garlic Lovers. Combining marinated beef, lettuce leaves, and vast quantities of raw garlic, it's a cook-it-yourself variation of traditional Korean barbecue. Less daunting are bulgogi (marinated filet of beef) or bulgabi (ribs) or any of the other tabletop grill options. Sizzling and deeply flavoured hot pots, assorted seafood preparations, and savagely good kimchi (the incendiary Korean pickle) round out the menu. The lunchtime barbecue buffet is an exceptional value. ■ *2211 Cambie St; 879-0990; map:T7; $$; full bar; AE, MC, V; no cheques; lunch, dinner every day.*

Ashiana Tandoori ★★ Ashiana moved from its decade-long, well-worn Victoria Drive location to emerge on Kingsway as the most upscale Indian restaurant in Vancouver. The new place features split-level seating divided into three rooms by unique mosque-shaped arches lushly decorated with brass wall platters and elaborate carvings. The owners spared no expense, and this includes the confident cooking in the kitchen. The tandoori dishes come sizzling from the oven to the table on cast-iron platters. The Chicken Tikka is tasty and moist; the Lamb Tikka superb—tender, fragrant, and rich from its marinade of yogurt, ginger, garlic, and spices. Murg Makhani—one of eleven chicken curries—is luscious and sweet and delectable on paneer naan deftly flavoured with fresh coriander. Speaking of breads, the whole-wheat paratha with cheese is a must with the Channa Masala—chickpeas stewed with garam masala, onions, and tomatoes. This is food that makes you happy. ■ *1440 Kingsway; 874-5060; map:R3; $$; full bar; AE, MC, V; no cheques; lunch, dinner every day.*

The Avenue Grill ★★ Eighteen years ago, chef Herve Fabre was the first chef at Umberto's Il Giardino. Today he's the new owner of "the Ave," a neighbourhood restaurant in Kerrisdale. We like Fabre's updated look, and bargain hunters and vegetarians will like the addition of his mix-and-match pasta combinations, 35 in total. A good bet is the black bean, red pepper, and scallops in sesame oil. Check out the chalkboard: every week there's a theme (salmon, chicken, oysters, lamb, etc.), with nothing over $14.95. We're happy he's left the superb pecan chicken with pommery mustard sauce on the menu. Still popular with the neighbourhood Kerrisdale crowd and one of the best places for weekend brunch (till 5pm), mainly because of the made-from-scratch pancakes cooked with seasonal fresh berries, eggs benny, and homemade marmalade. There's also a good selection of wines by the glass. ■ *2114 W 41st Ave; 266-8183; map:C4; $$; full bar; MC; cheques OK; breakfast Mon–Fri, lunch Mon–Sat, dinner every day.*

Bacchus Ristorante (The Wedgewood Hotel) ★★★ Dedicated hotelier Eleni Skalbania and executive chef Alan Groom have put Bacchus on the culinary map, and Groom's superb cooking is just what we want now: Northern Italian with an emphasis on fresh and simple, using the bounty of BC's local products. At lunchtime, Bacchus attracts the legal beagles from the neighbouring courthouse for penne with Gorgonzola, pizza rustica, or Il Taitano. A holdout from Skalbania's previous property, the Georgia Hotel, Il Taitano is a comforting trio of shrimp, avocado, and tomato on an English muffin with grilled fontina cheese. Afternoon tea (2 until 4pm) in front of the fireplace hits the spot, with finger sandwiches followed by freshly baked scones with dollops of Devon clotted cream, and tea pastries swished down by your favourite blend. The changing dinner menu might include grilled halibut with horseradish mashed potatoes, tiger prawns with lemongrass, or olive-crusted rack of lamb. Hope that the homey bread-and-butter pudding with sun-dried cranberries happens to be on the menu or surrender to the chocolate seduction for two. At press time, a rich new look is being planned, featuring a wraparound bar, cosy banquettes, and a cigar room. Nightly, except Sunday, a pianist tickles the ivories. ■ *845 Hornby St; 689-7777; map:S4; $$; full bar; AE, DC, MC, V; no cheques; breakfast, lunch, dinner every day; brunch Sat–Sun.* &

Bandi's ★★ You'll exit in a fog of garlic. At Bandi's, chef/owner Bandi Rinkhy produces the robust country food of Hungary, with mâitre d' and co-owner Kader Karaa's sense of humour providing the dash of paprika. Start with an excellent sour-cherry soup and the dangerously addictive langos, a deep-fried peasant bread served with raw garlic (order one for your friends, one for yourself, and one to take home). Duck aficionados who haven't experienced Bandi's signature dish—crisp duck served with red cabbage braised in Tokay wine—should by all means do so. Goulash is presented in a little kettle set over a portable flame. Hungary's best whites are on the wine list. ■ *1427 Howe St; 685-3391; map:R5; $$; full bar; AE, MC, V; no cheques; lunch Mon–Fri, dinner every day.*

The Beach House at Dundarave Pier ★★★ On sunny days, this waterside favourite, only metres away from Dundarave beach, offers unequaled Kodak moments on its year-round heated patio. Misty nights, when dining is accompanied by the basso profundo of distant foghorns, are equally appealing. First opened as a teahouse in 1912, this heritage building has been recently restored by designer Robin Ratcliffe. Wooden floors, creamy walls (check out the art by Jade Ratcliffe) and plenty of glass lend a warm neighbourhood feel. Chef Sonny Mendoza consistently puts out fine west coast dishes: a superb cornmeal-crusted Fanny Bay oysters, grilled salmon on a raft of asparagus in a sea of red chili. If offered the crème brûlée with toasted hazelnuts and an orange shortbread cookie, don't pass it up. And, by all means, take advantage of the tremendous wine list chosen by managing partner Ken Brooks. It features many good wines by the glass, the best of British Columbia estate wineries, an impressive mix of U.S. west coast, varietals and a sizable number of bottles from around the world. ▪ *150-25th St, West Vancouver; 922-1414; $$; full bar; AE, DC, MC, V; no cheques; lunch, dinner every day, brunch Sat–Sun.* &

Beach Side Cafe ★★★¹/₂ The Beach Side just keeps getting better and better. With their creative and varied approach to regional cuisine, owner Janet McGuire and chef Carol Chow have turned this little Ambleside haunt into the area's most serious kitchen. The summertime deck rates among the city's best, with views of Stanley Park and Kitsilano across the water. Choices are plentiful, with emphasis on daily specials as well as a cutting-edge list of better West Coast wines. Start with the warm cambazola with hazelnuts, roasted garlic, and toast points, or grilled Fanny Bay oysters with a lemon basil aioli. Definitely order pan-seared scallops with an oriental noodle pancake and a tomato black bean butter. Dessert lovers swear by the lemon meringue pie. Take advantage of the view, during a leisurely Sunday brunch, with a woodsy oyster mushroom omelette and freshly baked banana bread. A great place to do lunch too. ▪ *1362 Marine Dr, West Vancouver; 925-1945; map:D1; $$; full bar; AE, MC, V; no cheques; lunch Mon–Fri, dinner every day, brunch Sat–Sun.* &

Beetnix Pasta Bar and Grill ★★★ You can walk by Beetnix umpteen times without noticing it in its slightly subterranean location on a busy intersection. This would be a mistake. Once you enter this elegant little eatery, you'll discover an oasis of cool and calm in the busy city. Pale green walls, white-and-blue table settings, and fabulous art nouveau light fixtures provide the setting for some very fine food. Co-owners Kim Boyson and Adrienne Woolfries seem to specialize in the freshest of foods that pay homage both to local cuisine and the flavours of the Pacific Rim. Start with one of the big, pungent salads before embarking on a pasta adventure (the warm bread and tomato salad with greens and feta, olives, and balsamic vinegar is the best in town). Or try something from the grill, or the duck confit, redolent of intense flavours, or whatever the daily special is. A filet of sea bass arrived at our table, bringing with it a whimsical sense of the tropics—coconut crust, a whiff of curry, and a marvelously sunny fruit sauce. A selection of fresh sorbets and ice creams finish the meal—mix and match to suit your taste. ▪ *2459 Cambie St; 874-7133; map:T7; $$; full bar; MC, V; lunch Mon–Fri, dinner Mon–Sat.*

Bianco Nero ★★ Bianco Nero's bold black-and-white decor never fails to impress, though the service doesn't always live up to the surroundings. The well-prepared food, however, remains consistent and so does its proximity to the Queen Elizabeth Theatre. The kitchen has a healthy regard for garlic, onions, and olive oil (and a macho disregard for presentation).

Every Italian dish imaginable makes an appearance here, and we continue to love the tortellini alla nonna, the decidedly non-Italian sole in aquavit, and the osso bucco. The place is for lovers of Italian wine, with one of the most comprehensive selections in Canada, including a full range of vintage Barolo. ■ *475 W Georgia St; 682-6376; map:T4; $$$; full bar; AE, MC, V; no cheques; lunch Mon–Fri, dinner Mon–Sat.*

Bishop's ★★★★ No restaurant is as personal as this minimalist Kitsilano space, where master host John Bishop reigns. Bishop has cooked for Presidents Clinton and Yeltsin (he now has a standing invitation to the White House). Hollywood knows about Bishop's as well—Glenn Close, Robin Williams, Richard Gere, Robert De Niro, and others have been spotted here. Bishop warmly greets his guests (celebrity and otherwise) and, assisted by the most professionally polished young staff in the city, proceeds to demonstrate that he understands the true art of hospitality. Chef Dennis Green's entrées are uncomplicated. The rack of venison with goat cheese fritters and ginger-steamed halibut (in season) are standouts. So is the pan-seared scallops scented with lemongrass and topped with a crisp potato pancake. Everything bears the Bishop trademark of light, subtly complex flavours and bright, graphic colour. Desserts like the moist ginger cake, pooled in toffee sauce with homemade vanilla ice cream, and the Death by Chocolate are legendary. ■ *2183 W 4th Ave; 738-2025; map:O7; $$$; full bar; AE, DC, MC, V; no cheques; dinner every day (closed for two weeks in Jan).*

▼
**Top 175
Restaurants**
▲

Bodai Vegetarian Restaurant ★ The takeout deli showcases "pork," "squid," and "braised beef," but the restaurant is 100 percent vegetarian. These terms are merely masks for the elaborate and ingenious simulations crafted out of soy products and wheat gluten. Each of the 130-plus dishes is excellent—and not just for the many Chinese Buddhists who frequent the new Buddhist temple next door. Dumplings, steamed or Swatow style, and the fluffy lo-hon buns are all regular dim sum items. For dinner, try vegetables with winter melon soup, mock abalone in black bean sauce, crisp vegetarian duck, and the tasty salt and chile bean curd. While you're there, take the first step toward enlightenment: check out the calligraphy adorning the walls—it consists of Buddhist riddles pointing the way to nirvana. ■ *337 E Hastings St; 682-2666; map:V4; $; no alcohol; MC, V; no cheques; lunch, dinner Wed–Mon.*

Bo-Jik Vegetarian Restaurant ★ As part of a well-established Buddhist vegetarian tradition—there are hundreds of these restaurants in Hong Kong—Bo-Jik brings all the force of Chinese culinary tradition to bear on the problem of eating well without eating meat. Generally, you want to avoid the gluten dishes, which substitute textured soy protein for meat, and steer toward the vegetable dishes—the Bo-Jik veggie pancake, for example. It's a tangle of stir-fried vegetables, a generous stack of paper-thin Mandarin pancakes, and a hoisin sauce—mu-shu pork without the pork. Pair it with big fresh shiitake mushrooms on a bed of brilliant green sautéed gai lan, and you have, with a few bowls of rice and some tea, a splendid dinner for two for under $25. Portions are extremely large, and service is friendly, if somewhat disorganized. Unfortunately, the restaurant has all the atmo of a mall record store. ■ *820 W Broadway; 872-5556; map:S7; $; no alcohol; MC, V; no cheques; lunch, dinner every day.*

Boss Bakery and Restaurant The Boss is a slice of Hong Kong life transplanted intact from Asia's distant shores. Once beyond the sandblasted glass door, with its tongue-in-cheek silhouette of a man in a bowler smoking a pipe, you can easily imagine yourself transported across the Pacific. In one booth is a group of young teenagers reading to each other from their Chinese comics. In another, a businessman is taking lunch with an associate, and next to them three older men are debating the prowess of their favourite racehorse of the day. The menu is uniquely and eclectically Hong Kong-style cafe—a strange hybrid of East and West. Spaghetti is topped with baked seafood; macaroni is served up in soup with crunchy Chinese meatballs or strips of ham. Chinese noodle dishes and congees are also offered. If you are visiting Chinatown, the Boss is a must for both taste and fauna. Besides, where else are you going to get Ovaltine served hot, iced, or with a raw egg? ■ *532 Main St; 683-3860; map:V4; $; no alcohol; no credit cards; no cheques; lunch, dinner every day.*

▼
Top 175
Restaurants
▲

The Bread Garden ★ The Bread Garden is Vancouver's original bakery-cafe and still its most successful. Opened in 1981 as a croissant bakery, it quickly turned into an all-night coffee bar. The First Avenue location is still Kitsilano's happening scene for weekend breakfast, but now there are 10 Bread Gardens in the Lower Mainland (and two more in Colorado) to choose from. All but the suburban locations are open 24 hours a day, convenient whether you're looking for a late-night snack after an evening of dancing, a homey midweek dinner, a quick sit-down lunch, or just a muffin to go. As the franchise grows, the deli cases keep expanding, stuffed with salads, sandwiches, and ready-to-nuke fare such as quiches, frittatas, roast vegetable lasagna, and burritos. You can have a wholesome muffin or scone, or throw caution to the winds and let the dessert list tempt you with cheesecake or the New Orleans Bourbon Street pecan pie. ■ *1880 W 1st Ave (and branches); 738-6684; map:O6; $; beer and wine (1st Ave location only); MC, V; traveller's cheques OK; breakfast, lunch, dinner, midnight snacks every day.* &

Bridges ★★ One of the city's most popular hangouts has a superb setting on Granville Island. Seats on the outdoor deck, with sweeping views of downtown and the mountains, are at a premium on warm days. Bridges is actually three separate entities: a casual bistro, a pub, and a more formal upstairs dining room. The bistro's casual offerings are the best bet; upstairs, the kitchen takes its seafood seriously, but expect to pay for more than what you get. However, the recent move of chef Andrew Skorzewski from Raintree at the Landing has had a positive effect already. ■ *1696 Duranleau St (Granville Island); 687-4400; map:Q6; $$; full bar; AE, MC, V; no cheques; lunch, dinner every day, brunch Sun.* &

Cafe Centro [unrated] Phillip Mitchell of Cafe Norté has crossed two bridges to open Cafe Centro in Kitsilano, where Pepitas used to be. Classical and nonclassical out-of-the-rut Mexican dishes are made with the freshest ingredients and served in a lively room with two fireplaces and outdoor seating. ■ *2041 W 4th Ave; 734-5422; map:N7; $$; full bar; AE, MC, V; no cheques; lunch Mon–Sat, dinner every day.* &

Cafe de Paris ★★ Lace curtains at the window, paper covers on the table, a mirrored bar, and Piaf or Aznavour on the sound system: this is the bistro that takes you back to the Left Bank. Cafe de Paris' heart-of-the-West-End location draws locals and Francophiles alike. The frites—genuine french fries—have become a Vancouver legend; crisp and light, they accompany all entrées and have regulars begging for more. As in France, you can opt for the three-course table d'hôte menu or pick and choose from à la carte offerings. Among the latter: a savoury bouillabaisse dense with prawns, scallops, mussels, and monkfish, its broth infused with saffron and Pernod, and a deeply comforting cassoulet. Chef André Bernier also creates his own contemporary French cuisine: orange-glazed salmon slices perfumed with tarragon and flashed under a salamander; smoked rack of lamb. Table d'hôte offerings may include the leek and duck confit tarte, a satiny hot chicken parfait, or meltingly tender roast pork in a garlic cream sauce. Try this bistro for lunch or dinner, *naturellement*, and be sure to glance at the commendable wine list, with several surprises in store. Check out the couscous festival held in September. ■ *751 Denman St; 687-1418; map:Q2; $$$; full bar; AE, MC, V; no cheques; lunch Mon–Fri, dinner every day.*

Cafe Norté Mexican Restaurant ★★ Tucked away in Edgemont Village, this friendly spot is just minutes away from the north end of the Lions Gate Bridge. Peruse the menu while sampling the house salsa and tortilla chips. There's a full range of serious nachos: warm black bean guacamole, chile con queso topped with chorizo, sweet pineapple with jalapeño, and more. Smooth, rich, cream of crab soup comes with a garnish of finely chopped red peppers and parsley. Fajitas arrive with tender pieces of still-sizzling chicken nudged up against onions and green peppers. For diehard traditionalists, the refried beans are great and the margaritas perfectly slushy. Of the too few Mexican restaurants in Vancouver, Cafe Norté reigns supreme. ■ *3108 Edgemont Blvd; 255-1188; $$; full bar; AE, MC, V; no cheques; lunch Mon–Sat, dinner every day.* &

Caffe de Medici ★★★ As you enter Caffe de Medici, you are immediately made to feel like a favoured guest. The high moulded ceilings, serene portraits of members of the 15th-century Medici family, chairs and drapery in Renaissance green against crisp white table linen, and walls the colour of zabaglione create a slightly palatial feeling that is businesslike by day, romantic by night. Skip the soups and order the beautiful antipasto: a bright collage of marinated eggplant, artichoke hearts, peppers, olives, squid, and Italian meats. Pasta dishes are flat-out *magnifico*: a slightly chewy plateful of tortellini alla panna comes so rich with cheese you'll never order any of the others. Although it's mostly a Florentine restaurant (with a knockout version of beefsteak marinated in red wine and olive oil), we've also sampled a fine Roman-style rack of lamb. ■ *1025 Robson St; 669-9322; map:S3; $$$; full bar; AE, DC, MC, V; no cheques; lunch Mon–Fri, dinner every day.* &

The Cannery [unrated] Chef Peter Burge has departed The Cannery to produce cheese in New Zealand, and there's a new management team on board. This Vancouver original, serving "salmon by the sea" for more than 20 years, resides in a building that has been cleverly refurbished to look and feel even older than that. Nevertheless, it's badly in need of an update. So far, the menu's the same, with salmon selections running the gamut from house-smoked items to the restaurant's hallmark salmon Wellington. Stay tuned. ■ *2205 Commissioner St; 254-9606; map:F2; $$$; full bar; AE, DC, MC, V; no cheques; lunch Mon–Fri, dinner every day.*

Capers ★★ Healthy, holistic, fresh, inventive—pick practically any current cuisine buzzword and Capers fits the bill. Two locations used to serve up West Coast cuisine, but the Kits restaurant closed after a merger. There are now plans to expand and upgrade the cafe and move into fit-food takeout. What sets Capers apart from virtually any other establishment in the city is that you can shop in a country-store setting for glorious produce, unusual condiments, and a broad assortment of takeout dishes (Mediterranean wrap, Bali chicken wrap, smoked salmon). Less than a half-hour from downtown, the Dundarave location wows with water and city views from the outdoor terrace. Generous helpings and low prices draw local residents, who come for the apple and pear chutney, organic beef burgers, or pita pockets stuffed with organic turkey. Vegetarian emphasis translates into big-flavoured dishes. ■ *2496 Marine Dr, West Vancouver; 925-3374; $; beer and wine; AE, MC, V, debit cards; no cheques; breakfast, lunch every day, dinner Mon–Sat.*

Casa Sleigh ★ It's a good half-hour drive from Vancouver to the little fishing village of Steveston, so make an evening of it and schedule enough time for a preprandial saunter along the docks. After the building was fire-damaged, the original Sleigh's owners, British-born Stephen Sleigh and his Spanish wife Aurora, changed the name to Casa Sleigh to reflect the new emphasis on Spanish cooking. Chockablock with seafood and lusty with Iberian flavours, the paella is arguably BC's best. Fillet of salmon stuffed with avocado and spinach, uncomplicated prawn preparations, a fisherman's pot, a few meat dishes, and a vegetarian gypsy pot round out the menu. Many make a meal of the tapas: just-crisp patatas aioli is blanketed in a toothsome garlic mayonnaise. House special croquettes are crisp fingers filled with ham, chorizo, or shrimp in a creamy béchamel. Catalan pan con tomate is a triumph of simple flavours: toasted French bread spread with olive oil, garlic, and fresh tomato. You can always walk it off with another stroll after dinner. ■ *3711 Bayview St, Richmond (Stevenson); 275-5188; map:C7; $$; full bar; AE, MC, V; no cheques; lunch, dinner every day.*

▼

▲

Century Grill ★★ Whether you're checking out the action at the bar or slicing into the best beef in town, this urban, upscale steak house is great fun. Loud, friendly, and boisterous, it's a great place to hang with your friends—or to make some new ones. Typical of the trendy new Yaletown eateries, the Century Grill is built in an old warehouse, and much of the room's charm comes from the exposed wooden beams and industrial fittings. The kitchen opens on to the dining area, giving diners a great view of the cooks doing their pyrotechnics behind the counter. Go for the steak, whether beef or seafood. It's cooked to perfection and perfectly tender. The pepper steak is a meat-lover's dream, all spicy crust gentled with a creamy sauce and served with a mound of fluffy garlic mashed potatoes. Although the steak is the star here, salads and pastas are perfectly respectable, and there is a good selection of appetizers and side dishes to tempt as well. Servings are hearty and the food well-prepared. Don't, however, expect adventurous dining—or a cosy, romantic evening with your beloved. It is very noisy and popular with the trendy set, whom you'll see sipping martinis and smoking cigars at what's shaping up to be the city's hottest bar scene. ■ *1095 Hamilton St; 688-8088; map:S5; $$$; full bar; AE, MC, V; lunch, dinner every day, brunch Sun.*

Chartwell (The Four Seasons) ★★★★ Chartwell remains in the bold forefront of excellent hotel dining. It evokes an upper-class English men's club atmosphere. Executive chef Marc Miron, former executive chef of the award-winning Four

Seasons resort in Nevis, produces food of the highest quality that is generous both in proportion and in inspiration. Begin with his house-smoked salmon with onion and dill biscotti and lemon crème fraîche, and move on to Dungeness crab cakes with Fraser Valley greens drizzled with yellow pepper aioli. The rosy calf's liver with double-smoked bacon and garlic roasted onion confit with buttermilk herb mashed potatoes is world class. Master host Angelo Cecconi and his talented staff give Chartwell its distinctive stamp of personal service—warm, discreet, and attentive. A pre-theatre dinner menu with valet parking is an outstanding value. The wine list is an award winner, and the winemaker dinners are the most popular in the city. ■ *791 W Georgia St; 689-9333; map:S3; $$$; full bar; AE, DC, JCV, MC, V; no cheques; breakfast every day, lunch Sun–Fri, dinner every day.* ﹠

Chili Club Thai Restaurant ★★ Despite the name, with a few noteworthy exceptions, Chili Club's fare is not particularly hot. The staff members, however, are well informed and helpful, and if you want it spicy, they'll gladly oblige. We've enjoyed pork satay and Tom Yum Kung soup (prawns and mushrooms married in a good broth with hot spice and deep-scented lemongrass), and when giant smoked New Zealand mussels stuffed with a mild thick curry paste are available, order them; the same goes for solidly spiced chicken curry, made with coconut milk and bite-size Thai eggplant. There's plenty to choose from. Popular wines and beers are available at realistic prices. For the best view of False Creek, try the holding bar upstairs with ceiling-to-floor windows on all sides. Even when the food is fiery, the decor is rather cold. Chili Club is located close to the water, under the Burrard Street Bridge. ■ *1000 Beach Ave; 681-6000; map:Q5; $$; full bar; AE, DC, MC, V; cheques OK; lunch, dinner every day.* ﹠

Chiyoda ★★ In a town full of sushi restaurants with robata grills on the side, Chiyoda is a robata restaurant with a sushi bar on the side. Built on a generous scale, the robata bar was designed in Japan. Robata selections are arranged in wicker baskets on a layer of ice that separates the customer's side of the bar from the cook's side. Order from the simple menu (snapper, squid, oysters, scallops, eggplant, and shiitake). The cook prepares your choices and hands you the finished dishes across the bar on the end of a long wooden paddle. Seafood is excellent, but don't miss a foray into the cross-cultural world of robata-cooked garlic, potatoes, and corn. A popular spot for downtown businesspeople, the Chiyoda also attracts Japanese visitors exhausted from shopping in the huge gift shop downstairs. ■ *1050 Alberni St; 688-5050; map:S3; $$; full bar; AE, MC, V; no cheques; lunch Mon–Fri, dinner Mon–Sat.* ﹠

CinCin ★★★ *CinCin* is a hearty Italian toast, a wish of health and good cheer, all of which is implied in this sunny Mediterranean space. The scent from wood-burning ovens, the warm surroundings—what more could one need? Best seats are in the northeast corner by the window. CinCin's breadsticks and flatbreads (rosemary and oatmeal) are irresistible. Launch your meal with a saffron-scented cioppino, or carpaccio. Noodles are made fresh daily. Rigatoni is tossed with house-made sausage, clams, and fennel; linguine ribbons are laced with beef tenderloin and tomatoes; and penne is dotted with juicy morsels of roast chicken and capers. Another bonus: the wine list is not only one of the best in town but, because of a reduced markup on wines, economical. Desserts are all homemade in the best sense of the word. A great place to sip wine with the gang in the lounge (food's served until 11:30). ■ *1154 Robson St; 688-7338; map:R3; $$$; full bar; AE, DC, MC, V; no cheques; lunch Mon–Fri, dinner every day.*

Cipriano's Ristorante & Pizzeria ★★ This compact pasta-pizza house is approaching institution status for its basic and most plentiful portions. Strains of Tony Bennett and Frank Sinatra fill the air as straightforward Italian home cooking arrives at your table, preceded by fabulous garlic bread, dripping with butter and deluged with Parmesan. The giant caesar salad (made to share), an exercise in excess, is garlic-laden and crammed with croutons. Deep-dish pizza, pasta puttanesca, and chicken cacciatore are all worth your attention, though some sauces can be remarkably similar. Short routines from owner and onetime standup comedian Frank Cipriano punctuate the meal that wife Christina prepares. For atmosphere and value, few places compare: reservations are a must. ■ *3995 Main St; 879-0020; map:E3; $$; full bar; V; no cheques; dinner Tues–Sat.*

Corsi Trattoria ★★ This little family-run trattoria makes a great excuse for a mini-cruise via the SeaBus. The Corsi family was here on the North Shore before the SeaBus terminal and Lonsdale Quay Public Market existed. The family ran a trattoria in Italy, and the old-country touches still show. Twenty-odd homemade pastas include the house specialty, rotolo—pasta tubes stuffed with veal, spinach, and ricotta and topped with cream and tomato sauces. Or try trenette al salmone affumicata—pasta with smoked salmon, cream, olives, and tomatoes. Adventurous eaters might try the Roman food orgy (for a minimum of two big appetites): four pastas, mixed salad, a platter of lamb, veal, and prawns, followed by coffee and dessert. ■ *1 Lonsdale Ave (across from Lonsdale Market); 987-9910; map:E1; $$; full bar; AE, DC, MC, V; no cheques; lunch Mon–Fri, dinner Mon–Sat.* ♿

▼

**Top 175
Restaurants**

▲

Da Pasta Bar ★★ The concept of mixing and matching pasta with sauce isn't a new one, but it works better here than at most places. Aubergine-coloured walls, explosive artwork, and a kitchenside view of the action crank up the visual volume. The can't-miss location on Robson Street draws everyone from the Docs-and-jeans set to kids with their elderly aunts; the ebullient, pasta-literate servers make all feel welcome. The pastabilities are endless, with six different pastas and 14 assorted sauces adding up, theoretically, to more than 80 different dishes, but servers are strong at steering you to what best complements what. Perhaps they'll even suggest some intriguing fusions of West Coast produce and seafood with Asian ingredients. Good lunchtime deals on designer salad and pasta combos. There's a second location at 2201 West First Avenue in Kitsilano. ■ *1232 Robson St; 688-1288; map:R3; $; full bar; AE, DC, MC, V; no cheques; lunch, dinner every day.*

Dario's La Piazza Ristorante ★★ Dario's is not an upstart trendy restaurant where one is assured of classical competence at every turn. The decor is simple and functional. A salad and antipasto station displays the day's offering and splits the room in two. Large tropical plants and floral displays complete the comfortable illusion of dining in a courtyard instead of alongside the industrial artery on which the restaurant is located. The small bar extends into a floor-to-ceiling wall of wine racks, highlighting the restaurant's considerable inventory. Service is mature, understated, efficient, and seamlessly orchestrated— a pleasant change from the flamboyant casualness that seems to pervade the contemporary "concept" dining scene. The large menu at Dario's also bucks the trends and is full of familiar favourites now considered out of vogue: fettuccine alfredo, risotto al funghi, veal scalloppine with lemon and white wine. A glorious stracciatella soup of Parmesan, egg swirls, and spinach followed by a perfectly sauced plate of sun-dried tomato and sausage penne makes a very satisfying lunch. ■ *3075 Slocan St (Italian Centre); 430-2195; map:F3; $$; full bar; AE, MC, V; no cheques; lunch Mon–Fri, dinner Mon–Sat.*

Delilah's ★ Back in the old days, when was it tucked into the basement of the old Buchan Hotel, Delilah's was one of the city's best secrets. Cosy, romantic, and boisterous all at once, it was a voluptuous dining experience. Diners felt like the fortunate members of a special, in-the-know clique, and the restaurant's potentially annoying quirks—like the rule about no reservations for parties under six—merely added to its charm. But now Delilah's has moved uptown, only a few blocks in distance, but miles away in atmosphere. It still has the cheeky cupids painted on the ceiling, and the plush red velvet banquettes, and the fabulous martini menu—the city's first and still its best. Unfortunately, though, in expanding the room and let-

▼

Top 175
Restaurants

▲

ting in more light, Delilah's has lost a great deal of what made it so charming. Now the waitstaff seem too rushed to dish with the customers, the hour-long wait at the bar is irritating (why won't they take reservations?), and the multiple-choice menu a tad tiresome. The food itself is fresh and inventive, although the staff occasionally falls short on the preparation side of things. Luckily though, the wine list is extensive and reasonably priced, and it's worth dropping by just for the martinis, with names like the Blue Dolphin, the Surrealist, the Metropolitan, and nearly 30 others. Reservations are accepted only for groups of six or more. ■ *1739 Comox St; 687-3424; map:P2; $$; full bar; AE, DC, MC, V; no cheques; dinner every day.* &

Diva at the Met (Metropolitan Hotel) [unrated] An airy multi-tiered space with an exhibition kitchen has set the stage for imaginative, well-executed cooking at what's sure to become one of the finest hotel restaurants in the city. Thanks to some restaurant raiding, Michael Noble of the Four Seasons, David Griffiths of Alabaster, and Ray Henry of Waterfront Centre all have their spoons in the soup here. Whatever is served, it ranks with the best, but it's sometimes slow getting to you. However, it's worth a wait for the unique starter, a chilled tomato martini, and the entrées, the grilled prawns, avocado and Dungeness crab risotto, or a lamb rack with calamata olive butter. Brunchers will swoon over the smoked Alaskan black cod hash topped with poached eggs. All the desserts are winners, but the Stilton cheesecake is a must-order. No maître d' abuse here: ex-Le Crocodile manager John Blakeley strives for the highest standard of service. And the wine list is sure to win awards. ■ *645 Howe St; 602-7788; map:S3; $$; full bar; AE, DC, MC, V; no cheques; breakfast, lunch, dinner every day.*

Top 175 Restaurants

Earl's ★★ It's fast food, and it isn't. Each pearl in Earl's chain has the same sassy style and emphasis on high-quality, fresh-only ingredients, whether on pizzas, in pastas, or with burgers. Earl's follows food trends closely and trains its staff accordingly, once a year shipping the whole management team off to Tuscany (or wherever) to experience the cuisine firsthand. The menu caters to all tastes and ages, but you'll mostly find a younger crowd here. Specialty microbrews and a one-price wine list of 19 wines under $20. Open until midnight; some locations even later. There are now 22 Earl's restaurants in BC, 14 in the Lower Mainland. ■ *303 Marine Dr, North Vancouver (and branches); 984-4341; map:E1; $$; full bar; AE, MC, V; no cheques; lunch, dinner every day.*

El Caravan ★ Make a note to visit this Lebanese restaurant the next time you're downtown shopping or taking in a little Mozart at the nearby Orpheum Theatre. Levis or black tie, you'll be equally at home in El Caravan's roomy interior, where peachy walls and vases of pampas plumes subtly allude to sunnier climes. Original chef Mona Helfaoui has returned to her place in the kitchen, and she cooks the dishes she learned at her grandmother's elbow. Long on parsley, the tabbouleh is refreshing and clean to the taste buds. Partnering the usual Middle Eastern appetizers—hummus, baba ghanouj, and grape leaves—are her exceptionally spicy carrots. There are pita sandwiches filled with commendably good falafel and various souvlakia. All entrées—the prawns, lamb chops, chicken, spinach pie, moussaka, and souvlakia—come with the aforementioned spicy carrots and rice that's lightly tossed with vermicelli. ■ *809 Seymour St; 682-7000; map:S4; $$; full bar; AE, DC, MC, V; no cheques; lunch, dinner every day.*

English Bay Boathouse ★ The Boathouse presides over the sands of English Bay and, at day's end, some of the best sunsets in the world. The decor is shipshape and lean. Downstairs, a casual bistro with a summertime deck is a favourite spot. Upstairs, the serious eating takes place (but forget the wine list). A house specialty is rotisserie roasted prime rib. As expected, there is a fine selection of seafood, including Thai-spiced crab cakes and mesquite barbecued king crab. There is also a daily feature that is often delightfully and inventively toothsome. A good spot for family dining, beachside. ■ *1795 Beach Ave; 669-2225; map:P3; $$; full bar; AE, DC, MC, V; no cheques; lunch Mon–Sat, dinner every day, brunch Sun.* ♿

Ezogiku Noodle Cafe Ramen dishes are the order of the day at this 70-seater cafe. Ramen comes in regular (pork), miso, or soy broth, a fried noodle dish, a curried dish, and gyozas—and that's it. Ezogiku's focus is the secret to the large bowls of perfectly cooked chewy noodles in rich, steaming broth. Do what the old master in the movie *Tampopo* instructed: study, sniff, and savour. Other branches are in Honolulu and Tokyo. ■ *1329 Robson St; 685-8608; map:R3; $; no alcohol; no credit cards; no cheques; lunch, dinner every day.*

Farrago ★★ Dining doesn't come prettier than this. Farrago is, as the name suggests, a medley of lovely things: a modern restaurant in an antique building with rough brick walls, contemporary artworks, and delicate fixtures highlighted in purple, bronze, and gold. This Yaletown restaurant also has a patio in a former carriage turnaround that is possibly the most beautiful outdoor eating spot in town. The menu is an eclectic mix of flavours and ideas. Some dishes are exquisite, tantalizing all the senses while they please the palate. A squid ink fettuccine with shrimp, orange, and poppy-seed dressing is a marvel of design and delicate flavours, and the baby lettuces are just lightly bathed in a perfect, almost sweet, lemon-honey vinaigrette. Unfortunately, some of the dishes are better as concepts than as realities, being overflavoured and served with sides that don't readily balance them. The caesar salad, for instance, is overwhelmed by the oceanful of anchovies in the dressing; the slow-roasted duck needs a lighter, sharper partner than the rich stuffed red onion and pools of syrupy, sweet sauce. On the other hand, the room is so pretty and the wine list so reasonable, it becomes easy to ignore a few flaws. ■ *1138 Homer St; 684-4044; map:S5; $$$; full bar; AE, DC, MC, V; no cheques; dinner Mon–Sat.*

Favorito Pasta Trattoria ★★ It's 15 years since this beloved neighbourhood restaurant opened on Broadway's busy stretch of medical and office buildings, and in that decade and a half, Favorito has maintained one of the cosiest rooms in town. Small pink-clothed tables are close enough together to maintain an old-world hubbub of conversation. Although the room aspires to elegance, pretensions are dashed by the kitschy Italian mementos on the walls and the jars filled with dried pasta perched over the bar. In 1981, the food was adventurous for Vancouver; today it's pretty standard—though delicious—Italian fare. If you're ordering pasta, choose one of the tomato-based sauces, such as the linguine Siciliana, with eggplant, peppers, and just a hint of spiciness, or the linguine alla pescatora, a joyous mix of tender squid, shrimp, clams, and mussels in a zingy tomato sauce. Or choose the veal scalloppine, which is served with a variety of toppings. Finish with a zabaglione that will leave your taste buds tingling. As for wines, reasonable values and selection are to be had by the bottle; unfortunately, Favorito has a poor and pricey by-the-glass selection. ■ *552 W Broadway; 876-3534; map:S7; $$; full bar; AE, DC, MC, V; lunch Tues–Fri, dinner every day.*

Fiasco ★★ An eagerness to have their flagons filled and their palates sated is what draws a hip urban crowd to this easygoing westside eatery. The only thing cooler is the decor, a light and lofty room that, come summer, spills out onto the sidewalk. The skylit bar has its own faithfuls who come to watch the game on TV and sip Rickard's draft or Granville Island beer. The menu feels more Californian than Tuscan, the pizzas more Puck-ish than most. In the open kitchen with its wood-fired brick oven, you can watch the cook making a Cajun shrimp version or one topped with grilled zucchini, bocconcini, and oyster mushrooms. Or you can simply build your own. Pastas are esoteric: cannelloni are stuffed with chicken; tortellini are stuffed with salmon and Camembert. Live entertainment Thursday through Sunday. Bargain seekers should look for the weeknight specials. ■ *2486 Bayswater St; 734-1325; map:C3; $$; full bar; AE, MC, V; no cheques; lunch, dinner every day, brunch Sun.*

The Fish House at Stanley Park ★★★ Ever since high-profile restaurateur Bud Kanke put chef Karen Barnaby in the Fish House kitchen, he's been winning accolades from critics

▼

Top 175
Restaurants

▲

and diners alike. Here, seafood rules (salmon, seabass, shellfish of all kinds)—everything you'd expect and some things you wouldn't. As an appy, try the deep-fried cornmeal oysters with a chipotle-flavoured tartare sauce. It's the whole plate that impresses. Barnaby's vegetables aren't an afterthought; each is a discovery in itself: red cabbage with fennel, spaghetti squash with poppy seeds, and buttermilk mashed potatoes. Ahi tuna comes as two-fisted loins (a pair), barely grilled through and fork-tender in a green pepper sauce with buttermilk mashed potatoes. Barnaby's chocolate lava cake is lethal. ■ *2099 Beach Ave (entrance to Stanley Park); 681-7275; map:N1; $$; full bar; AE, DC, E, MC, V; no cheques; lunch Mon–Sat, dinner every day, brunch Sun.* &

Five Sails (Pan Pacific Hotel) ★★★ The drop-dead gorgeous harbour view at the Five Sails may lure diners here for the first time, but it's chef Cheryle Michio's imaginative way with fresh fish, soups, duck, and more that bring them back. Don't even think of not ordering the smoked Alaska black cod chowder. Second choice would be the seared scallops on wasabi mashed potatoes. Winning entrées include crispy seabass with sweet lemon and sour orange sauce, seared sesame salmon with hot-and-sour carrot butter sauce, and medallions of veal in a bacon wrap. Set sail on an individual baked Alaska. The eager-to-please service is icing on the cake. Become a member here of La Confrerie du Sabre d'Or by ordering champagne and sabreing the bottle. Free parking. ■ *999 Canada Place; 891-2892; map:T2; $$$; full bar; AE, DC, MC, V; no cheques; dinner every day.* &

Fleuri (Sutton Place Hotel) ★★★ Elegant all-day dining and a very civilized tea await those who venture through Sutton Place Hotel's chandeliered lobby to the newly re-named Fleuri. Hotel guests—corporate types and movie stars (celeb-spotting is a popular sport)—converse over classic English tea or a traditional Japanese tea ceremony with hand-whisked macha tea and bean jelly. For $15, you can nibble on finger sandwiches, pastries, and scones and cream. Buffets are a specialty: Friday and Saturday tables are laden with seafood and fish for the "Taste of Atlantis." On Thursday, Friday, and Saturday, the Chocoholic Bar has become a legend, and the Sunday brunch has been rated as the number one special occasion place in town. At press time, Sutton Place is closing the doors of its other restaurant, Le Club, and talented chef Kai Lermen is moving to Fleuri. A menu upgrade is planned—as if another reason to visit this elegant restaurant is necessary. ■ *845 Burrard St; 682-5511; map:S4; $$; full bar; AE, DC, MC, V; no cheques; breakfast, lunch, dinner every day, brunch Sun.* &

Floata Seafood Restaurant ★★ Vancouver's historical Chinatown begins its facelift as we speed forward into the new millennium, and the Floata Restaurant Group leads the pack with its opening of the largest restaurant in Vancouver to date. This cavernous, sparsely postmodern room seats 1,000 (yes, *1,000*). The room is equipped with wall-to-ceiling partitions that can carve up the impressive space, to order, into restaurant-size private dining rooms, each equipped with its very own karaoke sound system. An already brisk dim sum trade ensures fresh and very good nibbles for those who are there to enjoy this popular Chinese roving lunch-hour feast. Unfortunately, dinner experiences here have fallen short of the high quality one comes to expect at the group's other location in Richmond, where the succulent crispy-skin chicken, the tender lobster in cream sauce, the velvety braised Chinese mushrooms with mustard greens, and other Cantonese favourites are local standard-bearers of the cuisine. Hopefully, given time, this latest Chinatown landmark will come to deserve the vote of confidence its suburban elder sister received from a recent polling of Chinese diners, who voted it one of the top ten fine dining Chinese restaurants in the Lower Mainland. ■ *400-180 Keefer St; 602-0368; map:X4; $$; full bar; AE, DC, MC, V; no cheques; lunch (dim sum), dinner every day* ■ *1425-4380 No. 3 Rd (Parker Place Shopping Centre), Richmond; 270-8889; map:D5; $$; full bar; AE, V; no cheques; lunch, dinner every day.* &

Flying Wedge ★ Pizza is all they sell, but it's arguably the best in town in all five locations (including the airport). Join the lunchtime business crowd at Library Square and Royal Centre or the Kitsilano beach bunch on Cornwall Avenue, just south of the Burrard Street Bridge. You'll find funky, Crayola-coloured surroundings in all venues as well as generous wedges of thin-crusted pizza, served cafeteria-style, for $3.25 a pop. An old fave is Deep Purple, heady with marinated eggplant, and a good spicy Sichuan chicken; a new fave includes a pie with peaches and Black Forest ham. There is a wide choice of nonalcoholic drinks. Open till midnight weekends. Sundays is all-you-can-eat-day for $5.95. Royal Centre locale is closed Sunday, and Library Square serves only lunch. ■ *3499 Cambie (and branches); 874-8284; map:D3; $; no alcohol; no credit cards; no cheques; lunch, dinner every day.* &

Fortune House ★★ Awarded for creativity by a Chinese media restaurant poll, this upscale restaurant sports a menu that borrows from the diverse culinary regions of China, with delectable and innovative results. Steamed lobster and asparagus rolls in a dragon boat of carved winter melon flanked with paddles of braised ham slices; sautéed scallops, sea clams, and geoduck with jackfruit and lotus seeds; singing chicken in Mandarin wine sauce and steamed hairy squash with Buddha's feast are all excellent in both taste and presentation. The chef also makes a genuine effort to integrate local ingredients into his cooking. For instance, salmon, a fish seldom used in Chinese restaurants, is deep-fried, then smartly dressed in salt and chiles. It turns up again, succulent and delicious, in a sizzling clay pot braised with eggplant. Even the sometimes mundane permutations of dim sum manage to rise to new heights here, with wonderfully delicate items like tempura nori, tofu rolls, and scallop dumplings. Although the glass and brass interior of Fortune House borders on the generic, booth seating along one wall of the restaurant makes it quite comfortable and conducive to more intimate dining. ■ *5733 Cambie St (Oakridge Centre); 266-7728; map:D4; $$; full bar; AE, MC, V; no cheques; lunch, dinner every day.*

Gianni Restaurant and Norcineria ★★★ Spaghetti al tartufo Norcina or, to you and me, spaghetti with truffles. If for no other reason, visit Gianni's for this dish: you'll swear it was transported to earth by some heavenly messenger. Of course, the roasted meats, simple but packed with flavour, may also entice you; or the light-as-air tiramisu; or the good selection of Italian wines. The food is almost as appealing as the shy charm of chef/owner Gianni Picchi and his attentive waitstaff. Gianni used to cook at Umberto Menghi's Il Giardino and has brought all the lessons from that highly respected kitchen to a neighbourhood that sorely needed them. The classic dishes he serves are straightforward, husky, and simple, with strong earthy flavours that will assure you that this is just how food should taste. When Gianni took over the old, much-lamented Szasz deli on South Granville, he created an illusion of a walled Umbrian courtyard, with garden bric-a-brac, plants, and terracotta walls. It certainly appeals to local celebrities, who fill this wonderful spot with vibrant chatter. They're probably just there for the truffles. ■ *2881 Granville St; 738-7922; map:D3; $$$; full bar; AE, DC, MC, V; no cheques; lunch Mon–Fri, dinner Mon–Sat.*

▼

Top 175
Restaurants

▲

Giraffe ★★ This delightful, elegant neighbourhood restaurant in White Rock, with a view of Semiahmoo Bay, strongly believes in the three *G*s of California-style cooking—garlic, goat cheese, and grilling. As you peruse the menu, a basket of crisp pappadums is delivered to the table. Nobody will rush you through luxurious appetizers of crispy wonton skins filled with fresh crab and served with honey mustard, or a layered torta basilica of cream cheese, pesto, pine nuts, and sun-dried tomatoes with garlic crostini. The lamb loin in mustard herb sauce with caramelized onions is outstanding—ditto the boneless chicken breast with mixed berries. Save room for "The Graze"— a dessert sampler with an array of sweets that may include cheesecake, fruit and berry sorbets, or a rich chocolate cake. And owner/chef Corinne Poole constantly peeks out to ensure that everyone is finishing what's on their plates. ■ *15053 Marine*

Dr (across from the pier), White Rock; 538-6878; $$; full bar; MC, AE, V; no cheques; lunch, dinner every day, brunch Sun.

Grand King Seafood Restaurant ★★★ ½ Chef Lam Kam Shing and partner Simon Lee, the team behind the brief Camelot-like brilliance of the old Dynasty Restaurant in the Ramada Renaissance Hotel, are now wowing local and visiting lovers of Chinese food in their well-established restaurant located in the Holiday Inn on West Broadway. Granted, the decor here is no match for the elegant Dynasty, but the service, less formal, ever courteous, informative, and helpful, is unmatched. The menu is trademark Lam—a creative assimilation of his diverse experience in Chinese regional cuisines with innovative touches gleaned from Japanese and other Asian cooking styles. Local ingredients become new classics in dishes like pan-fried live spot prawns in chile soya, and stewed black cod with garlic and house-barbecued pork. Ideas both simple and complex are backed by thoughtful and impeccable execution in the kitchen. And with the chef's special menu changing monthly, it is easy to keep going back for more. One of our recent favourites is the Dungeness crab—the body meat steamed in its shell, laced with its rich roe, minced pork, and cellophane noodles, and surrounded by its legs crisp-fried with spicy rock salt. Another is superb double-boiled winter melon soup cooked inside the melon and laden with seafood. The list goes on. One more thing, you'll be happy to know that those addictive complimentary candied walnuts and their dynamite X.O. chile sauce are now bottled to go at the cashier's desk on your way out. ■ *705 W Broadway (Holiday Inn); 876-7855; map:R7; $$$; full bar; AE, MC, V; no cheques; lunch, dinner every day.*

▼

Top 175 Restaurants

▲

Griffins (Hotel Vancouver) ★★ The eminently respectable Hotel Vancouver (one of the historic Canadian Pacific châteaus that dot Canada) houses a bright and lively bistro. With taxi-cab-yellow walls, griffin-motif carpet, and a feeling of urban action, the place has energy to burn. Three meals a day are served à la carte, but the buffet meals are the way to go. The breakfast buffet lets you veer toward the healthy—muesli, fresh fruit compote, and such—or the hedonistic: carved Pepsi Cola-glazed ham. An Asian corner supplies early birds with a fix of grilled salmon and toasted nori. Make a dinner of smoked salmon or roasted peppers with basil at the appetizer bar, or work your way through entrées of silver-dollar scallops in garlic sauce, an exemplary steak, or a pasta dish, then take a run or three at the pastry bar. ■ *900 W Georgia St; 662-1900; map:S3; $$; full bar; AE, DC, MC, V; no cheques; breakfast, lunch, dinner every day.* ₺

Hamburger Mary's "Open 22 hours out of 24" says the sign, and in this neck of the woods the action lasts till the wee hours, when singles and couples wind up the night with a snack at good ol' Mary's. It's the diner we all grew up with gone upscale, with groovy chrome 'n' glass-block decor and heartachey songs on the jukebox. A West End fixture since 1979, Hamburger Mary's has stayed open by racing apace of fickle appetites. Thus, starters are whatever's hip, be it potato skins, chicken strips with plum sauce, or potstickers. Big burgers are the major draw here: served with bacon, cheese, and just about any other combo that strikes your fancy—with the Works for the undecided, the double-size Banquet Burger for the ravenous, and fish and chicken burgers for the quasi-vegetarians. Tuesday and Wednesday the attraction is a selection of twelve kinds of pasta for just $5.95. Not forgetting its diner roots, Hamburger Mary's also serves up chips with a side of mayo or gravy and humongous milkshakes in chrome containers. Genuine corned beef hash shows up occasionally as a special. Open till 4am. ■ *1202 Davie St; 687-1293; map:Q4; $; full bar; AE, DC, MC, V; no cheques; breakfast, lunch, dinner, midnight snacks every day.*

The Hermitage ★★ Owner chef Herve Martin (who was once chef to the late King Leopold of Belgium) sticks strongly by his French roots, although an innovative menu includes a few items that are more local in flavour. Like their owner, the surroundings are quiet and unassuming. Martin's menu varies, although he frequently prepares special requests with sufficient notice. Highlights often include veal—either a chop with a grainy mustard sauce or a tenderloin, gently sautéed with chanterelles. Local seafood might be plump prawns with sweet and sour apples in pomegranate juice. There is a carefully chosen wine list, and only a fool would pass up the crêpe with fresh berries and a scoop of vanilla ice cream warmed and served with a strawberry coulis. And while The Hermitage (as its name implies) may be hidden, it's well worth the looking. ■ *115-1025 Robson St; 689-3237; map:S3; $$; full bar; AE, DC, JCB, MC, V; no cheques; lunch Mon–Fri, dinner every day.*

Herons (Waterfront Centre Hotel) ★★ ½ In the Waterfront Centre, Herons' high-ceilinged dining room is a multipurpose bistro and restaurant with an open kitchen. Daryle Ryo Nagata is a rising young chef who's up to the challenge of attracting diners' attention away from the panoramic harbour view and the hustle and bustle of the hotel, both inside and out. His menu changes weekly, and there's a daily fresh sheet of contemporary Canadian cooking with a fusion flair. Start with an appetizer of musk ox carpaccio. It gets a lift from a shaving of Parmesan cheese and a roasted bell pepper aioli. Or share the salmon sampler—generous portions of salmon and Dungeness crab cakes, salmon tartare, Indian candy, warm pan-seared gravlax, alderwood smoked salmon, and salmon belly tempura. Everyone will appreciate Nagata's rooftop herb garden and his emphasis on healthy cuisine. Try the Imperial herbal soup, the citrus and gilly flower peppered salmon pasta, and the Similkameen peach cobbler with bee pollen and stevia crust. Or order a traditional clubhouse. On Sundays, a trio from Vancouver Symphony Orchestra plays during brunch. Warm, accommodating service despite the room's lack of intimacy. Innovative food and wine promotions. ■ *900 Canada Pl; 691-1991; map:T3; $$; full bar; AE, DC, E, JCV, MC, V; no cheques; breakfast, lunch, dinner every day, brunch Sun.*

Hon's Wun Tun House ★ Vancouverites have tracked the growth of Hon's from a diminutive space with windows that were continually steamed up by simmering stockpots to its present empire of multiple locations headquartered in one of Chinatown's newer retail complexes. The decor of the main Chinatown location may now be urbanly chic, but the lineups, noise level, rock-bottom prices, and basic menu remain reassuringly the same. Soups are a major draw: basic won ton, pig's feet, fish ball, and 90-odd variations— all in a rich, life-affirming broth. Equally noteworthy are Hon's trademark pot-stickers. Pan-fried or steamed, they come circled like wagons around a ginger-spiked dipping sauce. If you don't have time to sit down, Hon's now offers take-outs, ranging from barbecued meats and simple but tasty Cantonese-style dishes to a full line of frozen dim sum plus odd items like fresh frozen soy, yard-long beans, and, of course, fresh noodles galore. ■ *108-268 Keefer St (and branches); 688-0871; map:V4; $; no alcohol; no credit cards; no cheques; lunch, dinner every day.*

Horizons on Burnaby Mountain ★★ ¹/₂ A drive to the top of Burnaby Mountain leads right to this spacious room, whose numerous windows command a spectacular view of the city, snug in Burrard Inlet far below. A continuing emphasis on local fare in the hands of new chef John Garrett has produced a menu with specialties such as alder-grilled BC salmon, a scallop and prawn risotto, and seafood bouillabaisse. Many BC wines are featured on the restaurant's extensive list. Watch for seasonal food and wine promotions. ■ *100 Centennial Way; 299-1155; map:I2; $$; full bar; AE, E, MC, V; lunch, dinner every day, brunch Sun.*

Ikea Why would we suggest a meal in a furniture store? Two reasons. One, if you've never wandered through this phenomenally successful high-concept, low-priced, serve-yourself Swedish store, you're in for a treat. More to the point, it's the only place in and around Vancouver (20 minutes from downtown via the Knight Street Bridge) that serves Swedish food. It's also the only cafeteria—let alone furniture store—we know of that lets you sip a glass of wine with your meal. You'll find a variety of spiced or marinated pickled herring, liver pâtés,

cucumber salad, and robust smoked or spiced sausages round-
ing out the cold side of the buffet. Red cabbage and köttbullar
(Swedish meatballs) are usually among the hot dishes offered.
Open-faced hoagies and children's box lunches are also available. Nearby, you can gather an armload of such specialties as
lingonberry preserves, Swedish flatbread, or a bottle of 38-
proof Gammel Dansk bitters to take home. ▪ *3200 Sweden
Way, Richmond; 273-2051; map:C6; $; beer and wine; MC,
V; cheques OK; lunch every day, dinner Mon-Fri.* ⟨

Il Giardino di Umberto ★★★ Stars, stargazers, and the
movers and shakers come to Umberto Menghi's Il Giardino to
mingle amid the Tuscan villa decor: high ceilings, tiled floors,
winking candlelight, and a vine-draped terrace for dining alfresco
(no better place in summer). The emphasis is on pasta and game,
with an Italian nuova elegance: farm-raised pheasant with roasted-
pepper stuffing and port wine sauce, tender veal with a mélange
of lightly grilled wild mushrooms. Be warned: the prices on the
specials are in their own category. For dessert, go for the prize-
winning tiramisu—the best version of this pick-me-up in town.
▪ *1382 Hornby St; 669-2422; map:R5; $$$; full bar; AE, DC,
MC, V; no cheques; lunch Mon–Fri, dinner Mon–Sat.*

Imperial Chinese Seafood Restaurant ★★ The Imperial may
lay claim to being the most opulent Chinese dining room
around. There's a feeling of being in a grand ballroom of eras
past: a central staircase leads to the balustrade-lined mezza-
nine, diplomatic dignitaries and rock stars dine in luxurious
private rooms, and windows two storeys high look out onto
the panorama of Burrard Inlet and the North Shore moun-
tains. The food can be equally polished—lobster in black bean
sauce with fresh egg noodles, pan-fried scallops garnished with
coconut-laced deep-fried milk, sautéed spinach with minced
pork and Chinese anchovies, a superb pan-smoked black cod,
and the addictive beef sauté in chiles with honey walnuts. Dim
sum also is consistently good. However, reports of uneven ser-
vice continue to mar what otherwise might be a perfect restau-
rant in its class. Reservations recommended on weekdays.
▪ *355 Burrard St; 688-8191; map:S3; $$; full bar; AE, MC,
V; no cheques; lunch, dinner every day.*

Isadora's ★ Isadora's children's menu (clown-faced pizzas
and grilled cheese with potato chips), in-house play area, and
tables next to the outdoor water park in summer make this a
family favourite. The wholesome menu also features more
grown-up items, such as smoked wild salmon sandwiches, organic salads, great nut burgers, and plenty of choices for vegans. Isadora's is busiest at Sunday brunch. Service is generally
slow. ▪ *1540 Old Bridge St (Granville Island); 681-8816;
map:Q6; $; full bar; MC, V; no cheques; breakfast, lunch, din-
ner every day, brunch Sat–Sun.* ⟨

J J's Dining Room West Van matrons *adore* bringing their friends to this convenient spot for lunch and dinner. The food is well prepared, the service enthusiastic (if sometimes slow), and the prices—cheap, cheap, cheap. Attached to the Downtown Campus of Vancouver Community College, this '60s retro restaurant is a training ground for its chefs' program. There's good basic food served every day, but don't think basic means boring—it's not. Menus change from week to week but might include a crêpe with smoked salmon, a hearts of limestone lettuce salad with a roasted almond and raspberry vinaigrette, noisettes of lamb, or brochette of scallops. The Friday night buffet is a great deal at $14.95. A renovation is underway. Phone for reservations. ■ *250 W Pender St; 443-8479; map:U4; $; full bar; MC, V; no cheques; lunch, dinner every day.*

Joe Fortes ★★ ½ There's a strong focus on food here now thanks to super-cool chef Terry Multhauf, who's leading the pack in this Robson Street neighbourhood of terrific restaurants. You might be in New York or Boston: Joe Fortes—named for the city's best-loved lifeguard—has that kind of high-energy, uptown chophouse feel to it. "Joe's" is one of downtown's hippest watering holes, where Vancouver's glossiest young professionals flock after putting in a hard day at the stock exchange or ad agency. The draw is more than the big U-shaped bar where martinis and single-malt scotch are in equal demand. It's the oyster bar too, with Bob Skinner dispensing faultlessly fresh Quilchene or Malpeque or any of a dozen other varieties, all sold individually. Sipping, schmoozing, and sampling (starters include popcorn shrimp with Creole mayo, and clam and corn fritters, or Joe's appetizer platter for two) often segue seamlessly into the dinner hour. The fresh fish is a constant lure; order the chef's trio of fish: $15.95 gets you your choice of red snapper, ling cod, salmon, marlin, ahi tuna, or swordfish. The "Chaps" lunch ($11.95)—a "flat iron" grilled steak and eggs sunny-side up served with sautéed mushrooms, thick slices of fried tomatoes, hand-cut fries, and a spicy Creole sauce—is a winner for the cholesterol-deprived. Everyday Blue Plate specials from $6.95 to $9.95 might include turkey and black bean chili, jambalaya, and roast pork loin with a mash of garlic potatoes. Attentive service. ■ *777 Thurlow St; 669-1940; map:R3; $$; full bar; AE, DC, MC, V; no cheques; lunch Mon–Fri, dinner every day, brunch Sat–Sun.*

Kalamata Greek Taverna ★★ Not just your usual souvlakia-and-pita spot, Kalamata serves up excellent Greek classics with a modern touch. The cooks at this bright, lively restaurant take an unusually light hand to a cuisine that can often be overbearing and predictable. Fluffy zucchini rice and delicious roasted vegetables, including skewers of tart, grilled artichoke hearts, take the edge off the usual meat-heavy menu. The

▼
Top 175
Restaurants
▲

location is a bit unfortunate, right at a busy, loud intersection, and the service can be slow. But the truly good food and excellent prices make it worthwhile. ■ *478 W Broadway; 872-7050; map:T7; $$; full bar; AE, MC, V; no cheques: lunch Tues–Fri, dinner Tues–Sun.*

Kamei Sushi ★★ With five locations, Kamei may no longer be the best Japanese restaurant in town, but its simple, Westernized dishes certainly make it one of the most popular. The luxury-class Kamei Royale on West Georgia Street seats more than 300, with open and private tatami rooms. Combination platters contain all the standards, or try the red snapper usuzukui, thinly sliced and fanned on the plate, accompanied by a citrus sauce. Robata dishes are the special focus at the Broadway Plaza location and can be very good. ■ *1030 W Georgia St (and branches); 687-8588; map:S3; $$; full bar; AE, DC, MC, V; no cheques; lunch Mon–Sat, dinner every day.* &

Kam Gok Yuen If you're ravenous from souvenir shopping in Chinatown and can no longer resist the beckoning of barbecued ducks hanging in food store windows, head to the no-decor Kam Gok Yuen for an affordable repast. Its famous barbecued meats are sold out every day, so a near-empty window is not suspect but a sign that you should hurry in and order before the store runs out. Some of the best congee—rice porridge with meats or seafoods—in town are cooked to order over hissing burners in the open kitchen up front. Watch as wontons and noodles are tossed, caught, and dropped into bowls with a magical ease that borders on showmanship. Be sure to ask about specials posted on the walls in Chinese, since they can be some of the tastiest items. Brisk service. ■ *142 E Pender St; 683-3822; map:V4; $; no alcohol; no credit cards; no cheques; lunch, dinner every day.*

Kilimanjaro ★ Like East Africa itself, Amyn and Nargis Sunderji's restaurant is an intriguing melting pot—visually and culinarily. African masks and batiks mix with the deep pink walls, French provincial prints, and swirling ceiling fans to create the atmosphere of a chic Nairobi restaurant. Try the coconut fish soup, made on request from a recipe from Zanzibar of amazing complexity and depth; a Swahili specialty of curried goat; the prawns piri piri; or the uniquely African (specifically, Zairian) combination of chicken in ho-ho peppers, palm oil, and garlic. "Burning Spear"—lamb served flaming on a sword—is the house specialty. Desserts bring a fittingly exotic finale, from a tangerine cheesecake to a safari mango mousse. The Safari Bistro downstairs offers spicy ethnic fare as well as colonial indulgences like fish and chips for lunch or a late-night snack. ■ *332 Water St; 681-9913; map:U3; $$; full bar; AE, DC, MC, V; no cheques; lunch Mon–Fri, dinner every day. (Bistro open daily for lunch.)*

Kirin Mandarin Restaurant ▪ Kirin Seafood Restaurant ★★★

Kirin's postmodern decor—high ceilings, slate-green walls, black lacquer trim—is oriented around the two-storey-high mystical dragonlike creature that is the restaurant's namesake. The menu reads like a trilingual (Chinese, English, and Japanese) opus spanning the culinary capitals of China: Canton, Sichuan, Shanghai, and Beijing (live lobsters and crabs can be ordered in 11 different preparations). Remarkably, most of the vastly different regional cuisines are authentic and well executed, but the Northern Chinese specialties are the best. Peking duck is as good as it gets this side of China, and braised dishes such as sea cucumber with prawn roe sauce are "royal" treats. Atypical of Chinese restaurants, desserts can be excellent—try the red bean pie, a thin crêpe folded around a sweet bean filling and fried to a fluffy crispness. The Western-style service is attentive though sometimes a tad aggressive. Unless you are in the mood to splurge, stay away from the Cognac cart. The second, equally fine outpost is in City Square, with a passable view of the city. Here fresh seasonal seafood choices, such as drunken live spot prawns and whole Alaskan king crab, are often presented with dramatic tableside special effects. It also has great dim sum (including a definitive har gow or shrimp dumpling). ▪ *1166 Alberni St; 682-8833; map:R3; $$$; full bar; AE, DC, JCB, V; cheques OK; lunch, dinner every day* ▪ *201-555 W 12th Ave (City Square); 879-8038; map:D3; $$$; full bar; AE, DC, JCB, V; cheques OK; lunch, dinner every day.* ♿

▼

▲

Kitto Japanese Restaurant ★ Kitto opened to instant success in 1990 on the fashion strip on Robson Street (actually, on the corner of Robson and Bute). Now another thrives on theatre row on Granville Street. The reason for their success? Authentically flavoured, accessible Japanese food at rock-bottom prices—a '90s backlash against the trendy '80s gourmet mania. The high art of sushi and sashimi is not to be found here. Instead there are udons, ramens, sobas, and donburis—rice and noodle dishes that are fast and satisfying. Or try some robatas, including smoky yakitori chicken with green onions; fleshy velvety fresh shiitake mushrooms; zucchini with dry bonito flakes; and an incredible dish of hamachi gill. Two or three with a bowl of rice make a wonderful meal, with dinner for two comfortably priced around $10 a person. It's not a place to linger and hold hands—even though the booth seats are private and comfortable enough—but it's a great place for before or after a movie. ▪ *833 Bute St; 662-3333; map:R3; $; beer only; V; no cheques; lunch every day, dinner every day;* ▪ *833 Granville St; 687-6622; map:S4; $; beer only; V; no cheques; lunch, dinner every day.*

Koji Japanese Restaurant ★★ In our opinion, Koji has the most beautiful garden in a downtown Vancouver restaurant—

an island of pine trees and river rocks on a patio above Hornby Street. The best seats are the ones by the windows looking out on the garden or at the sushi and robata bars. The rest of the restaurant is crowded and often full of Japanese tourists. The sushi is not the best in town, but selections from the robata grill are dependable: grilled shiitake, topped with bonito flakes and tiny filaments of dry seaweed, are sublime. The Japanese boxed lunch might contain chicken kara-age, superb smoked black cod, prawn and vegetable tempura, two or three small salads, rice with black sesame seeds, pickled vegetables, miso soup, and fresh fruit— all for around $10. Finish with green tea ice cream. ■ *630 Hornby St; 685-7355; map:S3; $$; full bar; AE, DC, MC, V; no cheques; breakfast every day, lunch Mon–Fri, dinner every day,* &

La Belle Auberge ★★ Thirty minutes from Vancouver, owner/chef Bruno Marti seeks to preserve and enshrine traditional French cuisine at this old Victorian manse in Ladner. Marti is well known to Vancouverites as a member of the gold-medal-winning team at the 1984 Culinary Olympics. The duckling in blueberry sauce is, deservedly, the most popular dish on a predictable but superb menu offering rack of lamb, milk-fed veal, and some game dishes. ■ *4856 48th Ave, Ladner; 946-7717; $$$; full bar; AE, MC, V; no cheques; dinner every day.*

▼

Top 175 Restaurants

▲

La Cucina Italiana ★★ Stuck rather incongruously in the middle of North Vancouver's strip of car dealerships and video shops, La Cucina's rustic character overcomes its surroundings. The attractive dining room has Italian opera playing at just the right volume. When it's available, try bresaola—air-dried beef imported from Switzerland—as an appetizer, or the cold antipasto. Pastas range from traditional spaghetti with tomato and meat sauce to fettuccine with squid and sweet red peppers. Fish specials are usually good. Don't leave without sampling the homemade ice cream. ■ *1509 Marine Dr, North Vancouver; 986-1334; map:D1; $$; full bar; AE, MC, V; no cheques; lunch Mon–Fri, dinner Mon–Sat.* &

Landmark Hot Pot House ★★★ Hot potting—traditionally for the warming of body and soul on long wintry nights—seems to have transcended its seasonal limits to emerge as a Chinese culinary trend, and Landmark, Vancouver's first Hot Pot House, remains the best. If you are a Trekkie you may find yourself reaching for your com-badge upon first sight of state-of-the-art-extraction units needed to regulate the air quality and temperature in the room. But it will not take you long to discover that the picture-perfect presentation and uncompromised freshness of the food are earthly delights that no replicator can hope to provide. The gas stove inset into your table provides the basis for healthy, fun, do-it-yourself, fondue-style cooking. The menus are simply lists of available ingredients and prices.

Order the Duo Soup Base of satay and chicken broth, then, if it's your first time, start with the seafood combination. The initiated and not squeamish should attempt the still writhing live prawns when in season or the superb whole geoduck presented sashimi-style—cooking strictly discretional. Finish with noodles and dumplings and a soulful bowl of the rich broth. The cooling sour plum drink that follows is on the house. ■ *4023 Cambie St; 872-2868; map:D4; $$; full bar; MC, V; no cheques; dinner every day.* &

L'Arena [unrated] Tucked into Library Square, L'Arena is a new favourite among locals heading to the Ford theatre or the Queen E. A mostly Italian menu featuring antipasto, pizzas, pastas, and seafood, but the real star here is the warm spinach salad with Gorgonzola dressing. Service is friendly (they anticipate and expect the theatre crowd), and the ambiance is relaxed so you don't have to worry about missing the curtain call. A good range of wines at reasonable markups. ■ *300 W Georgia St; 687-5434; map:T4; $$; full bar; AE, DC, MC, V; no cheques; lunch Mon–Fri, dinner every day.*

Las Margaritas ★ *Olé!* Sombreros hanging from the ceiling, red-tiled floors, and white stuccoed archways all add up to quintessential Mexican restaurant decor in this lively Kitsilano cantina. The crowd changes with the hour. Early evenings, expect families (there's a good, inexpensive children's menu). Later, people come in for the margaritas: three sizes, eight flavours. This is a popular hangout for couples or the gang from the office. A little nacho-noshing or a few dips into Mexican cheese fondue with optional chorizo takes the edge off the appetite while you mull the relative advantages of tacos and enchiladas. Chile rellenos, chimichangas, and flautas—you'll find all the standards here, including combination plates for ditherers who can't decide. Servings are *¡muy amable!* and the margarita pie *¡muy bien!* ■ *1999 W 4th Ave; 734-7117; map:O7; $$; full bar; AE, E, MC, V; no cheques; lunch, dinner every day.*

La Toque Blanche ★★ This cosy, '70s retro-woodsy retreat tucked behind the Cypress Park Mohawk gas station is still a well-kept culinary secret. Owner John-Carlo Felicella has a passion for detail, manifest in appetizers such as smoked duck carpaccio, and wickedly rich lobster bisque. His entrées are no slouches either, as proved by salmon and crab cakes with seared scallops and red pepper butter, and rack of lamb crusted with figs, cooked perfectly pick. A moderately-priced wine list complements the menu. Prices are almost a bargain by today's standards—especially considering the quality, detail, and presentation. At press time, renovations are in the works to update the front of the house. ■ *4368 Marine Dr, West Vancouver; 926-1006; map:C1; $$; full bar; AE, MC, V; cheques OK, dinner Tues-Sun.* &

▼

**Top 175
Restaurants**

▲

La Villetta ★ ½ Inauspicious surroundings hide a romantic little Italian restaurant where first dates or flourishing relationships can find nourishment both on the menu and in the setting. In summer, the outdoor patio lures. Wintertime, habitués opt for the cosy dining room warmed by a fireplace. The draw apart from the decor? Simple, basic Italian food, perfectly cooked by chef Tony D'alessandro: golden roast chicken, its rosemary-and-oregano-flavoured pan juices poured over the top; clams in an herby tomato sauce; impeccably fresh mussels served with nothing but pepper, butter, parsley, and garlic. D'alessandro pastas, including homemade seafood cannelloni, linguine with assorted seafood, and homemade gnocchi, all have a staunch following. Specialties include a fish of the day (prawns if you're lucky), a quartet of veal dishes, a few chicken preparations, and rabbit, when available, simmered in herbs and wine. Don't miss the tiramisu. ■ *3901 E Hastings St; 299-3979; map:G2; $$; full bar; MC, V; local cheques only; lunch Mon–Fri, dinner Tues–Sun.*

Le Crocodile ★★★★ France without a passport—that's Le Crocodile. Chef and owner Michel Jacob named his bistro after his favourite restaurant in his hometown of Strasbourg, and his Franco-German culinary heritage is obvious. He accompanies a wonderfully savoury onion tart with chilled Alsatian wine in green-stemmed glasses. Salmon tartare and sautéed scallops in an herb sauce are both showstoppers. Luscious Dover sole, duck (crisp outside, moist inside) accompanied by a light orange sauce, calf's livers with spinach butter—it's a trauma to choose. The best desserts are the traditional ones. The well-thought-out wine list and European atmosphere make a dinner at Le Crocodile an affair to remember. ■ *100-909 Burrard St; 669-4298; map:R4; $$$; full bar; AE, DC, MC, V; no cheques; lunch Mon–Fri, dinner Mon–Sat.* &

Le Gavroche ★★★ Arguably the most romantic restaurant in the city, Le Gavroche is one of the city's leading French kitchens (with a Northwest influence), enhanced by a discreet upstairs room and complete with blazing fire and glimpses of the harbour and mountains. For starters, try the endive, pear, and Stilton salad with port orange vinaigrette. We loved the previous chef's seabass cassoulet with white beans, pancetta, spinach, and apple cider sauce, but at this writing, a new chef, Anna Anderson, has taken the reins, so new specialties may be in store. Service is formal but friendly and subtly attentive. For dessert, try the trademark lili cake—a soft almond and hazelnut meringue with an almond crème anglaise—even *Gourmet* magazine requested the recipe. Le Gavroche has one of the city's better wine cellars, with a range of better Bordeaux and Burgundies. ■ *1616 Alberni St; 685-3924; map:Q2; $$$; full bar; AE, DC, JCB, MC, V; no cheques; lunch Mon–Fri, dinner every day.*

Le Grec ★★ A hit from the moment it opened, Le Grec took a gutsy stance in the heart of Vancouver's Little Italy by focusing purely and simply on mezéthes: Greek-style tapas. With an ambience as cheerful as that of a Corfu taverna, big servings of consistently good food, and low prices for food and booze, this three-level restaurant is packed night after night with a lively crowd. Owner/chef Manolis Daroukakis knows what appeals. Kotopita encases rosemary-perfumed chicken in crackly filo pastry. An assertive, tartly refreshing artichoke salad is speckled with capers and sweet red pepper. Briam translates as roasted vegetables in their own savoury juices. Portions are generous and meant to be shared (really). Along with old friends like moussaka and souvlakia, the menu provides introductions to lesser-known dishes: skordalia, a rich, potato-based dip that shrieks with garlic; polentalike bobota simmered with tomatoes and feta; and the Greek version of salt cod, bakaliaros. Fabulous, not-too-sweet baklava rounds out the meal. Treat yourself to an after-dinner glass of raisiny Mavrodaphne. ■ *1447 Commercial Dr; 253-1253; map:Z6; $; full bar; AE, MC, V; no cheques; lunch, dinner Mon–Sat.*

Liliget Feast House ★ Architect Arthur Erickson designed this downstairs West End space for Vancouver's only First Nations restaurant (Muckamuck) almost 20 years ago. Dolly Watts, a Native caterer, opened Liliget when the second restaurant, Quilicum, closed in 1995. A meal here is certainly an unusual culinary foray. The bannock is Dolly's signature and you'll never taste better. You'll also sample dishes you never dreamed of—pan-fried oolicans, toasted seaweed, and wild blackberry pie with whipped sopalali. Another taste thrill is the Hagul Jam soup, a broth of salmon and vegetables. Coupled with the Wild Man Salad and Dolly's bannock, it's a meal in itself. The Liliget Feast platter for two ($39.95) is heaped with alder-grilled salmon, buffalo smokies, rabbit, halibut, and smoked oolicans and will easily serve three. The small wine list is well chosen, and there's even a chardonnay and a pinot noir from the Inkameep Reserve (Inniskillin). Only flub, vegetables appear to be an afterthought. But save room for dessert—upside-side down blueberry cobbler topped with real whipped cream is a winner. ■ *1724 Davie St; 681-7044; map:P3; $$; full bar; AE, MC, V; no cheques; dinner every day.*

Lok's Chinese Restaurant ★ And yes, they deliver. This long-time Vancouver east-side neighbourhood favourite continues to win converts at its second location on the upper floor of 2006 West Fourth Avenue. The tasteful, more upscale second-storey room means good food now comes with a bonus city view over the rooftops of this upwardly trendy Kitsilano strip. Lok's formula for success is simple—great, home-style Cantonese food in generous portions served up with a smile at easy-to-swallow

▼

**Top 175
Restaurants**

▲

prices. Its genuinely friendly, family-style service is a cut above that of any other restaurants of this type. Choose from great clay pot dishes: Cantonese satays and curries; fresh, well-prepared seafood dishes; wontons, noodles, and congee; and a solid repertoire of barbecued meats. The best are scrambled eggs with crunchy prawns, robust singing chicken, and succulent satay-spiced beef with sweet peppers. And if you don't feel like venturing out, delivery service is just a phone call away.
■ *4890 Victoria Dr; 439-1888; map:F4; $; beer and wine; MC, V; no cheques; breakfast, lunch, dinner every day.*

Lola's Restaurant ★★★ Lola's is a sexy, glamorous eatery, a ménage of chef Scott Kidd's excellent and adventurous cooking, the over-the-top team from Delilah's, and the antique opulence of the heritage building that houses them. Once the valet has whisked away your vehicle, you'll step into a baroque world that teeters giddily between sophistication and camp. An elegant marble foyer is watched over by a fresco of Renaissance angels. Inside, it's all crystal chandeliers, purple velvet draperies and banquettes, midnight blue ceiling, gilt trim, and a touch of turn-of-the-century Art Deco. Eclectic tunes set the mood—everything from Cole Porter to Nancy Sinatra—as neo-sophisticates sip champagne cocktails and martinis. The crowd tends to be young, hip, and urban, or older and moneyed. Kidd, who used to cook at Le Gavroche, prepares French classics with nuances of the West Coast and Pacific Rim. Sweetbreads, for instance, might come with a turnip pancake and Asian-inspired sauces; a crème brûlée is spiked with citrus and served in a lidded porcelain pot. The menu is ever-changing and creative, sometimes excessively so. The occasional shortcomings in the menu department, however, are compensated by the great cocktail and wine list. Lola's has brought the champagne cocktail back into style with more than a dozen varieties that range from the classic sugar-cube soaked in bitters to one garnished with a banana. The wine list includes both good, reasonably priced wines, mostly from North America; and in the "Whatever Lola wants, Lola gets" department are some rare, high-priced vintages. ■ *432 Richards St; 684-5652; map:T4; $$$; full bar; AE, MC, V, no cheques; lunch Mon–Fri, dinner every day.*

▼
Top 175 Restaurants
▲

Lumière ★★★ The minimalistic elegance of this room on the ever-expanding Broadway corridor showcases both the chef's exquisite creations and the Armani-clad clientele. Although the decor is a tad austere—very pale, very stark—the food luxuriates in the skill of Robert Feenie's kitchen. In fact, Lumière serves up some of the very best food the city has to offer, a sort of French gone modern. Whether Feenie is preparing a hearty dish like the exquisite stuffed saddle of rabbit loin on braised leeks or something lighter, he always seems to achieve a perfect balance of flavours and textures. Appetizers at Lumière are especially delicious and make choices especially difficult. For instance, how to decide between the caramelized onion and goat cheese tart with organic cherry tomatoes or the warm mille-feuille with shiitake and oyster mushrooms in a red wine butter reduction? A decent wine list accompanies the food. The palate-cleansing sorbet brought between courses ensures that each meal is a proper celebration of the dining experience. The service is informed, attentive, and helpful. ■ *2551 W Broadway; 739-8185; map:C3; $$$; full bar; AE, MC, V; no cheques; dinner Tues–Sun.*

Major The Gourmet Strictly speaking, this is not a restaurant but the perennially busy headquarters of caterer-about-town Nicky Major. No matter. Savvy Vancouverites know that this is the place—in fact, in this largely light industrial area, the only place within blocks—for a lunch that's as interesting as it is fast. Major spins the ingredients so that the menu is rarely the same, and there is an ever-changing panoply of specials. Grilled chicken might go on a daily pizza, be featured in a salad, or go mano a mano with Thai noodles. Curried lamb may show up, or a chicken and broccoli pasta. Vegetarian and meat lasagnes, hearty pot pies, and shepherd's pie are staples. Desserts and soups change daily. Tables outside in warmer months, with limited seating inside. Jet-setters often pause here en route to the airport for takeout that's classier than Business Class. ■ *102-8828 Heather St; 322-9211; map:D5; $; no alcohol; MC, V; no cheques; breakfast, lunch Mon–Fri.*

Mangiamo! ★★★ Let's eat! urges this chic eatery in Yaletown, and indeed we're delighted to do so. Mangiamo! is a happy collaboration between gastronomic guru Umberto Menghi and chef Ken Bogas, formerly of Saltimbocca in Kitsilano. At Mangiamo!, Bogas's occasionally wacky creations are beautifully mellowed by Umberto's sometimes staid insistence on quality. This creates a menu and an environment that are elegant and tasteful, yet fun and vibrant. (The cheesy puns on the menu help, too.) No wonder so many celebrities can be spotted at the white-cloth-covered tables. The room itself is gracious, with parchment-coloured walls, dark woods, and soft light coming in from the garden patio in back. And the wine list offers an extensive selection of Italian vino plus a respectable selection of wines by the glass. But it's the food that keeps bringing people back. Bogas takes traditional Italian dishes and gives them a bit of West Coast spin. Starters are hearty and innovative and soups seem to be a specialty. A shellfish soup is served with enoki mushrooms, a seasonal asparagus soup is adorned by a crunchy corn and Dungeness crab fritter. A green salad may come with seared portobello mushrooms and Gorgonzola croutons, all tossed in a tomato chipotle vinaigrette. The menu is extensive, with a focus on creatively prepared seafood—paillard of BC salmon with tequila lime fresca, for instance. Don't ignore the pastas, though: the penne with grilled, house-smoked wild-game chorizo is an unexpected treat for tired taste buds. ■ *1116 Mainland St; 687-1116; map:S5; $$$; full bar; AE, MC, V; no cheques; lunch Mon–Fri, dinner Mon–Sat.*

Maple Garden Restaurant ★★ Maple Garden was well received by its Richmond audience when it rode in on the crest of a wave of Hong Kong-style, high-end Chinese restaurants that opened in the Lower Mainland a few years ago. Rapid-fire expansions followed as it grew into a chain that now boasts five locations. The latest venture is Maple Garden Hot Pot on Number Three Road, which features a unique hot pot bar where one can point and choose while going it alone just as one would at a sushi bar. However, a downturn in the economy and fierce competition has all but eliminated the astonishingly large selection of prestigious and pricey items that once dominated the special feature menu—exotic preparations of game and the classic quartet of Chinese culinary treasures, abalone, dried sea cucumber, shark's fin, and fish maw. Instead, rustic choices such as sautéed squid with preserved mustard greens, steamed marinated duck with taro root, beef bedded on braised eggplants, and pan-fried chicken with scallops in hot bean sauce have made the menu more accessible. A somewhat condescending take-out menu designed to cater to Western tastes is also available, but the prices are on the high side for what you get. ■ *145-4751 Garden City Rd, Richmond (and branches); 278-2323; map:D7; $$; beer and wine; AE, MC, V; no cheques; breakfast, lunch, dinner every day.*

▼
Top 175
Restaurants
▲

Meinhardt Fine Foods ★★ Linda Meinhardt, the force behind the Bread Garden chain, took a health food store on South Granville and created a food shopper's paradise. In this lofty, white-painted room, stainless steel shelves carry the best in snack foods, sauces, spreads, oils, vinegars, dressings, and other condiments. Along with the small but well-stocked butcher shop, an extensive deli section offers excellent cheeses, olives, cold cuts, and sandwich fixings as well as prepared foods. There's a counter with 30 stools, so you can eat in or take out. Try the antipasto pasta salad, the chicken pot pie with mashed yams, the Moroccan lamb ragout, or the gravlax. The best bakers in town supply Meinhardt's with fresh loaves daily; but get there early or all the baguettes will be sold out. The store also offers decadent desserts, including an otherworldly carrot cake that consists of several layers of rich cake separated by inches of tangy frosting. Meinhardt's also showcases local food celebrities who put on cooking demos, and it sells a variety of kitchen gadgets, magazines, and flowers. The produce section is small but interesting, and we dare you to leave without succumbing to the temptation of Ghiradelli chocolates by the cash register.

■ *3002 Granville St; 732-4405; map:D3; $; no alcohol; AE, MC, V; no cheques; every day.*

Mescalero ★★ The very good Mescalero has become a most popular hangout (especially on Thursday nights) for southwestern food and atmosphere (the rustic decor works well). For best value, order from the tapas list; you can piece together a meal from garlic prawns, alder-baked stuffed sweet pepper, roasted mussels in sun-dried tomato chipotle cream, and grilled eggplant salad with fresh spinach leaves and tangy blue cheese dressing, generously garnished with pine nuts—among others. Roll out after a slice of white chocolate mango cheesecake. Lots of Chilean wines by the glass. ■ *1215 Bidwell St; 669-2399; map:P3; $$$; full bar; AE, MC, V; no cheques; lunch, dinner every day, brunch Sat–Sun.* &

Milestone's ★ Mega-servings of food (and booze), priced cheap, are the draw at Milestone's, which, despite being a chain, manages consistently to impress with its witty takes on West Coast food trends. The breakfasts are outstanding (and cheap!) and the dinners unfailingly good. Witness the appetizers (most big enough for a light lunch) and the southwestern chicken strips with ancho chile sauce and a cilantro-infused cream for dipping. Salads are generous: the caesar apparently uses an entire head of lettuce, and the seafood pasta salads are lavish with crab, shrimp, and smoked salmon. Pastas range from the mundane to the unusual, such as a Mongolian chicken penne (made by request). A fashionable menu includes Sicilian meatloaf rife with fresh herbs. Try the trademarked Rollups, whole-wheat tortillas encasing everything from smoked chicken or spiced brisket to grilled eggplant. Fresh fruit martinis, frozen Bellinis, and sinfully good desserts. ■ *1210 Denman St (and branches); 662-3431; map:P3; $; full bar; AE, DC, MC, V; no cheques; brunch, lunch, dinner every day.*

▼

**Top 175
Restaurants**

▲

Monterey Lounge & Grill (Pacific Palisades Hotel) [unrated]
The bounty of the BC harvest and an award-winning wine list star in the Pacific Palisades Hotel dining room on Robson. Chef Denis Blais (formerly of The Prow) is the Palisades newest chef. For starters, order his duck and spinach salad with ginger vinaigrette. Vegetarians will love the agnolotti pasta with wild mushrooms in a brandied roasted garlic and almond cream or the deep-dish-baked eggplant and potato pie layered with fresh basil cream. The chocolate hazelnut silk is a great way to end. The Pacific Palisades has welcomed a new age with its astrological dinner series. Each month, astrologer Jef Simpson is the main attraction at this bargain event ($38) that includes an astrologically correct three-course dinner, a personalized astrological chart, and free parking. On weekends, there's live jazz. ■ *1277 Robson St; 684-1277; map:R3; $$; full bar; AE, DC, MC, V; no cheques; breakfast, lunch, dinner every day.* &

Montri's Thai Restaurant ★★★ Why go anywhere else for Thai food when Montri's is simply the best in town? After more than a year's absence, Montri Rattanaraj is back and his food is better than ever. He presents an authentic cuisine not watered down for Vancouver tastes but with little touches all his own, like the salmon steak in red curry sauce. Thai cuisine is a careful balancing act, based on six interconnecting concepts: bitter, salty, sweet, hot, herbaceous, and fragrant. The heat content is rated on a scale of one to five chile symbols, five being the level for masochists and Thai nationals. What to order? Everything is good. Tom yum goong is Thailand's national soup, a lemony prawn broth, and it lives up to its name—yum. The tod mun fish cakes blended with prawns and chile curry are excellent, as is the salmon simmered in red curry and coconut sauce. Rattanaraj's Thai gai-yang, chicken marinated in coconut milk and broiled, is a close cousin to the chicken sold on the beach at Puhket. Have it with som-tam, a green papaya salad served with sticky rice and wedges of raw cabbage; the cabbage and the rice are coolants, and you *will* need them (Thailand's Singha beer also helps). ■ *3629 W Broadway; 738-9888; map:B3; $$; full bar; MC, V; no cheques; dinner every day.* ⅃

Moutai Mandarin Restaurant ★ The menu at this tiny restaurant was modelled after the one at the well-patronized Szechuan Chongqing; now West Enders don't have to leave their territory to get good versions of old favourites such as green beans with pork and plenty of chile pepper. We particularly like the specials: spicy clams in black bean sauce and the blistering stir-fry with tiger prawns known as dai ching. Moutai's acid-green tabletops and arborite trim in a pebble-pattern grey are miles removed from the red-dragon-tacky or Hong Kong-slick styles that seem to dominate the city's Chinese eateries. Being a stone's throw away from the very downtown strutting beach at English Bay, it somehow all fits. ■ *1710 Davie St; 681-2288; map:P3; $; full bar; AE, MC, V; no cheques; dinner every day.* ⅃

Mui Garden Restaurant ★ This two-year-old neighbourhood noodle-shop/eatery is a place to eat, not dine. Mui Garden features excellent authentic Chiu Chow-style noodles with fish, cuttlefish, and beef meatballs plus good Singapore-style satays, curries, and Hai Nan Chicken. Solid hot pot specials such as lamb and bean curd, singing chicken, and Hong Kong-style satay beef studded with pineapples are also worthy of note. Decor is minimalist Hong Kong coffee shop, but the food makes it an excellent bet among the legion of cheap and cheerful neighbourhood bargains. There's a second location on Victoria Drive. ■ *4264 Main St; 872-8232; map:E4; $; no alcohol; no credit cards; no cheques; lunch, dinner Wed–Mon* ■ *5797 Victoria*

Musashi Japanese Restaurant Sushi is high art in Japanese cooking, but for ordinary folks who have fallen in love with the stuff, a steady diet of it can prove costly. Not so at Musashi, where high art is offered nightly at low prices—usually to a packed house. You'll find no frills here. The decor is universal neigbourhood eatery, Japanese-style. The view out the window is only interesting during rush hour—if you take perverse pleasure in watching those strange things that BMW and Benz drivers do when they are stuck in traffic and think no one's watching. Value is the story here, and a remarkable story it is too. Nigiri sushi—shrimp, tuna, geoduck, sea urchin, and more—starts at $1 a piece and tops at a whopping $1.60 for the deluxe tsukimi ikura. Makis (rolled sushi), which yield four bite-size pieces, range from $2.10 to $5.50. A full range of soups, salads, appetizers, tempuras, rice and noodle dishes, and combination dinners are also available. ■ *780 Denman St; 687-0634; map:Q2; $; beer and wine; AE, MC, V; no cheques; dinner every day.*

Naam With its funky decor and friendly staff, the Naam, Vancouver's oldest vegetarian restaurant, is the last outpost of the era when West Fourth Avenue was hippie heaven. Lineups are common (maybe because the service is so slack). Summertime, we try to nab a seat in the tiny private garden patio. Winters, the candlelit Naam is as cosy as a Gulf Islands cabin. You can still sip dandelion tea and nibble at a bee pollen cookie, but the menu has broadened considerably over the years. Habitués breakfast on a mishmash of eggs, cheese, tofu, mushrooms, and tomatoes on toast. The house salad—a toppling heap of red cabbage, shredded lettuce, thickly sliced tomato, and sunflower seeds—is humongous. The veggie burrito is the size of a neck pillow. The menu wanders lazily around the world, offering stops for nachos, hummus and pita, Thai and caesar salads, sesame fries with miso gravy, and enormous pita pizzas. Naam, thankfully, is open 24 hours. ■ *2724 W 4th Ave; 738-7151; map:C2; $; beer and wine; MC, V; no cheques; breakfast, lunch, dinner, midnight snacks every day, brunch Sun.* &

▼

Top 175 Restaurants

▲

Natraj Natraj opened almost five years ago to rave reviews, when Vancouver's food scene was in the grip of ethnic experimentation. As the nearby Punjabi Market at Main Street and 49th Avenue grew and prospered, Natraj continued to benefit from its proximity. However, the decor of the restaurant has always been spartan at best. Beer cases stacked up in full view in one corner next to a filing cabinet don't help. But look past the neglect of the premises and you'll find a competent kitchen skilled in the magical application of spices that characterize Indian cooking. The Chicken Shahjahni Biryani is a fascinating mélange of flavours boasting the use of 21 exotic spices and served over aromatic basmati rice cooked with saffron. The mixed grill from the tandoor is a fine sampler of spicy beef Seekh Kabab, tender chunks of marinated chicken, and lamb with sweet wilted onions and tomatoes. Complete the meal with buttery patties of potatoes, vegetables, and cheese, called Malai Kofta, and an order of the Special Nan KW: stuffed with nuts and bits of chicken. ■ *5656 Fraser St; 327-6141; map:E4; $; full bar; MC, V; no cheques; dinner every day.*

Nat's New York Pizzeria ★★ Cousins Nat and Franco Bastone headed to their uncle's pizza parlour in Yonkers, where he taught them how to create Naples-style pizza. Then they opened up Nat's on Broadway's busy retail strip and now serve up some of the best thin-crust pizza around. Have it delivered or ask for it three-quarters baked and cook it crispy at home. Or pull up a chair under the Big Apple memorabilia and watch the world go by while you sink your teeth into some pie loaded with chorizo and mushrooms, or artichokes and pesto, or cappicolo and hot peppers. Or try the 5th Avenue (sweet onion, spinach, tomato, and feta cheese) or the Hot Veg (sun-dried tomatoes, hot peppers, and mushrooms). Top it off with the oven-baked garlic shavings or the selection of other condiments you can sprinkle on top. Avoid Nat's on weekdays between 11:30 and 12:15 (the local Kits high school breaks for lunch and they take over Nat's). If you're there before they leave you'll notice students squeezing honey on their leftover crust for dessert. ■ *2684 W Broadway; 737-0707; map:C3; $; no alcohol; no credit cards; no cheques; lunch, dinner Mon–Sat.*

Nazarre BBQ Chicken ★ There are rubber chickens on the turntables decorating the storefront, but only tender barbecued chicken finds its way onto your plate. French-born and Mexican-raised owner Gerry Moutal bastes the birds in a mixture of rum and spices in the rotisserie: the chickens drip their juices onto potatoes roasting and crackling below and are delivered with mild, hot, extra-hot, or hot garlic sauce. There are a few other goodies (vegetarian empanadas, tacos), but it's the chicken you really should not miss. Eat in, at one of the four tables—or take it to go. ■ *1859 Commercial Dr; 251-1844; map:Z7; $; no alcohol; no credit cards; no cheques; lunch, dinner every day.*

New Grand View Restaurant ★ In Vancouver's rapidly changing Chinese restaurant scene, New Grand View is almost like a granddaddy. They've add New to the name, but nothing else has changed. It has been there—same owner, same crew—for well over 10 years, carrying on business with the serenity of an elder, quietly setting the trends. Grand View was among the first to introduce weekend northern-style dim sum brunches, serving steamed pork dumplings, robust beef noodle soups, and foot-long fried dough with soya milk—salted or sweetened for dunking. A separate "vegetarian delights" section on the menu includes meatless versions of the garlicky Sichuan eggplant, hot-and-sour soup, and the Mah Po bean curd. Departing from convention, the chefs quick-fry geoduck in a spicy garlic sauce and substitute squid for chicken in a Kung-Pao-style sauté. Lamb dishes and the Shanghai-style, white-cooked pork in garlic and chiles deserve kudos. To revisit Grand View is to wonder how we could have stayed away so long. ▪ *60 W Broadway; 879-8885; map:V7; $; full bar; V; no cheques; lunch, dinner every day.*

New Japanese Deli House ★ This is the bargain beauty of the sushi crowd, right in the middle of old Japantown's grocery and fish stores. The Deli is an old, high-ceilinged room with big windows, arborite-topped tables, and all the sushi you can eat for $15.95. Quality is surprisingly good, especially if you arrive early. ▪ *381 Powell St; 681-6484; map:V3; $; beer only; no credit cards; no cheques; lunch Mon–Sat, early dinner Tues–Sat.*

900 West (Hotel Vancouver) [unrated] At press time, 900 West was on everybody's must-do lists. CP Hotels lured California chef Jeremiah Tower to Vancouver with a three-year contract to work with executive chef Robert Le Crom in creating an inspired menu. After a multimillion-dollar renovation, the fusty old Timber Club has been turned into one of the most fashionable rooms in the city. The restaurant is reminiscent of a cruise ship dining room, recalling the era when luxury liners were king. There's a wine bar area (you can order a snack from the lounge menu), an open kitchen, and live entertainment that keeps the action churning. Examples from the menu include a potato salmon lasagne with clam and a spit-roasted pheasant with blueberry yam pudding. The well-thought-out wine list complements the menu. ▪ *900 W Georgia St; 669-9378; map:S3; $$$; full bar; AE, DC, MC, V; no cheques; lunch Mon–Sat, dinner every day.* &

Noor Mahal ★ There's a new look at Noor Mahal and a tandoor oven, but the same hospitable, helpful service is still there along with the homey feel. Prices are still a bargain at $7 to $14 per dish. These are all full-meal deals, complete with rice, roti, chutney, pappadum, and salad. The food is hot and spicy but adjustable to order. The portions are substantial. Dosas—south Indian flatbreads made from rice, wheat, and lentil flour—are the specialty here. They come rolled, like crêpes, filled with your choice of 31 fillings, including, among others, chicken, shrimp, and vegetarian specialties, each accompanied by sambar—a lentil stew—and its traditional condiment, nariyal chatni—coconut chutney. ▪ *4354 Fraser St; 873-9263; map:E4; $; full bar; MC, V; no cheques; dinner every day.*

O-Tooz The Energie Bar ★ What started purely as a juice bar has become the darling of the health set, with its all-around-good-for-you-fast-food format. The mood is upbeat, with clean yellow and grey decor and contemporary black bar stools for those with enough time to sit while they down their energy boosters. A simplified menu includes the tasteful and healthful ricepot—basmati served with a choice of spicy peanut, spinach basil pesto, or hummus sauces, accompanied by raw vegetables. The same ingredients are served in the wrap, a whole-wheat tortilla shell. Steamed free-range chicken (the only meat you'll find here) is offered as an extra. Juices of choice are the BC trio of carrot, celery, and beet, and the Hi-C, with pineapple, orange, and carrot. Or try the shimmy shakes, made with frozen yogurt (a favourite is the creamsicle, a combination of orange and vanilla). The healthiest bar in town—with no hint of granola. O-Tooz has recently teamed up with Starbucks, so watch for them side by side at some locations. ■ *1068 Davie St (and branches); 689-0208; map:Q4; $; no alcohol; MC; no cheques; breakfast, lunch, dinner every day.*

Olympia Seafood Market and Grill ★ The Olympia has moved to new digs around the corner from its original Robson Street location. It's first and foremost a fish shop, but it purveys some of the best fish and chips in the Lower Mainland. Eleven years ago, fish merchant Carlo Sorace decided that what Robson Street really needed was a good place to get fish and chips. Whatever is on special in the store, which might be halibut cheeks, scallops, catfish, or calamari, is the day's special at the 12-seat counter and is served along with the tried-and-true halibut and cod versions. Soft drinks include Chinotto (Italian herbal and fruit-flavoured sparkling water) and root beer. Eat in or take out. ■ *820 Thurlow St; 685-0716; map:R3; $$; no alcohol; V; cheques OK; lunch, dinner every day.*

On Lock It took a friend—a gourmet at large who spends his summers in San Antonio, his winters in Singapore, and the rest of the year travelling the world seeking additions to his art collection—to point our way to one of the best bowls of wonton noodle soup in Vancouver. The rest of the food in this working-class restaurant is ordinary and bordering on greasy spoon, but the soup is in a class of its own. The wontons are fresh and a far cry from the standard soggy fare made with ground pork. Instead they are perfectly cooked, chewy chunky morsels, chock-full of diced pork and shrimp, as they should be. The noodles are toothsome and firm, served in a clear stock lightly perfumed with sun-dried flatfish—the Chinese answer to bonito—and topped with a sprinkling of fragrant green onions. All of this may sound simple, but this special attention to detail is what elevated this bowl of wonton soup from the ranks of mere belly filler to belonging in the repertoire of a gourmet. In

Hong Kong, there'd be taxis lined up along the street waiting to pick up the satisfied customers coming out of this joint. ■ *2010 E Hastings St; 253-3856; map:F2; $; beer and wine; MC, V; no cheques; lunch, dinner every day.*

The Only Seafood Cafe Vancouver's oldest restaurant, the Only opened for business in 1912 when out-of-town loggers came to East Hastings Street to spend their wages on liquor and flesh. Today, amid a neon sea of pawnshops and peep shows, a diverse sampling of humanity convenes for fresh no-frills fish. A periodic scrub and a coat of paint has brightened this greasy spoon over the years, but the time-worn design remains. There are two booths and a counter with stools, and you've got to be quick to nab one. When you do, order some fish and chips: halibut, sole, and lingcod are snatched from the deep fryer at the instant of just-cooked perfection and served with a side of fries. One bite tells you why this diner has become a Vancouver legend. ■ *20 E Hastings St; 681-6546; map:U4; $; no alcohol; no credit cards; no cheques; lunch, dinner Mon–Sat.*

Ouzeri ★★ Traditionally, the Greek ouzeri is a place to go to drink and eat tapas before going to dinner. In Vancouver, the Ouzeri is where you can go any time of the day and compose a meal of appetizers. The food here involves all the expected Greek specialties and then some. Moussaka Kitsilano-style is vegetarian; chicken livers are wonderful—crisp on the outside and tender on the inside. Prawns dressed with ouzo and mushrooms are simply amazing. Friendly, casual, happy (with surely the most reasonably priced menu this side of Athens), Ouzeri proves that being Greek doesn't mean you can't be trendy. Open until 2am on weekends. ■ *3189 W Broadway; 739-9378; map:C3; $$; full bar; AE, MC, DC, V; no cheques; lunch, dinner every day.* &

Paradiso ★★ Chef Bruno Born's version of paradise is a brightly coloured, cheery room with lots of noise, lots of people, and excellent Mediterranean-inspired food. The menu cleverly combines familiar foods with inspired seasonings. Meats are prepared simply but with panache; pastas are innovative and pleasing. A wild mushroom lasagne tempered the smokiness of the fungi with a soothing béchamel and piquant tomato sauce for a dish that was both light and satisfying. Born, who was most recently at the Wall Centre, also has a lively way with seafood, and fans flock to his restaurant for the yearly lobster festival, featuring classics (steamed lobster, lobster bisque) and unusual takes on the popular crustacean, such as the delicate lobster gyoza. Lunches, brunches (best in the city), and sidewalk seating in the summer are also great attractions in an increasing popular area of Kitsilano. ■ *3005 W Broadway; 734-3005; map:C3; $$$; full bar; AE, MC, V; no cheques; lunch Tue–Fri, dinner Mon–Sat, brunch Sun.*

Park Lock Seafood Restaurant ★ Amidst the changing streetscape of Vancouver's Chinatown, Park Lock appears to stand frozen in time. After more than 15 years and numerous renovations, this once top-ranked restaurant seems to look and feel exactly as it did when we first climbed its steep, narrow stairs in the early '80s. No trace of Hong Kong-style glitz here, just the simple, old-fashioned Cantonese dishes that so many of us cut our teeth on and have learned to crave. Egg foo yung comes in six varieties—including one with oysters. Black-peppered flank steak or scallops and prawns with black bean sauce still come sizzling to the table on scorching cast-iron platters. The tasty, dainty dishes of steamed spareribs with yellow plum sauce that are fast becoming an anachronism elsewhere are still proffered during the chaotic dim sum service every day. The cramped room is packed on a Monday with families and friends who all seem to know one another. We hope it will never change. ■ *544 Main St; 688-1581; map:V4; $; full bar; AE, MC, V; no cheques; lunch every day, dinner Tues–Sun.*

Phnom Penh Restaurant ★★★ Phnom Penh was once a treasure Vancouverites kept to themselves, but this restaurant now continues to win a steady stream of accolades from sources as diverse as local magazine polls to *The New York Times*. The decor is still basic, but the menu has expanded from its original rice and noodle focus to include the cuisines of China, Vietnam, and Cambodia. Pineapple-spiked hot and sour soup, with your choice of chicken, fish, or prawns, is richly flavoured and redolent with lemongrass and purple basil. An excellent appetizer of marinated beef sliced carpaccio-thin is seared rare and dressed with nuoc mam (a spicy, fishy sauce—the Vietnamese staple). Sautéed baby shrimp in prawn roe and tender slivers of salted pork cover hot, velvety steamed rice cakes—a real masterpiece. Grandma's recipe of garlic chile squid, prawns, or crab with lemon popper dip has been uniformly declared "unbeatable." The chicken salad with cabbage is a refreshing twist on a pedestrian vegetable, and the oyster omelette is a dream. If it's good enough for Julia Child, it should be good enough for you. Service is knowledgeable and friendly. ■ *244 E Georgia St; 682-5777; map:V4; $; full bar; AE, MC; no cheques; lunch, dinner Wed–Mon* ■ *955 W Broadway; 734-8898; map:R7; $; full bar; AE, MC; no cheques; lunch, dinner Wed–Mon.*

Pho Hoang ★ As common in Vietnam as the hamburger is here, pho is a quick balanced meal or a heart-warming snack and an incredible bargain besides. A large bowl of rich broth with rice stick noodles and your choice of flank, rump, brisket, tripe, and meatballs, or a dozen other permutations of the aforementioned, will cost you just over $5. You're served a side dish of bean sprouts, fresh basil, sliced green chiles, and lime to garnish as you see fit. A glass of super strong Vietnamese coffee, filter-brewed at the table, sweetened with condensed milk, then chilled with ice, is all you will need to complete a very satisfying meal. A second, equally busy, location is in Chinatown next door to the Phnom Penh. ■ *3610 Main St; 874-0810; map:E3; $; no alcohol; no credit cards; no cheques; breakfast, lunch, dinner every day* ■ *238 E Georgia St; 682-5666; map:I4; $; beer only; no credit cards; no cheques; breakfast, lunch, dinner every day.*

Pho Pasteur Vietnamese Restaurant ★ Other far-flung outlets of this successful, enterprising restaurant family hail from Toronto, Ontario, and Paris, France: and one can see why—good, interesting food served with utmost efficiency. The chopsticks, utensils, and condiments are all on the table when you arrive, so service is somewhat minimal but nevertheless friendly and fast. The menu offers mostly one bowl/plate meals of noodles and rice (76 items at last count) with everything from the classic pho variations—beef and more beef—to new and interesting combinations such as stewed duck in five-spice broth with lily buds and Chinese mushrooms. Other pleasant surprises include frogs' legs fried with lemongrass and chiles and a wonderful fried shrimp cake. Pho is open till 4am every day. ■ *290 E Hastings St; 689-8258; map:V4; $; full bar; AE, MC, V; no cheques; lunch, dinner every day.*

Picasso Café Staffed by a bunch of young people eager to make a change (the menu tells you the story) and operated by chef Gary Parks, Picasso offers an inventive menu whose key word is *modern*. Breakfast includes low-fat muffins or whole-grain toast with organic house-made preserves. Other times, fajitas, crêpes, and focaccia present a global village of favourites. Pizzalike pissaladires are topped with smoked salmon and dill or chicken, apricots, and almonds in a gentle curry sauce. Salads, in every shade of green, are spiked with exceptional dressings. The handful of meat entrées link simply cooked chicken, pork, or beef with unusually inventive sauces. Desserts run to the decadent: try the white chocolate or tofu chocolate cheesecakes. The superb crème caramel and the service give many a four-star restaurant a run for their money. ■ *1626 W Broadway; 732-3290; map:P7; $; beer and wine; MC, V; no cheques; breakfast, lunch Mon–Fri, dinner Mon–Sat, brunch Sun.*

Piccolo Mondo ★★★ Seldom do you meet people with as intense a dedication to fine food as the husband and wife team of George Baugh and Michele Geris, proprietors of this exquisite Italian restaurant. Their little world is one of Vancouver's best-kept secrets, a place where the setting is calm and elegant, the food absolutely authentic, the wine list phenomenal, and the service immaculate. This stately European room can seem stiff and formal at first. But just wait. Within minutes, Geris will have you feeling happy and comfortable,

and by the time you've taken your first sip of wine, you'll be right at home. The wine list is a marvel that is yearly honoured by *Wine Spectator* magazine. It is Baugh's mission to assemble the collection that ranges from reasonable table vino through excellent Chiantis, brunellos, and pinot grigios to the $1,200 special vintages. As for the food, chef Stephane Meyer oversees a menu that is small but nearly perfect. Each dish is packed with the intense flavours of Northern Italy, and the kitchen is dedicated to using only the best, freshest ingredients. To start, try the saffron-scented fish soup or one of the composed salads. Follow that up with, perhaps, the powerful risotto with duck, red pepper, and gorgonzola; the veal osso bucco with lemon and capers; or the house specialty, a creamy salted cod with pine nuts and raisins. By the time dessert comes around, you'll be convinced: this is the best of all possible worlds. ■ *850 Thurlow St; 688-1633; map:R3; $$$; full bar; AE, DC, MC, V; no cheques; lunch Mon–Fri, dinner Mon–Sat.*

The Pink Pearl ★★

Tanks of fresh fish are your first clue that the Cantonese menu is especially strong on seafood. If you order the crab sautéed with rock salt and chiles, you'll be further convinced. It's a spectacular dish—crisp, chile-hot, salty on the outside, and moist on the inside. A good dim sum is served every day (be sure to arrive early on weekends to avoid the lineups), and the cart jockeys always seem to have time to smile as you choose among sticky rice wrapped in lotus leaf, stuffed dumplings, and fried white turnip cakes. Table clearing is an event in itself. The tablecloth is actually a thick stack of white plastic sheets; when you're finished eating, a waiter will grab the corners of the top sheet and, with a quick flip, scoop everything up, dishes and all, and haul the lot away. A great place for kids. ■ *1132 E Hastings St; 253-4316; map:Y4; $$; full bar; AE, DC, MC, V; no cheques; breakfast, lunch, dinner every day, brunch Sat–Sun.* &

▼
Top 175
Restaurants
▲

Planet Hollywood [unrated]

Set in the old Vancouver Public Library building, you'll find the first Planet Hollywood in Canada. Owned by Arnie, Bruce, Demi, Sly, and Whoopi, this much-hyped Hollywood concept eatery is frequented by teens and tourists who line up outside to get inside, where they ogle memorabilia and buy T-shirts. The choices on the American menu should not be hard to guess: Texas nachos, Buffalo chicken wings, ceasar salad, BBQ pizza, pasta primavera, cheeseburgers, and apple strudel (from Arnie's mother) are just a few of the offerings. The ladies' and gents' rooms are pure Hollywood glitz. Help yourself to nail-polish remover, razors, hairdryers, hairspray, and perfume—but don't forget to tip the attendant. ■ *969 Robson St; 688-STAR; map:S4; $$; full bar; AE, MC, V; no cheques; lunch, dinner every day.*

Planet Veg ★★ There's hope for the slender wallet at Planet Veg. This new, mostly Indian fast-food spot is located in the heart of health-conscious Kitsilano and serves the juiciest veggie burger in BC. You can also get roti rolls (a meal in themselves), samosas, and potato salad. It's as inexpensive here as it is tasty. Inside seating is limited, so you may want to perch outdoors during the warmer months or avail yourself of its popular take-out. ■ *1941 Cornwall Ave; 734-1001; map:O6; $; no alcohol; no credit cards; no cheques; lunch, dinner every day.*

President Chinese Restaurant ★ It comes as no surprise that the Radisson President Hotel, located in the middle of "Little Asia" in Richmond, would harbour a great Chinese restaurant. The menu, although dotted with some Sichuan dishes like spicy eggplant in hotpot, is classically and creatively Cantonese and masterfully executed. A crabmeat egg foo yung is silky and packed with crab—a far cry from your average take-out fare. Shrimp and scallops are pan-fried with macadamia nuts in a truly winning combination, and another nutty must-try is diced chicken with honey walnuts. Be sure to finish with the popular Love Bird Fried Rice—half topped with creamy shrimp sauce and half with chicken in tomato sauce. Usual variety of dim sum is made to order. ■ *8181 Cambie Rd, Richmond; 276-8181; map:D5; $$; full bar; AE, MC, V; no cheques; lunch, dinner every day.*

The Prow ★★ Hidden away atop the bow of the ship-shaped Vancouver Trade and Convention Centre is a hideaway with a sweeping view of the North Shore mountains and the harbour. Book the Imax Theatre next door (there's a Prow discount coupon on your ticket) and take out-of-town family or friends to lunch or dinner. The location offers one of the most arresting outlooks in this view-rich city, but the creations of chef Thi Ngo—accompanied by selections from an award-winning wine list—easily rival the scenery. The menu has evolved into a tidy sort of West Coast cuisine, with small touches from Italy and Southeast Asia. A recent menu featured Fraser Valley ruby trout pan-fried in a hazelnut crust; Zarzuela, a simmered stew of fresh fish, prawns and shellfish; and a roast half-duck served with scallion cakes and a ginger-orange glaze. By all means reserve a window seat for an endless view of Burrard Inlet, but bring along a sweater: window tables can be drafty. Service could use polish. ■ *999 Canada Place; 684-1339; map:U2; $$$; full bar; AE, DC, MC, V; no cheques; lunch every day (Mon–Fri in winter), dinner every day, brunch Sat–Sun.*

Quattro on Fourth ★★★ Antonio Corsi took over the westside space that had been home to Montri's Thai Restaurant and turned it into one of the most comfortable Italian restaurants in the city. There's a high sense of *abbondanza* here. An impressive selection of antipasti includes no less than eight different carpaccio offerings; razor-thin sliced raw swordfish is superb, so too the grilled radicchio bocconcini and portobello mushrooms. Spaghetti Piga ("for Italians only") rewards with a well-spiced sauce of chicken, chiles, black beans, and plenty of garlic. Food prepared with lots of TLC from son Patrick and staff. Quattro recently added a heated patio that seats 35. ■ *2611 W 4th Ave; 734-4444; map:C4; $$; full bar; AE, DC, MC, V; no cheques; dinner every day.*

Raincity Grill [unrated] Raincity Grill is recognized for its extensive list of Pacific Northwest wines, but that's only one reason to visit this bright, contemporary restaurant. Fantastically situated at the happening intersection of Davie and Denman, Raincity provides diners with excellent views of English Bay all year round: in winter, from its tall windows; in summer, from the outdoor patio. Owner Harry Kambolis has welcomed a new chef, Chris Johnson (from Mayne Island's Oceanwood Country Inn), and at press time they were developing a new menu. ■ *1193 Denman St; 685-7337; map:P3; $$; full bar; AE, DC, MC, V; no cheques; lunch, dinner every day, brunch Sat–Sun.* ⟨

Raintree at the Landing [unrated] With the defection of chef Andrew Skorzewski to Bridges, Raintree's move to the Landing in Gastown, and a menu that's made a departure from West Coast cooking as we knew it on Alberni Street, we're sitting on the fence to see what happens. ■ *375 Water St; 688-5570; map:U3; $$$; full bar; AE, DC, MC, V; no cheques; dinner every day.* ⟨

Raku Kushiyaki ★★ This almost-too-stark restaurant sports an innovative fusion menu. It offers skewered tidbits and tiny preparations from the Far East, the Middle East, India, Thailand, France, and the Caribbean. There are some delicious surprises here and some pitfalls as well. Those looking for the unusual will find perfectly prepared Indonesian tamarind spiced beans and a combination of Japanese chicken rolls with chile rellenos. Too many liberties are taken with tuna carpaccio: instead of paper-thin slices, we were presented with a sashimi cut. You can nibble, nosh, and share at Raku, but watch out—it adds up. ■ *4422 W 10th Ave; 222-8188; map:B3; $$; full bar; DC, MC, V; cheques OK; dinner Tues–Sun.*

The Red Onion ★★ Forget drive-ins and head to Kerrisdale for the best double dogs, cheeseburgers, and fries (with a sour cream and dill dip) in town. The menu is designed to please everyone (we like the hot chicken salad; others pick the veggie soup). The wieners are the Onion's own, and so are the buns. At breakfast, the muffins (blueberry, chocolate chip, or banana) and aromatic cinnamon buns are baked on the premises. The best of its kind in the city. Take-out, too. ■ *2028 W 41st Ave; 263-0833; map:C4; $; beer and wine; MC, V; no cheques; breakfast, lunch, dinner every day.* ⟨

Romano's Macaroni Grill ★★ Meals are served with aplomb by singing waiters in this West End heritage mansion that's great theatre. Pizzas, toothsome pasta dishes (ask for extra sauce), and a hearty breaded veal with tomato sauce, asiago cream, and pasta are good bets. Wine is measured by the inch, and just about everything is worth the fair price. A great family place. Reservations for parties of eight plus can choose the bargain $16.95 family-style menu at dinner, $12.95 at lunch. Don't miss the frozen bellinis. On Sundays, there's a midday All-You-Can-Eat Pasta Bar for under $10. ▪ *1523 Davie St; 689-4334; map:P3; $$; full bar; AE, DC, MC, V; no cheques; lunch, dinner every day.* ♿

Rubina Tandoori ★★ Son Shaffeen Jamal is the congenial host; mother Krishna cooks the authentic East Indian fare. Rubina's menu is built around tandoori dishes, South Indian seafood, and Punjabi and Moghul dishes. Not surprisingly, tandoori breads are outstanding, and you can watch them being made in the new tandoori oven at the entrance of the restaurant. Fish masala is worth trying, as is a dry curry with potatoes— or any of the dishes that include Rubina's homemade paneer cheese. If you're a beginner at Indian food, try a duet (for two or more)—for example, Moglai Magic, a great, not-too-hot introduction to the cuisine. Don't pass up dessert, since the Gulab Jamun, deep-fried milk dough smothered in syrup and scented with rose water, is a soothing finale. The truly adventurous might want to sign up for the in-house cooking classes. ▪ *1962 Kingsway; 874-3621; map:E3; $$$; full bar; AE, MC, E, V; no cheques; lunch Mon–Fri, dinner Mon–Sat.*

The Salmon House on the Hill ★★ Northwest Coast Native artifacts reflect the origins of chef Dan Atkinson's Salmon House menu. The hallmark dish at Salmon House is BC salmon cooked over green alderwood, which delivers a distinctive, delicate, and smoky flavour—certainly worth the drive halfway to Horseshoe Bay (but only 10 minutes from downtown). There's a fresh sheet every day. Try the alder-grilled oysters with a jalapeño and bacon vinaigrette; they're perfectly prepared. The wine list favours good BC, Oregon, and Washington wines. There's a striking entrance area, but the lounge is smoky and somewhat uninviting despite the incredible view. Service is friendly and correct, and parking is free. Check out the annual salmon festival in October. ▪ *2229 Folkestone Way, West Vancouver; 926-3212; $$$; full bar; AE, DC, MC, V; no cheques; lunch, dinner every day, brunch Sun.*

Seasons in the Park ★★★ Considerable attention in the kitchen has contributed to Seasons in the Park's rapidly rising reputation. Although the Queen Elizabeth Park setting and the stunning view of downtown and the North Shore mountains still guarantee a line of tour buses outside, today's visitors to

Seasons (including visiting presidents Clinton and Yeltsin) come as much for the food as the view. Diners are treated to chef Pierre Delacorte's menu of just-picked produce, succulent seafood, and local wines. Popular dishes include a sun-dried tomato tart baked with Stilton, seared prawns and scallops sauced with Pernod and green peppercorns, and constantly changing wild or farmed Pacific or Atlantic salmon entrées. For dessert, the sun-burned lemon pie with fresh fruit coulis will end the meal on a high note. It's also a good place to get hitched—either on the patio or in the 60-seat gazebo. ■ *In Queen Elizabeth Park (Cambie St at W 33rd Ave); 874-8008; map:E3; $$; full bar; AE, MC, V; no cheques; lunch Mon–Fri, dinner every day, brunch Sat–Sun.* ♿

Settebello ★ You'll find splendid pizzas and pastas at Umberto Menghi's most casual restaurant. *Settebello* means "beautiful seven" (from an Italian card game), and, in contrast to Menghi's other establishments, this restaurant attempts to draw a younger crowd. Settebello is best on sunny days, as a respite from shopping, perhaps, when you can sit out on the rooftop patio nibbling at pasta or a collection of Italian tapas-style dishes. Begin with the fresh buffalo mozzarella with tomatoes, basil, and a touch of balsamico and extra virgin olive oil. Then order the first-rate trio of pastas featuring creamy tortellini, fettuccine sauced with spicy tomatoes, and the linguine with pesto. Try the salsiccia pizza, with hot Italian sausage, spinach, sun-dried tomatoes, and chile peppers. Excellent, moderately priced wine list. ■ *1131 Robson St; 681-7377; map:R3; $$; full bar; AE, DC, MC, V; no cheques; lunch, dinner every day.*

▼

Top 175 Restaurants

▲

Shabusen Yakiniku House ★ ½ *Yakiniku* is Japanese for "barbecue." The menu here highlights Korean food, and both of these big, glittery, action-packed, second-floor restaurants are more like what you'd expect to find in Hong Kong than in Tokyo. Everyone comes here sooner or later: families, couples (eating yakiniku can be a very sharing experience), and Japanese tourists marvelling at our cheap sushi. Ordering yakiniku gives you a choice of the familiar (chicken, beef, or salmon), or exotic (cuttlefish, beef tongue, or eel) to cook to your taste on the tabletop barbecue. Side dishes of pickled spinach and fiery kimchi, as well as a huge pot of rice, are included. Listings for shabu shabu—Japanese hot pots—offer a similar selection bolstered by live prawns, lobster, and geoduck. The Shabusen Special lets you eat your fill of yakiniku and shabu shabu. Sushi and sashimi round out the menu. ■ *2993 Granville St; 737-6888; map:D3; $$; full bar; AE, DC, MC, V; no cheques; lunch, dinner every day, brunch Sat–Sun* ■ *755 Burrard St; 669-3883; map:S3; $$; full bar; AE, MC, V; no cheques; lunch, dinner every day.*

Shanghai Chinese Bistro ★★ Consistently good food and cheerful servers with a formidable collective memory have made this tasteful, airy, L-shape "bistro moderne" a popular haunt for the downtown Chinese food cognoscenti. The unique and magical nightly noodle show provides another excuse to bring visitors along for a good nosh before heading next door for a bellow of karaoke. Hand-pulled noodles Shanghai-style are a must, of course, and so are the chile wontons. Both the pan-fried live spot prawns with chile paste and soya and the salt and chile crab are finger-licking good. For a balanced meal, try a plate of pea shoots lightly touched with garlic. The late-night hours (till 3am) are sure to be a welcomed alternative to the otherwise desolate downtown choices of pizzas, salads, and almost day-old pastries. ■ *1128 Alberni St; 683-8222; map:R3; $$; full bar; AE, JCB, MC, V; no cheques; lunch, dinner, midnight snacks every day.*

Shanghai Garden Restaurant ★★ For as long as we can remember, three restaurants have been located side by side on the east side of Fraser Street at 23rd Avenue. Like the three doors on the famous television game show, they don't always open to winners. In fact, doors one and three have changed hands so many times we've lost count. But door number two, the one in the middle, has always been a sure bet. Consistency and occasional brilliance are what one gets from Shanghai Garden's years of experience. Enter and you'll be rewarded with crispy fried duck—so tender you'll be tempted to eat the bones. Tofu steamed over sautéed spinach, wonderful five-spice beef, fat juicy Shanghai noodles, and silky drunken chicken are some of the other prizes. If you want to hit pay dirt, try a live crab out of the tank, deep-fried in peppered salt and tossed in garlic and chiles. In a word: outstanding. ■ *3932 Fraser St; 873-6123; map:E3; $; full bar; MC, V; no cheques; lunch, dinner Thur–Tues.*

Shanghai Lo Ching Hing Restaurant ★★★ Voted the best in both food and service by a recent radio poll (taken by a local Chinese station), this relative newcomer is poised to lead the revival of authentic Shanghai cuisine in the Lower Mainland. With 18 years of experience in the kitchen, 10 of them spent in the world-renowned Shanghai restaurant of the same name in Hong Kong, chef Chan is definitely the current star on Richmond's "Food Street"—Alexander Road. Start with wine-braised squab, sweet with the flavour of Shao Shing wine and laced with five-spice. Then try the subtle classic of shredded tofu stewed with prawns. The lingcod in rice wine sauce is a revelation and combines this wonderful local fish with superb Chinese technique. At lunch, traditional northern dim sum is featured, including daikon in puff pastry, steamed pork buns, and fabulous handmade noodles. ■ *1180-8391 Alexander Rd, Richmond; 821-1373; map:D6; $$; full bar; V; no cheques; lunch, dinner every day.*

Shijo Japanese Restaurant ★★ Shijo is a pleasant, uncluttered sushi bar serving excellent sushi, sashimi, and robata. Oysters, grilled on the half shell and painted with a light miso sauce, are a good bet, as are butterflied tiger prawns or shiitake foilyaki—mushrooms sprinkled with lemony ponzu sauce and cooked in foil. Meals end in a refreshing manner at this second-floor perch, with orange sherbet served in a hollowed-out orange. ■ *1926 W 4th Ave; 732-4676; map:O7; $$$; full bar; AE, JCB, MC, V; no cheques; lunch, dinner every day.* ᴖ

Shil-La Korean Restaurant ★ Shil-La can easily be mistaken for a private club. This second-storey restaurant on East Broadway has minimal signage, and the entrance hall at street level looks as if it belongs to a local branch of H & R Block. Upstairs, private rooms surround a central area with booth seating dominated by a giant mirror ball—all functionally decorated—with bulgogi grills on every table. The special combination for two (a hearty undertaking) is a bargain at $27: rib-eye steak slices, short ribs, chicken, prawns, and pork come neatly arranged on a large platter ready to be seared to taste, complemented by interesting side dishes of kimchi, pickled garlic, grilled dry minnows, sesamed spinach, and other vegetables. Sushi, tempura, and noodle dishes are also available, with sometimes inconsistent execution. But when they're good, they're very good. ■ *206-333 E Broadway; 875-6649; map:X7; $$; full bar; MC, V; cheques OK; lunch, dinner every day.*

Shiro ★★ Recently renovated, this hideaway in a mini-mall is one of Vancouver's neighbourhood haunts: a charming little restaurant run by Shiro Okano. Owner and sushi chef, he directs and stars in the show—and a highly entertaining show it is—from a stage-centre, banner-hung bar. It's a neighbourhood sushi place, and the neighbourhood loves it. Start with the cool noodle salad called wakame sunomono. Next, try Shiro's house-made gyoza, among the best in town, with its sharp and salty dipping sauce. Then order up some addictively good deep-fried squid. Or just sit at the bar, play it by ear, and eat the sushi as Shiro nimbly orchestrates. Donburi sushi, okonomi sushi, and the cone variety—temaki sushi—are all particularly good. This being the city for cuisine fusing, there's even a Tex-Mex variety made with chile sauce and mayonnaise. A happy place where you can't help but have a good time. You may have to wait on weekends, but you'll always be welcome. ■ *3096 Cambie St; 874-0027; map:D3; $; full bar; AE, MC, V; no cheques; lunch, dinner every day.*

Singapore Restaurant ★ The city at the crossroads of the world has bred a multicultural cuisine that's part Chinese and part Malaysian, yet has its own clear identity—as you'll discover at the Singapore. This small west-side eatery provides a cosy ambience, but it's the bargain-priced dishes, not the atmosphere, that keep customers coming in droves. Dishes are spice-rated with one to five stars; you decide how high to turn up the thermostat. At the top of the scale, sambal bunchies, a mix of green beans and pink prawns, can scorch your palate. Peanuty fried hokkien mee—noodles studded with squid and morsels of pork and omelette—offers a milder choice. Try the pungent Singapore eggplant, the satays, or the gado gado singapura salad. Other options? Smooth-as-a-kiss, coconut-milk-based curries, a complex yellow ginger rice, a pageful of clam, shrimp, and fish dishes, interesting noodles, and more. ■ *546 W Broadway; 874-6161; map:T7; $; full bar; MC, V; no cheques; lunch, dinner every day.*

Sophie's Cosmic Cafe ★★ Where "Leave It to Beaver" meets Pee Wee Herman—this funky diner-cum-garage-sale is a fun place to be. Don't worry about the wait—there's plenty to look at, including Sophie's collection of colourful lunch boxes and hats that were once stashed in her attic. People rave about the huge spicy burgers and chocolate shakes, but the best thing here is the stick-to-the-ribs-style breakfast: Mexican eggs (with sausage, peppers, and onions and spiced with hot pepper sauce poured from a wine bottle). ■ *2095 W 4th Ave; 732-6810; map:N7; $; beer and wine; MC, V; no cheques; breakfast, lunch, dinner every day, brunch Sat–Sun.* &

Spumante's Cafe Ristorante ★★ A standout in a street of good solid Italian neighbourhood restaurants, Spumante's is a haven for the indecisive. Dark green walls and gilt-framed paintings make for attractive surroundings, and the service is contagiously enthusiastic (they love their food, and they want you to love it too). But what sets Spumante's apart is one simple, brilliant idea: instead of having to choose between linguine in a marinated lamb sauce and chicken breast with a mint and cream sauce, you can enjoy both. Spaghetti alla carbonara gets paired with pork chops sautéed in milk with peppers, tomatoes, and a touch of curry. Egg fettuccine with vegetables is teamed with stuffed baked vegetables. All in all, there are 38 different "pasta and . . ." combinations to pick from, all priced the same: $9.95 at lunch and $14.95 at dinner (or $9.95 for pasta alone). Meals kick off with a little plate of stuzzichini—starters—on the house. There's a handful of appetizers and, as well as the combination dishes, a half-dozen additional entrées. Daytime regulars go for the inexpensive quick lunch menu. ■ *1736 Commercial Dr; 253-8899; map:Z6; $$; full bar; DC, MC, V; no cheques; lunch Tues–Fri, dinner Tues–Sat.*

Star Anise ★★ Recent changes in the kitchen mean this elegant South Granville eatery is in a state of transition, although it still maintains very high standards of service and food preparation. Owner Sam Lalji and his impeccably trained staff spoil their customers with attention. Chef Julian Bond's kitchen produces some of the most imaginative meals in town, with an emphasis on the fresh and local. The menu changes with the seasons and can run from the light—airy ricotta and leek tart or seafood sausage on wilted spinach salad—to the hearty and intense, such as the roasted duck or venison marinated with juniper berries. Exotic items add some spice to the simple local fare: tandoori, tabbouleh, roast ostrich, and enoki mushrooms, for instance. ■ *1485 W 12th Ave; 737-1485; map:D3; $$$; full bar; AE, DC, MC, V; no cheques; dinner every day.*

Starfish [unrated] Lovers of seafood had something to celebrate when chef Mark Potovsky and his French-Canadian co-chef, Frederic Desbiens, landed at Starfish (from Uforia). Potovsky, one of Vancouver's most talented chefs, is also one of its most hyperactive, rarely at the same restaurant for long. Desbiens is rattling the pots presently and we're holding back stars to see if the Potovsky talent rubs off. This lovely restaurant is tucked between a batch of high-rises on the waterfront right across False Creek from Granville Island. It is a very modern room, all floor-to-second-storey-ceiling glass that will give you a wonderful view of the sun setting behind the Burrard Street Bridge and the marina below it, whether you choose to sit outside on the patio or inside. Recent redecoration has brightened a once-chilly atmosphere with lively colours and friendly service. A nice selection of champagne cocktails, martinis, and reasonably priced wines are certainly welcoming, but it's the food that's the star at this spot. Potovsky has always served the most glamorous food in the city. Each dish is a work of art, a felicitous convergence of colour and flavour and texture. The smoked salmon and goat cheese parmentier is the prettiest appetizer to emerge from any local kitchen, all layers of creamy potato and delicate pink salmon topped with lightly toasted cheese. The grilled ahi tuna with a cabernet-horseradish glaze is so popular you'd be wise to get there early to get any at all. Luckily, a lobster risotto is a flavourful alternative, in case they've run out of the tuna. Desserts are witty takes on comfort-food favourites: an old-fashioned root beer float, starfish cookies with vanilla milk, or ginger chocolate cake. ■ *2-1600 Howe St; 681-8581; map:R6; $$$; full bar; AE, DC, MC, V; no cheques; lunch, dinner every day, brunch Sun.*

Stepho's Souvlakia ★ This is one of those little restaurants that just keeps on going, regardless of the economy or whether it's a Monday or Saturday night. This is basic, good Greek fair: lots of pungent tzatziki; mega-salads; decent-size hunks of

▼

Top 175 Restaurants

▲

pita—in a nutshell, great value, along with plenty of regulars and a staff that really seems to care. The interior is no-nonsense comfortable, with enough posters of the Parthenon to start a travel agency, bunches of fresh carnations on every table, and plenty of tiles and greenery. Despite the heavy traffic, it's also clean and the service is prompt and polite. Portions are generous: even a single, sizable brochette fights for space on a plate loaded with rice pilaf, giant buttery roast potatoes, Greek salad with plenty of black olives, parsley, tomato, feta and peppers, a healthy serving of tzatziki, and hot pita bread on the side for dipping. Good Greek food, cheap, with a well-priced wine list. At press time, Stepho's has taken over another space next door, so we're curious to see if fans will still have to wait in the rain to get in. ■ *1124 Davie St; 683-2555; map:Q4; $; full bar; AE, MC, V; no cheques; lunch, dinner every day.* &

Steveston Seafood House ★ Appropriately located near the Fraser River and the fishing docks, the Steveston Seafood House continues to earn its reputation as "that great little seafood place in Richmond." The decor is funky, with a nautical motif featuring overhead nets, glass floats, and corny seashell knickknacks. Seafood, simply prepared and generously served on large fish-shaped plates, delivers all it promises. We recommend any of the house specialties—even ones with names like Jonathan Livingston Seafood (a mixed seafood platter)—but you shouldn't overlook simple dishes such as the juicy pan-fried halibut with lemon butter. ■ *3951 Moncton St, Richmond (Steveston); 271-5252; map:C7; $$; full bar; AE, MC, V; no cheques; dinner every day.*

Subeez ★ Subeez has all of the urban edge that Vancouver can muster. Decor is neo-gothic, post-nuclear, and thrown into this postmodern cocktail are massive wax-encrusted medieval candelabras. It's as much a bar and meeting place as it is a restaurant. Almost everything has been recycled (the bathroom sinks are from Oakalla prison) in this 225 seater that you have to see to believe. It's great Vancouver theatre and it also has the best french fries going. They come with garlic mayo (order extra). All that, plus a thoughtful, well-priced wine list. Although it's clearly not the Main Event, the food is imaginative and sometimes quite good—the lamb on foccacia, chicken and brie sandwich, and veggie burger, for example. There's an ominous 30-speaker sound system with appropriately manic music. Keep earplugs handy. The kitchen's open till 1am. ■ *891 Homer St; 687-6107; map:S4; $; full bar; MC, V; no cheques; lunch, dinner, midnight snacks every day, brunch Sat–Sun.* &

Sun Sui Wah Seafood Restaurant ★★★ The splashy, new Sun Sui Wah, with its sail-like sculpture stretching across the glass-domed roof designed by Bing Thom, is fast becoming the talk of the town. This is *the* place for dim sum, and being named

▼

Top 175 Restaurants

▲

the best Cantonese restaurant in the Lower Mainland by a Canadian Chinese radio poll only serves to firmly set the jewel in the crown. Simon Chan brought the proven track record and signature dishes of this successful Hong Kong group to Vancouver a decade ago and his team has been playing to packed houses ever since, both in Vancouver and Richmond. The reasons are legion: crispy tender roasted squabs and sculpted Cantonese masterpieces such as the luscious broccoli-skirted steamed chicken interwoven with black mushrooms and Chinese ham; deftly steamed scallops on silky bean curd topped with creamy-crunchy tobikko (flying-fish roe) sauce; live Alaskan king crab dressed in wine and garlic; lobster hot pot with egg noodles; giant beach oysters steamed to perfection in black bean sauce; and lightly sautéed geoduck paired with deep-fried "milk"—fragrant with sweet coconut in a fluffy crust. Reserve early, as this is now the hot spot in town for weddings. ■ *4940 No 3 Rd (Alderbridge Plaza), Richmond; 273-8208; map:D6; $$; full bar; AE, MC, V; no cheques; lunch, dinner every day.* & ■ *3888 Main St; 872-8822; map:E3; $$; full bar; AE, MC, V; no cheques; lunch, dinner every day.*

Sun Wong Kee ★ The word is out: this little Chinese restaurant hidden away on Main Street offers some of the best, least expensive food in town. You'll find minimal decor and maximum attention to what's cooking, especially with the live crabs, rock cod, and lobsters priced just a tad above what they sell for at the market. The seafood is prepared steamed plain, served with butter and cream; baked with green pepper and black bean sauce; or baked with green onion and ginger—but the spicy, deep-fried version gets our vote. The 224-item menu runs the gamut of noodles, hot pots, congee, and pork, beef, and rice dishes; veers toward seafood (abalone to oysters); and includes such esoterica as fried milk with house special sauce. Five-course seafood dinners for four can be had for less than $30. ■ *4136 Main St; 879-7231; map:E3; $; beer and wine; MC, V; no cheques; lunch, dinner Wed–Mon.*

Surat Sweet ★ Formerly located in Vancouver's East Indian neighbourhood, Surat Sweet became so popular with west siders, the owners decided to relocate to Kitsilano. Serving freshly made Gujarati food (and therefore by definition vegetarian), this updated 50-seat restaurant draws a steady stream of regulars looking for a curry fix. Samosas are fresh and commendably nongreasy. Bhajia—chickpea-floured potato slices—are deep-fried and served with tamarind sauce and fresh grated coconut. Thalis, depending on their size (the special feeds two), include one or two curries spiced with the subtlety of a maestro. The mind-blowingly sweet desserts are all good, but don't miss the shrikhand—thickened yogurt tinted with saffron and speckled with cardamom seeds and finely chopped pistachios.

■ *1938 W 4th Ave; 733-7363; map:O7; $; wine & beer; DC, MC, V; no cheques; lunch Tues–Sat, dinner Tues–Sun.*

Szechuan Chongqing Restaurant ■ Szechuan Chongqing Seafood Restaurant ★★

In 1993, a new era began for Szechuan Chongqing. Playing catch-up to increasing demand, the family-run eatery that, once upon a time, anchored the foot of Victoria Drive, went through a series of rapid metamorphoses. First it moved to the corner of Commercial and 12th. Then it ventured into the west side with the opening of its posh Broadway location, strategically adding the ranking of "seafood" restaurant to its well-known name. Shortly after, the Commercial Drive restaurant, still operating today as Szechuan Chongqing Restaurant (sans "Seafood"), was sold to different owners. Last September, a new 280-seat Kingsway branch of Chongqing Seafood opened in Burnaby, making it that much easier to sate our cravings for those chile-spiked garlicky green beans that had us lining up at its doors a generation ago. After some initial reports of uneven service, both locations are now in true form, serving up the robust flavours, the piquant sauces, and the searing heat of fresh and dry chiles that the family has long established as familiar signposts of Sichuan food in Vancouver. Added to the memorable repertoire of General Tso's Chicken, magnificent fried prawns with chile sauce, lingering orange beef, melt-in-your-mouth sliced pork with garlic, and rich, silky-crunchy Tan Tan noodles are popular seafood treasures, including steamed Alaskan king crab in garlic and braised sea cucumbers with black mushrooms. We can now recommend all three branches: It looks as though the new Chongqing dynasty is going to be long-lived. ■ *2808 Commercial Dr (and branches); 254-7434; map:E3; $$; full bar; AE, MC, V; no cheques; breakfast, lunch, dinner every day.*

▼

Top 175
Restaurants

▲

Tang's Noodle House ★

As Vancouver's Asian population swells, noodle houses pop up overnight like mushrooms. Tang's is still one of the best, thanks largely to owner Eddie Tang's rigorous quality control (MSG is verboten) and insistence on giving good value. Here, in bubblegum-pink and grey surroundings, you'll find locals rubbing elbows with those who have trekked in from the distant 'burbs for a serving of fried spicy black cod or shredded pork in garlic and sour sauce. The 100-plus dishes on the menu include rice with barbecued duck, chicken, pork, or brisket; warming hot pots; and vegetarian dishes. Aficionados of incendiary dishes (thoughtfully marked with an *H*) shouldn't miss the wonton in spicy garlic and chile. Gentler flavours are found in the Singapore noodles—a golden curry-flavoured dish crunchy with bean sprouts, green pepper, and onion and generously sprinkled with shrimp and slivers of barbecued pork. Terrific hot and sour soup and bargain-priced lunch specials. ■ *2805-2807 W Broadway; 737-1278; map:C3; $; beer and wine; MC, V; no cheques; lunch, dinner Mon–Sat.*

The Teahouse at Ferguson Point ★★ This stunning location in Stanley Park is a magnet for tourists, with its park setting and spectacular view of English Bay, but a faithful following of locals attests to the consistency of fare. Appetizers run the gamut from Teahouse stuffed mushrooms (crab, shrimp, Emmentaler) to steamed mussels in a saffron-anchovy broth. Salmon is always a good bet, served with seasonal sauces. Executive chef Dino Gazzola's rack of lamb in fresh herb crust is a perennial favourite—even without the view attached. Desserts include a dark and milk chocolate torta milano with mascarpone mousse or the lemon hazelnut parfait with a blackberry coulis. If you're planning a summer wedding, check out the sunset patio overlooking English Bay. ■ *7501 Stanley Park Dr (in Stanley Park); 669-3281; map:C7; $$; full bar; AE, MC, V; no cheques; lunch Mon–Fri, dinner every day, brunch Sat–Sun.* ♿

Tio Pepe ★ Tio Pepe—a shoebox of a restaurant with one long, narrow room crammed full of tables and a kitchen at the back—has reasonable prices and food unlike any other Mexican restaurant in town. Start with margaritas and a double order of chicken flautas. Charbroiled lamb is marinated in wine and spices with a haunting, bittersweet taste of Seville oranges. *Pascaya con huevo*—date-palm shoots fried in an egg batter and served with tomato sauce—is an unusual appetizer, with a pleasantly astringent taste. The food has a flavourful mildness typical of Yucatán cooking. If fire is your style, however, shake on some habaero hot sauce, distilled from the hottest peppers known to anyone. ■ *1134 Commercial Dr; 254-8999; map:Z6; $; full bar; MC, V; no cheques; dinner Mon–Sat.* ♿

Tojo's ★★★★ Tojo Hidekazu *is* Tojo's. One of the best-known sushi maestros in Vancouver, this beaming Japanese chef has a loyal clientele that regularly fills his spacious upstairs restaurant, though most people want to sit at the 10-seat sushi bar—not big enough for all his devoted patrons. He's endlessly innovative, surgically precise, and committed to fresh ingredients. Show an interest in the food, and he might offer you a bit of this and that from the kitchen: Tojo tuna or perhaps special beef (very thin beef wrapped around asparagus and shrimp) or shrimp dumplings with hot mustard sauce. Getting to be a regular is not difficult, and it's highly recommended. The dining room has a view of the stunning North Shore mountains and plenty of table seating; Japanese menu standards like tempura and teriyaki are always reliable, and daily specials are usually superb: pine mushroom soup in the fall, steamed monkfish liver from October to May, and cherry blossoms with scallops and sautéed halibut cheeks with shiitake in the spring. Plum wine and fresh orange pieces complete the meal. ■ *202-777*

The Tomahawk ★ The Tomahawk must be the original in-spiration for all those hokey, totem-pole theme restaurants on highways across North America. In Vancouver, it's a 70-plus-year institution, famous for its hungry-man-size meals. Everyone comes for the eye-opening Yukon Breakfast—five rashers of bacon, two eggs, hash browns, and toast ($7.70)—served all day. For lunch, there are several hamburger platters (named after Native chiefs), sandwiches, fried chicken, fish and chips, and even oysters. Pies (lemon meringue, Dutch apple, banana cream) are baked on the premises, and the staff will gladly wrap one to go. ▪ *1550 Philip Ave, North Vancouver; 988-2612; map:D1; $; no alcohol; AE, DC, MC, V; no cheques; breakfast, lunch, dinner every day.*

Tomato Fresh Food Cafe ★ Chef on the run Diane Clement and partners have a real neighbourhood joint here. But when you slip into a wooden booth, you're in for some serious eating. For years, this was a greasy spoon; now it has an overlay of young, retro energy, most lucidly expressed in the big, chunky, wildly coloured bowls used for serving specialties such as "tea-puccino"—cappuccino made with tea. Young waitstaff serve a variation of mom food: vegetarian chile with really good corn bread, a whacking slab of turkey in the turkey sandwich, and real milk shakes. There's also great take-out from Tomato To Go (open Mon–Sat, just around the corner). ▪ *3305 Cambie St; 874-6020; map:D3; $; beer and wine; MC, V; no cheques; breakfast, lunch, dinner Mon–Fri, brunch Sat–Sun.*

▼

**Top 175
Restaurants**

▲

Top Gun Chinese Seafood Restaurant ★★ A visit to Top Gun is never just a culinary experience, it's also a crash course on Pacific Rim cultural immersion. The Hong Kong-style Aberdeen Shopping Centre in which it's located, together with the adjacent Yaohan Centre and nearby Parker Place, is part of an area nicknamed "Little Asia". In these few square blocks are an education centre, a Buddhist temple, bookstores, barbecue shops, bakeries, video arcades, herbalist clinics, and even a Bonsai studio. All this makes weekend dim sum here seem more like an excursion than a meal. Expect a lineup and sometimes indifferent service. The dinner menu is generic Cantonese, but specials can be quite interesting. Try sautéed spiced frogs' legs with fagara, baby abalone on mustard greens, or sea scallops with jackfruit and fresh pears in a potato nest. For dessert, amble across the mall to Rhino's Cafe (next to the bowling alley) and try some of the unusual Eurasian cakes and pastries that are featured there. ▪ *2110-4151 Hazelbridge Way (Aberdeen Shopping Centre), Richmond; 273-2883; map:D5; $$; full bar; V; no cheques; lunch, dinner every day.* ᕁ

Tropika Malaysian Cuisine ★ The only Malaysian restaurant in town was a truck stop on Kingsway until Tropika came along offering authentic Malaysian fare. Try the spicy spinach, pungently flavoured with dried shrimp and fish sauce. Less fiery is the tender Hainan chicken served with ginger, scallions, and a sambal dip. Rendang lembu, a beef curry, retains an element of heat, though it's smoothed with soothing coconut milk. Two rice dishes also stand out on the menu: a luxurious coconut rice and a warm, porridgy, sweet black-rice pudding. The latter is served in Bali as breakfast and makes a comforting late-morning meal here too. ■ *3105 W Broadway; 737-6002; map:B3; $$; full bar; AE, MC; no cheques; lunch, dinner every day* ■ *1-8280 Lansdowne, Richmond; 278-6002; map:D6; $$; full bar; MC; no cheques; lunch, dinner every day.*

Umberto Al Porto Umberto Menghi's least expensive restaurant, Al Porto, has a lively, colour-splashed decor. We recommend the antipasto plate or the excellent carpaccio as a starter. Pastas range from good to excellent; only the canneloni falls short of expectations, and it would have been redeemed had it been cooked longer. The chicken piccata is tender and plentiful, the sauce appropriately lemony and light. Serious grape nuts are drawn to the basement of this Gastown warehouse not only to choose from an estimable wine list, cleverly divided by region, but also to attend Umberto Wine Club events. ■ *321 Water St; 683-8376; map:U3; $$; full bar; AE, DC, MC, V; no cheques; lunch Mon–Fri, dinner Mon–Sat.*

▼

▲

Uncle Herbert's Fish & Chip Shop ★★ At Uncle Herbert's, owner Ken Mertens has crafted an old English village street atmosphere, with individually styled rooms lining either side of a main "street." The walls in one room are covered with tea towels from every English town big enough to print one, and the Windsor Room is stocked with royal memorabilia dating back to George V. Stop by from 2 to 4 for afternoon tea. For $6.95, you get a pot of tea, finger sandwiches, and scones with clotted cream and sweets. But it's the top-quality fish (lingcod or halibut) and chips that draw the crowds. The roster of pub food includes Cornish pasties, English pork pies, Scotch eggs, sausage rolls, New England clam chowder, and Yorkshire fish cakes (two large slices of potato with fish between them, like a sandwich, battered and deep-fried). Mertens imports as many English beers as he can get. ■ *4866 Delta St, Ladner; 946-8222; $; beer and wine; MC, V; no cheques; lunch Tues–Sat, dinner Tues–Sun.*

Vassilis Taverna ★★ You'll feel transported to the Mediterranean: the paper place mats are even adorned with maps of the Greek islands. Vassilis, one of Vancouver's original Greek restaurants, is located in what is loosely referred to as Little Greece. The menu is quite traditional, but the quality is

consistent. Worthy starters include lightly battered calamari
and rich, salty, scalding-hot saganaki (Greek kefalotiri cheese
fried in oil and sprinkled with lemon juice). The house specialty
is a perfectly juicy kotopoulo—chicken pounded flat, simply
seasoned with lemon juice, garlic, and oregano, and then barbecued. The Greek salad makes a meal in itself, especially with
a succulent pile of quick-fried baby smelts on the side. Honey-
sweet baklava or a luscious navarino make fantastic desserts.
In summer, the restaurant opens onto the sidewalk. ▪ *2884 W
Broadway; 733-3231; map:C3; $$; full bar; AE, MC, V; no
cheques; lunch Tues–Fri, dinner Tues–Sun.* &

Victoria Chinese Restaurant ★★ This upmarket, well-
maintained, professional restaurant in the Royal Centre adja-
cent to the Hyatt Regency Hotel is now a downtown favourite.
Superb dim sum is made to order from a sizable menu featur-
ing tasty bites such as shrimp salad roll, egg rolls with shrimp
and mayonnaise filling, satay calamari, and, on a good day, os-
trich pot-stickers. The dinner menu travels all Chinese culinary
regions. Standouts include finger-licking lettuce wrap with
minced squab; succulent, perfectly cooked salt and chile black
cod; creamy braised napa cabbage; and a superior pan-fried
prawns in soya. The older sister restaurant, East Ocean Seafood
Restaurant at 108-777 West Broadway, was among the very first

of the new style Chinese dining rooms to cross the Pacific from
Hong Kong and remains one of the most popular. ▪ *1088
Melville St (Royal Centre); 669-8383; map:S3; $$; full bar;
AE, MC; no cheques; lunch, dinner every day.*

Vij's ★★ A civilized change from ersatz curry houses. Vikram
Vij dishes up home-cooked Indian fare that evolves at whim.
His seasonal menu changes every three months but almost always includes a mean curry or a killer saag. Courtesy and simplicity rule as Vik waits carefully on all who arrive early enough
to get in—first greeting them with a glass of chai before dis-
cussing the menu. The prices are civilized too. ▪ *1480 W 11th
Ave; 736-6664; map:D3; $; beer and wine; AE, MC, V; no
cheques; dinner Mon–Sat.* &

Villa del Lupo ★★★ Owners Julio Gonzalez Perini and Vince
Piccolo boast culinary pedigrees, and it shows. The "house of
the wolf" is a simple, elegant space warmed with a sunny Tuscan palette that balances heritage with contemporary. Prices
tend to be high, but portions are generous. Almost everything
is wonderful: a simply broiled lamb chop with a carrot and basil
reduction is accompanied by herb mashed potatoes to soak up
the juices; fresh salmon and shrimp cakes are served with a piquant saffron and lime mayonnaise. The osso bucco is a constant and for serious appetites only. Italy isn't the only region
on the wine list, and grappa and eaux-de-vie are available as
well. Service is always correct. ▪ *869 Hamilton St; 688-7436;*

map:S5; $$$; full bar; AE, DC, MC, V; no cheques; dinner every day.

Vivace! ★★ Bring your appetite if you're headed to Vivace!. This fun and lively spot is a good place to take the family or a group of friends for huge servings of excellent pastas, tasty grilled meats, and hearty appetizers. Until recently, this was the location of Cafe Roma, a longtime '70s-style Italian restaurant that has been reworked into a breezy, open room with red-and-gold columns, colourful tiles, and lots of light streaming in through huge windows with a view of the harbour and city. The menu features reasonable prices for both wine and food, and a fairly creative—and big!—selection of dishes. Start your meal with the steamed clams or mussels; they nestle in a spicy broth of either saffron or tomato and hot pepper. Or try the appetizer portions of prawns hot off the grill. The grill works overtime at Vivace!, cooking up seafood, chicken, and a beef tenderloin in a reduction of balsamic vinegar. The choice of pastas is extensive as well, so it's a good thing you can have an enormous three-pasta combo that costs about $14 a person. The hot, tomatoey spaghetti vivace is advertised as "for Italians only—hot, hot, hot," and while it doesn't quite live up to its billing, it *is* very tasty. Meanwhile, the squid-ink fettuccine with scallops in a pesto cream sauce is a delicate and lovely choice. ■ *60 Semisch Way, North Vancouver; 984-0274; map:E1; $$; full bar; AE, DC, MC, V; lunch Mon–Fri, dinner every day.*

Vong's Kitchen ★★ At least two generations of Vancouverites cut their teeth on the Vong family's cooking. After inheriting the secrets from Mom, then putting in time in Hong Kong, Tony Vong, the hippest Chinese chef in town, is now manning the giant woks in his tiny kitchen in between filming commercials for Chinese TV. For a unique opener, Tony's fried curried beef wontons are a must-try. Follow that with Jade Chicken, named for its jewel-like garnish of deep-fried spinach surrounding tender morsels of Sichuan peppercorn-spiced chicken. Then garlic chili prawns, honey orange beef, seafood and vegetables in a deep-fried potato nest . . . we never seem able to stop ordering more than we should. But somehow, we always manage to find room for those banana fritters that come with the bill. Note the new location with its cheery canary-yellow paint job (courtesy of number two son), which matches the ever spritely service of number one daughter—a winning combination that completes the picture of an exemplary family operation. ■ *4298 Fraser St; 879-4298; map:E4; $; no alcohol; no credit cards; no cheques; dinner Tues–Sun.*

Water Street Cafe ★ 1/2 Across the street from Gastown's steam-powered clock, this small corner cafe is the restaurant of choice for homemade focaccia, buttery carpaccio, and Southern Italian pastas. A delightful find, especially when you can sit outside at the sidewalk tables (best to call ahead and reserve one at lunch). The menu's not long, but, lunch or dinner, there's always something that's exactly right: calamari, deep-fried with a cucumber and dill yogurt; salmon marinated in soy and balsamic vinegar, sautéed and served on a bed of greens; spaghetti tossed with chicken, sun-dried tomatoes, and fresh basil; and for dessert, a rich, smooth tiramisu. The staff is warm and welcoming, providing a great place to dine alla famiglia. Two rooms upstairs (one seats 12 and has a fireplace; the other seats 45) are used for private parties. ■ *300 Water St; 689-2832; map:U3; $$; full bar; MC, V; no cheques; lunch, dinner every day.*

White Spot It's as much a part of the city as Stanley Park, and Vancouverites driving into town after months or years away have been known to stop first for a chocolate milkshake and a Legendary Burger Platter, which includes a Triple O Burger lavishly garnished with a "secret sauce." The first Spot opened as a hamburger joint in 1928, went on to become the first drive-in restaurant in Canada, and now has more than 45 locations. It continues to be a fave among even the most fussy foodies. The freshly baked muffins, the clam chowder, the clubhouse sandwich, and the Pirate Pak for kids are the stuff of legend. You'll also find the ultimate in comfort foods: liver and onions, a hot turkey sandwich, meat loaf, and chicken pot pie. In keeping with the culinary correctness of the '90s, White Spot has broadened its listings to include pastas and stir-frys as well as garden salads and Heart Smart items. Signature desserts include the cheesecake and boysenberry pie. And its even got a hip website. ■ *1616 W Georgia St (and branches); 681-8034; map:T4; $; full bar; MC, V; no cheques; breakfast, lunch, dinner every day.*

The William Tell (The Georgian Court Hotel) ★★★ ½ This is special-occasion dining at its very best, thanks to owner Erwin Doebeli. Doebeli, the consummate restaurateur, is possibly the most charming man in Vancouver and will personally ensure that you have a wonderful meal. His restaurant reflects his old-world dedication to excellent food and service. Recent renovations have only improved things; the old-fashioned darkness of the room has been lightened and it's now a bright, elegant spot for dining, drinks before the theatre, late-night dessert, or any special celebration. Proximity to the Queen Elizabeth and Ford Theatres makes this a perfect place for a big night out—have an early dinner then come back after the show for dessert and a spectacular flaming caffé diablo. Outstanding appetizers include rabbit rillettes in phyllo pastry and BC salmon tartare with fennel and wild mushrooms on toasted homemade brioche. A revitalized menu ranges from the traditional (chateaubriand for two) to Swiss-inspired dishes (veal scalloppine with morel mushrooms in cream sauce) to the light and flavourful, such as the fish braid of salmon, Arctic char, and sea bass. The desserts are pure decadence: meringue glace au chocolat, hot fruit soufflés, and opulently rich crêpes Suzette prepared at your table. The sommelier reigns over one of the best wine cellars in the city (aficionados should ask to see the reserved wine menu). Sunday night is family dining with a Swiss farmer's buffet (no à la carte menu). ■ *765 Beatty St; 688-3504; map:T5; $$$; full bar; AE, DC, MC, V; no cheques; breakfast every day, lunch Mon–Fri, dinner every day.* ㅗ

Won More Szechuan Cuisine ★ Whether you eat in or take out, Sichuan is the fieriest of Chinese cuisines. Go for the diced chicken with hot garlic sauce or dried tangerine peel, or the three-alarm spicy pork with peanuts and hot chile. Milder appetites can be appeased, but will never be bored, with a zingy lemon chicken or fresh squid with mixed vegetables. Not everything is spicy: mu-shu pork is subtly flavoured and good. With its intensely flavoured broth and savoury stuffed noodles, the Won More's wonton soup elevates a cliché to a classic. Particularly commendable are the Singapore noodles, lightly curry flavoured and tangled with shrimp, barbecued pork, shredded omelette, and crispy bean sprouts, every bite different. Vegetarians will have a field day here. At either location, consider take-out, then stroll down to the beach, take in the sunset, and consider coming back for just won more. ■ *201-1184 Denman St; 688-8856; map:O7; $; beer and wine; MC, V; no cheques; dinner every day.* ■ *1944 W 4th Ave; 737-2889; map:P3; $; beer and wine; MC, V; no cheques; dinner every day.*

Wonton King ★★ They should have changed the name when they spiffed up this surprisingly secret spot from its former shabby incarnation. After being voted best family-style restaurant by Canadian Chinese Radio AM1470 listeners, it will now be a little harder to keep the lid on this find. Skip the wonton and the regular menu and ask for a translation of the preset special menu printed in Chinese. Don't miss the crispy, meaty, succulent spareribs in salt and chiles or the cool, velvety, hand-shredded chicken. For around $50, you get a full meal consisting of your choice of four dishes from about 40 selections, a double-boiled soup, and an appetizer of Peking duck in crêpes. It's enough to feed four to six. For the quality, it's a bargain. ■ *620 SE Marine Dr; 321-4433; map:E5; $$; full bar; V; no cheques; lunch, dinner Wed–Mon.*

Wonton Noodle Restaurant ★ ½ Don't be put off by the out-of-the-way location on an otherwise charmless strip of Hastings Street. Or by the fact that apart from the couple of tables that offer a peekaboo mountain view, decor is basic. Or that the service, though pleasant, is brisk. The food makes up for all of these shortcomings. The menu lists 176 items. Wonton soup,

Peking duck, sweet and sour, hot and sour: chances are good you'll find any Cantonese dish you've ever heard of, and then some. Servings are generous. The medium-size bowl of Seaweed Bean Cake Seafood Soup, a bewitching complexity of textures and flavours, feeds three. The listing for chicken's feet, duck's tongues, and various tripe dishes is written in Chinese only, but the staff is happy to make a stab at translation. Worth a separate trip are the rock-bottom-priced, snack-size specials: a single crisp-skinned, butterflied quail or pai dan—the preserved duck egg whose yolk is the colour of green marble. Worth trying too are the half-moon-shaped dumplings, the eggplant and deep-fried bean curd in hot garlic sauce, and superlative pan-fried squid with salt and hot pepper. A newer location is on Cambie Street. ■ *1991 E Hastings St; 253-8418; map:E2; $; full bar; MC; no cheques; lunch, dinner every day* ■ *4008 Cambie St; 877-1253; map:D3; $; full bar; MC; no cheques; lunch, dinner every day, brunch Sat–Sun.*

Zeppo's Trattoria ★★ ½ Lively, upbeat atmosphere in a setting as warm as a Tuscan family reunion. A ho-hum location, but the hip and hungry crowd willingly drives kilometres for the food as, with élan and bravado, chef Tim Johnstone finesses lusty peasant flavours into memorable and often elegant dishes. There's complementary focaccia and silken pâté to start. Antipasto is a must, hot or cold, the hot big enough to share and including shrimp, oysters, sausage, some spicy pepperonata, and a solitary escargot. What about that insanely rich polenta next? It's topped with more pepperonata and reclining on a bed of decadently rich sauce—an amalgam of Romano, Parmesan, and Edam—wicked as original sin. Fettuccine with scallops; fork-tender lamb shanks; angel hair pasta with two sauces neatly divided by a row of grill-marked tiger prawns; gnocchi with Gorgonzola cream; shell pasta stuffed with chicken, fennel, and chorizo—they're all good. The menu's re-jigged every couple of weeks to accommodate seasonal tastes, but you get the general idea. Pray that the triple cream of mushroom soup is still on the menu. ■ *1967 W Broadway; 737-7444; map:O7; $$; full bar; AE, DC, MC, V; no cheques; lunch Mon–Fri, dinner every day.*

NIGHTLIFE

Alternative
DV8
The Gate
Graceland
Luv-A-Fair
The Odyssey
The Piccadilly Pub
The Starfish Room
The Underground
The World

Blues
Arts Club Theatre
    Backstage Lounge
Darby D. Dawes
Delaney's
The Fairview
Jake O'Grady's
The Railway Club
The Town Pump
The Yale

Comedy Club
Yuk Yuk's

Country
Boone County
Pancho & Lefty's
The Railway Club

DJ
The Avalon
Bar-None
Big Bam Boo
Cat and Fiddle Pub
    and Bistro
Celebrities Nightclub
Chameleon Urban
    Lounge
Fiasco
Graceland
It's a Secret Pub and
    Lounge
Kits New West
Kits On Broadway
Lotus Club
Luv-A-Fair
Madison's
MaRS Restaurant and
    Nightclub

Mavericks Sports
    Cabaret and Grill
Mavericks Sports Grill
    on the Waterfront
Montana's Sports Bar
The Mountain Shadow
    Pub
Niagara Hotel
Numbers Cabaret
The Odyssey
The Purple Onion
    Cabaret
The Rage
Shark Club Bar and
    Grill
Steel Monkey
The Odyssey
The Underground
The Wild Coyote
The World

Gay Bars
Celebrities Nightclub
Denman Station
The Edge
Lotus Club
Numbers Cabaret
The Odyssey
Uncle Charlie's Lounge
The Underground

Irish
Blarney Stone

Jazz
Carnegie's
Casbah Jazzbah
Chameleon Urban
    Lounge
Hot Jazz
The Purple Onion
    Cabaret

Karaoke
Denman Station
The Purple Onion
    Cabaret

Nonalcoholic
The Edge
The World

Peeler Bars
The Drake Show
    Lounge
The Marble Arch
No. 5 Orange

Piano Bars
Carnegie's
The Garden Terrace
Gerard Lounge
Jake O'Grady's
Wedgewood Hotel
    Lounge

Rock
The Avalon
Bar-None
Celebrities Nightclub
Fiasco
Gastown Music Hall
The Gate
Graceland
It's a Secret Pub and
    Lounge
The John B
    Neighbourhood Pub
Kits New West
Kits On Broadway
Luv-A-Fair
Madison's
MaRS Restaurant and
    Nightclub
The Mountain Shadow
    Pub
Niagara Hotel
Numbers Cabaret
The Piccadilly Pub
Railway Club
Richard's on Richards
The Roxy
Shark Club Bar and
    Grill
Steel Monkey
The Town Pump
The Wild Coyote

Singles
The Avalon
Bar-None
Big Bam Boo

Carnegie's
Cat and Fiddle Pub and
  Bistro
Chameleon Urban
  Lounge
Fiasco
Fred's Uptown Tavern
Georgia Street Bar and
  Grill
Graceland
It's a Secret Pub and
  Lounge
Jake and Elwood's
  Sports Bar
Joe Fortes

The John B
  Neighbourhood Pub
Kits New West
Kits on Broadway
Luv-A-Fair
Madison's
MaRS Restaurant and
  Nightclub
Mavericks Sports
  Cabaret and Grill
Mavericks Sports Grill
  on the Waterfront
Mescalero
Montana's Sports Bar

The Mountain Shadow
  Pub
Numbers Cabaret
The Odyssey
The Purple Onion
  Cabaret
The Rage
Richard's on Richards
The Roxy
Shark Club Bar and
  Grill
Steel Monkey
The Underground
The Wild Coyote
The World

LOCATION

Burnaby
Delaney's
Fiesta's
Mavericks Sports
  Cabaret and Grill
The Mountain Shadow
  Pub

Coquitlam
Boone County
Cat and Fiddle Pub and
  Bistro
The John B
  Neighbourhood Pub
Steel Monkey

Downtown
Automotive
Bar-None
Bayside Lounge
Beatty St. Bar and Grill
Blarney Stone
Casbah Jazzbah
Celebrities Nightclub
Chameleon Urban
  Lounge
Denman Station
The Drake Show
  Lounge
DV8
The Edge
Fred's Uptown Tavern
The Garden Terrace
Gastown Music Hall
The Gate

Georgia Street Bar and
  Grill
Gerard Lounge
Graceland
It's a Secret Pub and
  Lounge
Joe Fortes
Luv-A-Fair
Madison's
The Marble Arch
MaRS Restaurant and
  Nightclub
Mavericks Sports Grill
  on the Waterfront
Mescalero
Niagara Hotel
No. 5 Orange
Numbers Cabaret
The Odyssey
The Piccadilly Pub
The Purple Onion
  Cabaret
The Rage
The Railway Club
Richard's on Richards
The Roxy
Steamworks Brewing
  Company
Shark Club Bar and
  Grill
Soho Cafe
The Starfish Room
The Town Pump
Uncle Charlie's Lounge

The Underground
Wedgewood Hotel
  Lounge
The World
The Yale
Yuk Yuk's

East Vancouver
Hot Jazz
Jake O'Grady's

New Westminster
Kits New West

North Shore
The Avalon
Jack Lonsdale's
Jake and Elwood's
  Sports Bar
Sailor Hagar's
Montana's Sports Bar

South Vancouver
The Wild Coyote

Surrey
Pancho & Lefty's

West Side
Arts Club Theatre
  Backstage Lounge
Big Bam Boo
Carnegie's
Darby D. Dawes
The Fairview
Fiasco
Kits on Broadway

Nightlife

NIGHTCLUBS

Big Bam Boo Several club owners pooled their methods and their moola with the goal of taking on the popular Richard's on Richards for the title of number one nightspot. The result is this funky playroom where 19-to-49-year-olds can frolic while dressed to the nines and looking for 10s. Sports, pool, and sushi are upstairs. Downstairs, the singles cruise the aisles and dance to retro '80s and Top 40 sounds or live music on Friday. Wednesday and Saturday offer the hottest Ladies' Night in the city. ■ *1236 W Broadway; 733-2220; map:Q7; full bar; Wed–Sun.*

Blarney Stone The Blarney Stone proves that there's more to Irish music than U2. This rollicking Gastown club turns every weekend into a St. Patty's Day celebration and every patron into an honorary native of the Emerald Isle. The decor is Olde Irish pub. Don't be surprised to see entire families partying together. ■ *216 Carrall St; 687-4322; map:V3; full bar; Tues–Sat.*

Boone County Why do cowboy hats turn up at the sides? So you can fit four people into a pickup and 300 into Boone County on weekends. This place is raucous, with a cramped layout that makes it seem busier than it really is. A large square bar fills much of the back half of the place, and raised tables and a decent-sized dance floor fill the rest. Weekends are so busy you'll have to grease your chaps to slide into a standing-room spot, so mosey in early to grab a seat. ■ *801 Brunette Ave, Coquitlam; 525-3144; map:K2; full bar; Mon–Sat.*

Celebrities Nightclub Since its auspicious beginning as the Retinal Circus,where the Grateful Dead came to play and the '60s hippies came to trip out, this room has been best known for its revolving marquee. Step through the doors into a massive, square, two-storey room encircled by an upper balcony and centred by a giant dance floor, Vancouver's hottest place to dance. An amplifier the size of an Oldsmobile pushes out modern dance and rock. Strippers take it off Tuesdays at 10:30pm, and a drag show takes the floor Wednesday nights at 11:30 pm. ■ *1022 Davie St; 689-3180; map:R5; full bar; Tues–Sun.*

Chameleon Urban Lounge Deep in the bowels of the Georgian Court Hotel awaits the Chameleon. The room itself is a narrow space dripping in cool basic black, with only red velvet antique couches and splashes of halogen-lit original art to warm the visual landscape. Here the crowd is as cool as the black marble underfoot. Well-dressed, very urban 20-to-40-year-olds congregate to sip the latest trendy beverages. You won't find much of a dance floor, but you're more than welcome to sway where you stand. A lounge lizard lineup is in place from 9:30pm till 1am on weekends, so slither in early. ■ *801 W Georgia St; 669-0806; map:S3; full bar; Mon–Sat.*

The Edge As other clubs close, the Edge fills with club-weary revellers looking for a jolt of caffeine or a last chance at romance. A pair of polished heat ducts and a lively mural run the length of this narrow room. If the recorded dance music doesn't energize the gay crowd, a full list of espresso drinks or desserts should do the trick. Open until 4am (2am on Sundays). ■ *1148 Davie St; 688-3395; map:R5; no alcohol; every day.*

Fred's Uptown Tavern After running the gauntlet of panhandlers on Granville Street, you'll want to catch your breath and a cool one in Fred's Uptown Tavern. This is the latest offering from the fertile brain trust that made the Roxy one of Vancouver's longest-running success stories. Their stated goal was to create a nightspot with the ambience of a U.S. tavern, and they must have succeeded because Fred's has been busy since day one. Belly up to the large rectangular bar that dominates the centre of the room or perch on the periphery at a table. At Fred's, the usual ceiling-mounted TV screens have been eschewed in favour of built-in mahogany bookshelves and high-quality TVs, which show an eclectic mélange of rock videos, cartoons, and other short cinematic surprises. The canned tunes are equally diverse: everything from modern rock to '60s numbers and TV themes are all delivered at a comfortable volume. An open kitchen turns out surprisingly good grub, which keeps the 19-to-50-year-old customers well fed and friendly. ■ *1006 Granville St; 331-7979; map:S5; full bar; every day.*

Gastown Music Hall At the Gastown Music Hall the decor is simple and so is the menu: live bands, original tunes. The crowd consists mainly of the friends and relatives of whichever local act is banging away onstage. Hence, it's not uncommon to see a grandparent or two, looking terribly out of place but bravely tapping their orthopaedic shoes to whatever racket their grandkid is emitting. ▪ *6 Powell St; 689-0649; map:V3; full bar; Thurs–Sat.*

The Gate From beast to beauty, this room has gone from a seedy heroin-hangout to possibly the best live room in town. The decor is sensational: a wall of weathered brick and a long bar with recessed lighting line one side, and the large elevated stage is easily seen from every seat in the house. The Gate books original local acts and occasional touring biggies; you won't find a better place to see them. ▪ *1176 Granville St; 608-4283; map:R5; full bar; every day.*

Graceland You won't find Elvis in this humongous warehouse-size club, where the 4,000-watt sound system works almost too well. The music is cutting edge, alternative, obscure, and programmed with the notion that anything a month old is a golden oldie; needless to say, the crowd is young, hip, and dressed in black. A line forms by 10pm on weekends. Different music every night—Monday, '80s; Tuesday, progressive house; Wednesday, reggae; Thursday, soul; Friday, Eurotronics; Saturday, alternative. ▪ *1250 Richards St; 688-2648; map:R6; full bar; Mon–Sat.*

Hot Jazz Those hard-to-find big band and swing sounds are served up here at Vancouver's jazz institution, a real favourite among the city's jazz fans who pack the dance floor for a blast from the past. Cover charge varies. ▪ *2120 Main St; 873-4131; map:V7; full bar; Fri–Sun.*

It's a Secret Pub and Lounge With a professed goal of becoming the McDonald's of the bar biz, one of Vancouver's newest clubs won't be a secret for long. With almost 500 seats and recorded music that covers everything from rock to dance to '50s favourites, this place is quickly catching on. The next time you head to the Roxy and find yourself at the tail end of a long lineup, stroll a block down Granville Street and let yourself in on this town's worst-kept secret. ▪ *1221 Granville St; 688-7751; map:R5; full bar; every day.*

Jake O'Grady's Make a run for the border, where Burnaby meets Vancouver and thirsty locals meet the blues. The decor is nothing special, just a square, windowed, 140-seat room that could just as easily be a family restaurant—were it not for a minute stage flanked by framed pictures of musical greats and loaded with musical gear. When the band starts, the small dance floor fills and the unrhythmical hit the dart boards. A tasty menu is offered from noon till 11pm, with food and drink specials every day and nine beers on tap. Live music Friday and Saturday, piano bar Wednesday. ▪ *3684 E Hastings St; 298-1434; map:F2; full bar; every day.*

▼

▲

Luv-A-Fair Luv-A-Fair plays host to a very young crowd of suburbanites in trendy threads who bop nonstop to equally trendy tunes (industrial, acid house, etc.) played at ear-splitting volume. This is one of the most successful places in town, and there's usually a line out the door. ■ *1275 Seymour St; 685-3288; map:S5; full bar; every day.*

Madison's A night at Madison's is like spending eight hours locked in the trunk of one of those boom cars that cruise Robson Street. The decor is glitzy, the nonstop canned dance music is loud, and the fashion-conscious patrons range in age from 19 to 19½. Valet parking. ■ *398 Richards St; 687-5007; map:T3; full bar; Wed–Sat.*

MaRS Restaurant and Nightclub The next time you're all dressed up, there *is* somewhere to go. The MaRS Restaurant and Nightclub is 1994's resurrection of Saturno, an ambitious project that sat idle for a few years. This time around it's working, and deservedly so. MaRS is world-class—from the hardwood floors with recessed illuminated stars to the DMX fibre-optic technology that re-creates the Milky Way on the ceiling three stories above. The back wall is a computer-controlled hydroponic garden complete with running brook, banana trees, and live volcano. One bar serves shooters, the others feature good wine and champagne selections, a perfect complement to the five-star offerings of the culinary team. Spinning above the ample dance floor is the Vortex, an 11.5-metre (38-foot) titanium, robotic, lighting structure with cybernetic technology that issues an array of dazzling effects. Meanwhile, the sound system (designed for Michael Jackson's tour) pumps out distortion-free dance music that centres on the dancers and keeps the level tolerable elsewhere in the room. Throw in the world's most powerful video system, a 6.5-metre (22-foot) fibre-optics screen, a world-exclusive nitrogen fog screen, and Hollywood special effects, and you have a truly interplanetary experience. Memberships offer privileges at future MaRS locations in LA and New York. Nonmembers pay a cover charge after 9pm unless they're dining in. ■ *1320 Richards St; 662-7707; map:R6; full bar; Wed–Sat.*

Mavericks Sports Cabaret and Grill At Mavericks, a good sport is anyone who buys someone a drink and doesn't expect to be invited back to her or his place afterward. This is a party room for twentysomethings, with a DJ playing a bit of everything. Mavericks is a fun spot when you really want to let loose and get down. ■ *6669 Kingsway, Burnaby; 430-9594; map:H4; full bar; Wed–Sat.*

Mavericks Sports Grill on the Waterfront Born during Expo 86, the place celebrated its infancy as the most popular hangout in the entire fair. Finally, the event was over and the baby

▼
Nightclubs
▲

didn't seem so cute anymore, saddled as it was with a location on the desolate, out-of-the-way Expo grounds. Now, thanks to new owners and the gradual residential development of the fairgrounds, the newly rechristened restaurant/bar is a place worth checking out. Rich oak decor, live entertainment, and the city's largest outdoor patio make for a pretty successful combination. A full kitchen pumps out passable food at decent prices. This place is huge, so lineups are uncommon. ■ *770 Pacific Blvd S; 683-4436; map:U6; full bar; every day.*

Montana's Sports Bar Montana's—a sports bar? Perhaps, if they include the act of picking someone up as a form of weightlifting. Until then, Montana's remains simply the hottest "meating" place on the North Shore. This was one of the first nightspots to set an age requirement of 25 years or older on weekends, and according to management the move has virtually eliminated fights and unruly behaviour. Though the younger set has taken to referring to Montana's as the "Prune Saloon," the place is a huge success. A large dance floor throbs to the beat of classic rock, while darts, a pair of satellite dishes, and a few pool tables offer diversion to those who are rhythmically challenged. Weekends are jammed, so get an early start to avoid the lineup. Large menu of pizza and pastas. ■ *135 W 1st St, North Vancouver; 980-7722; map:E1; full bar; Tues–Sat.*

Numbers Cabaret Regulars of all ages squeeze into Levi's and leather and cram into a room that's as interesting as the gay clientele. Corridors connect four split-levels and a pair of bars. Grab a stool down below in the Kok-Pit or head up top and practise your stroke on a trio of pool tables. The dance tunes are cranked up at 10pm nightly, and the mid-level dance floor fills until closing with gyrating patrons. Never a cover charge (except New Year's Eve). ■ *1042 Davie St; 685-4077; map:R5; full bar; every day.*

The Odyssey At the Odyssey, a large contingent of bisexuals mingle with gays and a growing number of straight patrons, which has motivated management to pluck gay people from the ever-present lineup. Work up a sweat on the dance floor and then cool off by stepping outside to the rear garden—or strip naked and lather yourself in an elevated shower on Thursdays. Rubba dubba hubba hubba. ■ *1251 Howe St; 689-5256; map:R5; full bar; every day.*

Pancho & Lefty's There's no better place to kick back and listen to music about blue-collar people than the kind of blue-collar suburb from which they came. Pancho & Lefty's is stationed in the deepest, darkest heart of Surrey, a flat, rectangular, one-storey addition to the Flamingo Hotel. Rub elbows with an eclectic mix of cowpokes, greaseballs, and plain old Surrey folks. Oddly enough, the atmosphere is peaceful and friendly, and although it's comfortably full on weekends, there never seems to be a lineup. The bands are usually topnotch and can be seen from anywhere in the room. ■ *10768 King George Hwy, Surrey; 583-3536; map:K5; full bar; Mon–Sat.*

The Purple Onion Cabaret The Purple Onion has risen like a tuberous phoenix from the ashes of a defunct comedy club, and this time around, the only ones laughing are the owners—all the way to the bank. In the heart of Gastown, two flights up from historic Water Street, the Purple Onion offers two great choices to suit your mood. For live jazz, check out the lounge: the room itself is nothing special but the music definitely is. A snorting selection of local and imported jazzbos weave an aural tapestry of cool blues, zesty salsa, and sinewy Latin rhythms. Watch white-bread suburban kids enter and seemingly transform from geek to chic quicker than you can say Thelonious Monk. If moody jazz isn't for you, the cabaret just may be. This place is crammed with tony and well-toned 19-to-25-year-olds. Indulge in a selection of appys, bagels, and sandwiches, or shake a leg to an interesting mix of recorded salsa, Latin, and funk. The Purple Onion is one of Vancouver's hot spots, so expect to cool your heels in a two-hour lineup on Friday (from 9pm) and Saturday (from 8:30pm) nights. ■ *15 Water St; 602-9442; map:V4; full bar; every day.*

The Rage The rumour is that house lights dim in a 12-block radius when the Rage turns on its sound system. Very loud and very young, the Rage is one of this city's prime places to bebop to hip-hop. The club's rule of thumb on music is, basically, if you've heard it before, you won't hear it at the Rage. Progressive dance and obscure European releases. ■ *750 Pacific Blvd S; 685-5585; map:U6; full bar; Fri–Sat.*

The Railway Club The setting is intimate and the entertainment is innovative, with acts running the gamut from folk to country to blues to rock or a combination thereof. This casual, second-storey spot is narrow, with a large square bar cutting the room in two. Try to arrive early enough to grab a seat in the front section; you'll be glad you did. Although the Railway is a club, nonmembers are welcome at a slightly higher cover charge. ■ *579 Dunsmuir St; 681-1625; map:T4; full bar; every day.*

Richard's on Richards Better known as Dick's on Dicks, this is Vancouver's most venerable "meet market"—a place where hair is piled high, hemlines show lots of thigh, and silk shirts are open to the navel. Richards is also a popular live venue, with the accent on dinner tunes, R & B, and occasional one-nighters by touring artists. The second level offers a shooter bar and a bird's-eye view of the dance floor, so if you're balding and like to comb it over, you won't be fooling anyone. Expect long lines on weekends. ■ *1036 Richards St; 687-6794; map:S5; full bar; Tues–Sat.*

The Roxy After the young suburbanites hit the mall and the college crowd hits the books, they all hit the Roxy for classic rock. Behind three bars the gin slingers do their Tom Cruise imitations, juggling joy juice, catching bottles behind their backs, and clanging a hanging bell whenever a generous donation makes its way into their tip jar. A pair of house bands splits the week. Don't miss the Surreal McCoys, Sunday through Tuesday. Casual dress, with retro '60s attire in abundance. ■ *932 Granville St; 684-7699; map:R5; full bar; every day.*

Shark Club Bar and Grill The Shark Club is an upscale, tiered sports bar offering a soothing decor of oak and brass punctuated by an array of sports memorabilia. In addition to the usual assortment of interpersonal games being played among the crowd, you'll find 30 screens showing games of other kinds, along with the requisite pool tables. At 8pm sharp, a DJ fires up Top 40 and classic rock ditties and the dance floor fills fast. There's a long oak bar (offering 22 beers on tap) and a kitchen that pumps out Italian cuisine for lunch and dinner. All 180 seats are filled and a lineup in place by 9pm on Thursdays and 8pm on weekends. Reservations are accepted until 5:30pm. A valet docks your vessel Thursday through Saturday evenings, or you can do it yourself in the underground parking lot. ■ *180 W Georgia St; 687-4275; map:T5; full bar; every day.*

The Starfish Room Live alternative music is the lure that attracts schools of new-music aficionados to the Starfish. It's intimate, smoky, and high volume, with good sightlines to the stage. Be cautious on the dance floor—it often fills up with an eel-like tangle of moshing maniacs. Expect fine local talent and some stellar international acts. Cover charge varies. ■ *1055 Homer St; 682-4171; map:S5; full bar; Tues–Sat.*

Steel Monkey On Tuesdays, Cheap Drink Night, this place has the feel of an out-of-control house party—not surprising, since highballs sell for an unbelievable 99 cents. Probably the hottest Tuesday night in the city, with lines forming at 7:30pm (the doors don't even open until 8pm). Popular dance and rock tunes keep the floor jumping, with two large dance boxes that let the exhibitionists strut their stuff. Things simmer down the rest of the week, until Ladies' Night on Friday, which is usually standing room only. ■ *2745 Barnet Hwy, Coquitlam; 941-3128; map:K2; full bar; Tues–Sat.*

The Town Pump Touring acts of all kinds and all statures have played on this stage, and the club remains one of the city's most popular concert spots—in spite of some of the poorest sight lines in town. The long, narrow room has a middle-mounted stage that faces sideways, leaving those in the seating area with a side view. If you want a front view, you'll have to stand on the dance floor. The feeling is casual and rustic, with a front lounge area for those intent on conversation. ■ *66 Water St; 683-6695; map:U3; full bar; every day.*

The Underground In the Underground, the decor is rough and so are the patrons, as black paint and bare floors meet up with black leather and bare flesh. This is a cruiser bar that offers two choices: grab a stool and impress someone with your witty repartee in the bar-room, or undulate your way into their heart in the dance room where an ear-numbing sound system dishes out jungle rhythms and a mirror ball twinkles overhead. ■ *1082 Granville St; 681-8732; map:R5; full bar; every day.*

The Wild Coyote The Wild Coyote proves there are more than trolls lurking under the Arthur Lang Bridge. The club is packing 'em in, despite an unlikely location on the south end of Granville Street. The lively young crowd hails mainly from Richmond and Kits. The Coyote features a main-level dance floor with a second level overlooking the action. Get there early. ■ *1312 SW Marine Dr; 264-ROCK (7625); map:D5; full bar; Thurs–Sat.*

The World Insomniacs share this space with those who can't get enough and those who've already had too much, proving there's never a dull moment at Vancouver's premier after-hours joint. The tunes are loud and alternative, the refreshments are nonalcoholic, and the doors are open from midnight until 5am. ■ *1369 Richards St; 688-7806; map:R6; no alcohol; Thurs–Sat.*

Yuk Yuk's This venue originated as the Flying Club during Expo 86 and is still going strong as a member of the world's largest comedy-club chain. This is the perfect place for comedy, just the right size (218 seats), with a theatre-style setting that ensures a perfect vantage point from any seat in the house. Three hilarious touring acts are featured each night, Wednesday through Sunday. ■ *750 Pacific Blvd S; 687-LAFF (5233); map:U6; full bar; Wed–Sun.*

PUBS

The Avalon On weekends, this hotel lounge resembles a future Volvo-owners convention as young middle-class North Vancouverites come out to play. An up-tempo, upscale energy fills the air as a DJ spins popular, rock, and dance music (Sunday through Thursday), and the revellers bop till they drop or till 2am, whichever comes first. Live music on Friday and Saturday. ■ *1025 Marine Dr, North Vancouver; 985-4181; map:R1; full bar; every day.*

Bar-None This relative newcomer to the club scene is one of the trendiest and most popular places in town. The well-dressed, well-coiffed, and well-heeled under-40 set queue up for a chance to stand crammed together like sardines, hunch over a long row of built-in backgammon boards or checkerboards, or play pool to the sounds of recorded music, from acid jazz to Top 40. Come early, stay late, and keep your stomach sucked in. ■ *1222 Hamilton St; 689-7000; map:R6; full bar; every day.*

Cat and Fiddle Pub and Bistro Cradled among the warehouses and auto-supply wholesalers of Port Coquitlam's industrial district sits one of the Lower Mainland's most successful pubs. Abundant oak and a low ceiling make for a fairly dark atmosphere, which does nothing to diminish the festive feel of the place. By 9pm, Thursday through Saturday, pub-goers are lined up out the door, but the real wingding is Wednesday, when the place is jammed by 5pm for Cheap Wing Night. (Saturday mornings find Cheap Wings here, too—if you can rouse yourself that early.) ■ *1979 Brown St, Port Coquitlam; 941-8822; map:L3; full bar; every day.*

Darby D. Dawes Many Kitsilano residents start their evening in Darby's warm, convivial confines and then head over to the Fairview at closing time. Friday and Saturday you'll find live music, and good food is served up seven days a week. ■ *2001 Macdonald St; 731-0617; map:C2; full bar; every day.*

Delaney's Customers range from suits to bikers, from 19 to fossilized, and they seem to be a sociable lot. The pub's entire front wall consists of garage doors that slide up (weather permitting) and open on to a fresh-air patio, providing relief to non-smokers. Bonuses are the occasional live blues acts, a pair of pool tables, and a cosy corner offering comfortable couches and a fireplace. The budget-conscious will appreciate the daily food and drink specials. ■ *170-5665 Kingsway, Burnaby; 433-8942; map:G4; full bar; every day.*

Denman Station Denman Station calls itself a neighbourhood nightclub, but it feels more like a pub. Its recorded music is at a well-modulated volume so you can converse without shouting. The decibel and energy level climb a bit later in the evening on Friday and Saturday as the predominately gay clientele takes to the dance floor. The popular Electra Lush and Electra Soul Lounges give everybody a chance to drape themselves in something slinky and accessorize with a martini on Thursdays and Fridays. Denman Station offers a pool table, dart board, and a big-screen TV. ■ *860 Denman St; 669-3448; map:Q2; full bar; every day.*

The Drake Show Lounge When they say their staff bends over backwards to satisfy the customer, they're not kidding. The servers are known as "the Drakettes," and when they're not whizzing to your table with refreshments, they're doffing their uniforms (clingy red micro-shorts and low-cut bodysuits) on-stage. Ironically, the stage is shaped like a cross and is flanked by a pair of 1-metre (3-foot) hexagonal ministages, where the Drakettes occasionally put on a minishow in response to your special request. Sports screens, pool tables, and decent pub grub. ■ *606 Powell St; 254-2826; map:X3; full bar; every day.*

The Fairview The Ramada Inn may seem like an unusual location for a blues club, but this is one bar that showcases some of the city's best players. Although not comfy enough to be considered intimate, the room is just the right size and there isn't a bad seat in the house. A small dance floor sits in front of the tiny stage, and when the band gets cooking, so do the dancers. The atmosphere is casual, so come as you are. ■ *898 W Broadway; 872-1262; map:S7; full bar; every day.*

Fiesta's On Fridays you'll be hard-pressed to find an empty chair in this happening little pub in a very nonhappening location on Kingsway. The multilevelled setting is fairly intimate, and the clientele likes to party hearty. Bang some balls on the pool tables or take roost on the outdoor patio and savour the hospitable atmosphere and wholesome bistro food. ■ *6879 Kingsway, Burnaby; 525-7414; map:H4; full bar; every day.*

Jack Lonsdale's A fave among the mountain-grown grown-ups of North Vancouver, this haunt delivers everything you'd expect from a pub—clean, comfortable surroundings, decent food, live entertainment on weekends, and a good selection of beer. Pop in after a day on the slopes during ski season. ■ *1433 Lonsdale Ave, North Vancouver; 986-7333; map:E1; full bar; every day.*

Jake and Elwood's Sports Bar Much like its namesakes, Jake and Elwood Blues (the Blues Brothers), this little spot will do its best to drive your blues away. The atmosphere is as bubbly as the liquid concoctions hoisted by the armchair athletes who flock to Jake and Elwood's to satisfy their thirst for sports. Here four satellite dishes serve up four different games at once, with the most prominent displayed on the North Shore's largest screen. Test your memory on the Interactive National Trivia Network or demonstrate your skills at foosball, bubble hockey, pinball, pool, backgammon, chess, or checkers. With only 88 places to park it, Jake and Elwood's offers almost as many things to do as it does seats. Any event night is a hot one, especially Monday Night Football and any Canuck or Grizzly game. ■ *1080 Park Royal S, West Vancouver; 922-8399; map:C1; full bar; every day.*

The John B Neighbourhood Pub Live classic rock and a boisterous but well-mannered contingent of 25-to-40-year-old regulars keep the energy level high. A freestanding gas fireplace dominates an upper no-smoking section, and 16 stools await those who choose to belly up to the gorgeous oak bar with its ceiling-high backdrop of liquor bottles. The patio wins awards for its garden. The food's great, too, with Wing Night every Monday and Nacho Tuesdays. ■ *1000 Austin Ave, Coquitlam; 931-5115; map:J3; full bar; every day.*

Kits On Broadway ■ Kits New West Check your attitude and your leathers at the door. This place is strictly casual: come as you are and leave as you wannabe. Both pubs are noisy and energetic, with a good-size dance floor where the crowd gyrates to canned classic rock and Top 40. You'll find pool tables in back and a line out front, so cruise in early. The New Westminster location has a slightly younger clientele. ■ *1424 W Broadway; 736-5811; map:Q2; full bar; every day.* ■ *535 Front St, New Westminster; 525-2353; map:I5; full bar; Thurs–Sat.*

The Marble Arch Canadian laws allow exotic dancers to take it all off, whereas U.S. lawmakers permit them to strip to the G-string only. So it's no wonder businessmen and rock stars alike love the Marble Arch's downtown location. Lunchtime finds them seated suit to suit, shoulder to shoulder. All 280 seats are well served by not one but three stages, which are often found in simultaneous operation—an event known as "triple stage mania." Sports screens, video games, pool tables, food, and a courtesy phone for calling home. ■ *518 Richards St; 681-5435; map:T4; full bar; every day.*

▼

Pubs

▲

The Mountain Shadow Pub Clad in weathered wood and stained glass, this Tudor-style inn is as good-looking as the 20-to-35-year-olds who fill it to the rafters. There's an upper level overlooking an open centre section, allowing you either to hide away upstairs for a bird's-eye view of the frivolities or to mix it up in the main floor action, where there's a pool table and dart boards. Live music occasionally. Weekends are jam-packed. ■ *7174 Barnet Rd, Burnaby; 291-9322; map:I2; full bar; every day.*

Niagara Hotel As the sun sets, this venerable old beer parlour transforms from rubby to clubby as the local derelicts shuffle out and the young and trendy shuffle in. For mid-week mayhem you can't beat Wednesday night, an event dubbed "The Gin and Sin Lounge." On this night the youngun's wrap themselves in '40s and '50s retro rags and schmingle while soaking up the DJ's soundtrack of croon-tunes from Tony Bennett and the like. The furnishings are pure early '50s kitsch and suit the mood perfectly. On weekends, live music takes the stage with some of the city's hottest rock acts holding court and keeping the dance floor and all 260 seats full. ■ *435 W Pender; 688-7574; map:T4; full bar; every day.*

No. 5 Orange Vancouver peeler bars: where women shower for men who don't. This hallowed hall of hedonism has been fuelling fantasies for 25 years, meaning it's older than most of the ladies who dance there. The decor and food are okay but the location is on the grotty side. ■ *203 Main St; 687-3483; map:V3; full bar; every day.*

The Piccadilly Pub The pub managers at the Pic, as it is known, recently tired of operating a typical downtown beer parlour where aging chairs are filled with aging men, shoulders stooped and heads bowed. Their solution was to add life with an injection of live original rock bands, and the result is a very successful addition to Vancouver's growing list of live rock venues. Here the music is the star, with two bands on weekends, acid jazz on Thursdays, and a world jam every Tuesday. ■ *620 W Pender St; 682-3221; map:T3; full bar; Mon–Sat.*

The Yale To fully appreciate the blues, they should be enjoyed in the same atmosphere in which they were created—a tattered old place in the tough part of town. Welcome to the Yale. The building has been around for more than 100 years, and so, it seems, have many of the imported bluesmen who play there. The room is long and narrow, with a teeny stage that's hard to see from the back, but you can always squeeze yourself onto the stage-front dance floor for a closer peek. Suburban blues lovers and seedy-looking characters share the surroundings. ■ *1300 Granville St; 681-YALE (9253); map:R5; full bar; every day.*

▼

Pubs

▲

BREWPUBS

Sailor Hagar's The Lower Mainland's new breed of brew pubs has elevated the downing of beer to the level of a fine art. On-site microbreweries, like the gleaming stainless-steel example on display at Sailor Hagar's, have tweaked the palate and expanded the vocabulary of the beer-drinking regular. These days discussions of sports and fast cars are liable to give way to fervent discourse on the colour, clarity, and head of one of the on-tap elixirs. Sailor Hagar's boasts of stocking the city's largest selection of West Coast cottage, microbrewed, and import beers in addition to a fine array of wines, ciders, and coolers. The beers are pushed through temperature-controlled lines to a set of original British beer engines and taps. Just a two-block stroll from the Lonsdale Quay and SeaBus, the brew pub offers inviting decor that features a solid-oak carved fireplace and bar, an excellent menu of pub fare and Scandinavian delights, satellite sports, and a heated patio with an outstanding view of Vancouver. Thursday night is the hot time to hoist a few. ■ *86 Semish Ave, North Vancouver; 984-3087; map:E4; full bar; every day.*

Steamworks Brewing Company Standing guard at the entrance to Gastown is the Steamworks Brewing Company. The main floor holds a pub with the ambience of an old English study; antique books line one wall waiting to be read (don't hold your breath), while a bank of windows offer a semicircular vista of railyards, the inlet, and the North Shore. If you venture down a set of spiral mahogany stairs, you'll find an even cosier 35-seat lounge. Pull up a cushy leather chair, sink in, and divide your attentions between the inlet view and the thermal charms of a rock fireplace. Or you can shoot some stick at a pair of pool tables and shoot the breeze with one of the 25-to-45-year-old suits who make this place hop. Friday is the big night, especially 4:30 till 9pm (with a queue in place 5:30 till 7pm). Try their home brew—it's justly famed—or take advantage of the fine restaurant on site. ▪ *375 Water St; 689-2739; map:T3; full bar; every day.*

LOUNGES

Arts Club Theatre Backstage Lounge Originally designed as a spot where theatre patrons could exit a play and embark on a little play of their own, the Backstage Lounge has succeeded almost too well. So many young and old west-siders pop by on weekends to listen to live blues that the theatre-goers can barely squeeze in. The room is simple, the crowd is well-mannered and jubilant, and the grub's not bad either. ▪ *1585 Johnston St, Granville Island; 687-1354; map:Q6; full bar; every day.*

Bayside Lounge If you're looking for a cosy spot where you and your sweetie can look out over the ocean at English Bay, don't overlook the Bayside Lounge. The decor is soft and loungelike, but things get rollicking on the weekend. There are telephones between tables to call someone across the room or to call your boss. Popular with the 25-to-40-year-olds. ▪ *1755 Davie St; 682-1831; map:P3; full bar; every day.*

Beatty St. Bar and Grill If you're having trouble getting Mr. Couch Potato out of the house and away from the tube, hook his La-Z-Boy to the family car and tow him to the Beatty St. Bar and Grill. With 15 83-centimetre (33-inch) TV screens awaiting, the only thing he'll miss is the remote control. Let him try his stroke on the pool tables (during commercials) or sample the tasty array of snacks prepared by the adjoining and world-renowned William Tell Restaurant. This is a nice quiet spot to enjoy a beverage after an event at BC Place Stadium or GM Place. ▪ *765 Beatty St; 682-6265; map:T5; full bar, every day.*

Carnegie's Sax and sex combine with a delightful result in this very happening spot. The jazz is warm and mellow—so mellow it's ignored by most of the well-dressed singles who mingle in the stand-up lounge area. A pianist holds court with a special guest Thursday through Saturday—perhaps a vocalist, sax player, or guitarist. Things heat up on Fridays, when many of the local Kits crowd stop by after work to commence the weekend festivities with a couple of cool ones in the warm, antique-oak environment. ■ *1619 W Broadway; 733-4141; map:P7; full bar; Mon–Sat.*

Casbah Jazzbah   The next time you have your taste set on tabbouleh and trombone—or perhaps couscous and a crooner—set your sights on the Casbah Jazzbah. Middle Eastern cuisine and middle-of-the-road jazz? It's an unusual combo, but it works. The small room, like a tiny Arabian oasis, is resplendent in tapestries; and the patron saint of lounge lizards, Kenny Colman, belts out the standards to the beat of some of this town's best jazz cats. It's the closest thing to Sinatra this side of Vegas, and unlike Frank, Kenny isn't liable to punch you in the head if you say hello to him. The Casbah Jazzbah is a super place for a drink after attending the nearby Queen Elizabeth Theatre, Ford Centre for the Performing Arts, or GM Place. ■ *175 W Pender St; 669-0837; map:U4; full bar; Tues–Sat.*

DV8   The refrain "last call for alcohol" sets many a downtown party animal scurrying for Vancouver's newest after-hours haunt. You're greeted by a tall narrow room done in basic black, the walls peppered with original art and black-and-white nude photos. Off to the side a wood-fired oven dispenses the pizza and quesadillas that share the menu with salad, pastas, burgers, and salmon. The atmosphere ranges from bubbly to downright clamourous, and the sound system struggles to compete with the raucous revellers. Its weapon—a mix of rap, hip-hop, and alternative tunes. The full bar is pouring until 2am and the kitchen operates until 3am weeknights and 4am on weekends, so leave the nightclub early and have a last round at DV8 to guarantee yourself a seat. ■ *515 Davie St; 682-4388; map:S5; full bar; every day.*

Fiasco   Fiasco has proved to be anything but for the owners of this trendy Evian watering hole, where meeting takes precedence over eating. In the Cal-Ital restaurant, the scent of a wood-burning oven mingles with the fragrance of expensive perfume, and designer clothing is de rigueur. Expect long lines on Thursdays. ■ *2486 Bayswater St; 734-1325; map:P3; full bar; every day.*

The Garden Terrace   Sure to impress those out-of-town guests, the Garden Terrace, in the Four Seasons Hotel, is a stunning destination. A towering, atrium-style roof covers 120 seats set in what seems like a jungle but what is actually an award-winning garden full of rare flora from Africa. The result is a soothing lounge, where the soft clinking of cocktail glasses mingles with the soft tinkling of a grand piano. A drink will cost you what a case used to, but the decor is impressive, and the full restaurant menu offers another excuse to drink it all in. ▪ *791 W Georgia St; 689-9333; map:S4; full bar; Mon–Sat.*

Georgia Street Bar and Grill A rich 30.5-metre (100-foot) ribbon of oak bar snakes its way through this tastefully appointed watering hole. Choose your poison from hundreds of backlit bottles lining the wall, then choose your roost from a selection of fireside tables, cosy nooks, window seats, and bar stools. Suit-clad lawyers, brokers, and bankers peruse, schmooze, and nosh their way through burgers, appys, panini, and other bistro offerings. The hottest times are Thursday and Friday after work and Thursday through Saturday after 10pm, as the overflow from the overfull Chameleon Lounge downtown makes its way up here. ▪ *801 W Georgia St; 602-0994; map:S4; full bar; every day.*

Gerard Lounge How does the other half live? Very well, thank you, if this lounge in the Sutton Place Hotel is any indication. The decor is posh, with an understated elegance—about what you'd expect from Western Canada's best place for celebrity-watching. After a hard day on the set, the movie crews and stars repair to Gerard's to let their famous butts sink into the comfy couches around the fireplace. Kirstie Alley, Richard Gere, Sharon Stone—if they're in town, eventually they'll be at Gerard's. There are only 50 seats, but a promenade with 25 more awaits, and you'll still hear the piano from there. ▪ *845 Burrard St; 682-5511; map:R4; full bar; every day.*

Joe Fortes Lawyers, stockbrokers, and even decent people start their weekend festivities with a visit to the lounge area of this gorgeous restaurant named after a turn-of-the-century lifeguard. Friday afternoon finds it packed with well-heeled movers and shakers clad in suits and well-cut business attire. The mood is jubilant, and the decor resembles that of a U.S. chophouse. ▪ *777 Thurlow; 669-1940; map:R3; full bar; every day.*

Mescalero Despite its small size, the lounge area of Mescalero manages to hold a big place in the hearts of the oh-so-trendy well-monied sorts who haunt its confines. Rough plaster walls stretch from the tile floors to the lofty two-storey ceiling, while folk-art furnishings and subdued lighting complete a very attractive picture. Park yourself on a bar stool or lounge in a Mexican leather chair and let the rootsy scent of the wood-fired adobe-brick oven mingle with your designer cologne. ▪ *1215 Bidwell; 669-2399; map:P3; full bar; every day.*

Uncle Charlie's Lounge ▪ Lotus Club Perched where Chinatown, Skid Row, and downtown converge, this antiquated Heritage House Hotel is a cultured oasis in a sea of decay. On the main floor is Uncle Charlie's Lounge, a toasty hideaway that caters to a gay crowd. A pair of opulent chandeliers, gorgeous antique furnishings, and warm colours complete the room. Snuggle into a cushy corner and swoon as the croon of Nat King Cole oozes from the speakers. Prices are reasonable. Down a flight of marble stairs is the **Lotus Club**, a small, pillared room where the ceiling is low and the attitude high. A mixed crowd dances to Top 40 on the smallish dance floor weeknights and Saturday. Friday night is women-only. A bright spot in a blighted part of town. ■ *455 Abbott St; 685-7777; map:U4; full bar; every day.*

Wedgewood Hotel Lounge Nestled in one of the city's best hotels, this elegant retreat is a 120-seat sensation. A piano player rules the roost weekdays during cocktail hours (5 to 8), and a combo often sets up on weekends to serenade imbibers with everything from soft rock to old standards. Attire is dressy, with wall-to-wall suits in attendance Friday and Saturday nights. Call ahead for a reservation. ■ *845 Hornby St; 689-7777; map:S4; full bar; every day.*

POOL HALLS

Automotive The pool hall used to be strictly a male domain—a place where monosyllabic greasers, smelling of Brylcreem and leather, would congregate to smoke, squint, and swear. Automotive is an example of how much things have changed in Vancouver. This hip Yaletown billiard room is ensconced in a former auto dealership. White walls, a high ceiling, and abundant windows keep it bright and cheery, and the original garage door swings open (weather permitting) to keep the air as fresh as the juices and bistro snacks that are offered up front. You'll wait about 15 minutes in the '60s-furnished holding lounge if you arrive between 8pm and 1am. ■ *1095 Homer St; 682-0040; map:S5; beer and wine; every day.*

Soho Cafe You can credit this establishment with instigating the wave of upscale pool haunts washing over the city. Since day one, the seats and pool tables have been full of Kitsilano yupsters and Yaletown hipsters. The walls are clad in the original rustic brick, and the place looks and feels super. The food alone is worth a visit. ■ *1144 Homer St; 688-1180; map:S5; beer and wine; every day.*

The Arts

The Vancouver arts community is alive, thriving, and enthusiastically reflecting the diversity of the city. Art events such as multicultural festivals, traditional and innovative art exhibits, and impromptu performances abound, and, in any given week, you might catch Shakespeare on the beach, opera by the lake, or music in the mountains.

The daily and weekly newspapers and special event publications do a good job of providing current listings for a broad spectrum of happenings, but the **Arts Hotline** is probably the best source of up-to-date information. Staffed by the Vancouver Cultural Alliance (VCA), an umbrella service organization for some 200 members, the hotline is accessible 24 hours a day. Call 684-ARTS (2787), visit the VCA's office at 938 Howe Street (map:S4), or check its very comprehensive website at http://www.culturenet.ca/vca.

ART IN PUBLIC PLACES

Vancouverites make the most of their city's moderate climate, spending a lot of time outdoors. And the outdoors is almost as well-decorated as is the indoors. The brilliant banners that blossom on lamp standards in many of the city's main areas and on bridges about town are an institution almost 40 years old and always herald the beginning of summer for local residents. Many BC artists have designed banners, including Jack Shadbolt, Bill Reid, Sam Black, Robert Davidson, Toni Onley, Barbara Shelly, and Joe Average. The practice was first sponsored by the city, but now local merchants' associations display their own banners in many areas.

Vancouver is a festive city, and art is everywhere—in the

air, on street corners, in parks, in gardens, and in public buildings. You can also find it in a few unexpected places. Visitors who fly into Vancouver and enter through the new international terminal building are greeted by an astounding display of the rich art and culture of the Musqueam people, the Coast Salish inhabitants of the lands around the **airport**. Susan A. Point designed and carved the six-metre-wide (almost 20 footwide) *Spindle Whorl*. (Spindle whorls 15 cm (6 inches) in diameter were used by the Musqueam to spin raw wool into yarn for weaving and are a signature motif for Point.) She has used this traditional implement in a contemporary design that depicts the theme of flight. Point also carved the female of the pair of monumental (5.5-metre/18-foot) red cedar *Welcome Figures* that stand at the entrance to the arrivals hall. The male figure is by Shane Pointe. Adjacent to the *Welcome Figures* are four large weavings by five Musqueam weavers: Debra Sparrow, Robyn Sparrow, Krista Point, Gina Grant, and Helen Calibreath. Musqueam weaving was once a lost art and has only been relearned over the past two decades or so. The focal point of the new terminal is pre-eminent Northwest Coast Native artist Bill Reid's magnificent 6-tonne (almost 6-ton) bronze sculpture, *The Spirit of Haida Gwaii, the Jade Canoe*. The sculpture sits on level three of the terminal, spectacularly displayed on a bed of polished jade-coloured marble. Behind it is *The Great Wave Wall*, a 10 x 40 metre (33 x 131 foot) art glass wall created by Lutz Haufschild, one of Canada's most respected glass artists. Outside the arrivals level are three totems carved in the 1960s at the Native centre of 'Ksan in the Skeena Valley of northwestern BC, two by veteran carver Earl Muldoe and one by Walter Harris. Scattered throughout the terminal are 14 showcases featuring works by various local artists. These works are for sale. In the Pacific Market is Dan Planko's 4 x 8 metre (13 x 26 foot) three-dimensional interactive sculpture of Vancouver's skyline.

▼

**Art in
Public Places**

▲

Back downtown, *The Search*, Seward Johnson's bronze of a woman rummaging in her purse while sitting on a park bench, sits near the entrance to Stanley Park and has caused more than one motorist to do a double take. At Robson Square, Inuit artist Etungat's bronze *Bird of Spring* is solidly elegant. Outside 700 W Pender you can enjoy Robert Dow Reid's fibreglass *Canada Geese in Flight*. Franklin Allen's *Terry Fox Memorial*, which pays homage to the courage of a young man, stands outside BC Place Stadium. Outside the Pacific Press building on Granville Street just south of the bridge is Jack Harman's *Family Group*, which caused a furore when it was unveiled in 1966 because the boy in the group is nude. Pacific Press is moving to new leased offices at the north foot of Granville Street in 1997, but at press time no decision had been made on the fate of the family.

Close by "PacPress," as it is known, on a grassy area near the bridge, is the stone carving *100*, which was erected in 1986 for Vancouver's centennial. In *Continuity*, the work of Letha Keate, two nude cherubic children balance on a log outside Brock House, 3975 Point Grey Road, near Jericho Beach. Farther west along the beach, at Spanish Banks West, is Christel Fuoss-Moore's fittingly nautical concrete *Anchor*.

The lobby of the Waterfront Hotel displays a map of Captain George Vancouver's third and final voyage to the Pacific Northwest in 1790. Beautifully mounted on a mirrored wall, the antiqued map, entitled *Voyage of Discovery*, includes hand-lettered quotes from his journal, some proclaiming that the Strait of Juan de Fuca does not exist. The map was created by Emily Standley and Peggy Vanbianchi of Seattle. In fact, walking anywhere in the hotel is much like wandering around an art gallery. The main wall of the Garden Lounge at the Four Seasons Hotel gives the same feeling, dominated as it is by a large, striking, Inuit felt hanging appliquéd with caribou-skin figures and depicting objects from everyday Inuit life. These seals, bears, sleds, huskies, and fishermen are the work of Susan Sinnisiaks Seelo of Eskimo Point, Northwest Territories.

First-time visitors to the airy atrium of the Hongkong Bank of Canada Building on Georgia Street invariably react by ducking when they see the 27.5-metre-long (90-foot-long) shining pendulum of buffed aluminum gliding silently toward them. Suspended 30.5 metres (100 feet) above the floor, the pendulum, by BC sculptor Alan Storey, has a hypnotic rhythm.

Art that actually reacts to people adorns the lobby of Cathedral Place on West Georgia. This vast fragment of fractured glass and brass circles, called *Navigational Device,* has lights and brass pipes that respond to the movement and number of people in the lobby. The device is a mythical icon created by local glass artist Robert Studer, and part of the myth is that this glass was found on Lyell Island in the Queen Charlotte Islands. The etched hieroglyphics on the glass are indecipherable. Around the corner in the lobby of Park Place, a glowing pink glass high rise, hangs a brilliant weaving by fibre artist Joanna Staniszkis. Woven in wonderfully tactile strips, the hanging echoes scenes from the busy harbour nearby—mountains, ocean, buildings, and boats. Although it is impossible to outdo nature in Vancouver, the vast ceramic mural entitled *The Fathomless Richness of the Seabed* in the lobby of the Guinness Tower of West Hastings comes close. Myriad textures of the ocean floor—ripple marks, fronds of coral, tubes and vents, the movement of currents, and the supple shapes of sea creatures—are captured in gentle shades of blue, green, cream, and tan. The work is by Québec artist Jordi Bonet.

Vancouver's parks and gardens contain many sculptures and fountains. **Stanley Park** alone has about two dozen, many of which are mentioned elsewhere in this book. The UBC campus is also home to at least 20 excellent works, but any discussion of public art is incomplete without a mention of Charles Marega's pair of magnificent concrete lions guarding the south end of the Lions Gate Bridge.

GALLERIES

Inside, outside, upstairs, and downstairs, Vancouver has a wealth of public and private galleries. Many are on South Granville Street, between the bridge and 16th Avenue; others are scattered throughout downtown, in Gastown, or on Granville Island. Small galleries and artists' spaces are popping up on, or relocating to, the streets around Victory Square (Hastings and Cambie). It's worth exploring the area for new developments.

Artist-run spaces include the refreshingly irreverent **Western Front** (876-9343), now a quarter of a century old, **Video In/Video Out** (872-8337), and **Basic Inquiry** (681-2855).

ART

▼

**Art in
Public Places**

▲

Art Beatus Art Beatus is one of Vancouver's newest galleries. Its goal is to present and promote contemporary international art, and its special focus is artists of Asian origin, both local and offshore. The gallery's directors feel Asian artists are not being represented and promoted in the West, with the result that their work is both under-appreciated and underpriced. The first Art Beatus opened in Hong Kong in 1992. ▪ *M1 888 Nelson St; 688-2633; map:R4; Tues–Sat.*

Bau-Xi Gallery The Bau-Xi specializes in the works of Canadian artists such as Tony Urquhart, Joe Plaskett, and the venerable Jack Shadbolt. Uncrowded paintings are displayed against a minimalist background, and open storage allows visitors access to a lot more than what's on display. This is one of Vancouver's oldest private galleries. ▪ *3045 Granville St; 733-7011; map:D3; Mon–Sat.*

Burnaby Art Gallery Housed in an elegant heritage building, with sweeping staircases, curved wooden railings, and leaded glass windows, this gallery specializes in 20th-century art, which is shown to advantage in this gracious setting. ▪ *6344 Deer Lake Ave, Burnaby; 291-9441; map:H4; Tues–Sun.*

Buschlen–Mowatt Gallery This modern gallery on the edge of Stanley Park, overlooking Coal Harbour, focuses on international contemporary art, from the truly challenging avant-garde to huge, splashy, romantic works. Artists include Bill Reid, Bernard Cathelin, Yehouda Chaki, Otto Rogers, and J. Fenwick Lansdowne, to name a few. ▪ *111-1445 W Georgia St; 682-1234; map:R3; every day.*

Diane Farris Gallery The almost-industrial feeling of this gallery is not an accident. Farris specializes in artists who work on enormous canvases, and the movable walls and high ceilings are essential. Farris nurtures many young artists, including enfant terrible Attila Richard Lukacs, who had the international art world lining up at his Berlin studio door and is now in New York. Other artists include Laurie Papou and David Bierk. The cutting edge of contemporary local and national art. ▪ *1565 W 7th Ave; 737-2629; map:P7; Tues–Sat.*

Equinox Gallery Another long-established, serious Vancouver gallery, the Equinox Gallery handles only the very best North American painters and graphic artists. Works are beautifully displayed in serene surroundings. ▪ *2321 Granville St; 736-2405; map:P7; Tues–Sat.*

Federation Gallery The Federation of Canadian Artists runs this delightfully elegant gallery and workshop, which presents the works of many of British Columbia's best artists. Group of Seven artist Lawren Harris was its first president in 1941. Less formal than many other art spaces, the gallery mounts excellent exhibits that change frequently. ▪ *1241 Cartwright St, Granville Island; 681-8534; map:Q7; Tues–Sun.*

Heffel Gallery Elegantly housed in a historic stone building, the Heffel Gallery specializes in works by the august **Group of Seven** and many respected Canadian landscape artists. Exhibits can be spread over three floors, with lots of little spaces for quiet contemplation of a special work. ▪ *2247 Granville St; 732-6505; map:P7; Mon–Sat.*

John Ramsay Contemporary Art This gallery has an exciting roster of contemporary artists whose work may be bold and beautiful or small and exquisite but is always respected across the continent. Shows range from cool still lifes to the starkly contemporary. ▪ *2423 Granville St; 737-8458; map:P7; Tues–Sat.*

Morris and Helen Belkin Art Gallery The UBC Fine Arts Gallery has its own new building, opened in 1995, and a new name, but it still features ever-changing exhibitions of contemporary art and hosts lecture series and special events. ▪ *UBC, 1825 Main Mall; 822-2759; map:B2; Tues–Sat.*

Or Gallery Society Conceptual, quirky, and cutting edge, the Or is a great showcase for local artists. Located on the seamy end of Hastings Street, it's a must-see for the best in contemporary art. Located at the back of the Or Gallery is the **Kootenay School of Writing**. Known as KSW, this is the place to go for the extreme in experimental poetry and fiction. Obscure, obtuse, and mind-bending in its approach to writing, it's one of the pulses of the literary fringe. Check its listing in the *Georgia*

▼

Galleries

Art

▲

Straight. ■ *112 W Hastings St; 683-7395 (Or Gallery) and 688-6001 (KSW); map:T4; Tues-Sat.*

Presentation House This is one of the oldest galleries in the city that is still faithful to photographic art. From elegant black and white to contemporary full colour, exhibitions are exciting and beautifully showcased in this attractive older building. ■ *333 Chesterfield Ave, North Vancouver; 986-1351; map:E1; Wed–Sun (summer hours vary).*

Richmond Art Gallery [KIDS] Local and international artists are exhibited at this gallery, which is also very involved in the community. Each show has programming for children and adults, including such events as artist-run workshops, talks, and tours. Each year a show is specifically mounted for children. ■ *180–7700 Minoru Gate (Minoru Blvd and Granville Ave), Richmond; 231-6440; map:D6; every day.*

Surrey Art Gallery [KIDS] This cool, spacious gallery is part of the Surrey Arts Centre and benefits from strong community involvement. Exhibitions range from soothing to cutting-edge contemporary and from local to international. The gallery and the arts centre hold imaginative art-appreciation programs for adults and children. ■ *13750-88th Ave, Surrey; 501-5580; map:K6; every day.*

Vancouver Art Gallery See Major Attractions in the Exploring chapter.

NORTHWEST COAST NATIVE AND INUIT ART

Gallery of Tribal Art The main focus of this gallery is contemporary First Nations art from the West Coast and Alberta, but exhibits also include art from aboriginal Australia and Papua New Guinea. ■ *2329 Granville St; 732-4555; map:P7; Tues–Sat.*

Images for a Canadian Heritage This large Gastown gallery specializes in Northwest Coast Native wood carvings (which account for its pleasantly aromatic smell), Eskimo carvings in stone and bone, as well as graphics, some crafts, sculpture in bronze and glass, and pottery. It also carries stone carvings by BC artists and houses a wide variety of limited-edition prints and artworks. ■ *164 Water St; 685-7046; map:U3; every day (extended summer hours).*

Inuit Gallery This longtime Gastown gallery has a well-deserved reputation as North America's leading Inuit art gallery. Collectors from around the globe buy here, and some of the beautifully produced show catalogues are collector's items. Northwest Coast work includes masks, wood carvings, and jewellery. Gallery employees know their subject and are usually delighted to share their knowledge. ■ *345 Water St; 688-7323; map:T3; every day.*

Leona Lattimer Gallery Housed in a traditional cedar long-house on the edge of Granville Island, this gallery has an impressive collection of Northwest Coast Native art. Works vary from limited-edition prints to carvings and from bent boxes and masks to button blankets. In addition, the gallery displays traditionally engraved gold and silver jewellery and some argillite carvings. ■ *1590 W 2nd Ave; 732-4556; map:Q7; every day.*

Marion Scott Gallery One of the oldest galleries around, Marion Scott has moved north a bit to a light and airy new spot with three times the display space. Once known for both Inuit and Northwest Coast Native art, the gallery now concentrates solely on Inuit art, and always has some absolutely stunning works. ■ *481 Howe St; 685-1934; map:S3; every day.*

The Three Vets Vancouver's best-kept Native art secret. Behind all the outdoor equipment, clothing, and great little gadgets is a gallery/storage room filled with Northwest Native art from more than 300 of BC's Native peoples. Paintings, prints, masks, carvings, jewellery, rattles, talking sticks, bowls, and plaques are all represented, having been collected over a 10-year period by curator Jerry Wolfman. ■ *2200 Yukon St; 872-5475; map:U7; Mon–Sat.*

CRAFT

The Canadian Craft Museum See Museums in this chapter.

Circle Craft Unique pottery, creative weaving, innovative jewellery, and challenging toys are just some of the items displayed in this cooperative gallery. The work is all jury-selected and is the best of the best. ■ *1-1666 Johnston St, Granville Island; 669-8021; map:Q6; every day.*

Crafthouse Gallery This popular nonprofit gallery/shop on Granville Island is run by the Crafts Association of BC. An amazing array of clay, glass, fibre, metal, wood, and papier-mâché pieces illustrates the many talents of BC's finest craftspeople. A small side gallery showcases something special each month. ■ *1386 Cartwright St, Granville Island; 687-7270; map:Q7; Tues–Sat (extended summer hours).*

Gallery of BC Ceramics The teapot as a functional work of art is quite the norm in this gallery, which showcases the sometimes-amazing pottery of more than 60 BC artists. From funky to beautiful, useful to decorative, there isn't a clunky piece in sight. ■ *1359 Cartwright St, Granville Island; 669-5645; map:Q7; Tues–Sat (extended summer hours).*

Robert Held Art Glass Watch how glass is blown in this cavernous workshop/studio, where the red-hot furnaces lend an unreal background to the exquisite works of art created by local artisans. Elegant vases, goblets, glasses, candlesticks, and decorative pieces are swirled through with colour, emphasizing their unique, fragile shapes. ▪ *2130 Pine St; 737-0020; map:P7; Mon–Sat.*

MUSEUMS

From large, world-renowned museums to tiny specialized collections tucked into remote corners, Vancouver has a museum for just about everyone—aviation buffs, ancient culture nuts, even those who are considering cloning a dinosaur.

BC Museum of Mining [KIDS] [FREE] Take an hour-long drive along the scenic Sea to Sky Highway toward Squamish to this mine and museum, now a National Historic Site. The old Britannia Copper Mine, which in the 1920s was one of the largest copper mines in the world, once processed more than 6.4 million kilograms (14.1 million pounds) of ore daily. Guided underground tours on electric trains give a glimpse of what working life was like for the miners, and there are demonstrations of diamond drilling and copper mining. The museum exhibits include hundreds of old photographs, artifacts, and a slideshow. You can also pan for gold. "Recovery guaranteed" means visitors are sure to find traces of gold dust in their pans. Prearranged tours are available (minimum 20). ▪ *Take Hwy 99 to Britannia Beach on Howe Sound; 688-8735 or 896-2233; days and hours vary, call for information.*

BC Sports Hall of Fame and Museum This is the home of BC's most extensive collection of artifacts and archival materials chronicling the province's professional and amateur sports and recreation history. Multimedia exhibits showcase BC's Olympic, Commonwealth, Stanley Cup, and Grey Cup champions. The heroic journeys of BC disabled athletes Terry Fox and Rick Hansen are commemorated in dedicated galleries. Hands-on exhibits allow visitors the chance to test their skill at climbing, throwing, or racing like the pros. ▪ *Gate A, BC Place Stadium (east foot of Robson St), 777 Pacific Blvd S; 687-5520; map:T5; every day.*

Burnaby Village Museum [KIDS] This delightful re-creation of a turn-of-the-century town was built to honour BC's centennial in 1958. Step backward through time and visit a blacksmith's shop, an 1890 dentist's office, a sawmill, or a printer. In all, there are more than 30 buildings and outdoor displays depicting daily life from 1890 to 1925. Authentically costumed "residents" welcome you into their homes—which might be a pioneer log cabin—and workplaces. A church, which can be booked for weddings, and a schoolhouse have also been re-created, and the ice-cream parlour (available for birthday parties) is operational. A lovingly restored 1912 carousel, called "Carry-us-All," was once an attraction at the Pacific National Exhibition. Kids and adults alike will delight in a ride on this beautiful antique. ▪ *6501 Deer Lake Ave, Burnaby (Canada Way at*

Sperling); 293-6501; map:I3; days and hours vary, call for information.

Canadian Craft Museum [KIDS] [FREE] Located off an elegant courtyard tucked behind the impressive facade of Cathedral Place, the Canadian Craft Museum is Canada's first national museum devoted to crafts. Local, national, and international pieces all emphasize the beauty of handmade items and reflect the patience and care that go into these mostly one-of-a-kind pieces. A permanent collection and changing exhibits include everything from fragile glass perfume bottles to large pieces of furniture. Exhibits include tapestries, pottery, glass, jewellery, baskets, and sculptures. There is an excellent gallery gift shop. ■ *639 Hornby St (in the courtyard of Cathedral Place); 687-8266; map:S3; every day.*

Canadian Museum of Flight and Transportation The fascination with vintage aircraft is evident at this mainly outdoor museum, which has moved from Surrey to the Langley airport (where it now has a hangar). The collection of early aircraft includes a Tiger Moth, a Sopwith Camel, a Harvard, and an Avro Canuck. The transparent skin of a lumbering Second World War supply plane, the *Lysander*, reveals just how they do fly. Those interested in the technical side of things can browse in the library and the gift shop. The museum is an hour's drive from downtown Vancouver. ■ *Langley Airport, 5333 216th St, Langley; 532-0035; every day.*

▼

Museums

▲

Geology Museum—UBC [KIDS] [FREE] Pieces of glowing amber and 80-million-year-old Lambeosaurus dinosaur bones are just some of the treasures to be found in this fascinating place. Displays of glittering crystals and minerals, as well as fossils that are so beautiful they outshine gemstones, encompass about 4.5 billion years of mineral and fossil history. More than 9,000 specimens are exhibited. ■ *Geological Science Centre, UBC, 6339 Stores Rd; 822-2449; map:A2; Mon–Fri.*

Hastings Mill Store Museum [FREE] The handmade glass is wavy and distorts the beach scene visible through the windows, but it only adds to the charm of this cluttered museum inside Vancouver's oldest building, one of only a handful to survive the fire of 1886. Set in a little park beside the Royal Vancouver Yacht Club, this building started life as a company store for a lumber operation and, before Vancouver became a city, was the fledgling town of Granville's first post office. Old muskets, Native baskets, satin clothing, chiming clocks, and a coach are only some of the items sheltered in the cool, dim interior. ■ *1575 Alma St; 734-1212; map:C2; every day June–mid-Sept, Sat–Sun rest of year.*

Museum of Anthropology [KIDS] "Stunning" seems an inadequate word to describe this soaring, Arthur Erickson-designed glass-and-concrete building overlooking the Strait of Georgia. Founded in 1947, it is Canada's largest teaching museum and winner of the 1989 "Tourist Attraction of the Year—Canada" award. From the moment you walk through the carved wooden doors, it is difficult to know which is more awe-inspiring—the building or its contents. In the Great Hall, monumental totem poles studded with carvings of ravens, bears, eagles, frogs, and beavers gaze into the distance, seemingly imbued with the spirit of their Northwest Coast Native artisans. Spot-lit on the podium of the Great Hall is Haida artist Bill Reid's *The Raven and the First Men*, depicting how the mythic Raven tricked the first people into emerging from their clamshell. In 1994, a new permanent display of Reid's smaller works in gold, silver, wood, and argillite was opened. The museum uses visible storage: visitors are encouraged to open any of the hundreds of drawers that contain one of the most comprehensive collections of Northwest Coast Native artifacts in the world, as well as objects from other cultures (for comparison). The Koerner Ceramics Gallery displays a collection of 600 European ceramics unique to North America as well as specially commissioned ceramics and textiles by contemporary Vancouver artists. The Masterpiece Gallery exhibits carved works in silver, gold, stone, and wood. Besides this amazing permanent collection, there are ever-changing temporary exhibits and many special events. The gift shop is excellent. [FREE] Tuesdays, admission is free from 5–9pm.

▼

Museums

▲

[KIDS] [FREE] Outside, between the museum and the Point Grey cliffs, is the outdoor sculpture garden, which includes 10 totem poles towering over grassy knolls and two beautifully carved Haida houses that blend perfectly into the cliff-side setting. The work is that of some of the finest contemporary First Nations artists of the Coast, including Bill Reid, Douglas Cranmer, Norman Tait, Walter Harris, Joe David, Jim Hart, and the late Mungo Martin. Signs give information about the spirit beings represented on the poles, as well as the history of the buildings. You can enjoy the totem poles and the breathtaking views from this little park whether the museum is open or not. ■ *UBC, 6393 NW Marine Dr; 822-3825; map:A2; Tues–Sun (extended summer hours)*.

Vancouver Maritime Museum and *St. Roch* [KIDS] Vancouver's seagoing tradition is spectacularly documented in this museum, suitably perched on the southern shore of English Bay. A Kwakiutl totem pole stands near the entrance, a replica of the 30.5-metre (100-foot) pole presented to Queen Elizabeth to mark BC's 1958 centennial. The museum is the home of the 1928 ketch the *St. Roch*, now a National Historic Site. This Royal Canadian Mounted Police patrol boat was the first sailing vessel to navigate the Northwest Passage from west to east,

a dangerous voyage of 28 months. The museum's permanent displays honour the city's growth as a port, the modern fishing industry, and 18th-century explorers. The museum also holds workshops, talks, and demonstrations—all with a nautical flavour. The new Children's Maritime Discovery Centre is a fun interactive area that offers a manoeuvrable underwater robot, computer games, a telescope, discovery drawers, and an operational replica of a tug's wheelhouse. Stroll along the docks of the Heritage Harbour for a changing scene of vessels, both historic and modern. ▪ *1905 Ogden Ave, Vanier Park; 257-8300; map:O5; every day Victoria Day–Labour Day, Tues–Sun rest of year.*

Vancouver Museum [KIDS] Part of the planetarium complex, this museum has a white, cone-shaped roof based on the woven hats worn by Coast Salish peoples. Thousands of artifacts include archaeological and ethnological items, ceremonial objects, carvings, and intricate masks both ancient and contemporary. Displays feature the early settlement of the BC coast, the pioneers, and the growth of Vancouver from a rough-and-ready mill town to a major city in less than 100 years. Memorabilia range from railroad passenger cars and a replica of a sawmill to elaborate 19th-century evening dresses, Victorian bedrooms, and beautifully carved Native cradles. Regularly changing exhibits usually have a Pacific Rim theme or highlight one of the city's many cultures. ▪ *1100 Chestnut St, Vanier Park; 736-4431; map:O5; every day May–Sept, Tues–Sun rest of year.*

▼

Dance

▲

Vancouver Police Centennial Museum From clues to ancient unsolved murders to gambling displays to counterfeit money, this little museum has it all. Old photographs from the days when the police wore British bobby helmets contrast with gleaming modern guns and the grim faces of some of Vancouver's most notorious crooks. Uniforms, badges, and other artifacts are also on display. The museum has recently been completely remodelled, and, along with new exhibits, an admission charge was added. ▪ *240 E Cordova St; 665-3346; map:V4; Mon–Sat May–Labour Day, Mon–Fri rest of year.*

DANCE

British Columbia is developing a reputation as a hotbed of contemporary dance, attracting dancers and independent choreographers from all over Canada, the United States, and abroad who offer lively and original performances to appreciative audiences. Look for regular programs by Vancouver-based choreographers Karen Jamieson, Jennifer Mascall, and Judith Marcuse.

Ballet British Columbia Since its inception in 1986, BC's premier contemporary ballet company has earned a glowing reputation for its bold, exciting performances. Under the artistic directorship of noted choreographer John Alleyne, the energetic company offers dance enthusiasts a potpourri of modern and classical dance each September through June as part of its popular danceAlive! series. Five programs and three special events each season range from the exquisite grace of Canada's National Ballet to the invigorating passion of Alvin Ailey's Dance Theatre of America. Ballet BC performs two programs each season, including Canadian or world premieres of innovative works by master choreographers. ■ *Queen Elizabeth Theatre, Hamilton St at W Georgia St; 732-5003; map:T4.*

Dancing on the Edge Festival Dubbed North America's largest festival of independent choreographers, this two-week celebration of new dance, held each July, attracts international leaders in choreography from around the globe. Always fresh and daring, some 60 to 70 shows are offered throughout the day, from early afternoon to the wee hours of the morning. Venues can be as adventurous as the dance itself—from Vancouver's incomparable beaches to street corners. Most, however, appear on the traditional stage of the Firehall Arts Centre. ■ *Various locations; 689-0926.*

Firehall Arts Centre The Firehall Arts Centre Dance Series is best known as a vehicle for emerging dance artists. If the name will be on everyone's tongue tomorrow, it's on the boards at the Firehall today. From October to June you can catch contemporary dance productions, including works by such well-established Vancouver companies as Karen Jamieson Dance, JumpStart Performances, and Kokoro Dance. The Firehall also presents several theatre productions each season, with an emphasis on Canadian theatre that reflects the cultural diversity of the nation. Axis Mime is a resident company, which, in addition to performing at the Firehall, puts on plays for children in schools throughout the province. ■ *280 E Cordova St; 689-0926; map:V4.*

The Kiss Project [KIDS] From mid-January to the last week of February every year, the Kiss Project celebrates dance, theatre, and music at Granville Island's Performance Works Theatre. The heart of the festival is the Kiss Commissions, in which 10 choreographers and 10 playwrights each produce a five-minute piece that includes a kiss. These works are performed over the Project's last two weeks. What makes this festival unique is the hands-on—or should we say feet-on—workshops that invite audiences to try flamenco or ballroom dancing, play improvisational theatre games, or simply bang some Japanese taiko drums. The program also includes plenty of performances and workshops for children. Kiss is produced by Judith Marcuse's Dance Arts Vancouver. ■ *1218 Cartwright St; 606-6425; map:Q7.*

Vancouver East Cultural Centre From September to June, the
Vancouver East Cultural Centre—known affectionately as the
Cultch—presents the finest Canada has to offer in contemporary dance. If it's on the cutting edge, you'll find it at the Cultch.
Past programs have included innovative dance and theatre
artists from Montreal, including La La La Human Steps, Paul-
Andre Fortier, and Peggy Baker, as well as the cream of Vancouver's rich dance scene and some international artists. See
also Theatre in this chapter. ▪ *1895 Venables St; 254-9578;
map:E2.*

THEATRE

Vancouver's theatre scene is flourishing, offering a mosaic of
live performances that range from glorious extravaganzas to
impromptu events and practically everything in between. Two
large-scale companies and many small, innovative groups keep
theatregoers entertained year-round with a wealth of diverse
performances. The University of British Columbia, Simon
Fraser University, and Langara College mount excellent productions while classes are in session. Other companies, performing in Vancouver and on tour, include Coconut Theatre;
Ruby Slippers; Pink Ink; the Headlines Theatre Company,
which does "powerplay theatre," concentrating on plays about
social issues; and the Tamahnous Theatre, which gave much
of the city's senior talent its start.

The Arts Club Theatre Situated in the heart of lively Granville
Island, the Arts Club Theatre and the neighbouring Arts Club
Revue Theatre, both run by Bill Millerd, have become local institutions. This is the largest regional theatre in Western
Canada, and the year-long offerings on the main stage include
a smorgasbord of drama, comedy, and musical classics, with a
focus on 20th-century works. For those who enjoy a drink with
their theatre, the cabaret-style Revue Theatre is the perfect
spot for light theatre and musical comedy. Intermission on the
False Creek dock or at the bustling Arts Club bar is an added
attraction. The bar, which supports the theatre, has its own programs and is also a popular spot to hang out with musicians and
artists and enjoy some music. By the fall of 1997, the Arts Club
hopes to have a third stage in the Stanley Theatre on Granville
Street near 13th Avenue. A fund-raising campaign to convert
the Stanley from cinema to live theatre is under way. ▪ *1585
Johnston St, Granville Island; 687-1644; map:Q6.*

Bard on the Beach Imagine—Shakespeare all summer long,
set against a magnificent backdrop of city, sea, and mountains.
Colourful red-and-white tents provide the stage for the two
Shakespearean masterpieces that are offered in repertory during the summer months. Come as you are in comfortable and

layered clothing: the sunsets are breathtaking, but it can be cool. Ticket prices are not quite as low as they were in the 17th century, but they are a pleasant surprise nonetheless. Cushions recommended. ▪ *Vanier Park; 733-1910 (summer tickets); 325-5955 (year-round); map:P5.*

Ellie King Summer Arts Festival For many years, the eccentric charm of suburban White Rock has included a summer set of plays in repertory. Expanding on the theme is the Ellie King Summer Arts Festival, which runs from late June until the end of August and includes not only theatre but also jazz and poetry nights, a mini-fringe festival, writers' readings, and more. ▪ *White Rock Playhouse, 1532 Johnston Rd, White Rock; 534-9747.*

Firehall Arts Centre See Dance in this chapter.

Ford Centre for the Performing Arts Vancouver's new home of the mega-musical was launched by a splashy opening in November 1995, featuring Cranbrook-born Brent Carver, a Tony Award winner for his performance in *Kiss of the Spider Woman*. Then the curtain rose on *Showboat* for a run of almost a year, followed by *Sunset Boulevard*, with more always in the wings. The $24.5-million, 1,824-seat theatre was designed by Moshe Safdie, who also designed the oh-so-controversial Library Centre across the street. The two most striking features of the theatre are the intimacy of the auditorium and the visual power of the seven-storey, mirrored wall grand staircase that unites all the levels. "The auditorium is more intimate and warm than even I expected," Safdie said on opening night. Livent Inc., headed by Toronto's entertainment *wunderkind* Garth Drabinsky, is the co-owner and operator of this new addition to Vancouver's theatre space. ▪ *777 Homer St; 602-0616; map:T4.*

▼

Theatre

▲

The Fringe Festival The good, the bad, and the adventurous are "Alive on the Drive" every September at the second-largest fringe theatre festival in North America. Billed as "an uncensored opportunity for performers to express ideas, challenge conventions, and stage innovative works with minimum financial risk," this theatre extravaganza features all ages and levels of experience. All this in 500 performances over 11 days in 10 indoor theatres and outdoor stages on and around Commercial Drive. The 100 companies are accepted on a first-come, first-served basis—there is no jury process—and content includes everything from outrageous comedy to challenging drama to performance art. Admission is extremely reasonable. ▪ *Various locations; 873-3646.*

Queen Elizabeth Theatre and Playhouse On the Queen E's spacious stage, gorgeous glitz and glitter are commonplace. This elegant, comfortable 2,800-plus-seat theatre is still one of Vancouver's main venues for lavish touring musicals each spring and summer, dance, rock, and pop concerts and many multicultural shows the rest of the year. It's also home to the Vancouver Opera and Ballet British Columbia. The complex includes the Queen Elizabeth restaurant for the option of a gourmet buffet before the show. ■ *Hamilton St at W Georgia St; 665-3050; map:T4.*

The Shadbolt Centre for the Arts (formerly Burnaby Arts Centre)

So successful is this performance and teaching centre that it recently expanded by 3,250 square metres (35,000 square feet), adding a second theatre, banquet facilities, and multi-use studios. It was renamed in honour of artist Jack Shadbolt and his wife, writer Doris Shadbolt, who are residents of Burnaby. Although it holds some performances, the centre focuses on teaching, and classes include dance, acting, music, and the visual arts. Michael J. Fox and the Kimura Parker brothers have taken part in Centre activities. ■ *6450 Deer Lake Ave, Burnaby; 291-6864; map:H4.*

Theatre under the Stars [KIDS]

The sweetly familiar strains of "Some Enchanted Evening" take on new meaning at a performance of Theatre under the Stars (TUTS). Two Broadway musicals are offered in repertory from mid-July through mid-August each summer in Canada's only truly open-air theatre. Casts feature a combination of professional and amateur performers, lending the event a wonderful enthusiasm that makes for perfect family entertainment. Festival seating accommodates some 1,200 people amid a spectacular backdrop of forests, stars, and the moon—who could ask for anything more? Bring a cushion and warm clothing and be sure to wear socks to protect your ankles from the mosquitoes. ■ *Malkin Bowl, Stanley Park; 687-0174; map:Q1.*

Vancouver East Cultural Centre [KIDS]

This beautifully restored 1914 church is one of Vancouver's most intriguing performance venues, where the tried and true shares the stage with the brand new. Known to locals simply as the Cultch, the centre, which opened in 1973, makes diversity the key ingredient in its programming. Daring dance, alternative theatre and performance art, as well as music to keep your toes tapping or your heart swelling, it all comes alive in this intimate 350-seat theatre space, which was undergoing a facelift at press time. The popular Kids' Series offers theatre, music, and madness for children, including a performance by the highly acclaimed resident company Green Thumb Theatre for Young People, which specializes in developing lighthearted and intelligent scripts based on complex social issues. The Cultch is also home to Masterpiece Music, a delightful six-Sunday chamber music series, where the city's top musicians gather to pool their creative talents. Touchstone Theatre is newly resident, as is the Modern Baroque Opera. ■ *1895 E Venables St; 254-9578; map:E2.*

Vancouver International Children's Festival See Vanier Park in the Exploring chapter.

Vancouver International Comedy Festival [KIDS] They call it the funniest festival of all. For 10 days at the beginning of every August, Granville Island is transformed into a veritable comedy lover's paradise. With more than 100 free performances and some 30 ticketed events, mime artists, jugglers, and comedians seem to be everywhere. From noon to five each afternoon, roaming performers entertain onlookers, and each evening paying audiences savour the humour in clubs around the city. Performers hail from around the globe, but as the saying goes, the language of a smile is universal. ▪ *Granville Island; 683-0883; map:Q6-R7.*

The Vancouver Playhouse Theatre Company The Vancouver Playhouse produces six shows during its October through May season. One of western Canada's largest regional theatre companies, the Playhouse blends the classic and the modern in its repertoire, including Canadian premieres and Broadway plays. The 670-seat theatre (every seat a good seat) is home to many of Canada's finest actors, and productions are invariably top quality, with spectacular sets, luscious costumes, and terrific soundscapes. Friends of Chamber Music, the Vancouver Opera, and dance companies also use the space. ▪ *Hamilton St at Dunsmuir; 873-3311; map:T4.*

Theatre

Vancouver TheatreSports League Murder, talk shows, politics—nothing is sacred when in the hands of the Vancouver TheatreSports League. A six-time world improvisational champion, TheatreSports offers hilarious, affordable entertainment. The content of this Canadian creation varies—on any given night the 30-member ensemble might improvise on a specific theme, satirize the hottest TV shows, or stage competitions in which three-member teams vie for audience approval as they create vignettes based on audience suggestions. Expect the riotously unexpected. ▪ *By September 1997, TheatreSports should be at home on the second stage of the Stanley Theatre, sharing the former cinema with the Arts Club Theatre; map:Q6. Until then the group is playing various venues. To find out where, call 738-7013.* •

MUSIC SERIES

Vancouver has always enjoyed a vital music scene, but over the last decade the city has witnessed a renaissance in the proliferation of classical, jazz, and world music. Musical institutions such as the Vancouver Symphony and the Vancouver Opera have spread their wings, and smaller chamber music series are flourishing.

Coastal Jazz and Blues Society and the du Maurier Jazz Festival

It's the rebirth of cool. Jazz has witnessed an incredible renaissance in Vancouver during the last decade, thanks to the indefatigable efforts of the Coastal Jazz and Blues Society. To find out about the eclectic mix of alternative, avant-garde, and straight-ahead performances throughout the year, pick up the Society's newsletter at record stores or libraries, or call to get on the mailing list. In late June comes the superb **du Maurier International Jazz Festival**, considered by many to be the best jazz festival in North America. For approximately 10 days, the city is transformed into a jazz mecca that spans the entire jazz spectrum, with hundreds of ticketed performances and free music everywhere. ■ *Various locations; 682-0706.*

Early Music Vancouver and Vancouver Early Music Summer Festival

In times past, early music seemed to be the domain of a select following, but more and more converts are discovering these sublime sounds. Early Music presents a series of performances, including various recitals, chamber orchestras, and choirs, held in churches and concert halls throughout the city from fall through spring. Music from the Middle Ages to the 18th century is performed on original instruments by some of the finest early music specialists. As an extension of the organization's main season, each summer the sounds of harpsichords, lutes, and violas da gamba sweeten the UBC campus. From mid-July through mid-August, local and international proponents of early music share the stage and classrooms, providing a feast of musical pleasures for both the novice listener and the advanced music scholar. ■ *Various locations; 732-1610.*

▼

Music Series

▲

Enchanted Evenings

In spring and summer, the Dr. Sun Yat-Sen Classical Chinese Garden presents Enchanted Evenings. The grounds are illuminated with lanterns, providing a soft glow for music and dancing. [KIDS] Storytelling for children, afternoons in summer. ■ *578 Carrall St, at the garden; 662-3207; map:V4.*

Friends of Chamber Music

Devotees of chamber music may feel they have discovered manna with this 10-concert series. From October through April (all concerts are on Tuesdays), Friends of Chamber Music presents the crème de la crème of chamber music ensembles, such as the Emerson String Quartet. The group has received accolades for its special presentation of the complete Beethoven quartets, featuring the renowned Bartok String Quartet. The Orpheum Theatre is also a venue for this renowned series (see the Vancouver Symphony Orchestra in this chapter for address). ■ *Vancouver Playhouse, Hamilton St at Dunsmuir; 437-5747; map:T4.*

Masterpiece Music

See Vancouver East Cultural Centre in Theatre section of this chapter.

Music in the Morning Concert Society Experience the grace of the European salons of the 18th century with a visit to one of Music in the Morning's concerts. Born in the living room of artistic director June Goldsmith almost 10 years ago, the concert series has blossomed into a well-respected and innovative event. The repertoire includes the old and the new, performed by local or imported artists. The society also presents the Musical Conversation series for those who want to learn more about music in a relaxed setting. ■ *Vancouver Academy of Music, 1270 Chestnut, Vanier Park; 873-4612; map:P5.*

Rogue Folk Club The music is mainly Celtic at the Rogue Folk Club, a nonprofit organization that presents a year-round series of folk music concerts and dances, most at the funky WISE Hall in East Vancouver. Seating is cabaret-style on school gymnasium-type chairs. Events are licensed (the honey ale always goes fast), kids are welcome, and if you feel the urge, get up and dance. There's also regular country dances, including instruction for beginners. The Folk Club is run by Steve Edge, also on a not-for-profit—or even pay—basis, and he works hard to bring in performers you may never have another chance to hear. Along with the Celts, there are also the nonconformists—Tom Russell, for instance. Become a member ($16) and get concert discounts and the monthly newsletter; be a volunteer and they might let you see the concert gratis. The club's website includes links to the British soccer scores for those who share Steve's other passion. ■ *WISE Hall, 1882 Adanac St (off Victoria Dr); 736-3022; map:E2; http://mindlink.net/Roguefolk.*

Vancouver New Music Society Eclectic, alternative, on the cutting edge—whichever expression you choose, the Vancouver New Music Society has earned a reputation for presenting the hottest composers of contemporary music on an international scale. As unlikely as it may seem, you may well be hearing music history in the making. The majority of concerts are staged at the Vancouver East Cultural Centre, where the intimacy of the hall makes for a wonderful ambience. Concerts are also held at other venues scattered throughout the city. ■ *Various locations; 606-6440.*

Vancouver Recital Society For a preview of who's going to be who in the classical music world in the years to come, catch one of the seven concerts in this recital series. Artistic director and general manager Leila Getz seems to have an uncanny sixth sense about young, up-and-coming artists, and that, matched with her impeccable taste, has enabled Vancouver audiences to hear some of today's foremost performers when they were aspiring musicians. In addition, the society presents a handful of superstars each season—for example, the enchanting singer Cecilia Bartoli, pianist Jon Kimura Parker, and violin master Itzhak Perlman. ■ *Vancouver Playhouse, Hamilton St at Dunsmuir; 602-0363; map:T4.*

Vancouver Symphony Orchestra [KIDS] This granddaddy of the classical music scene makes its home in the magnificent 1927 Orpheum Theatre, where thick red carpets, ornate rococo gilding, and sweeping staircases transport you back to an earlier, more gracious era. Under the leadership of maestro Sergiu Comissiona, the 74-member orchestra has reached new heights of artistic splendour. Eleven subscription series offer music lovers a wide variety of aural delicacies, from traditional symphonic fare to a more adventurous repertoire to pops concerts. An ever-increasing focus on Canadian artists and repertoire has added a new dimension to the VSO's offerings, although a number of illustrious soloists, such as Yo-Yo Ma, Issac Stern, and Pinchas Zukerman, continue to grace the Orpheum stage. The popular Kids' Koncerts provide an opportunity for children to experience the joys of symphonic music in a fun, relaxed atmosphere. Recently, the symphony has been collaborating with rock, pop, and Celtic groups to reach different audiences. These include the Maritimes' Ashley MacIsaac and local North Shore Celtic rock band Spirit of the West. Together, Spirit of the West and the VSO cut the CD, Open Heart Symphony. ■ *Orpheum Theatre, Granville St at Smithe St; 876-3434; map:S4.*

▼

Choral Music

▲

In addition to its main-stage concerts and special events, the VSO also performs in the parks and on the beaches of the Lower Mainland during the summer. The high point of a symphonic summer is the annual Whistler mountaintop concert, where glorious music resounds amid the mountain peaks. The orchestra also plays a series in New Westminster and tours the province every year.

CHORAL MUSIC

Choral music is always popular and enjoys a healthy following locally. Both amateur and professional groups, such as the **Vancouver Cantata Singers**, the **Vancouver Chamber Choir**, and the **Vancouver Bach Choir**, perform in various theatres, hotels, and churches throughout Vancouver. The Vancouver Bach Choir is known for its adventurous repertoire, and the **Elektra Women's Chorus** always dazzles audiences with its exquisite renditions of works that span the generations. The **Vancouver Men's Chorus** is also highly popular and well-supported and has its own season. For choral phone listings and all other arts information, call the Arts Hotline at 684-ARTS.

OPERA

Chinese Cultural Centre Chinese opera is just one of the many events presented at the centre by local organizations in the

Chinese community and from around the world. The centre is also a venue for fascinating exhibitions of paintings and photography as well as book launchings and dance programs. Classes in language and arts and crafts are also offered. ▪ *50 E Pender St; 687-0729; map:V4.*

Vancouver Opera Association Opera is once again firmly entrenched in the Vancouver arts scene. Once the domain of the "ladies who lunch," it is now one of the hippest tickets in town. And thanks to clever marketing, a re-evaluation of the organization's artistic vision in recent years, and the influence of megamusicals such as *Phantom of the Opera*, audiences have flocked to the opera in droves. Under the astute leadership of general director Robert J. Hallam and music director David Agler, the Opera Association presents five productions each season, a mix of contemporary and traditional works. The sets are spectacular and the artists are of international calibre. In addition, some of Canada's brightest singing talents frequently grace the stage of the Queen Elizabeth Theatre. ▪ *Queen Elizabeth Theatre, Hamilton St at W Georgia St; 683-0222; map:T4.*

FILM

▼

Opera

▲

Vancouver is often called Hollywood North, and for good reason. Stargazing, for locals, is no longer the novelty it was a decade ago. Hollywood discovered Vancouver in 1935, when powerful MGM mogul Louis B. Mayer sent cast and crew northward to shoot Mountie scenes for his classic film *Rose Marie*. In 1969, director Robert Altman encountered the adaptable charms of the city while filming *That Cold Day in the Park*; he returned the following year to shoot *McCabe & Mrs. Miller*. Since then, the film industry has become one of the leading money makers for the province and has attracted international filmmakers. The list of stars who have worked in the area during recent years grows steadily: Warren Beatty, Mel Gibson, Goldie Hawn, Alicia Silverstone, Robin Williams, Kirstie Alley, Brad Pitt, John Travolta, Richard Gere, Sharon Stone, Steve Martin, Glenn Close, Robert De Niro, Sean Penn, Jodie Foster, and Sylvester Stallone. A few local actors—Michael J. Fox, Cameron Bancroft, Jason Priestly, and Cynthia Stevenson—have made it big in Hollywood after beginning their careers in Vancouver.

American producers flock to Vancouver to shoot feature films, television series, and TV movies-of-the-week (they say we have some of the most interesting alleys in North America for movie shoots). Several television series shoot here year-round: *The X-Files, Millennium, The Outer Limits, Poltergeist, Sliders, The Sentinel,* and *Highlander*; recent features filmed here include *Jumanji, Excess Baggage, Deep Rising, Free*

Willy 3 and *The Sixth Man.* The most-used locations in Vancouver are the **Vancouver Art Gallery** on Hornby Street, **Blood Alley** just off Carrall Street in Gastown, and the alley south of Hastings Street between Cambie and Abbott Streets.

If you'd like to see yourself on the big screen just once, or if you'd like to be an extra, there are lots of opportunities here. You'll like the work if you're already financially secure, your ego is intact, and you don't take the whole thing too seriously. The hours are long, the food's mediocre (you don't get to eat with the stars), the money isn't great (about $11 an hour), the work is sporadic, and you'll be herded around like a heifer on a cattle drive. But hey, you might get to meet your favourite star. Extras casting is done by several local agencies. Try **Universal** at 689-9056 or **Local Color** at 685-0315. You'll need a few head shots for their files, and you may be required to pay a one-time fee (between $20 and $40) to register. Other talent agencies include **Characters**, 733-9800; **Lucas Talent**, 685-0345; **Twentyfirst Century Artists Inc.**, 736-8786; and **Hodgson & Company**, 687-7676.

The **Vancouver International Film Festival**, in its 15th year, is the third largest in North America and typically presents more than 400 screenings of some 250 first-run feature films from more than 45 countries (screened in seven centrally located theatres). Every October viewers can catch the traditional to the avant-garde, and the obscure to the mainstream, from a selection of documentaries, dramatic features, animated shorts, and comedies new to the Vancouver scene. Call for more information, 685-0260.

For up-to-the-minute local movie news read "The Insider," a Friday column in the *Province* newspaper. Entertainment reporter **Lynne McNamara** goes behind the scenes on Vancouver film sets to interview the stars for BCTV's *Star Tracks* (Cable 11) every Monday at 5:20pm. *Playback*, a tabloid-format industry newspaper, publishes every two weeks; *Reel West* is a bimonthly industry magazine. *Reel West Digest*, published annually, lists production personnel, studios, performers, writers, and agents. It can be picked up at most major news-stands or ordered by calling 294-4122. The *BC Film Commission's Film List* of projects currently in production may be picked up at the BC Business Info Centre, main floor, 601 W Cordova, weekdays; map:T3. Or call the **BC Film Commission Hot Line** (660-3569) for film-listing updates.

Film fest fans and aficionados frequent the **Dunbar** (228-9912; map:B3), **Vancouver Centre Cinemas** (669-4442; map:S4), **Park** (290-0500; map:D3), **Varsity** (222-2235; map:B3) and **Fifth Avenue Cinemas** (734-7469; map:P7), where they can find an eclectic selection of independent movies and where they can often catch screenings missed during the festival. The **Ridge** (738-6311; map:C3) and the **Hollywood** (738-3211;

Exploring

DOWNTOWN VANCOUVER
Between Beach Ave and Hastings St, Chilco St and Pacific Blvd; map:Q1-T5

Vancouver's sprawling downtown stretches over numerous city blocks with no real main core. Glance north down any street and, catching glimpses of the mountains between buildings, you will see that the city ends at the water. All around, glass-sheathed high rises glitter in the sunlight, offering stunning reflections of the neighbouring buildings. Many buildings are set back from the street, with flower-filled courtyards built around fountains or pools.

These glass and steel office towers are in striking contrast to the mellow stone of lovely old **Christ Church Cathedral** (Burrard and Georgia Streets), the oldest surviving church in Vancouver. Across from the cathedral is the venerable **Hotel Vancouver**, with its famous griffins and gargoyles, green copper roof, and hushed, spacious lobby. Behind the hotel is the former main branch of the **Vancouver Public Library** (Burrard and Robson Streets). The completely renovated building is now the site of a Virgin Records Megastore, a virtual-reality amusement park, and a Planet Hollywood restaurant (see Restaurants chapter). The central library is now located in the dramatic **Library Square** complex (Robson and Homer Streets). Designed by world-renowned architect Moshe Safdie (he is also responsible for the Ford Centre across the street), the library is a marvel. Like they did with the Roman Colosseum that inspired it, people come by the thousands daily. Instead of gladiators, it is books, magazines, audio and video tapes, CDs, and multimedia tools that await the curious. Across Homer Street is the **Ford Centre for the Performing Arts**, which showcases touring musicals. Vancouver's two biggest sports venues, **General Motors Place** (Pacific Boulevard and Griffiths Way) and **BC Place Stadium** (at the foot of Robson Street), are neighbours. GM Place is the 19,000-seat home of the NHL Vancouver Canucks and NBA Grizzlies, and the BC Lions play under the big white roof of BC Place. Rock concerts and trade shows appear at both buildings from time to time, and just inside gate A of BC Place Stadium is the **BC Sports Hall of Fame and Museum** (see Museums in The Arts chapter). Separating the shores of False Creek from BC Place is the **Plaza of Nations**, which was the main entrance and gathering area during the Expo 86 World's Fair. It is now home to nightclubs, restaurants, and a casino. The bandshell is the site of rock concerts in the spring and summer. Among the Plaza's biggest annual events are the Dragon Boat Festival in mid-June and the Molson Indy car race on Labour Day weekend. The three-day Indy event causes the closure of a large portion of Pacific Boulevard to regular traffic.

On the harbour's edge at the north side of Vancouver's downtown peninsula, the gleaming white stylized sails of **Canada Place** at the bottom of Howe Street are a city landmark. Canada Place, another of the four Expo 86 legacy complexes, incorporates Vancouver's convention centre, Pan Pacific Hotel, cruise ship terminal, World Trade Centre, government offices, and the CN IMAX Theatre. **[FREE]** Walk around the "decks," enjoy the sea breeze, and admire the views. The **Marine Building** (Hastings and Burrard Streets) is an art deco masterpiece, and for a decade after it opened in 1930 it was the tallest building in the British Commonwealth. The intricate, richly diverse carvings and sculptures in and outside this building emphasize a marine and transportation theme in terra-cotta, brass, stone, and marble. **Cathedral Place** (Georgia Street near Hornby Street), with its gargoyles and elegant facade, is newly "old." Across the street is the **Vancouver Art Gallery**, which once housed the provincial courthouse. (See Major Attractions in this chapter.)

Three of the city's major department and specialty stores are clustered at the corners of Granville and Georgia Streets—the ornate facade of **The Bay** contrasting with the modern **Eaton's** building and the **Holt Renfrew** store, called Holt's by locals.

Robson is the city's most fashionable shopping street. Once called Robsonstrasse because of its many German delis and hearty restaurants, it has now been taken over by designer boutiques and cafes. It is often compared to Beverly Hills' posh Rodeo Drive, and not just because of its high-end merchandise.

Some of its habitués are pretty high-end as well, and if you're there at the right time, you may even spot a Hollywood star in one of the shops or fine restaurants. It is the liveliest place in Vancouver in late evening, as people stroll along window-shopping, lingering in sidewalk cafes, meeting friends, or people-watching from a chair in one of the many gourmet coffee bars, like the two **Starbucks** kitty-corner from each other on the corner of Thurlow and Robson Streets.

The Vancouver Art Gallery and **Robson Square** (Hornby and Robson Streets) are across from the **Law Courts**, a soaring glass structure designed by West Coast architect Arthur Erickson. Embellished with trailing greenery, the site of Vancouver's provincial supreme courts resembles a dignified greenhouse.

CHINATOWN
Between Abbott St and Heatley St, Prior St and Powell St; map:V4

[KIDS] [FREE] Vancouver has North America's second-largest Chinatown district; only San Francisco's is larger. Chinese immigrants began arriving in Vancouver in the late 1850s. In the 1880s, thousands of Chinese arrived to work on the building of the railway across the West. By 1890, Vancouver's Chinatown had a population of more than 1,000, many of whom ran their own businesses.

Today's Chinatown, which lies mostly between Carrall Street and Gore Avenue, is a crowded, bustling area where shop owners loudly advertise their wares. Stores sell fruit and vegetables, jade, ivory, rattan, brass, china, silk, and brocade. It's easy to spend hours browsing through the cramped, incense-perfumed stores, unearthing delicately embroidered tablecloths or blouses. Enticing aromas waft from bakeries and restaurants. Wander along the busy streets, dodging women laden with bulging shopping bags, and admire streetlights decorated with golden dragons, phone booths topped with pagoda-style roofs, and ornamental street signs in both Chinese and English. Parking is difficult, though new parkades have been constructed to ease the congestion and stem the flow of shoppers to the modern Chinese shopping malls on Number Three Road in suburban Richmond. Browse outdoors in warm summer breezes: Chinatown's newest attraction is the **open air night market**, which runs from 6pm to midnight at Main and Keefer Streets during summer months.

On the corner of Pender and Carrall Streets is the famous **world's narrowest office building**. The **Sam Kee Building**, built in 1913, is only 1.8 metres (6 feet) wide and two storeys tall. Once a store that sold beautiful silks, it is now an insurance office.

GASTOWN
Between Hastings St and Water St,
Homer St and Columbia St; map:U3-V4

[KIDS] [FREE] Vancouver's first community was called Granville and was located where Gastown now stands. In the 1860s, it grew up around the Globe Saloon, owned by **Gassy Jack Deighton**, a former river pilot renowned for his volubility—hence the nickname. After a fire levelled the infant city in 1886, the city centre moved westward and changed its name to Vancouver. The old Gastown gradually disintegrated into the city's skid-row area.

In the late 1960s, the renovation and restoration of the district began. The streets were paved with cobblestones or red brick, decorative street lamps were installed, and trees were planted in front of the boutiques and restaurants that had just moved in. In 1971, Gastown was designated a heritage site.

In Gastown, all roads—Carrall, Powell, Water, and Alexander Streets—lead to **Maple Tree Square**. Nightclubs, art galleries, antique stores, coffee bars, and jazz and rock music clubs all add to the attractions of this pleasant place. Tucked into corners are flower-filled courtyards with names like Gaoler's Mews and Blood Alley, and, except for the presence of some elegant boutiques, they seem unchanged from the turn of the century. Gassy Jack himself has not been forgotten—his statue stands proudly near the centre of Maple Tree Square.

▼

Major Attractions

Gastown

▲

[KIDS] [FREE] The 2-tonne (almost 2-ton) **Gastown Steam Clock**, on the corner of Cambie and Water Streets, operates on steam tapped from the underground pipes of nearby buildings. The five-metre-tall (16.4-foot-tall) clock whistles every 15 minutes and sends forth clouds of steam every hour. With its big, four-sided glass face, 20-kilogram (44-pound) gold-plated pendulum, and gothic roof, the clock is a popular stop for photographers. Around the corner and beside the train tracks, Ray Saunders, who designed the clock, has a store filled with antique timepieces.

GRANVILLE ISLAND AND FALSE CREEK
Beneath south end of Granville Street Bridge;
666-5784; map:Q6

[KIDS] [FREE] Granville Island is a success story that has confounded critics who argued that derelict warehouses and crumbling boathouses were pretty shaky foundations on which to build a vision. In 1917, the island, which is really a peninsula, was a filled-in mudflat that held the city's main industrial area. As the city expanded, businesses gradually moved away and the island became a grimy embarrassment. In the early 1970s, two Vancouver businessmen decided the area had potential and began developing one small part of it, arousing enough interest to get the federal government involved. Now, with imaginative buildings that are faithful to its industrial beginnings, this bustling people place is as popular with locals as it is with visitors.

The way to enjoy the island is at a leisurely pace. Allow lots of time to wander and wonder at the endless marine traffic (from canoes to yachts to picturesque paddlewheelers), the airy art galleries, the fearless seagulls looking for lunch, the downtown skyline, the uptown skyline, the pottery, jewellery, books, and blossoms—and the people. You'll want to stop at many of the colourful stalls, heaped high with fruits and vegetables, candy, bread, fish, and meat. For nightlife, the island boasts two theatres and an eclectic mix of restaurants, and you can still watch the boats—and the people.

As is the case with many urban success stories, there is still an obstacle to overcome when visiting Granville Island: parking. The problem is especially acute on weekend mornings, despite the addition of covered pay parking places to supplement the free outside spaces. Try parking around Fourth Avenue and Fir Street and take the Granville Island bus. There's also the tiny shuttle **Aquabus** from the downtown side of serene False Creek to the island.

▼

Major
Attractions

*Granville
Island and
False Creek*

▲

[KIDS] The **Kids Only Market** on Cartwright Street near the entrance to the island is filled with everything a child (or an adult) could wish for. Games, gifts, hobbies, art and craft supplies, toys, video games, and live entertainers all contribute to the fun.

At the west end of the island is the waterside wharf edging Broker's Bay. Millions of dollars' worth of yachts are berthed here, and it's a good place to rent or charter a boat.

The sprawling public market is housed in a huge renovated warehouse on the north corner of the island on Johnston Street (which bisects the island east to west). Here you will find more than 50 shops and stalls offering fresh produce, pasta, fudge, fish, crafts, and much more. The market is open daily except Mondays in the winter months. On Thursdays, from late May to October, there's the **Truck Farmers' Market** in the Arts Club Theatre parking lot, where BC farmers set local fruit, vegetables, and flowers from the backs of their trucks. Nearby, the **NetLoft** contains small shops and big craft displays, with everything from beads to Northwest Coast native carvings under one roof. All around are wonderful aromatic bakeries, bookshops for browsing, and art and craft galleries. Boat shops, boat rentals, and boat repairs are on Duranleau Street; floating homes and marinas are on False Creek; and the Emily Carr Institute of Art and Design is on Johnston Street.

[FREE] [KIDS] Visit the **Water Park** and adventure playground off Cartwright Street beside grassy Sutcliffe Park. Most restaurants on Granville Island have capitalized on the waterfront setting, and there's no shortage of sights to take in as you relax over coffee or a meal.

There's a pleasant walk along the seawall, a wide water-front walkway paved in a mixture of surfaces—flagstones, wood, or concrete—where you will find sheltered courtyards, inviting plazas, and grassy, landscaped areas as well as benches where you can sit and watch all the activity. Canada geese perch on boulders rising from the large duck pond. Cormorants wait patiently for dinner to swim by. Three marinas cluster along the shore of False Creek, where sailboats, kayaks, and canoes abound.

The seawall divides into a cycle path and walkway to form a loop around the north and south shores of False Creek. Start at Granville Island and wander east to the Cambie Street Bridge, then head north over the bridge and turn west to pick up the path that parallels the north shore. Follow the path west under the Granville Street Bridge and continue for a few minutes more to the west side of the Burrard Street Bridge, where you can take the Aquabus across False Creek back to the island. The loop takes about two hours to walk.

[KIDS] Each June is the **Canadian International Dragon Boat Festival** (688-2382). Slender, brilliantly coloured, exotically decorated boats come from around the world to take part in the races. Each one is paddled by 20 people, with rhythmic assistance from a drummer and a steersman. The best viewing is on the north shore of False Creek near the Plaza of Nations or near Leg-in-Boot Square on the south side. The festival also includes an international food fair and entertainment stage.

GROUSE MOUNTAIN
*6400 Nancy Greene Way, top of Capilano Rd,
North Vancouver; 984-0661.*

[KIDS] Sailing 1,128 metres (3,700 feet) through the sky in an aerial tramway could be considered one of the more pleasurable ways to scale a mountain. The scenery is amazing: feathery firs stand just beneath you, the city spread out at your feet, and Washington State's San Juan Islands are more than 160 kilometres (100 miles) to the south. Well known as a ski resort, Grouse Mountain is a different place in summer. For energetic hikers and those who prefer relaxing strolls, Grouse, just a 15-minute drive from downtown Vancouver, has something to please everyone. The **Skyride**, an enclosed gondola, glides up the mountain and drops you into the centre of the alpine activities. The peak chairlift will take you right to the top of the mountain for additional breathtaking views and enchanting sunsets.

A notice board outside the Skyride station has general information and a map of the trails. The nearby **Blue Grouse Trail** winds gently through the trees to a picturesque lake, which supplies the resort with its water. Swimming is not allowed, but it's a perfect place for a picnic. Although this 15-minute hike is ideal for small children, only experienced hikers should tackle the challenging **Goat Ridge Trail** and the **Grouse Grind**, which takes about six hours, round trip. In between are hikes for every level of fitness. Kids also flock to the adventure playground, and in summer there are pony rides, horse-drawn wagons, and helicopter tours. Round out the perfect day with a visit to the multimedia **Theatre in the Sky** or attend one of a series of summer concerts.

HARBOUR CENTRE TOWER
555 W Hastings St; 689-7304; map:T3

[KIDS] Get a bird's-eye view of Vancouver and never leave the ground—take a trip to the top of the Harbour Centre Tower. Glass elevators whisk you up 167 metres (548 feet) in less than a minute to a 360-degree vista of the city. Burrard Inlet, the North Shore mountains, Burnaby Mountain with Simon Fraser University perched on top, the Port of Vancouver, Stanley Park, downtown, West Vancouver, Bowen Island—all are on display. There are also photo-fact plaques, historical displays, and a video on Vancouver. Enjoy a meal or a snack in the revolving restaurant while you take in the view.

QUEEN ELIZABETH PARK AND ARBORETUM
Cambie St and 33rd Ave; map:D3

[KIDS] [FREE] This jewel of a park is set on the highest point of the city, 150 metres (500 feet) above sea level, offering a stunning full-circle view of the surrounding area. Beautifully landscaped, the park has visual treats at every turn—fountains, rock gardens, waterfalls, flower beds bursting with brilliant blossoms, and a placid pond where ducks preen beneath graceful willow trees.

This park was created from two old quarries—the crushed volcanic rock was used to pave the city's first roads—and the paths swoop up and down or twist around the steep sides. Landscaping of the largest quarry was finished in 1954, and the second quarry was finished in 1961, in time for Vancouver's 75th anniversary.

In spring the park's grassy slopes glow with colour from rhododendrons, azaleas, and other indigenous BC shrubs. When Vancouver revels in a rare snowfall, these slopes are quickly claimed by young tobogganers. The rose garden is a perfumed delight, as is the tiny Japanese garden with its stone lantern surrounded by dwarf trees and small fountain.

At the top of Little Mountain, as the park was called before the name was changed to commemorate a visit from King George VI and Queen Elizabeth, an open reservoir has been filled and transformed into a spacious plaza with water gardens and fountains. A beautiful bronze sculpture by Henry Moore,

▼

**Major
Attractions**

*Queen
Elizabeth
Park and
Arboretum*

▲

Knife Edge—Two Pieces, graces the plaza and is a favourite with children, who squeeze between the sculpture's two sections. The park's popularity as a setting for wedding party photographs is reflected in another bronze sculpture—a life-sized family group by Seward Johnson called *Photo Session*. Tennis courts, pitch-and-putt, and lawn bowling add to the attractions of this family park. **Seasons in the Park** (874-8008) is one of the city's finest restaurants, known for its fine cuisine and fantastic views.

[KIDS] The silver triodetic dome of the **Bloedel Conservatory** is the crowning point of the park—1,490 little Plexiglas bubbles that are illuminated at night. From the walkway around the conservatory, you get a panoramic view of Vancouver, the harbour, the North Shore mountains, the Fraser River delta, and the Strait of Georgia. Plaques along the way tell you which mountains you are looking at and how high they are.

Inside the dome is a warm, moist rain forest and a miniature desert. Tropical plants and shrubs from Mexico, Africa, Australia, and South America spread their leafy branches overhead. Brightly hued birds flit through the trees or peck at cunningly disguised feeders. A curving path winds through the shrubbery, leading to a little desert where cacti flourish. The floral displays change with the seasons—at Christmastime, the conservatory is a blaze of crimson poinsettias (257-8570).

At the northeast foot of the park is **Nat Bailey Stadium**, a minor league baseball park that is home to the Vancouver Canadians of the Pacific Coast League. It's a great place to catch the major league's stars of the future, from May to September (872-5232).

SCIENCE WORLD
1455 Quebec St; 268-6363; map:V5

[KIDS] Fondly known as the city's "golf ball," Science World is housed in what was the Expo Centre at the 1986 World's Fair. Now this futuristic building on the False Creek waterfront features permanent and travelling exhibits that dazzle the senses, offering hands-on experiences that range from buzzing around a beehive to mastering the essentials of light and sound. Three main galleries explore the realms of biology, physics, and music; the fourth gallery is reserved for travelling exhibits. Uncover the secrets of the universe and still be home in time for dinner. There is a great gift shop with a science-oriented theme.

At the **Omnimax Theatre** in Science World, one of the largest wraparound screens in the world puts you right in the picture. Admittance is from Science World, though package rates are available.

SEABUS AND LONSDALE QUAY
Foot of Lonsdale Ave, North Vancouver; 521-0400; map:E1

[KIDS] Take a boat ride on a "bus"—the SeaBus that hustles back and forth across the harbour from downtown Vancouver to the North Shore. The Vancouver terminal is in the beautifully renovated **Waterfront Station**, the former Canadian Pacific Railway Station, at Cordova and Granville Streets. Here, above the small shops and coffee bars, a series of wonderful paintings depicts views of the Rocky Mountains. It's also the Vancouver terminus for the **SkyTrain** automated light rapid transit service and the **West Coast Express** commuter train to the Fraser Valley. On the North Shore, the SeaBus Terminal is in Lonsdale Quay, a lively area of boutiques, coffee shops, restaurants, and a public market. Beside the terminal is Waterfront Park, a delightful place to stroll along the oceanside and view the city from a different angle.

The SS *Burrard Beaver* and the SS *Burrard Otter* take 12 minutes to sail across the sheltered waters of Vancouver's inner harbour. This is history repeating itself. In 1900, years before any major bridges were built, a ferry linked Vancouver and the then-small North Shore population.

Activity is all around as the SeaBus sails serenely across Burrard Inlet. Freighters steam by to load and unload, while sailboats, and even the occasional windsurfer, skim over the waves. To the north loom the Coast Mountains, and to the west lies the green bulk of Stanley Park, framed by the Lions Gate Bridge. During the four-month summer season, gleaming cruise ships glide by en route to Alaska. Southward, office towers and high rises cluster behind the shining sails of Canada Place. The SeaBus is also a wonderful mini-cruise to take at night, when the city lights are reflected on the water.

Lonsdale Quay shelters three levels of shops, boutiques, and restaurants. At ground level the public market offers an array of fruits and vegetables, fish, breads, flowers, and meats. Have coffee outside in the sunshine and admire the stunning view. On the second level are gift shops and boutiques, and on the third level is the entrance to the Lonsdale Quay Hotel.

[KIDS] Take a left turn at the SeaBus Terminal for Waterfront Park. There's plenty to see on a stroll around the paved walkway that circumnavigates the small park. Along the seawall, plaques identify several outstanding downtown buildings, and a huge modernistic sculpture, *Cathedral*, by Douglas Senft, sits on the lawn. At **Sailor's Point Plaza**, dedicated to those who have lost their lives at sea, sits an elegant sundial by Tim Osborne titled *Timelines*. A plaque also commemorates Captain George Vancouver, the Englishman who discovered and named Burrard Inlet. At the far end of the park the **Pacific Marine Training Institute** is full of boats, ropes, and outboard engines for students working toward a marine career.

During the summer this park is busy. Concerts are held on many Sunday afternoons, and numerous clubs hold festivals, exhibits, dances, and competitions here.

STANLEY PARK
Vancouver Parks and Recreation Board,
2099 Beach Ave; 257-8400; map:D1

[KIDS] [FREE] Thanks to the farsightedness of Vancouver's city founders, the 400 glorious hectares (1,000 acres) that became Stanley Park were set aside in 1886. The park was officially opened by Mayor David Oppenheimer in September 1888. Long before the Spanish explorers and Captain Vancouver arrived in the late 18th century, Chief Khahtsahlano lived at Chaythoos, now **Prospect Point**, the highest area of the park.

Natural woodlands, manicured gardens, sports facilities, winding trails, ocean beaches, calm lagoons, an aquarium, a summer theatre, a haven for wildlife, and a wonderful park to spend a day (or several days) exploring—Stanley Park is all this and more. Much of Vancouver's reputation as a beautiful city is linked with the wonders of Stanley Park, one of the largest urban parks in North America.

Attractions are spread throughout the park, but the best way to get acquainted with its many charms is to walk, run, in-line skate, or cycle the **Stanley Park seawall**. (Bike rental outlets are at Georgia and Denman Streets near the park entrance). The seawall, the longest in Canada, is 10.5 kilometres (6.5 miles) long and was constructed over a period of 60 years; it was finally completed in 1980. A brisk walk takes two hours, or you can take a day to stroll around it, veering off to check out the surrounding attractions, stopping for coffee or lunch, or sitting in the sun marvelling at the views, which are always incredible. Horse-drawn tours around the park are also available May to October through **Triple-A Horse and Carriage**, beginning at the lower zoo parking lot (681-5115).

Start at **Lost Lagoon**, a haven for Canada geese, trumpeter swans, and more. The fountain in the centre, built in 1936 to mark the park's Golden Jubilee, is illuminated at night. (A path around the lagoon is separate from the seawall.) Single sculls and eights from the **Vancouver Rowing Club** can often be seen skimming over the harbour waters. A statue of Scottish poet **Robbie Burns** is opposite the Rowing Club. Near a statue of **Lord Stanley** are the **Rose Gardens**, just a few minutes' walk from the seawall. Nearby, in a country-gardenlike setting, is the **Stanley Park Pavilion Cafeteria**, built in 1932 and now a heritage building. It looks out onto **Malkin Bowl**, an outdoor theatre where revivals of classic Broadway plays are staged during July and August. Artists display their wares along a walkway in an informal, outdoor gallery atmosphere.

Intriguing totem poles of the Squamish people, the first inhabitants of this coast, stand near **Brockton Point**—a prime spot for photographs. The **Nine O'clock Gun**, which used to call fishermen home at night, is still used by residents to check their watches. Be warned, it is loud! On summer weekends

▼

Major Attractions

Stanley Park

▲

watch an unhurried cricket match at **Brockton Oval**. At low tide you can see a bronze statue entitled *Girl in a Wet Suit*, created by Elek Imredy. A wooden fire-breathing dragon on the seawall here is a replica of the figurehead from the old *Empress of Japan*, a passenger ship that regularly called at Vancouver.

[KIDS] [FREE] The popular **Lumberman's Arch** is made of Douglas fir and was erected in 1952 to pay tribute to those in the logging industry. It sits in a meadow perfect for picnics or playing, with a delightful children's water park by the ocean and a busy concession stand nearby. Watch for brave bunnies who hop in and out of the bushes. This lively, cheerful area was once a Native village, and literally tonnes of shells from the village midden were used to surface the first road into the park in 1888.

The most developed area of the park is the **Vancouver Aquarium**. (See Vancouver Aquarium in this chapter.) Kids of all ages love the miniature train that puffs over 1.2 kilometres (0.75 mile) through forest and lake (weather permitting).

Beaver Lake, speckled with water lilies, is a quiet place for contemplation or a gentle walk. Behind the lake are numerous forest trails weaving through hemlock, cedar, Douglas fir, maple, and spruce. Popular with walkers and joggers, these isolated trails should not be tackled solo.

Besides offering a North Shore panorama, Prospect Point (north of Beaver Lake on the seawall) also displays a cairn in memory of the Pacific Coast's pioneer steamship, the SS *Beaver*, which sank near here in 1888. Nearby is a popular restaurant with an outdoor deck overlooking the Lions Gate Bridge, as well as the large, grassy Prospect Point picnic area, suitable for groups. Stanley Park Drive leads past the remains of the once-mighty **Hollow Tree** (large enough for automobiles to park inside) and on to **Siwash Rock**. The rocky pinnacle has defied the elements for centuries. Various Native legends have grown up around this rock, which has one tiny tree clinging to its top. **Third Beach**, a wide, sandy swimming beach, is also near here. At **Ferguson Point**, locals take visitors to the **Teahouse Restaurant** to admire the scenery.

[KIDS] **Second Beach** is one of the best places in town to watch the sunset, and children love the playground and picnic area. [FREE] Several nights a week in summer, the paved area is awash with dancers—Scottish dancers, ballroom dancers, and square dancers all kick up their heels here. This is also a sports area, with pitch-and-putt golf, shuffleboard, lawn bowling, and busy tennis courts. The excellent **Fish House at Stanley Park** restaurant is a good place for either a casual lunch or a more formal dinner.

Numerous annual events are held in Stanley Park; call the Parks and Recreation Board office for information and maps (257-8400).

▼

Major Attractions

Stanley Park

▲

UNIVERSITY OF BRITISH COLUMBIA
2075 Wesbrook Mall; 822-2211; map:A2-B3

With a student population of more than 40,000, it is hardly surprising that the University of British Columbia is a city within a city. Founded in 1908, the university is in a spectacular setting on Point Grey, a wooded peninsula stretching into the Strait of Georgia less than half an hour from downtown. Beaches and cliffs, dense woods and meadows, flower gardens, expansive lawns, towering trees, and spectacular views of the surrounding mountains make this one of the most beautiful campuses in the country. Buildings range from old and imposing to modern and spare.

There are four main entrance roads into the campus: W 16th, which becomes SW Marine Drive; W 10th, which becomes University Boulevard; W Fourth, which divides into Chancellor Boulevard and NW Marine Drive; and SW Marine Drive. W Fourth and W 10th have frequent bus service.

Part of **Pacific Spirit Park** and the **University Endowment Lands** is on the south side of W 16th, which leads to the **Thunderbird Stadium** (home of the UBC football team, the Thunderbirds) and the **Botanical Gardens**. Nearby is the **Thunderbird Winter Sports Centre**, with ice rinks and curling, racquetball, and squash courts all open to the public at specific times. Student residences and many of the largest student parking lots—some are a 15-minute walk or more from lecture and laboratory facilities—are found in this area. University Boulevard ends at the [KIDS] **Aquatic Centre and Empire Pool**, which includes excellent indoor and outdoor (seasonal) swimming pools, the **Student Activity Centre**, and **War Memorial Gym**. [KIDS] [FREE] Children are entranced by the **Geology Museum**. The spacious **UBC Bookstore** stocks more than 70,000 titles for study, with special sections devoted to children and general interest, computers and accessories, and souvenirs. The **Main Library**, the second-largest library in Canada, is nearby. It is open to everyone, though library cards for nonstudents and nonstaff come at a premium. The library's elegant old facade and sweeping steps are popular with the many film and television people working in Vancouver and have appeared in numerous productions, as has the **Ladner Clock Tower** opposite. The **Astronomical Observatory** and the **Geophysical Observatory** both offer fascinating tours (822-3131). From Chancellor Boulevard and NW Marine Drive the superior **Museum of Anthropology**, as well as the **Beach Trails**, the **SUB** (the Student Union Building), **Nitobe Gardens**, and the **Faculty Club** are all easily accessible. So is the **Frederic Wood Theatre**, where students put on several excellent productions each year (822-2678). The **Music Building** hosts concerts, an opera, and summer events (822-5574).

To get an idea of the university's size, scope, and facilities, you need a map. In summer, some student residences are available as visitor accommodations, one of the best bargains in the city (822-1010). (See Alternatives section in the Lodgings chapter.) Reservations are required.

VANCOUVER AQUARIUM
Stanley Park; 685-3364; map:D1

[KIDS] Guarding the entrance to the Vancouver Aquarium in Stanley Park is Haida artist Bill Reid's magnificent 5.5-metre (18-foot) bronze killer whale sculpture in its own reflecting pool. Inside, everything from the Arctic to the Amazon awaits you. The aquarium is Canada's largest and is rated as one of the best in North America. With more than 8,000 species of aquatic life, representing almost 600 separate species from the world's seas and oceans, the aquarium is also an important educational and research facility and provides tours, talks, films, and field trips.

A highlight of the aquarium is the **beluga and killer whale presentations**, held in the $14-million marine mammal area. Small bays, beaches, and rubbing rocks around the pool closely replicate the beluga and killer whales' natural environment. The whales eat up to 60 kilograms (132 pounds) each day. While cavorting as they do in the wild, with breaching and other manoeuvres, they also soak the unwary—the splash area by the pool is well named.

▼

*Major
Attractions*

*Vancouver
Art Gallery*

▲

The **Pacific Northwest Habitat** offers a close look at the inhabitants of local waters, from playful sea otters to gliding octopuses. Scuba divers feed the fish and harvest the fronds of kelp. **The Amazon Gallery**, 10 years in planning, is the only exhibition of its kind in Canada and re-creates part of the Amazon Basin. Fish, reptiles, birds, insects, and plants thrive in the tropical humidity, created partly by computer-generated tropical rainstorms. The creatures in the gallery are amazing—four-eyed fish, scarlet ibises, anacondas, and fluorescent fish.

The **Arctic Canada** exhibition allows visitors to hear the language of the whales, walruses, and seals that live in the cold blue world beneath the ice. Fascinating displays illustrate just how fragile this hostile northern environment is, and you can go nose to nose with a smiling, curious beluga whale.

VANCOUVER ART GALLERY
750 Hornby St; 662-4719; map:S4

Designed in 1907 by Victoria architect Francis Rattenbury—who also designed Victoria's Empress Hotel and Legislative Buildings—the imposing structure of the former provincial courthouse, with its impressive stone lions and Greek columns, now houses the Vancouver Art Gallery. Another famous architect, Arthur Erickson, transformed the cramped interior into four spacious floors flooded with light from the new glass-topped dome above the elegant rotunda.

The **Emily Carr Gallery** is filled with the glowing works

of British Columbia's most revered artist. A native of Vancouver Island, Emily Carr captured the majesty of the coastal rain forests, the towering totem poles, and the Natives who created them. Many of these works are from the turn of the century. The gallery has a permanent collection of contemporary local and Canadian artists, and a collection of European and North American masters, including the Group of Seven and such luminaries as Pablo Picasso. Frequently changing travelling exhibits offer everything from photography to videos to sculpture.

[KIDS] The **Children's Gallery** also has changing exhibits. Short talks are held several times a week. There are children's and adult workshops as well as concerts (682-5621).

The **Gift Shop**, off the main lobby, is an excellent place for souvenirs as well as postcards, posters, jewellery, books, and prints. Visit the **Gallery Cafe** for coffee or lunch. Sit outside if weather permits and watch the crowds on Robson Street. On the Georgia Street side of the Vancouver Art Gallery are attractive, well-kept gardens and the **Centennial Fountain**. Surrounded by a blue, green, and white mosaic, the rough-hewn rock in the centre has carvings depicting Celtic legends. Designed in 1966 by R.H. Savery, the fountain commemorates the union of the Crown colonies of BC and Vancouver Island in 1866.

▼

**Major
Attractions**

*Vancouver
Art Gallery*

▲

YALETOWN
Between Pacific Blvd, Homer St, and Nelson St; map:S5-T6

This roughly triangle-shaped area was first settled in the 1890s by workers from the nearby Canadian Pacific Railway line on the shores of False Creek. Yaletown evolved into the city's warehouse district, but in the late '80s and early '90s many of those warehouses became home to funky cafes, bars, billiard halls, boutiques, art galleries and studios, offices, and condominiums. Redevelopment of the nearby former CPR yards on Pacific Boulevard, the site of Expo 86, is part of the massive Concord Pacific Place project. **The Roundhouse** is the area's most historic building, where the first Trans-Canada passenger train ended its 1887 voyage. You'll find engine 374 in the building's atrium.

PARKS AND BEACHES

Whether you're looking for a seaside stroll or a strenuous workout, dazzling views or deep aromatic forests, tennis courts or a shady picnic spot, one of Vancouver's more than 160 parks will provide it. And, most likely, there's a beach nearby for good measure.

Ambleside Park [KIDS] This aptly named West Vancouver park is an ideal place to amble along the seawall, enjoying the superb scenery that forms a backdrop for the marine traffic. For the energetic, there are playing fields, pitch-and-putt golf, a fitness circuit, and jogging trails as well as picnic areas and a playground. The beach is popular with families on summer days. Impromptu volleyball games take place most evenings. Bird-watchers appreciate the bird sanctuary on an artificial island in the tidal slough. ■ *Along Marine Dr, turning south at 13th St, West Vancouver; map:D1.*

Andy Livingstone Park An all-weather playing surface in an all-weather city—amateur (and even the occasional professional) soccer, baseball, and field hockey players make good use of these fields across from the Sun Yat-Sen garden on the fringe of Chinatown. Floodlights make it ideal for late-night practices and games. Outdoor basketball courts and an adventure playground are almost in the shadow of GM Place. ■ *Keefer St and Columbia St; map:V5.*

Barnet Beach Park [KIDS] Once the site of a busy mill town, this heritage park in north Burnaby is the perfect place to spend a day by the water. Traces of the old mill workings, which resemble a medieval castle, are a joy to youngsters. Safe, guarded swimming areas, a wharf for fishing and crabbing, picnic areas, barbecue pits, and a nonpowered boat launch area make this park a local favourite. On summer weekends the parking lot is often full, but there's plenty of parking on nearby side streets. ■ *East along Inlet Dr to Barnet Rd, Burnaby; map:I2.*

Belcarra Regional Park [KIDS] It's well worth the hour's drive from downtown Vancouver to this park, which is really two parks in one—Belcarra and White Pine Beach. The huge, grassy sweep of the Belcarra picnic area slopes gently down to Indian Arm on Burrard Inlet and is ideal for individual and group picnics. Sasamat Lake has one of the warmest beaches on the Lower Mainland. There are also well-marked trails that edge the ocean at White Pine Beach, and the sheltered caves make perfect picnic and sunning spots. Tidal pools with their varied marine life are an endless source of entertainment. Crabbers and fishers bask in the sunshine on the dock, waiting for a bite (permit required). Kids love the imaginative adventure playground. Mudflats on the southern tip of Bedwell Bay provide interesting beachcombing. Busy on weekends. Signs along Ioco Road tell you if the park is full. ■ *Along Hastings/Barnet Hwy to Ioco Rd N and N to 1st Ave (follow signs); group picnic reservations, 432-6352; map:I1-J2.*

Burnaby Lake Regional Park The focal point of this huge, 300-hectare (740-acre) park is 12,000-year-old Burnaby Lake, which has the best rowing facilities in the province. There's a public canoe launch area at the Rowing Pavilion, and other sports facilities include tennis courts, grass hockey, rugby, soccer fields, a skating rink, a swimming pool, and an archery range.

In addition, there's a fitness circuit and an equestrian centre with riding rings and a large network of trails. The **Nature House** (432-6351) has children's programs in summer. Throughout the park, pleasant walking trails are liberally scattered with birdhouses, providing accommodation for everything from tiny chickadees to wood ducks. A bird-watching tower offers a sweeping view of the lake, which is usually busy with rowboats and canoes. ▪ *Between Kensington Ave and Caribou Rd, Hwy 1 and Winston St, Burnaby; map:H3-I4.*

Capilano Regional Park [KIDS] This park spans North and West Vancouver and ranges from the urban to the wild. The immense **Cleveland Dam**, named after Vancouver's first water commissioner, Ernest Cleveland, harnesses the Capilano River and supplies Vancouver's water. There are great viewpoints of the spillway from clearings beside the dam. Pleasant picnic areas abound near the colourful flower gardens. **[FREE]** Follow signs through the woods to the fish hatchery (666-1790), where a glass-fronted observation area shows the fishways that assist salmon battling their way upriver to return to their birthplace. Displays chronicle the life cycle of the Pacific salmon, and breeding tanks hold minute salmon and trout fry. Below the hatchery is wilderness, with long and short hikes beside the rushing river and inland. The **Capilano Suspension Bridge** (985-7474) is a swinging, 137-metre (450-foot) bridge that spans the Capilano River Canyon and is the area's oldest tourist attraction. Fishing in the Capilano River can be rewarding. ▪ *Along Capilano Rd N at the fish hatchery, North Vancouver; map:D1.*

Capilano and Coquitlam Watersheds [FREE] Though off-limits to the public most of the year, the Greater Vancouver Regional District's two main sources of drinking water are open for limited guided tours, Thursday to Sunday from June to September. Tours of the lakes in the mountainous marvels of the Coast Range are conducted in rain or shine and last approximately four hours. ▪ *Reservations required: 432-6430.*

Central Park [KIDS] One of the oldest parks in the city, straddling the boundary between Vancouver and Burnaby, this lovely park was named after its New York counterpart. Once a military reserve for the defence of New Westminster, the park has an award-winning playground specially designed with disabled children in mind. On the trails around the lake, which is rimmed with elegant weeping willows, you are likely to be waylaid by ducks looking for handouts. The ducks, however, are smart enough to keep clear of the remote-controlled boats on the nearby artificial lake. Longer trails for joggers and cyclists meander through the park. In spring, rhododendron blossoms make a brilliant display. Horseshoe pitches, pitch-and-putt golf, tennis courts, a swimming pool, and lawn bowling greens ensure this park has something for everyone. Vancouver's professional soccer team, the **86ers**, play their home games at newly renovated **Swangard Stadium** during spring and summer. ■ *Between Boundary Rd and Patterson Ave, Kingsway and Imperial St, Burnaby; map:G4.*

Chester Johnson Park Amidst the bustle of Vancouver's new airport terminal is a calm, quiet sample of the West Coast's temperate rain forests. Named for the chairman of the airport board who oversaw the facility's expansion, the park is a small but lush green oasis of waterfalls, trees, and totem poles. ■ *Vancouver International Airport main entrance, Richmond; 276-6101; map:C5.*

Cypress Bowl and Provincial Park This West Vancouver park is perfect for those who like their wilderness manageable. Trails are steep and can be muddy and rough, but they are well marked. Trees are huge and old, with thick, textured bark. Swirling mist in the treetops adds to the feeling that you are a long way from civilization, when, in fact, the parking lot is a short walk away. Cypress Creek has carved a deep, narrow canyon, and the roar of the water foaming through the steep walls echoes around the park. From the canyon, the creek plunges in a spectacular cascade to the wide creek bed and its smooth, waterworn boulders. The main trail, which can be muddy and slippery, climbs steadily upward through heavy forest and underbrush, occasionally opening into natural viewpoints. Downhill and cross-country skiing, and tobogganing are popular activities at the **Cypress Bowl Ski Area** (926-5612) in winter. ■ *Along Hwy 1 west to Woodgreen Dr and Woodgreen Pl, West Vancouver.*

David Lam Park [KIDS] [FREE] Named for a Chinese-Canadian philanthropist and former lieutenant-governor of BC, this park is one of the biggest green spaces in the mammoth Concord Pacific redevelopment of the south shore of False Creek. ■ *Pacific Blvd between the south foot of Homer St and Drake St; map:S6.*

English Bay Beach [KIDS] In the 1920s and 1930s, throngs of Vancouverites would gather on this wide, sandy beach and along the pier. Plays were performed on the roof of the 1931 English Bay bathhouse, where a windsurfing school now operates. A Jamaican seaman, Joe Fortes, lived in a little cottage on the beach and for 25 years was a self-appointed lifeguard, teaching many youngsters to swim. A bronze drinking fountain in tiny Alexandra Park, across Beach Avenue, stands in tribute to Fortes. [FREE] There is also a delightful gingerbread-embellished bandstand here, where the band plays on warm Sunday afternoons. The pier is gone, but crowds still come to swim and sunbathe. In July and August, English Bay

▼

Parks and Beaches

▲

is the setting for the **Symphony of Fire** (738-4303), an international fireworks competition that takes place over four nights. On the last Sunday in July, the annual **Nanaimo-to-Vancouver Bathtub Race** finishes near Kitsilano Beach on the south side of the bay. Dozens of hardy souls brave the Strait of Georgia in motorized bathtubs. Every New Year's Day, Vancouver's traditional **Polar Bear Swim** (732-2304) takes place near the bathhouse off Beach Avenue. The number of onlookers is always larger than the number of brave swimmers who begin the year with a chilly dip. ■ *Along Pacific St and Beach Ave between Denman St and Burrard St; map:O2-P3.*

Fraser River Park [KIDS] The wooden boardwalk parallelling the Fraser River in this Marpole-area park bridges ponds and marshy areas where thick grasses attract birds and insects. Signs set at intervals along this walk relate the history of the river and its delta and the river's importance as a marine highway, highlighting local wildlife, geology, and Native history. The Interpretive Court at the south end of the park offers additional information. Have a seat on one of the benches to watch the endless river traffic, or sit on one of several huge logs strewn along the riverbank. An open grassy area is popular with picnickers and Frisbee throwers, and a long wooden pier jutting into the river puts you almost within touching distance of log booms. Wading children delight in waiting until the last possible moment before running from the waves thrown up by passing tugboats. This park is a wonderful place to watch the sunset and to view planes landing and taking off from Vancouver International Airport, across the river on Sea Island. ■ *Along 75th Ave between Barnard St and Bentley St; map:D5.*

Garry Point Park [KIDS] This park on the extreme southwestern tip of **Lulu Island** is rich with the history of boat-building and the lore of fish canneries. At the turn of the century more than 2,000 fishing boats waited at the mouth of the Fraser to set out into the Strait of Georgia. The nearby town of Steveston is preserved much as it was a century ago, when the first cannery went into operation. It is still an important fishing area. You can buy fish fresh off the boat from Steveston quay or enjoy a meal in one of the many excellent fish and chip restaurants nearby. This is also the perfect place to watch freighter traffic heading up the main arm of the Fraser. Equally popular is picnicking in one of the many sandy bays that edge this park (beach fires permitted). A small Japanese garden pays tribute to the strong Japanese presence in Steveston. Kite fliers flock to the open grassy field where steady breezes from the strait provide a challenge. North from the park are scenic riverside trails along Richmond's dykes, which are well used by walkers and cyclists. ■ *7th Ave at Chatham St, Richmond; map:B7.*

George C. Reifel Migratory Bird Sanctuary A bird-watcher's paradise (946-6980). The 260 hectares (650 acres) of former tidal flats were reclaimed through dyking and eventually transformed from a hunting ground to a rest stop for hundreds of species of migrating waterfowl and other winged creatures. (See also Nature Observation in the Recreation chapter.) ▪ *Follow Westham Island Rd to Robertson Rd, Ladner.*

Iona Beach Park [KIDS] Based on the premise that if you can't hide it, flaunt it, one of Vancouver's major sewage outfall pipes has been transformed into a unique walking and cycling path that extends 4 kilometres (2.5 miles) into the Strait of Georgia. The pathway, which is on top of the pipe, evokes the sensation of being at sea on an ocean liner. At the end of the walkway a viewing tower gives a bird's-eye view of the strait and, on clear days, distant glimpses of Vancouver Island and the mountains of the Olympic Peninsula. [KIDS] Beaches are sandy and flat, ideal for kite flying, swimming, and sunning. The waters are sheltered for canoeing and kayaking. Driftwood rims the shore, and the river marsh on the island's south side is a haven for migrating birds that stop over on their way to and from Arctic breeding grounds. Ducks, songbirds, and sandpipers congregate here in vast numbers. ▪ *Along Ferguson Rd near the airport's south terminal to Iona Island Causeway, Richmond; map:B4.*

Kitsilano Beach [KIDS] This great sandy sweep of beach was once part of a Native reserve and is named after Chief Khahtsahlano of the Squamish band. In summer, families flock to its warm, safe swimming area, while sun worshippers pack the grassy area towel to towel. Tennis courts, a children's play area, and basketball courts are equally busy. [KIDS] **Kitsilano Pool**, open seasonally, is the largest outdoor pool in Vancouver, with areas for serious swimmers and for small children as well as a generous anything-goes section. This heated saltwater pool is always crowded. [FREE] On the south side of the pool is the **Kitsilano Showboat**, a local institution that has been providing beachside entertainment every summer since 1935. Local amateur groups sing and dance three evenings a week, weather permitting. The shoreline path is the perfect place for a summer evening stroll, and benches allow comfortable people-watching. Cyclists use this path too. The route curves along the beach, past the Maritime Museum, the Vancouver Museum, and the Planetarium, all the way to Granville Island, a pleasant 30-minute walk. ▪ *Along Cornwall Ave and Point Grey Rd, between Arbutus St and Trafalgar, Kitsilano Pool; 731-0011; map:N5-N6.*

Lighthouse Park Driving along West Vancouver's Marine Drive, where houses are perched atop cliffs, you might anticipate a beach park. Instead, you find a dense forest edged with rock. No logging has been allowed here since the area was set aside as a reserve in 1881. Numerous trails, long and short, meander through the park and to the tidal pools. Allow at least half a day for exploring. There are maps and information boards in the large parking lot, which can fill early on summer Sundays. The main trail to the ocean and the Point Atkinson lighthouse (built in 1914) is well-marked and is a mere 10-minute downhill walk through gigantic Douglas firs, some 61 metres (200 feet) tall and 2 metres (6.5 feet) in diameter. [KIDS] [FREE] Tours of the lighthouse are given daily in summer—just show up. Take a sweater, since it can be cool in the woods. Unspoiled wilderness only 30 minutes from downtown Vancouver, spectacular sunsets. ■ *Along Marine Dr to Beacon Lane, West Vancouver.*

Locarno and Jericho Beaches [KIDS] Locarno is the oldest settlement in Point Grey. Bones and shells that were once part of a Native midden date back 3,000 years. This is also one of the most spectacular beaches in the city. At low tide it seems as if you can walk to West Vancouver across miles of tide-rippled sand speckled with shallow tidal pools. Warmed by the sun, these pools are perfect for children. Seagulls stalk around the water's edge, herons hunch in the shallows, and eagles sometimes circle overhead. A wide dirt path, well used by walkers and cyclists, runs along the top of the beach. Between the path and the road is a broad, grassy area with picnic tables and benches. A few trees bestow shade. All along this shoreline beach you can see the green of Stanley Park, the wilderness of Lighthouse Park, and the gleaming fingers of the high rises in the West End. Locarno and Jericho Beaches blend into each other, creating a beach lover's, windsurfer's, and sailor's paradise. ■ *Along NW Marine Dr between Trimble St and Blanca St; map:B2.*

Lynn Canyon and Mount Seymour Provincial Park The North Shore's other provincial park shares many similarities with Cypress, its West Vancouver counterpart. Downhill and cross-country skiing are popular in the winter (986-2261). When the snow melts it's a prime location for hiking. On a clear day, BC's Gulf Islands and Washington State's San Juan Islands can be seen in the distance from several trails and lookouts. Farther down the mountain in the 5,600-hectare (14,000-acre) **Seymour Demonstration Forest** you will find some of Vancouver's most popular routes for in-line skating and mountain biking (987-1273). [KIDS] [FREE] The **Lynn Canyon Suspension Bridge and Ecology Centre** is near the entrance to the 250-hectare (617-acre) **Lynn Headwaters Regional Park**. The ecology centre, an educational resource and interpretive facility, is considered the ideal location to begin a hike (981-3103). Guided walks are available. ■ *Lynn Canyon entrance on Park Rd, past Lynn Valley Rd; Mount Seymour, along Mt Seymour Pkwy; map:G1-H1.*

Pacific Spirit Park Pacific Spirit Park is one of the Greater Vancouver Regional District's newest parks, offering more than 800 hectares (2,000 acres) of wilderness adjacent to the University of British Columbia. Some 55 kilometres (34 miles) of trails (designated for walkers, cyclists, and horseback riders) plunge through thick second-growth forest, edge deep ravines, and wind along cliff tops overlooking beaches with spectacular views of English Bay, Howe Sound, and the north arm of the Fraser River. There's plenty of small wildlife here, and early in the morning you may even catch a glimpse of a coyote. Just above the Locarno Beach cliffs on the Spanish Trail is an open area covered with wild roses, fireweed, and salmonberry bushes. It's called the Plains of Abraham, and a dairy farm operated here at the turn of the century (traces of the brick foundation remain on the south edge). A serene forest on the edge of the city, Pacific Spirit Park is well-named.
■ *Between NW Marine Dr and SW Marine Dr, Camosun St and UBC; map:B3.*

Portside Park [FREE] Exactly as its name implies, Portside Park is nestled among the Port of Vancouver on the north side of Burrard Inlet and is an excellent site for viewing the freighters, cruise ships, and fishing boats that sail by, especially at sunset when Canada Place is silhouetted. A short walk across the train tracks from Gastown. ■ *Follow the overpass at the foot of Main St to E Commissioner St; map:V3.*

▼

Parks and Beaches

Stanley Park See Major Attractions in this chapter.

▲

Vanier Park [KIDS] Ocean breezes blowing over this wide, grassy space on English Bay make it one of the best places in town to fly a kite. There's also the **H. R. MacMillan Planetarium** (738-7827), considered one of the best planetariums in North America and an anchor attraction of the new Pacific Space Centre, slated to "blast off" in 1997. The planetarium and the **Vancouver Museum** (736-4431), which has displays chronicling the history of Vancouver and the Lower Mainland, offer frequently changing shows. Both are in the building with the conical roof in the shape of a traditional Native woven cedar-bark hat, a fitting tribute to the coastal people who once lived on this tip of land jutting into English Bay. Outside the building is the wishing pool guarded by George Norris's stainless steel fountain, *The Crab*. On the west side of the museum parking lot is the [KIDS] **Maritime Museum** (257-8300), which shelters the historic RCMP vessel the *St. Roch* as well as offering fascinating information about Vancouver's seagoing heritage. [FREE] Nearby is **Heritage Harbour**, where a unique collection of ordinary and unusual vessels, including a Chinese junk and a Haida canoe, are moored. At the end of May, families flock to the red-and-white-striped tents of the **Vancouver International Children's Festival** (687-7697), where performers from around the world entertain multitudes of children with an amazing variety of theatre, music, dance, circus, storytelling, and multimedia productions. During the summer months, Shakespearean plays are presented by the **Bard on the Beach** troupe (739-0559). ▪ *Just west of the Burrard St Bridge, north of Cornwall Ave at Chestnut St; map:P5.*

Wreck Beach Take it off or keep it on—the choice is yours. Vancouver's famous (and only) nude beach lies down a steep trail beneath the cliffs toward the northern tip of the University of British Columbia. Over the years it has generated strong criticism, but more recently a live-and-let-live attitude seems to prevail. Vendors weave between the sun worshippers, offering cold drinks and a variety of food. Fun in the sun with no tan lines. ▪ *Below NW Marine Dr at the UBC; map:A2.*

GARDENS

Vancouver's temperate climate and soft, plentiful rains encourage exuberant growth in limitless combinations of species. All over the city, gardens, parks, and green spaces are tucked into the corners of lots, squeezed between houses, stretched across a campus, or set in front of public buildings. High on a mountainside or beside the ocean are tiny private domains as well as sprawling hectares for public pleasure. The dogwood is British Columbia's provincial flower, and in spring the spreading trees are clothed in fragile, creamy blossoms. Following are descriptions of some of Vancouver's wonderful gardens.

Dr. Sun Yat-Sen Classical Chinese Garden This authentic Ming Dynasty (1368–1644) garden is the first of its kind to be built either inside or outside China since 1492. Rocks, wood, plants, and water are used with deceptive simplicity, but gradually contrasts are revealed—large and small, dark and light, hard and soft, straight and curved, artificial and natural. Windows frame courtyards, intricate carvings, or a rock whose heavily textured surface changes with the play of light. Pavilions connected by covered walkways edge the milky jade waters of the pond, whose surface is speckled with water lilies. Most of the materials were imported from Suzhou, China's foremost garden city. Adjoining this serene, starkly elegant garden is Dr. Sun Yat-Sen Park, a simplified version of the main garden. ▪ *578 Carrall St; 662-3207; map:V4.*

Nitobe Memorial Garden This tranquil garden should be explored at leisure. As you stroll along gently curving paths, note the care that went into the placement of every rock, tree, and shrub: each element harmonizes with nature. Wander counterclockwise, accompanied by the soothing sounds of the lake, waterfalls, and tiny streams, for the gardens move from a beginning through growth and change to an ending. Native and imported plants and trees, azaleas, flowering cherry, irises, and maples provide colour the year round. ▪ *UBC; 822-6038; map:A3.*

Park and Tilford Gardens [FREE] Created in 1968, these glorious gardens are a popular place for summer weddings, and it's easy to understand why. A choice of eight theme gardens provides the perfect setting—from a stunning display of roses to the cool formality of the **White Garden**. The **Display Garden** features colourful spring bulbs and spreading annuals. The **Oriental Garden** showcases traditional bonsai trees and a tranquil pond, and in the **Native Garden**, a footpath winds through a small, aromatic Pacific Coast forest. There's also the **Herb Garden** and the shady **Colonnade Garden**, with its soothing rock pool and numerous other botanical delights. Located on the site of a former winery/distillery, which is now a shopping centre and movie studio complex. ▪ *440-333 Brooksbank Ave, North Vancouver; 984-8200; map:F1.*

University of British Columbia Botanical Gardens The oldest, and one of the finest, botanical gardens in Canada, the UBC Botanical Gardens is really five gardens in one. Each has a different theme and character. Spread over 28 hectares (70 acres), the gardens launch you on a trip around the botanical world. The **Asian Garden**, nestled in a second-growth coastal forest of firs, cedars, and hemlocks, has fragile magnolias and more than 400 varieties of brilliant rhododendrons. Climbing roses and flowering vines twine around the trees, and the rare blue Himalayan poppy and giant Himalayan lily bloom here. The **BC Native Garden**, displaying more than 3,500 plants found in the province, offers more than 3 hectares (8 acres) of diversity, encompassing water meadows, dunes, bogs, and a desert. The **Alpine Garden** lives up to the challenge of growing high-elevation plants at sea level. Specially imported soil, boulders, and rocks give protection for vibrant, rare, low-growing mountain plants from Australia, South America, Europe, Asia, and Africa. The **Physick Garden** re-creates a 16th-century monastic herb garden. The traditional plants, which grow in raised brick beds, are all used for medicinal purposes. The **Food Garden** is an amazing example of efficient gardening. Tucked into a 1/10 of a hectare (.75 acre), it's a patchwork of a dozen raised beds and more than 180 fruit trees that successfully grow a cornucopia of crops, including warm-season ones like cantaloupes. Fruit and vegetables are harvested regularly and donated to the Salvation Army. Regular lectures, on everything from pruning to growing trees in tubs, are given for gardeners. ▪ *UBC, SW Marine Dr; 822-9666; map:A3.*

VanDusen Botanical Gardens [KIDS] Once a golf course, the gardens are named for W. J. Van Dusen, who was president of the Vancouver Foundation when it joined forces with the city

▼

Gardens

▲

and the provincial government to buy the rolling 22.25-hectare (55-acre) site and transform it into a botanical garden. Set against the distant backdrop of the North Shore mountains, the garden is a series of small, specialized gardens within the framework of the main garden. **Sprinklers** restaurant (261-0011) offers dining in a serene garden setting. The gardens boast Canada's largest collection of rhododendrons, which in springtime line the Rhododendron Walk with blazing colour. The hexagonal Korean Pavilion is a focal point for the garden's Asian plant collection. Sculptures abound on the lawns, under trees, and between shrubs, and several are in the Children's Garden, where a chubby cherub presides over a wishing fountain. A latticework of paths wanders through 40 theme gardens—skirting lakes and ponds, crossing bridges, and winding through stands of bamboo and giant redwoods. ■ *5251 Oak St, 878-9274; map:D3.*

ORGANIZED TOURS

Sometimes the best way to get to know what's going on (and where) is to take a tour. Tours by land, sea, and air, by bus, boat, train, plane, bicycle, motorized trolley, and foot are all available. In addition to organized tours, there are plenty of individual ones, including walking tours, horse-drawn buggy tours, luxury limo tours, tours of the university, museum tours, and art tours.

Don't overlook the obvious. Investigate **BC Transit's** (521-0400) flexible *Discover Vancouver on Transit Guidebook,* and ride the bus, SkyTrain, and SeaBus to places far and near. Available at Travel InfoCentres.

BUS TOURS

Gray Line Most city tours take about 3 ½ hours. Evening excursions may include a stop for dinner at an ethnic restaurant, a boat tour, or a drive along the North Shore. The choice is up to you. ■ *879-3363.*

Pacific Coach Lines The long and the short and the tall. Pacific Coach Lines has half a dozen tours, from a short tour of major attractions to an all-day tour that includes an Aquabus to Granville Island and the Grouse Mountain Skyride. ■ *662-7575.*

West Coast City and Nature Sightseeing West Coast City and Nature Sightseeing Tours whisks you through the city in a comfortable minibus that stops at museums and allows time for shopping and exploring at other attractions. ■ *451-1600.*

CYCLING

Velo-City Cycle Tours The **Grouse Mountain West Coaster** is billed as Vancouver's first gravity-assisted mountain bike adventure tour. The 25 kilometre (15.5 mile) downhill trek begins at the summit of the Grouse Mountain peak and takes riders at an unhurried pace to the bottom of the North Shore via its rain forests and river canyons. The 4 ½ hour guided tour includes use of a 21-speed mountain bike and transportation on the Grouse Mountain Skyride aerial tram. Sunrise and afternoon tours available. Snacks included. Rain or shine, May through September. ▪ *924-0288.*

HIKING

Rockwood Adventures **Rainforest Walks** are an opportunity for visitors to get out of the city without going very far at all. All year round, Rockwood offers tours by knowledgeable guides through Stanley Park, Capilano River Canyon, Lighthouse Park, Lynn Canyon and Cypress Falls, and Bowen Island in nearby Howe Sound. Hiking experience is not necessary, as Rockwood allows participants to savour the stunning, temperate rain forest wilderness at a leisurely pace. Frequent stops are made along the trails for brief, informal nature lectures or to view wildlife. Any of the Rainforest Walks are the ideal way to cap a visit to the Lower Mainland, though the Lighthouse Park tour is a favourite. The last first-growth forest in the area is home to towering cedars, Douglas firs, and hemlocks, some of which are 600 years old and taller than many of the downtown buildings that can be seen in the distance from the rocky shoreline. Half-day or full-day tours available. Meals are included (owner Manfred Scholermann is a Culinary Olympics chef), as is the shuttle bus from downtown hotels. The Bowen Island trek includes a ferry ride, though seaplane transportation is optional. ▪ *926-7705.*

TROLLEY

The Vancouver Trolley Company [KIDS] Take a jolly ride upon a trolley. It's an ideal way to familiarize yourself with the myriad charms of Vancouver. At any one of 15 stops you can jump off and explore some of Vancouver's most favourite attractions, catching the next trolley 30 minutes or even three hours later—and you pay only once. Reproductions of the trolleys common on Vancouver's streets around 1890, these bright red and gold vehicles trundle you unhurriedly through the city. A relaxing, fun way to explore. ▪ *451-5581.*

TRAINS AND BOATS

Aquabus [KIDS] Vancouver's cutest way to get around. The fleet of 12-passenger ferries serves a network of five stations along the False Creek shoreline, 7am to 10pm daily. Sightseeing mini-cruises of False Creek are offered year round. Special summer cruises to English Bay aboard the vintage 1930s Tymac ferry are summer only. ▪ *Main terminal, south foot of Hornby St; 689-5858.*

Lotus Land Tours Lotus Land's "paddle power" four-hour guided tours on the waters of Indian Arm are just the thing for those seeking something more relaxing than "pedal power." Lotus Land uses two-person, folding kayaks: small craft that are wide and stable like a canoe, yet sleek like a kayak. Prior experience is not necessary, but comfortable shoes, clothes, and a windbreaker are. A barbecued salmon lunch (with a strawberries and whipped cream dessert) on a small island in the fantastic glacial fjord is included, as is free pickup and drop-off in Vancouver. ▪ *684-4922.*

Rocky Mountaineer Railtours The Canadian Rockies offer some of the most breathtaking scenery in all of North America, but most trains travelling from Vancouver to Jasper or Banff National Parks cross the magnificent mountain range in the dark. Not so with the Rocky Mountaineer. It stops in Kamloops overnight and then crosses the Rockies during daylight hours on the second day. Meals are served to you at your seat. Extended trips to Alaska or the Columbia Ice Fields are available. Custom and group packages available. ▪ *Pacific Central Station, 130-1150 Station St; 606-7250 or (800) 665-7245.*

▼

Organized Tours

Trains and Boats

▲

Royal Hudson [KIDS] It's a steamy experience—riding the rails on the Royal Hudson Steam Train. Engine 2860, the sole survivor of the 65 steam trains that crisscrossed Canada 50 years ago, takes you on a majestic trip along spectacular Howe Sound to Squamish, 65 kilometres (40 miles) north of Vancouver. There's a 90-minute stop in Squamish for sightseeing and lunch. June to September; reservations are essential. ▪ *Royal Hudson Steam Train, BC Rail, W 1st Ave between Pemberton Ave and Philip Ave, North Vancouver; 984-5246.*

Royal Hudson and MV *Britannia* [KIDS] Take the Royal Hudson one way and the MV *Britannia* the other way. It's almost the same scenic trip, but cruising on the water offers a different perspective of the same views. ▪ *MV Britannia, Harbour Ferries (north foot of Denman St); 688-7246.*

Paddle Wheelers [KIDS] Take to the water in another way—Harbour Ferries offers a 90-minute tour of the city in the MPV *Constitution*, a delightful paddlewheeler that churns through Burrard Inlet. ▪ *Harbour Ferries (north foot of Denman St); 687-9558.*

One Stop Charter Explore the matchless scenery around Vancouver and take a cruise on the *Abitibi*, a 42-metre (140-foot) classic ship, or the *Gulfstream II*, a 34-metre (114-foot) classic yacht. Enjoy large decks, a dance floor, on-board food, and other amenities. The *Gulfstream II* even has a hot tub. ▪ *Tradewinds Marina, Coal Harbour; 681-2915.*

Fraser River Connection The variety of Fraser River excursions on board the MV *Native* are unparalleled. To begin with, the *Native* is the last remaining working sternwheeler on the river. Built in 1985 (though you'd hardly know it), the *Native* plies the waters from New Westminster, BC's first capital city, to Fort Langley, the 150-year-old former Hudson's Bay Co. trading post. Along the way, friendly crew members dressed in turn-of-the century costumes provide historical perspective and witty anecdotes about the colourful, pioneering men and women of the 19th century whose lives and livelihoods relied upon the Fraser and surrounding communities. A unique way to experience BC's greatest waterway, where wildlife still abounds despite increasing industrial use. Cruises feature luncheon buffet and bar service. Evening dinner and dance cruises, as well as special occasions voyages, are available.
■ *Fraser River Connection; 525-4465.*

Starline Tours British Columbia's history is closely tied to that of the mighty Fraser River, where Native peoples fished for salmon, explorers paddled canoes, and prospectors discovered gold. A Fraser River tour allows a close-up of hardworking little tugs hauling log booms, impressive freighters, and other assorted vessels that work this busy waterway. Eagles, seals, and sea lions are not uncommon sights along the banks. Cruises up some of the Fraser's tributaries, like Harrison Lake and Pitt Lake (the world's largest freshwater tidal lake), are also available. ■ *Starline Tours; 272-9187 (Steveston) or 522-3506 (New Westminster).*

▼

Organized Tours

Planes and Helicopters

▲

PLANES AND HELICOPTERS

Harbour Air or Vancouver Helicopters You can cover a lot of ground in an airplane and avoid traffic problems to boot. Several different tours are available, depending on the amount of time you want to spend and what you want to include. There's a special thrill to walking on ancient glacier ice, and on one of the chopper trips you can do just that. Various flights from downtown or Grouse Mountain. ■ *Harbour Air, 688-1277; Vancouver Helicopters, 270-1484.*

SHOPPING

Shopping

Chinatown Although the Chinese-Canadian population of Vancouver is spread throughout the Lower Mainland, the old Chinatown is still a vital and interesting area to visit and shop in. You'll find it a few blocks east and west of Main Street on Pender and Keefer Streets. The little stores look as though they've been there for generations, and of course many of them have, so you'll get a good idea of the architecture of Vancouver in the first few decades of the 20th century. The Dr. Sun Yat-Sen Classical Chinese Garden at 578 Carrall Street is definitely worth a visit. Many of the buildings there were built by Chinese artisans in a style that cannot be found anywhere else outside China. Other stores to check out include the original Ming Wo cookware shop at 23 E Pender Street and Chinese Jade and Crafts at 38 E Pender. Be sure to stop at the original Hon's Wun-Tun House at 268 Keefer or at its other Chinatown location at 288 E Pender—the locals do! Try the Man Sing Meat Centre at 224 E Pender for a little barbecued pork or duck, and try the Ten Ren Tea & Ginseng Co. at 550 Main Street. During the summer, there's a **night market** at Main and Keefer. ■ *Map:U4-V4.*

Commercial Drive Once known as Little Italy, the section of Commercial Drive between Venables Street and 12th Avenue is now an amalgamation of many different cultures. The Italian Cultural Centre is the hub of the still-thriving Italian community, but many other Latin, Caribbean, and Asian peoples live in the area, and the stores along "the Drive" reflect this diversity. ■ *Map:Z5-Z7.*

Downtown The area between Beach Avenue and Hastings Street, and Chilco Street and Pacific Boulevard has experienced a lot of growth recently. Notable buildings to see include the Marine Building at Pender and Hastings Streets (a tribute to Art Deco inside and out), the refurbished Hotel Vancouver at Burrard and Georgia Streets, the fabulous old Orpheum Theatre on Granville Street, and the Hudson's Bay Building at the corner of Georgia and Granville Streets. There's also the magnificent Canada Place at the foot of Burrard Street, with its sails perpetually raised. But, like many centres, the shopping action has moved underground to malls such as the Pacific Centre, Vancouver Centre, Royal Centre, Bentall Centre, and Harbour Centre. ■ *Map:N1-V5.*

Gastown Downtown also encompasses historic Gastown, a quaint and cobbled tourist "must-see." The old warehouses and office buildings have been restored and refurbished, and summer and weekends find the streets bursting with visitors seeking food, fashion, and tourist-schlocky tourist souvenirs. Drop by The Landing, a particularly handsome refit of an antique structure. It's conveniently close to the old CPR station, which now serves as a terminus to the SkyTrain and the SeaBus transit options. ■ *Map:T3-V3.*

▼

**Shopping
Districts**

▲

Granville Island Under the Granville Street Bridge, across False Creek from the now-burgeoning old Expo 86 site, warehouses and factories have been transformed into a public market and craft shops. Locals and tourists flock to the public market for a tremendous selection of fresh food and gourmet items. It's a walk along the seawall from the many False Creek condos, co-ops, and townhouses; or a ferry ride from the apartments of the West End. Most of the shops are closed Mondays during winter. ■ *Map:Q6-Q7.*

Kerrisdale This area is arguably the best shopping neighbourhood in town for variety and quality of selection. You can find it spread along 41st Avenue from Maple to Balsam and along W Boulevard from around 39th to 49th Avenues. There is a decidedly English flavour to the area. Stores are well maintained, and the strong residential community that supports them includes a community centre with a pool and library. You'll find lots of fashion shops, like Margareta and Hill's, as well as shops for the home decorator (Hobbs and Ragfinders are two notable ones). Specialty shops abound, offering everything from cheese to chocolates. No wonder Kerrisdale shoppers are so loyal: they have no reason to wander. ■ *Map:C4.*

Kitsilano Along W Fourth Avenue, from Burrard to Alma, is **Kits**. The roots of its rebirth in the '60s as a hippie haven can still be found in its vegetarian restaurants, such as the original—very original—Naam and Sophie's Cosmic Cafe as well as in the original and eclectic furnishings at Mōtív and Kaya Kaya. The bohemian flavour is all but gone, eaten up by top restaurants (Bishop's and Quattro on Fourth), chains (Capers and Shoppers Drug Mart), unique bookstores (Sportsbook Plus and Wanderlust), and elegant shops (The Avant Gardener and Wear Else?). The neighbourhood's proximity to the beach and its view of the mountains appear to inspire the outdoor life; sport-minded equipment and fashions can be found along the length of W Fourth. ■ *Map:B2-C2.*

Point Grey This university district runs along W 10th Avenue from Discovery to the gates of the University of British Columbia at Blanca. Specialty shops run from decorator stores like Peasantries, the Cloth Shop, and Splish Splash Bath Boutique, to stores like Bali Bali, which sells imported fashions, to the very practical Hewer Home Hardware. There is also a Safeway (with lots of parking). This is a great area for browsing because crowds are sparse and the quality of the merchandise is very high. It has a true neighbourhood feel to it, and it is set in an old and prestigious part of town. ■ *Map:B2.*

Robson Street This street is the meeting place of cultures and couture, as *tout le monde* can be found strolling among its many shops every day. Weekends can be very crowded, but there's lots to see since the street runs from the Granville Mall right down to Denman Street in the West End. You'll find the Vancouver Art Gallery, the Provincial Courthouse and its below-street-level Robson Square, and a number of designer boutiques, coffee shops, and neat little international-flavour restaurants. If you want to venture in an easterly direction from Granville, just head toward the fabric dome of BC Place. Along the way you'll find the new Ford Centre for the Performing Arts, just across Homer Street from the splendid new Vancouver Public Library. Here you will find Bŏok'-märk: The Library Store, offering little gifts for literary folk here and abroad. ■ *Map:Q2-U4.*

South Granville The area from the Granville Bridge in the north to 16th Avenue in the south is rich with an abundance of galleries, eateries, and specialty shops full of high-end merchandise. In terms of destinations, it might be said that the area reaches from Uno Langmann (antiques) in the north to Suki's (hair and body care) in the south. In between you'll find Asian green grocers, cappuccino bars, and traditional shops that cater to the carriage trade in this highly browsable area. ■ *Map:D3.*

West Vancouver Apart from the massive Park Royal Shopping Centre, the shops along Marine Drive in West Vancouver reflect the British heritage of the area's original European settlers (note the name of the areas—Ambleside and Dundarave).

The stores are quaint but, in general, carry a good stock of quality merchandise, whatever they may be selling. There are some nice little restaurants and galleries too. West Vancouver is one of the more prestigious neighbourhoods in the Lower Mainland, so expect prices to reflect that. ▪ *Map:C1-D1.*

Yaletown Once just a cluster of dilapidated warehouses across the tracks from False Creek's mills and factories, Yaletown is now a highly desirable piece of history-crammed real estate. Industry has been banished from False Creek, soon to be replaced by parks and residential high rises. And in Yaletown, brick warehouses have been transformed into loft apartments, chic shops, and restaurants. Even the recent and ubiquitous condominium towers that sit cheek by jowl with the old brick buildings have been designed to (more or less) fit in with the prosaic and practical Edwardian architecture. Bounded on the north by the new library on Robson Street, it has become the destination of choice for exciting and eccentric fashion for oneself and one's home. ▪ *Map:S5-T6.*

SHOPPING CENTRES

Arbutus Village Square (4255 Arbutus St; 732-4255; map:C3; every day) is one of Vancouver's earliest experiments with mall life. This centre was renovated a few years ago to incorporate an atrium and carriage-trade decor, while **Bentall Centre Mall** (595 Burrard St; 661-5656; map:S3; every day) connects with the Burrard SkyTrain Station and meanders under the Bentall Towers.

City Square (555 W 12th Ave; 876-5102; map:D3; every day) is the result of a unique recycling project, in which two old school buildings were integrated into a stone, steel, and glass shopping centre. It's right across from Vancouver's City Hall at 12th Avenue and Cambie Street, but dress tends to be casual thanks to the Fitness World on the top floor. **Coquitlam Centre** (2929 Barnet Hwy, Coquitlam; 464-1414; map:L2; every day), on the other hand, is one of the largest—and snazziest—of the *suburban* shopping centres. This mall holds a special place in our hearts because its baby-sitting service saved the sanity of many a bedroom-community-bound mom. Another mall mothers will love is the **Kids Only Market** (1496 Cartwright, Granville Island; 689-8447; map:Q6; every day). It's a great place to visit with kids—and even without them. There are toys, shoes, clothes, and even a special hairdressing salon for kids.

The Landing (375 Water St; 687-1144; map:U3; every day) is very convenient to Gastown and the SeaBus and is worth a look just because it is a clever renovation of an old waterfront building. Soda's Cafe, inside, is a fun place to grab a burger, too. **Pacific Centre** (700 W Georgia St – 777 Dunsmuir St; 688-7236; map:T4; every day) was carved out of the subterranean depths beneath downtown's busiest business section. You can enter the Eaton's store on Robson Street and shop your way under Georgia Street, then under or over Dunsmuir, until you're nearly at Pender Street. And if you travel via the SkyTrain and disembark at Granville Station under The Bay, you can shop all the way from Metrotown in Burnaby to the Pacific Centre without every going outside! Given its convenient location, and its 200-name list of outlets, this mall is crowded all year-round.

Lansdowne Park (5300 No. 3 Rd, Richmond; 270-1344; map:D6; every day) was originally a race course and could once have easily taken home the trophy for most confusing layout. A subsequent reno has solved most of the navigation problems, and, of course, there is the lure of free parking. **Lonsdale Quay Market** (123 Carrie Cates Ct, North Vancouver; 985-6261; map:E1; every day) is a delightful conclusion to a SeaBus ride, and this "open market" centre contains a surprising number of intriguing shops. There are lots of food outlets, so be prepared; but fashions for adults and kids, fresh and dried flowers, and specialty shops (Girder & Beams Construction Toys and The Games People) also abound. Parking is abundant.

The North Shore's largest and most prestigious shopping centre, **Park Royal** (100 Park Royal S, West Vancouver; 922-3211; map:D1; every day), straddles Marine Drive in West Vancouver, just across the Lions Gate Bridge from Stanley Park. (Out-of-town visitors note: it's too far to walk, so take the bus or drive.) Parking is free and plentiful but wear your most comfortable shoes, as you may be covering acres of shops.

As the suburb of Surrey grew, so did **Guildford Town Centre** (104th Ave and 152nd St, Surrey; 584-4890; map:L5; every day), its first mall, so it has a sort of "chopped-up" feel to it. Be that as it may, it has everything a good mall should: two department stores, lots of smaller shops, and movie theatres. Another place to catch a flick between bargain-hunting is **Vancouver Centre** (650 W Georgia St; 688-5658; map:T4; every day), which is tucked under the Scotia Tower and connected to Pacific Centre at one end and The Bay at the other. There are just twenty or so shops here, but one of them is the enormous Bollum's Books.

Metrotown (4800 Kingsway, Burnaby; 438-2444; map:G4; every day) is actually two malls for the price of one—anchored by three department stores and having two very different atmospheres. In Eaton Centre Metrotown, you'll find crowds, noise, and the majority of the stores as well as the best food fair in the area. The Bay section is much quieter, and with good reason. The stores are larger, there are fewer of them, and the crowds just don't venture across the connecting bridge. Because the mall is right on the SkyTrain route, a visit can be

▼

Shopping
Centres

▲

an important part of your shopping experience. You can start and end in downtown Vancouver and, in between, take the Sky-Train out to Metrotown. **Oakridge Centre** (650 W 41st Ave; 261-2511; map:D4; every day) has been Vancouver's favourite shopping centre for a couple of generations, and it has worn the years well. Large and bright, it sits right in the middle of the Oakridge residential district. Originally built up around the now-defunct Woodward's store, the centre currently contains both The Bay and Zellers department stores and the only Vancouver outlet for British-based Marks & Spencer: so if you're nostalgic for a touch of old Blightly, be sure to visit "Marks & Sparks" and the Crabtree & Evelyn store.

Back when Richmond was still "out of town," The Bay opened a small shopping centre. Sears came along, and the whole thing grew like Topsy until recently, when a giant renovation changed **Richmond Centre** (6551 No. 3 Rd, Richmond; 273-4828; map:D6; every day), a tired old mall, into a marble-and-glass fashion mecca. You'll still find The Bay and Sears, but in between are bright and breezy malls with delightful stores. A personal favourite is Dundee Hobby Craft—well worth a visit. **Sinclair Centre** (757 W Hastings St; 666-4438; map:T3; every day) is not a large shopping centre, but it bears a look for two very good reasons. First, it is a striking example of the "reclaimed-heritage" school of architecture, where fine old buildings are put to good use without destroying their charm. Second, it contains Leone Fashions, Gianni Versace, Plaza Escada, and several other expensive but wonderful luxury fashion stores. Sinful indulgence may be satisfied at a lower cost at Miriam's Ice Cream & Scones.

ACCESSORIES AND LUGGAGE

Edie Hats Owner Edie Orenstein has been a mainstay of the local fashion scene for years. The store carries her own delicious creations as well as those of other local milliners. Imports too. ■ *1666 Johnston St, Granville Island; 683-4280; map:Q6; every day.*

Eleanor Mack A visit to this shop makes you nostalgic for the days when every well-dressed woman wore a hat. A great selection of chic imports as well as custom pieces. ■ *1453A Bellevue (Walker Place), West Vancouver; 922-4630; Mon–Sat.*

Satchel Shop A local favourite for purses, handbags, good-looking backpacks, and luggage. Lots of convenient locations. ■ *1060 Robson St (and branches); 662-3424; map:R3; every day.*

Weston Luggage Repair Weston has a well-established reputation for suitcase repairs. Most repairs completed while you wait. ■ *1111 Homer St; 685-9749; map:S5; Mon–Sat.*

ANTIQUES

Canada West Antiques Authentic pine antiques from Eastern Canada mix with country furniture and decorator pieces. Be sure to see the selection of grandmotherly folk crafts—quilts, hooked rugs, and more. ■ *3607 W Broadway; 733-3212; map:B3; every day.*

Folkart Antiques Besides antiques, this charming and fanciful place features unique pieces of folk art that are simply irresistible. There's a good selection of pine furniture as well. ■ *3715 W 10th Ave; 228-1011; map:B3; every day.*

Old Country Antiques A homey atmosphere and a wide selection of pine furniture. Be sure to pick up a jar of the shop's own antique pine wax for the care of your purchase. The delightful garden and patio statuary and benches are perfect for your own "secret garden." ■ *3720 W 10th Ave; 224-8664; map:B3; every day.*

R. H. V. Tee & Son (England) The provenance of this stately shop goes back almost as far as some of the antiques. The current Mr. Tee is the fourth generation of his family in the business, and he personally selects the pieces for the shop on his many trips to England. ■ *7963 Granville St; 263-2791; map:D4; Tues–Sat.*

Uno Langmann Ltd. This long-established, internationally recognized gallery specializes in European and North American paintings from the 18th, 19th, and early 20th centuries. Langmann also features furniture, porcelain, and silver. ■ *2117 Granville St; 736-8825; map:P7; Tues–Sat.*

▼

Apparel

▲

APPAREL

Aritzia Six locations feature high-end, high-tech fashions for the girl on the go. Hot, in, definite fashion statements for the very brave or the very young. Designers like Vancouver-based Talula Baton, Parallel, and Rugby North America grace the racks. Aritzia is also the sole retailer for the France-based line, Kookai, in Western Canada. Look for the classic retro-chic Hush Puppies comfort shoes, too. ■ *2125 W 41st Ave (in Hill's of Kerrisdale) (and branches); 266-6446; map:C4; every day.*

Bacci's For the bold and the beautiful. Are you ready for Madonna's favourite designer, Jean-Paul Gaultier? Other high-fashion designers for the *autre-couture* are also sold here. ■ *2788 Granville St; 733-4933; map:D3; Mon–Sat.*

Bali Bali An eclectic combination of imported and domestic fashions. Owner Mooh Hood shops the exotic East for fashions, accessories, and jewellery. ■ *4462 W 10th Ave; 224-2347; map:B3; every day.*

Boboli The stone archway is fabled to have come from a ruined Mexican cathedral. Inside, designer fashions and footwear await discriminating shoppers. The adventurous gentleman will find many imports, including Claude Montana, Issey Miyake, Pal Zileri, and Yohji Yamamoto. The lady can rub fashionably clad elbows with such names as Blumarine, Issey Miyake, Armani, and Alberta Ferretti; also shoes, jewellery, accessories; as God is your witness, you'll never go naked again. ■ *2776 Granville St; 736-3458; map:D3; Mon–Sat.*

Boutique Zolé Shoes and accessories from designers such as Adrienne Vittadini, Fendi, Armani, and many more. ■ *763 Hornby St; 688-8160; map:S4; every day.*

Boys' Co The venerated king of ready-to-wear in Vancouver, Murray Goldman, spawned this upmarket, youth-oriented chain-of-three; and the BOYS have done their old man proud. Imported suits from Germany, England, and Italy, with lots of imported shirts and accessories from Europe. The Yaletown General Store and Cafe offers tasty culinary treats also served to those who sit and wait. ■ *Pacific Centre (and branches); 683-0022; map:T4; every day.*

Cabbages & Kinx Fashions for those who like to make it up as they go along. Leggings, tops, boots, leather, and lace in very interesting combinations. For the very, very chic. ■ *315 W Hastings St; 669-4238; map:U4; every day.*

Can America Custom Shirtmakers The staff has more than 60 years of experience, through high collars and button-downs, so you know you're in good hands. The selection of cotton and polyester/cotton is very good. Both men's and women's shirts are available here, but their clientele is largely businessmen. ■ *609 W Pender St; 669-1128; map:T3; Mon–Sat.*

Celine Sophisticated fashion imported from France. ■ *755 Burrard St; 685-2353; map:S3; every day.*

C'est Ca This classically hip shop for women is located in the same trendy Yaletown building as Quorum Fashion Emporium Menswear. The owners have exquisite taste and a strong sense of their market. Oliver by Valentino, Le Garage Paris, Gruppo Americano New York, and other exclusive European and American designers are available. You can also get jewellery, accessories, and handbags. ■ *206-1008 Homer St; 684-5154; map:S5; every day.*

Chanel The little store that Coco built can include Vancouver as part of its far-flung empire. This shop carries Chanel fashions, accessories, and perfume, and its ebullient francophone staff is a pleasure to visit. ■ *755 Burrard St; 682-0522; map:S3; every day.*

Chapy's Wardrobe for Gentlewomen This classically elegant shop caters to classically elegant women, and specializes in updated traditional imports from Europe and Britain. ■ *833 W Pender St (in Edward Chapman Men's Wear); 685-6207; map:S3; Mon–Sat* ■ *2135 W 41st Ave; 261-5128; map:C4; every day.*

Chevalier Creations Definitely for the man on the way up. Custom suits from tailor Gabriel Kalfon in linen or mohair blends and 100 percent wool. Custom-made shirts in silk, linen, or cotton. Make an appointment. ■ *620 Seymour St; 687-8428; map:T4; Mon–Sat.*

Cottonental Superlative women's sportswear fashioned in (predominantly) 100 percent cotton. Top lines include Calvin Klein, Inwear, and Part Two (imported from Copenhagen) and locally made Moratti. Also Dim and Elita underfashions. ■ *2207 W 4th Ave; 733-6553; map:N7; every day.*

E. A. Lee for Men ■ E. A. Lee for Women Two adjacent stores with classic designs for men and women, many imported. *Pour monsieur:* Pal Zileri, Hugo Boss, and Warren K. Cook. *Pour madame:* Stenesse and Georges Rech. Expensive and worth it. ■ *466 Howe St; 683-2457; map:T3; Mon–Sat.*

Edward Chapman Ladies Shop For more than 100 years, this name has been synonymous with quality imported women's wear. Somewhat conservative in its selection, the store carries top names from England and Europe (notably Germany) in well-cut, well-made fashions. Mother may have got her tweeds here, but the shop is very popular with the career women downtown, too. ■ *2596 Granville St (and branches); 732-3394; map:D3; every day.*

▼

Apparel

▲

Edward Chapman Men's Wear Traditional in every sense of the word, Edward Chapman has been *the* place for classic British clothing for four generations. The store carries Liberty of London, Burberrys, and other British designers. ■ *833 W Pender St; 685-6207; map:S3; Mon–Sat.*

Enda B A warning to casual browsers: this store has a large selection of designer natural-fibre fashions and the savviest wardrobe consultants in town. Don't enter unless you're fully prepared to walk out with something you love. DKNY, Anne Klein II, Lida Baday, Inwear, A-Line, Steilmann, and Jones New York, among others, fill the store. You'll also find accessories and jewellery, a good shoe section, a children's play area, and a cappuccino bar. ■ *4346 W 10th Ave; 228-1214; map:B3; every day.*

Esmode Boutique High-quality, authoritative clothing by Canadian designers. Renowned local designer and owner RozeMerie Cuevas has fashioned her Jacqueline Conoir line to be classic and confident. ▪ *3035 Granville St; 732-4209; map:D3; every day.*

Exquisite Boutique The loyal female clientele is addicted to exclusive European imports such as Laborn Modell, Louis Feraud, and Jobis. Fashions for work, play, and evening—many are one of a kind. ▪ *Park Royal North, West Vancouver; 922-5211; map:D1; every day.*

Ferragamo Extraordinary fashions in an exclusive international boutique. This is the only Canadian operation of this company that can be found in major cities around the world. Shoes, handbags, separates, and accessories are offered, along with a handsome selection of men's footwear and accessories. ▪ *918 Robson St; 669-4495; map:S3; every day.*

Harry Rosen Another long-time supplier of natty men's attire. The two stores offer a complete selection of sportswear, shirts, and accessories as well as designer suits from world-famous makers. ▪ *Pacific Centre; 683-6861; map:T4* ▪ *Oakridge Centre; 266-1172; map:D4; every day.*

Hill's of Kerrisdale Top-quality clothing with labels such as Wilke Rodriguez, Replay, A-Line, and Teenflo; and shoes from Hush Puppies and others. Local jewellery designs bedeck counter displays; the store also houses an Aritzia in-store boutique stocking fashion-forward lines such as Kookai and Dollhouse. There is something for everyone in the family. ▪ *2125 W 41st Ave; 266-9177; map:C4; every day.*

▼

Apparel

▲

Is It Legal? A great find for those in the legal profession (and those who wish they were) who want more than polyester. Beverli Barnes has designed a collection (for both men and women) of robes, skirts, pants, cotton shirts, and coat dresses in 100 percent wool, mohair blends, and cottons. Affordable if you're on the bench. ▪ *206-1040 Hamilton St; 681-7977; map:T3; every day.*

Laura Ashley The English country style popularized throughout the world by these stores is still going strong. This shop carries women's fashions from the Laura Ashley Collection and will special-order wallpaper and fabrics for your home. ▪ *1171 Robson St; 688-8729; map:R3; every day.*

Leone Worth a visit—if only for the sheer architectural splendour of it all. Set like a jewel in the exquisite Sinclair Centre, this store showcases international women's designers in separate galleries—Versace, Armani, Donna Karan, DKNY, and many more. Many designers are exclusive to Leone, and the store carries a very fine house label—A-Wear—from its talented team of local designers. Complete lines of accessories and fragrances for men and women. ▪ *Sinclair Centre; 683-1133; map:T3; every day.*

Lesliejane This store has been a mainstay in West Vancouver for many years, and shoppers depend on it for a good selection of wearable, versatile designer clothing. Several exclusive lines and a good range of accessories. ▪ *1480 Marine Dr, West Vancouver; 922-8612; map:D1; every day.*

Margareta Design Classics, designed and manufactured for the store's own label. Styles range from the elegant to the casual. Custom-made and custom-fitted fashions are a specialty. ▪ *1441 Bellevue Ave, West Vancouver; 926-2113; map:D1* ▪ *5591 W Blvd; 266-6211; map:C4; every day.*

Mark James Everything for the fashionable man, from classic jeans to suits from Armani and Boss. Designer shirts and accessories. Savvy shoppers on the store's large mailing list get in on tremendous savings during its big biannual sales. ▪ *2941 W Broadway; 734-2381; map:C3; every day.*

MaxMara Associated with its neighbour, Boboli, this women's clothing shop stocks the entire MaxMara clothing and accessory line. These chic but casual Italians include SportMax, Weekend, and Blues Club. ▪ *2756 Granville St; 736-4827; map:D3; Mon–Sat.*

The May Sun Custom Shirt Company Both men and women patronize these two shops. They handle mostly cotton and polyester/cotton blends, but if you bring in your own fabric, they'll make it up into a finely finished shirt. ▪ *5881 Victoria Dr; 324-6771; map:E3* ▪ *3673 Main St; 875-9116; map:F4; Mon–Sat.*

Michael McBride Casual men's clothes, including a lovely selection of sweaters and shirts. A great place to stock up on suspenders and bow ties. ▪ *4426 W 10th Ave; 222-4433; map:B3; every day.*

Nancy Lord There have been some monumental and technological changes in this one-of-a-kind store. Although the store is still known for its soft, supple leather fashions in classic and eclectic styling, it also creates women's fashions in Italian and Swiss fabrics personally selected in Europe and exclusive in the U.S. and Canada. Clothes are manufactured by the shop, and made-to-measure styles are available—in 24 hours if necessary! The colours are beautiful and the quality is high. Shop from home at http://www.nancylord.com. ▪ *1666 Johnston St, Granville Island; 689-3972 or (800) 586-8555; map:Q6; every day.*

Quality Custom Shirtmakers Close to Granville and Broadway, you'll find top-quality custom shirts made from cotton in Japan, England, and Italy. Very nice. Mostly men, but some women frequent this small shop. A stock of top-quality shirts is also available. ▪ *2531 Granville St; 731-9190; map:D3; Mon–Sat.*

Quorum Fashion Emporium Designer names in a sleek setting for the man with more taste than money. Quorum offers prices up to 25 percent lower than you'll find elsewhere. A little hard to find but worth the search. ■ *206-1008 Homer St; 684-1223; map:S5; every day.*

Rodier Paris Boutique Members of the fashionable chain you see all over the world, these shops feature European-style women's knitwear and matching accessories. ■ *Oakridge Centre; 261-5121; map:D4* ■ *Park Royal South, West Vancouver; 925-7660; map:D1; every day.*

Romeo Gigli ■ **Instante** Side by side on Hornby Street and cheek by jowl with the business world and the carriage trade, these two boutiques boast designer fashions, knowledgeable staffs, and elite clienteles. Gianni Versace perfumes and china are available at Instante. ■ *769 Hornby St; 669-8080; map:S3* ■ *773 Hornby St; 669-8398; map:S3; every day.*

Roots The Vancouver area boasts eleven of this popular North American chain's shops, carrying casual, ruggedly styled clothes and shoes for men, women, and children. The shops also sport a good selection of accessories perfect for weekends in the great outdoors. ■ *Pacific Centre (and branches); 683-5465; map:T4; every day.*

▼

Apparel

▲

S. Lampman Set in a building with charming trompe l'oeil second-storey windows, this men's shop stocks sporty separates from designers like Calvin Klein, T. Lipson & Sons, Lyle & Scott, and Alan Paine. Suits available by order. ■ *2126 W 41st Ave; 261-2750; map:C4; every day.*

Seawinds at Waterfront Centre Truly Canadian fashions and gifts. Separates and coordinates in distinctive fabrics plus Victorian nightgowns from Spence Designs, Puffins babywear, and the Clown Group of children's togs. Quilts and accessories are also sold. ■ *200 Burrard St (Waterfront Centre); 688-1612; map:T3; every day.*

Simply Grand Clothing Co. A great selection of comfortably chic women's fashions in sizes 14 to 56, including evening and business wear and casual separates. Ask about the store's customer files for out-of-town orders. ■ *4695 Central Blvd, Burnaby; 439-1313; map:H4* ■ *126-1959 52nd St (Windsor Square Mall), White Rock; 536-1936; every day.*

Suzanne Bell's Fashions A generous collection of the latest fashions and fabrics for women size 16 and up, both imported and created by Canadian designers. The shop carries both casual wear and dresswear, and customer sizes and preferences are kept on file for future orders. ■ *5794 Victoria Dr; 324-7394; map:F4; Mon-Sat.*

Tilley Endurables Adventure Clothing For the truly adventurous—or those who want to look as though they are. Functional yet somehow funky, these incredibly practical clothes for men and women have been worn all around the world. The Tilley fame is built on hidden vents, secret pockets, and durable fabrics. Top it all off with one of those fabulous Tilley hats. ▪ *2401 Granville St; 732-4287; map:P7; every day.* ▪ *1194 Marine Dr, North Vancouver; 987-6424; map:E1; Mon–Sat.*

Versus Kitty-corner from two of Vancouver's larger hotels, this shop caters lavishly to the tourists as well as to well-clad locals. Versus, Versace Jeans Couture, and Gianni Versace *parfums pour madame et monsieur.* ▪ *1008 W Georgia St; 688-8938; map:S3; every day.*

Wear Else? The dependable fashion consultants can outfit you with an entire wardrobe—or the classic pieces that will be its foundation. Both international and Canadian designers are represented, and there is a large selection of accessories. Wear Else Weekend is available at the W Fourth Avenue location and offers casual clothing and accessories for leisure wear. There's a Wear Else Clearance at 78 E 2nd Ave. ▪ *2360 W 4th Ave (and branches); 732-3521; map:N7; every day.*

▼

Auctions

▲

Zig Zag Boutique Great mix of singularly attractive accessories, shoes, handbags, and separates. ▪ *4424 W 10th Ave; 224-2421; map:B3; every day.*

Zonda Nellis Unique loomed fabrics are used to create simple yet distinctive fashions. Nellis is a local designer with an international clientele. ▪ *2203 Granville St; 736-5668; map:Q7; Mon–Sat.*

AUCTIONS

Love's Since 1912, Love's has been helping bargain hunters get the best prices on all kinds of items. Auctions are held every Wednesday at noon and at 7pm. Watch the papers for items to be auctioned. Merchandise varies: one day you could pick up a priceless antique; the next, some repossessed restaurant equipment. Love's also does appraisals. ▪ *1635 W Broadway; 733-1157; map:Q7; Mon–Fri.*

Maynard's Another longtime Vancouver fixture, Maynard's has been around since 1902. Auctions are held every Wednesday at 7pm, and you're invited to view your potential treasures on Tuesdays between 10am and 6pm. The store also has a large retail area, where liquidated inventories go for a song. There's quite a range of quality and price, but some genuine bargains can be found. Constant vigilance is the key. ▪ *415 W 2nd Ave; 876-6787; map:U7; every day (Sunday retail only).*

Tyldesley's The store may have been around since 1917, but it has kept up with communications technology. You can call the Talking Yellow Pages at 299-9000 and punch in 4238 for up-to-date info on upcoming auctions. Auctions are held every Tuesday; viewing of items is Monday afternoons. ■ *1339 Kingsway; 874-4238; map:F3; Mon-Fri.*

BAKERIES

La Baguette et L'echalotte Undoubtedly the best baguettes (crispy on the outside; dense, moist, and sweetly fragrant on the inside) are to be found here on Granville Island. Owners Mario Armitano and Louise Turgeon create classic French-baked goods, such as their pain de compagne, a country-style baguette, decadent chocolate truffles, and seasonal fruit flans. For those on special diets, they bake loaves with no yeast, no sugar, and no salt. ■ *1680 Johnston St, Granville Island; 684-1351; map:Q6; every day.*

Bon Ton Pastry & Confectionery *(See Coffee and Tea)*

Ecco il Pane Christopher Brown and Pamela Gaudreault are the hardworking duo behind Ecco il Pane, and they create wholesome Italian country breads in their upscale west-side bakery cafes. They produce incredible ficelle, a small cousin to the French baguette, complete with crunchy crust and moist, porous interior. Topping off their selection of breads is our favourite, dolce mio, a buttery and fragrant version of raisin bread with orange zest, anise, Marsala, currants, and walnuts; the fantastic chocolate cherry loaf comes in a very close second. Wonderful Christmas gift packs and a whole line of incredible biscotti are available. ■ *238 W 5th Ave; 873-6888; map:U7* ■ *2563 W Broadway; 739-1314; map:C3; every day.*

Pâtisserie Bordeaux An authentic French bakeshop, Pâtisserie Bordeaux rolls up the best chocolate-filled croissants in town. You'll also find aromatic baguettes, croquembouche, Paris Brest, St. Honoré, mousses, savarin, tourtieres, gateaux, and, of course, an *assortiment des petits-four exquis.* ■ *3675 West 10th Ave; 731-6551; map:B3; Tues–Sun.*

Qualitie Made Bakeries Many folks believe this is the best source of hot-cross buns, seasonal pumpkin pies, and Eccles cakes in town, which may account for the fact that they run out of them early in the day. ■ *2068 W 41st Ave; 261-7010; map:C4* ■ *4474 Dunbar St; 733-3737; map:B4; every day.*

Siegel's Bagels For bagel-bingers who love a chewy bagel with a homey handmade look. Several varieties—pumpernickel, cinnamon-raisin, caraway, multigrain, onion, sesame, orange poppyseed, etc. Also knishes stuffed with potato or spinach and a vegetable roll. Try the Montreal smoked meat

▼

Auctions

▲

or lox and cream cheese. Eat-in or take-out 24 hours at this location. ▪ *1883 Cornwall Ave (and branches); 737-8151; map:O6; every day.*

Terra Breads Michael Lansky's Terra Breads has an avid clientele for its crusty hearth-baked breads, which are baked fresh every morning in a stone-deck oven and naturally leavened by a slow process using natural yeast starters. Terra's French baguettes are made in the authentic French tradition—the bakers use only unbleached flour without additives, fillers, or preservatives. The staff serves cinnamon rolls and coffee cake, fresh sandwiches, cappuccino and other coffees, herb and regular teas, and Terra's special biscotti, fresh-baked on the premises. Among the exceptional breads are white or levain rounds, fabulous black olive or rosemary and olive oil loaves, Italian cheese bread, rye raisin, fig with anise, a very fine focaccia, and a grape and pine nut loaf. ▪ *2380 W 4th Ave; 736-1838; map:N7* ▪ *Granville Island Public Market; 685-3102; map:Q6; every day.*

Uprising Breads A well-known Vancouver establishment, Uprising Breads features the best in wholesome breads, buns, and goodies. An expanded retail area now includes a selection of cheeses, cakes, cheesecakes, and German chocolate, among other items. There's a full range of deli salads and spelt flour bread for those with allergies. ▪ *1697 Venables St; 254-5635; map:Z5; Mon–Sat.*

BOOKS, MAPS, MAGAZINES

Aerotraining Products Appropriately located at the Vancouver Airport's South Terminal, this store has really taken off but remains strictly for those with no fear of flying. It has increased its sections on technical aspects of aviation, which should thrill engineers, designers, and mechanics right to the wild blue yonder. The store still has shelfloads of handbooks, regulation books, maintenance manuals—even video-format pilot training programs. ▪ *4680 Cowley Cres (South Terminal Bldg, Vancouver Airport South); 278-8021; map:C6; Mon–Sat.*

Albion Books A very personal mecca for people who love old books and jazz, and like to talk about them with other kindred souls. It's well-stocked with used books: fiction, science fiction galore, and large dollops of philosophy, chess, and art books. The big difference is the selection of jazz vinyl records, CDs, and sheet music. Want to listen to a piece of music? Albion employees will cheerfully play it for you. ▪ *523 Richards St; 662-3113; map:T3; every day.*

Antiquarius In Antiquarius you can spend anywhere from fifty cents to $3,000 on ancient paper ephemera. Used books, posters, magazines, labels, letters, signed portraits—everything is original. Browsing is encouraged, and you can do it for hours, gazing at such memorabilia as a passenger list from the steamship Queen Mary, autographed letters of McKenzie King or FDR, old car magazines and Life magazines from the past, or a 60-year-old menu from the Hotel Vancouver. This store is definitely one of a kind. ▪ *341 W Pender St; 669-7288; map:T4; Mon–Sat.*

Banyen Books ▪ Banyen Sound Known for its extensive stock of New Age and self-help books, Banyen Books also has a great selection of vegetarian cookbooks, religious texts, and tarot cards. The store provides hours of contented browsing in a quiet, friendly atmosphere. Banyen Sound, next door, has New Age music recordings and spoken text cassette tapes. Many unique-to-the-area offerings. ▪ *2671 W Broadway; 732-7912; map:C2 ▪ 2669 W Broadway; 737-8858; map:C2; every day.*

Blackberry Books Bright and attractive locations provide the perfect backdrop for extensive selections of popular fiction and nonfiction books. There are satisfying classic and craft sections as well. Appealing book reviews can be found at the Broadway location, where staff read books and post their comments for customers. ▪ *1663 Duranleau St, Granville Island; 685-6188; map:Q6 ▪ 2855 W Broadway; 739-8116; map:C3; every day.*

Bollum's Books With 85,000 titles to peruse, you may want to take your time—and you should. Tantalizingly arrayed over two floors, Bollum's books, videos, and magazines tempt you to linger. You can enjoy a coffee or a snack in the Last Word Cafe, and the special orders desk has a comprehensive database of North American books in print. The staff aims to please, with superlative service; during high-volume shopping periods, shoppers trapped in lineups are soothed and entertained by the antics of the "Maintenance" crew. ▪ *Vancouver Centre; 687-0083; map:S4; every day.*

Chapters Book Superstore This ever-expanding chain of stores has two in the Lower Mainland, one of which, the Metrotown location, is the largest bookstore in Western Canada (2,322 squares meters or 25,000 square feet). The stores offer a long list of features: 25 percent discount on the Top 40 bestselling titles, 15 percent discounts on 20 titles chosen by staff, music on Friday nights, author readings, and Children's Storytime on Tuesdays and Saturdays. Each store also contains a Starbucks outlet. A downtown branch is scheduled to open on Robson Street. ▪ *Metrotown, Burnaby; 431-0463; map:G4 ▪ 8171 Ackroyd Rd (Richport Centre), Richmond; 303-7392; map:D6; every day.*

The Comicshop It's true that the books here are comic books, but the shop has such a comprehensive collection that it deserves mention. For 22 years it has served Vancouver's comic connoisseurs with new issues and collector's items. ■ *2089 W 4th Ave; 738-8122; map:O7; every day.*

Duthie Books The true bibliophile must make a pilgrimage to one of Duthie's locations. There are eight now, not counting the Virtual Book Store that exists only in pixels (http://www.literascape.com/; e-mail: infodesk@duthiebooks.com). Since 1957, Duthie Books has been serving the literati and the hoi polloi alike with its comprehensive selection of the popular and the obscure. Helpful, knowledgeable staff. A new outlet has opened at the new Library Square (345 Robson St; 602-0610; map: T4), and another can be found in the new International Terminal at the Vancouver airport (303-3073; map:C5). ■ *919 Robson St (and branches); 684-4496; map:S4* ■ *Foreign language books and periodicals at Manhattan Books and Magazines, 1089 Robson St; 681-9074; map:R4* ■ *Duthie's Technical & Professional Books, 1701 W 3rd Ave; 732-1448; map:P7; every day.*

Granville Book Company This store is a browse-fest for book lovers, with a good selection of the latest bestsellers and a very good sci-fi/fantasy section. ■ *850 Granville St; 687-2213; map:S4; every day.*

Hager Books This cosy Kerrisdale shop contains all the latest bestsellers and has an excellent children's selection. ■ *2176 W 41st Ave; 263-9412; map:C4; every day.*

Kidsbooks To say this store is dedicated to children's literature is to make a terrible understatement. There are books and book talks, book readings, and book launchings. And did we mention the books? The staff are especially helpful in choosing gifts for out-of-town children. ■ *3083 W Broadway; 738-5335; map:C3* ■ *3040 Edgemont Blvd, North Vancouver; 986-6190; map:E1; every day.*

Little Sister's Book And Art Emporium You don't have to be gay to enjoy Little Sister's—especially in its new expanded location—but it helps. Little Sister's is not only the biggest, it's the *only* gay and lesbian bookstore in Western Canada, and it is lavishly stocked with books on subjects ranging from coffee-table erotica to travel. Every cranny is filled with divertissements—calendars, T-shirts (Queerly Canadian), kites, candles, Sex Grease, sex toys, greeting cards.Come to think of it, this store will also tickle people who enjoy a rainbow of sexualities. If you're shopping with the kids and want to stop in, there's a totally separate hideaway where children can play with toys and puzzles and draw pictures on the walls. Little Sister's has received a lot of press coverage because of its court challenge to Canada Customs, which is inclined to periodically seize its books at the border. ■ *1238 Davie St; 669-1753; map:Q4; every day.*

MacLeod's Books Walking into MacLeod's is like walking into a Dickens novel: layers and mazes of books are piled to the ceiling. One can get lost for hours. Each area of antiquarian books and collectibles is meticulously classified, and the store is heavily into history: British Columbian, Asian, Military, Marine, Native (broken down into sub-categories: Plains, Northeast, etc.). Ninety percent of the stock is used and out of print. If you can't find what you want on the shelves, owner Don Stewart can likely dig it up for you. ■ *455 W Pender St; 681-7654; map:T4; every day.*

Magpie Magazine Gallery An intimate neighbourhood magazine store with a bookstore atmosphere, Magpie has halogen track lighting, a background of jazz music, and a curious and attentive staff who will track down the most obscure rag. The store is packed with tightly focused magazines you'll find nowhere else, from jazz guitar to the latest conspiracy theory updates. Take a break and send a friend e-mail on the Magpie Terminal for a buck per half hour. ■ *1319 Commercial Dr; 253-6666; map:Z6; every day.*

Mayfair News Can't find your hometown newspaper? Need a copy of an obscure magazine? Try the Mayfair News collection of more than 3,000 periodicals. ■ *1535 W Broadway; 738-8951; map:P7* ■ *Royal Centre; 687-8951; map:S3; every day.*

The Mystery Merchant Bookstore You can find the latest bestsellers in any bookstore, but here mystery is a fetish and so are used and out-of-print mysteries. If you can't remember the title or author but have some idea of the plot (or the car the sleuth drives), owner Sandra Lees will track it down for you. Dick Francis and Elizabeth George head for this store when they're in town to sign their books. Lees hosts gatherings once a month, featuring authors, PI's, RCMP officers, or anyone involved in crime. Just sign up to get on the list. They've taken out a web page on the Internet, so you can post mini-reviews and get a list of upcoming authors who will be paying a visit. ■ *1952 West 4th St; 739-4311; map:O7; every day.*

The Pink Peppercorn Before you head down to the Granville Island Public Market, drop by and pick up a new cookbook from the Pink Peppercorn's selection of more than 5,000. Every taste is catered to, from that of the connoisseur to that of the fast-food fanatic. Knowledgeable staff. The storewide summer sale offers some real bargains. ■ *2686 W Broadway; 736-4213; map:C3; every day.*

Sportsbook Plus Fewer than a dozen bookstores in the world are dedicated solely to sports, and Vancouver boasts one of the best. If a book has been written about a sport, chances are owner Mike Harling will have it in his stock of more than 5,000. The fitness section is particularly strong, and there are some excellent selections on sports nutrition. ■ *2100 W 4th Ave; 733-7323; map:N7; every day.*

The Travel Bug Off to the Serengeti? The Outback? The Bronx? Owner Dwight Elliot can find you just the right travel guide and foreign language phrase book from his stock of more than 6,000 titles. Then he'll equip you with the essential travel accessories, from money belts (security holster, sock safe) to teleplug-ins for computers to travellers' sleep sacks (an essential item for the hosteller). He can even provide the carry-on luggage in which to stow it all. ■ *2667 W Broadway; 737-1122; map:C2; every day.*

UBC Bookstore For a bookstore, it's huge—the biggest in Western Canada, and the most incredibly thorough. If you can muster the strength, you can look through at least 100,000 titles, from anatomy to zoology. Veer off into another section and you'll find B.C. pottery, jackets with UBC logos, art supplies, clay, cameras, fax machines, and a major computer department. Don't let the fact that it sounds like a mall put you off. The staff is dedicated to books, and there are comfy chairs where you can sit and read. As a bonus, look into their book clubs for adults, children, and frequent buyers. Another bonus: special times are reserved for children, with hands-on science happenings and Saturday afternoon readings. ■ *6200 University Blvd; 822-2665; map:B2; Mon–Sat.*

▼

Books, Maps, Magazines

▲

Wanderlust When it's time for those boot heels to go wanderin', Tony McCurdy and his helpful staff can make sure you're ready to go anywhere. They carry thousands of books about foreign lands, with entire bookcases devoted to some countries. Travel accessories include water purifiers, mosquito nets treated with repellent, safety whistles, convertible packs, and language tapes. ■ *1929 W 4th Ave; 739-2182; map:O7; every day.*

White Dwarf Books For a vacation in another dimension, get one of the science fiction or fantasy tomes in White Dwarf's incredible selection. ■ *4368 W 10th Ave; 228-8223; map:B3; every day.*

Women in Print Books by women, for women, on women's issues. Also books by men on topics of interest to women, plus cool T-shirts, cards, and puzzles. ■ *3566 W 4th Ave; 732-4128; map:B2; every day.*

World Wide Books and Maps Wherever you're going, this store can help you find your way. It has one of the largest map and travel guide selections in Canada. ■ *736A Granville St (downstairs); 687-3320; map:T4; every day.*

CAMERAS

Kerrisdale Cameras This locally owned chain has seven locations—and the largest selection of new and used cameras in Western Canada. As well as providing expert advice and darkroom and photofinishing equipment, staff members assure us that they sell "everything photographic" and even take trade-ins. ■ *2170 W 41st Ave (and branches); 263-3221; map:C4; Mon–Sat.*

Lens & Shutter Cameras Serious, dedicated shutterbugs will tell you it's not the camera that costs so much, it's the accessories. That's why they shop here. This chain of stores has its own line of accessories as well as every single thing you ever wanted in the photography line. The knowledgeable staff of photographic professionals doesn't intimidate. ■ *2912 W Broadway (and branches); 736-3461; map:C3; Mon–Sat.*

Leo's Camera Supply This store has an unprepossessing exterior in one of the seedier sections of the Granville Mall, but inside is a shutterbug's dream. The store boasts of being one of the country's largest dealers of professional supplies and carries a huge selection of used photo equipment. If you're looking for a hard-to-find antique camera, chances are you'll find it here. Franchised for all the major manufacturers. Shipping available. ■ *1055 Granville St; 685-5331; map:S4; Mon–Sat.*

London Drugs This store is a local phenomenon, and although it's technically a drugstore, it isn't in the true sense of the word. London Drugs has an exceptional selection of moderately priced cameras at competitive prices. The staff is helpful and can usually answer any questions that beginners might have. Small electrical appliances are the specialty here, and London Drugs sells sound and video equipment as well. Brand names include Braun and Minolta to Canon and Sony. Computers too. Oh yes—you can also get your prescription filled, your film developed, and find your favourite hair and skin care products. ■ *665 W Broadway (and branches); 872-8114 (Camera dept.); map:S7; every day.*

CANDIES AND CHOCOLATE

Bernard Callebaut Chocolaterie Yes, there really is a Bernard Callebaut, and he supplies his stores with what may be the best chocolate in the world. (We know everyone says that, but we can't find anyone to argue with this claim.) There are 27 of these Canadian-owned stores across the country, with three in the Lower Mainland. You can select from a sumptuous array of chocolates, chocolate-related giftware, and chocolate shavings to mix with hot milk. ■ *2698 Granville St (and branches); 736-5890; map:D3; Mon–Sat.*

Chocolate Arts Greg Hook collaborated with Native artist Robert Davidson to open this sweet shop and has created fabulous-tasting chocolates that look like fine art. The perfect gift to impress out-of-towners is chocolate medallions with Haida designs. And Hook's liquor-laced truffles are incredible. ■ *2037 West 4th Ave; 739-0475; map:N7; every day.*

Daniel Le Chocolat Belge In 1987, Daniel supplied his secret-formula chocolates to heads of state attending Vancouver's Commonwealth Conference, testimony to his highly developed sense of presentation, packaging, and decoration—not to mention his exquisite array of hazelnut paste, creamy caramel, delicious ganache creams, and liquor truffles sleekly enrobed in pure, rich chocolate. Further, Daniel's "gift gallery" has recently been expanded, offering the discriminating chocoholic an even more abundant array of exclusive items. ■ *1105 Robson St (and branches); 688-9624; map:S3; every day.*

Lazy Gourmet Tops locally for a unique BC delicacy—a chocolatey, gooey, almost-too-sweet (but that never stopped us) confection known as the Nanaimo bar. ■ *1595 W 6th Ave; 734-2507; map:P7; every day.*

Lee's Candies A local legend, Lee's Candies is located next to the Varsity Theatre and is the mainstay of many a chocolate-starved UBC student. All candies are handmade on the premises. Seconds sell for $5.45/lb and are bagged each Saturday, when they usually sell out fast. If you miss out and can plan a return visit, you can order seconds for pick-up the next day at the same discount price. Lee's has the largest selection of novelty chocolate moulds in the city. ■ *4361 W 10th Ave; 224-5450; map:B3; Mon–Sat.*

▼

Candies and Chocolate

▲

Olde World Fudge Here's the most reliable source we know for fabulous fudge. More than 10 varieties are available, with special novelty types for sale from time to time. ■ *1689 Johnston St, Granville Island (and branches); 687-7355; map:Q6; every day.*

Purdy's Purdy's is another Vancouver institution and the place to fill up a stocking or Easter basket. Chocolate-maker Tom Cinnamon has introduced a new line of European-style cream chocolates called Bonté; the espresso anisette, Kir, and Poire are addictive. The factory store (2777 Kingway St) always has prepackaged seconds as well as a clerk who will parcel up what you want from loose seconds. ■ *Pacific Centre (and branches); 681-7814; map:T4; every day.*

Rocky Mountain Chocolate Factory Here the revered bean is available in every form—chocolates, fudge, popcorn, brittles, and, many claim, the best ice cream in the region. For the skiers in your life, there are also chocolate moguls (like Turtles) and even moguls that die-hard dieters will love—no sugar and no salt. Besides the Robson Street location, Rocky Mountain can be found at malls throughout the Lower Mainland and Whistler. ■ *1017 Robson St (and branches); 688-4100; map:S3; every day.*

Sutton Place Chocoholic Bar A legend in its own time, this decadent buffet of desserts simply overwhelms. Fresh fruit, French crêpes made to order, a variety of cheesecakes and squares, passionfruit, raspberry, or chocolate sauce, and a selection of liquor syrups await. ■ *845 Burrard St; 682-5511 (ask for Cafe Fleuri); map:S3; Thurs–Sat.*

CHILDREN'S CLOTHING

Bobbit's For Kids! This newborn/little kids store specializes in Kinderslings carriers, designer diaper bags, Medda breast pumps, and really, really neat gift ideas. ■ *2951A W 4th Ave; 738-0333; map:C2; Mon–Sat.*

Bratz Stroll down South Granville until you come to a window full of colourful, adorable, definitely wearable children's clothing. Haircuts and hair styling specifically for tots is also available. ■ *2828 Granville St; 734-4344; map:D3; Mon–Sat.*

▼

Candies and Chocolate

▲

Hula Hupp Fashions and accessories for the young, well-dressed set (newborn to 16), with a large selection of imported styles. ■ *Metrotown, Burnaby (and branches); 433-1771; map:G4; Mon–Sat.*

Isola Bella Exclusive designer togs for tots—much of the stock is imported from France and Italy—with European quality. You'll also find footwear for fashionable little feet and beautiful gift items for children. From newborn to size 16. ■ *5692 Yew St; 266-8808; map:C4; Mon–Sat.*

Please Mum Fun and functional clothing for the junior jet set. ■ *2951 W Broadway (and branches); 732-4574; map:B3; every day.*

Spoilt Designed and made locally, these classic children's fashions are constructed to last through several hand-me-downs. The helpful staff is very tolerant of tired and temperamental tots. ■ *Oakridge Centre; 261-2311; map:D4; every day.*

COFFEE AND TEA

Bean Around the World Together with its sister stores on Granville Street and in West Van, this retail roasting shop helps supply Vancouver's blossoming addiction to fresh roasted beans. It's an inviting cosy-sweater kind of place that serves a mix of sippers: early-bird exercisers, retired folk, students, and parents with kids in tow. This coffeehouse gives its beans a slightly lighter roast than many other beaneries. Not only does this preserve varietal distinctions, it provides more caffeine kick in the cup. Forty varieties of take-home beans are offered, along with the very popular fruit pies and rhubarb muffins. There's a 45-cent discount on take-out coffee (you provide the mug) and 50-cent refills. Curl up by the roaster and warm your cheeks over a latte served in a filling, consoling bowl. ■ *4456 W 10th Ave (and branches); 222-1400; map:B3; every day.*

Blenz Coffee Vancouverites are as fond of coffee as the rest of the planet, and lately we have found ourselves in the throes of a caffeine frenzy. So it's nice to know we've got a Canadian-owned company supplying our favourite beverage. Blenz is a local outfit with several key locations—it serves the "suits" at the Stock Exchange counter and the hoi polloi at Library Square and Robson Street. Ten private-label blends, some flavoured coffees, coffee-related paraphernalia, and light snacks are offered, and Blenz staff roasts and blends the beans itself. Blenz has gained a faithful following among the loyal locals. ■ *1201 Robson St (and branches); 681-8092; map:R3; every day.*

Bon Ton Pastry & Confectionery Mr. Notte came from Italy, Mrs. Notte came from France, and sometime in the early '30s they opened a tea shop. Second-generation Nottes still labour away behind the scenes, creating the kind of picture-perfect pastries you remember from your childhood. Unless you're heavily into plastic geraniums, the back-room tearoom is unassuming at best. But here, motherly waitresses serve up some of the most wickedly delicious pastries in the city: mocha filbert meringues, chocolate éclairs, cream puffs, Napoleons, and diplomat cake. A selection, under a plastic dome, gets left on your table. Only the most ascetic can stop at one. This place is a Vancouver tradition, and around teatime you can have your tea leaves or tarot cards read by itinerant fortune-tellers. ■ *874 Granville St; 681-3058; map:S4; Tues–Sat.*

British Home The name says it all. This experience, so authentic it causes tears to well in the eyes of expatriates, calls for a 30- to 40-minute drive south from Vancouver to the fishing village of Steveston. Here, Ray and Mary Carter have duplicated the corner store you find on every street corner in Britain. If you've ever watched Coronation Street, you've seen its kind—shelves stocked with marmite, treacle pudding, and other delicacies dear to the hearts of the British. From a counter backed by a wall crammed with pictures of royalty, the Carters dispense haggis, black pudding, boiled sweets, and tea. The $2.95 "cream tea" includes scones and jam, both made by Mary, plus Devonshire cream and a pot of tea that comes with its own knitted cosy. If you forgo the cream, it's only $2.10. Jolly nice, either way. ■ *3986 Moncton at No. 1 Rd, Steveston; 274-2261; map:C7; every day.*

▼

Coffee and Tea

▲

Fleuri (Sutton Place Hotel) Blissfully tranquil surroundings and a very civilized tea await those who venture through the hotel's chandeliered lobby. But what tea to choose? Chinese? Or the traditional Japanese tea ceremony with hand-whisked macha tea and bean jelly? Classic English tea? Most of the hotel guests, the corporate types and the movie stars (celeb-spotting is a popular sport), go for the latter. Fifteen bucks gets you finger sandwiches, pastries, scones, and cream. Half the price buys a duo of warm, currant-studded scones, a generous bowl of thick cream, and a trio of little pots of English preserves. ■ *845 Burrard St; 682-5511; map:S4; Mon–Sat.*

Ciao Espresso Bar Not only is smoking permitted, it's practically mandatory at this smouldering '70s cafe. Here, black brew and tobacco provide the stimulus, both for those who come to talk and for the writers residing in worn booths. Try the Americano—an exquisitely thick and caramelly concoction with beautiful crema. Ciao also serves up a modest selection of Italian sandwiches, fresh juices and desserts, beer and wine, and its popular low-fat muffins. ■ *1074 Denman St; 682-0112; map:P3; every day.*

▼

Coffee and Tea

▲

Coloiera Coffee Like Continental Coffee down the street, Coloiera is a local pioneer and its reputation lives on under new ownership. Throughout the '70s, Coloiera's beans were roasted at this harshly lit shop. Demand grew locally as well as down south, requiring the roasting operation to move to larger facilities in Richmond. It's a serious place, offering bean varietals and more than 10 blends over the pink Formica counter along with reasonably priced espresso drinks (like the cappuccino for $1.50). If you like, you can sit and sip in the quiet fluorescence of this tiny room. The minimalist decor welcomes you to focus on the essence of your drink and not be manipulated by jazzy music, trendy gimmicks, or fanciful presentations. ■ *2206 Commercial Dr; 254-3723; map:Z7; Mon–Sat.*

The Expressohead Coffee House At the caffeine-induced hallucination that is Expressohead, honey-coloured afternoon light slants through the generous southern exposure windows while patrons work their way through provocative pleasures like Expresso Bolt, Steamed Moo, or Mario's Glory. The popular Mocha Head is a mocha with a chocolate-whipped cream head. The nonsmoking Expressohead has chosen its caterer well, offering outstanding desserts and yeast-free goodies from around the city. Renowned among Kitsilano regulars are the mile-high lemon meringue and hazelnut dacquoise. Why not add to your pleasures with a unique take-home bean blend such as Sigmund's Waltz or Zappatta Hot Wire? ■ *1945 Cornwall Ave; 739-1069; map:O7; every day.*

The Fine Grind The Fine Grind is the *first* shop in the Lower Mainland to successfully meet the demands of Vancouverites for fresh-roasted coffee and beans. This compact custom coffeehouse roasts very small batches every one to two days, so beans are consistently the freshest available (roast dates are quickly quoted). The outstanding freshness along with the custom blending service helps supply a booming mail-order business for owners Reg and Brenda James. Introduce yourself to this exciting store: choose from more than 50 beans and blends, or phone in and time your arrival with the roasting of your favourite varietal or custom blend (the aroma of roasting beans will greet you at the door). Shuttle the warm beans back home. Grind, brew, and discover what fresh coffee tastes like. There are also 25 flavours of hot chocolate—try the caramel. Fine Grind also has a branch in Banff, Alberta. ■ *2297 W 41st Ave; 264-1270; map:C4; every day.*

Hotel Vancouver The city's venerable grande dame among hostelries has recently renovated its chic Lobby Lounge, and "Afternoon Tea" is once more reigning supreme. A bargain $2.25 gets you a silver pot of any one of more than a dozen different teas, but few can resist the full service "Tea," featuring munchies such as scones with Devonshire cream, sandwiches and pastries, and a very grand finale of strawberries and cream. ■ *900 W Georgia St; 684-3131; map:S3; every day.*

Joe's Cafe Intellectuals, bohemian philosophers, poets, feminists, and political agitators mix with pool-hustling locals at this vigorous pool hall and cafe. Joe's doesn't glamorize espresso or otherwise try to be popular; it just happens. All Joe needs to do is serve up his comely drinks with the famed foam. Despite the seedy decor and laundromat lighting, the place has the feeling of a well-worn neighbourhood living room. Knowing, deliberate hands prepare espresso standards, along with hybrids like Espresso Bica, Double Cappuccino, and Butterscotch Milk. The Carioca lait coffee is a dwarf-size latte and can be ordered with a refreshing slice of lemon. (For coffee abstainers, juices, pop, flavoured malts, and average snacks are offered.) But be prepared—after the last mouthful . . . clank! Cup and saucer are jettisoned out from under you and whisked back to the bar. This encourages you to get up and take part in the activity (i.e., play pool)—or to leave. ■ *1150 Commercial Dr; number unlisted; map:Z6; every day.*

Murchie's Tea & Coffee The current coffee scene reveals how the city is flavoured by Europe these days, yet Vancouver's roots are in Britain, and some of those roots were brought over by John Murchie in the late 1800s. After working for the Melrose Tea Company in his native Scotland, John and family emigrated to BC and opened the first Murchie's Tea Shop in New

▼

Coffee and Tea

▲

Westminster in 1894. In 1908, John began roasting fine coffee beans at his first Vancouver location—an oasis in an otherwise bleak coffee scene. Murchie's has been educating and refining itself as well as the palates of Vancouverites for 100 years now. It has chosen a lighter roast to bring out and preserve varietal nuance, and beans are always fresh (any beans that post-roast get dumped after seven days). Choose from more than 40 blends and varietals, including the house blend (Murchie's Best). There are some 50 varieties and blends of tea: loose and bagged. John Murchie's No. 10 blend is literally world renowned. It's sold by mail in more than 40 countries. This longtime merchant has assembled an engaging collection of brewing paraphernalia and gifts, from clay teapots and English bone china to samplers, gift boxes, and traditional chocolate-coated ginger. ■ *970 Robson St (and branches); 669-0783; map:S3; every day.*

Secret Garden Tea Co. Ltd. Care to partake of a full afternoon tea? Sip perfectly brewed tea and nibble finger sandwiches, pastries, and scones? This is the place. Snugly settled in staid Kerrisdale, the Secret Garden offers a choice of more than 100 types of tea from around the world and traditional treats baked right on premises. Take some tea away for home brewing. ■ *5559 W Blvd; 261-3070; map:C4; every day.*

▼

**Coffee
and Tea**

▲

Starbucks Vancouver coffee bars can thank Starbucks for making coffee fashionable here in 1991. After a successful market probe of its first Vancouver location (under another name), the Seattle-based company brought its ebony roast to the city and hit the jackpot. Passersby find it hard to resist that distinct aroma wafting from open transoms. Service is rapid and drinks well executed by a highly trained young team of swirling baristas who are eager to share their knowledge. Snag a cup on the run, or sit down in the sleek, Italian-style bar and put on your cheaters to eyeball and be eyeballed. Choose from 33 blends, varietals, and seasonal offerings. Committed to freshness and service, Starbucks gives local charities any beans that do not sell in seven days. You can also enjoy a sampling of pies, oat bars, and Belgian brownies. Like the other 60-plus outlets, the shop stocks affordable and upscale brewing paraphernalia, including the ever-popular Bodum. ■ *1099 Robson Street (and branches); 685-1099; map:R3; every day.*

The Tearoom at Plaza Escada Hidden away in this savagely pricey designer store is a coolly sophisticated, granite-and-black-leather spot for tea—the flagship Canadian venue for Banana Republic founder Mel Ziegler's "Republic of Tea." To showcase his exquisitely packaged offerings, this tearoom offers tea for free, provided you're content to sip Cinnamon Plum or Earl Greyer or whatever else they're sampling that day. Otherwise, it's three bucks a pop, a charge they waive should you do any shopping, which is easy enough. Surrounding you are both teas and the accoutrements of tea-making, such as handsomely designed teapots and various gourmet nibbles—all highly tempting and all for sale. ∎ *757 West Hastings St; 688-8558; map:T3; Mon–Sat.*

Tearoom T It's nice to find people who take an interest in their work, but these folks are obsessed! In a sedate, polite way, of course. This tea shop offers 170 different tea leaves and blends, including non-caffeinated teas, fruit tisanes, and herbals. Drop by for a tea tasting on the first Sunday of the month, or take a tea tour. And if you're just coming in for an afternoon "cuppa," they'll do their best to do it the traditional way; either English, with locally made scones and Devonshire cream, or in a special Chinese tea service that gets the most from each infusion. They carry an extensive selection of tea ware, cups, pots, and kettles from Alessi, Cardew, and Prandelli. They really know their stuff, and they're happy to make up gift baskets or put together an order for mail order. ∎ *2460 Heather St; 874-8320; map:S7; every day.*

Ten Ren Tea & Ginseng Co. Bordered by the sensory pleasures of Chinatown and the squalor of Skid Row, a visit to Ten Ren is a unique, vigorous experience. You'll find no chrome tea balls or cosies here. One of 78 shops worldwide, Ten Ren offers many varieties and grades of Chinese tea: loose or in bags, green, baked or fermented. Popular are Ti Kwan, jasmine, and King's Tea (the Ten Ren blend). Fortify yourself as you browse with a ginger or ginseng tea on tap. To the newcomer, the staff can seem anxious for you to buy—it's really just enthusiastic to share its delicious teas. If you show even a slight interest, you'll likely be invited to share a private tea ceremony, where you will learn much about the art and rites of Chinese brewing. Why not request to try something particular? The north wall showcases many types and grades of ginseng. Most of it arrives not from the east but from the ideal climate and soil of Wisconsin. Beyond tea and ginseng, many tiny clay pots are presented—handcrafted works of art. Those burdened with cash can drop $300 on a service for six; however, less pricey accoutrements are also offered. Despite the Lower Mainlands' craze for coffee, that insidious drink gets a thumbs down from Ten Ren. Tea is as popular as ever here. ∎ *550 Main St; 684-1566; map:V4; every day.*

Urban Expresso Hewed into the concrete base of a downtown building, this dimly lit grotto offers fast coffee, sandwiches, salads, and baked edibles to fortify the BC Tel bunch by day. By night, Urban's black brew fortifies the younger crowd while noise from the street blends with the pulse of the music and the hiss of the cappuccino maker. Bring your own mug to avoid paper cups. ∎ *605 Robson St; 681-3987; map:T4; every day.*

▼
Coffee and Tea
▲

CONSIGNMENT

The Comeback A consignment shop with designer labels. There's a fast turnover, so shop often. ■ *3050 Edgemont Blvd, North Vancouver; 984-2551; map:E1; Mon–Sat.*

Kisa's of Kerrisdale Down the stairs through the ivy-bedecked entrance, you'll find a very nice selection of designer consignment fashion, jewellery, shoes, handbags, and accessories. Owner Christine Farris has an eye for the unique and offers new or gently worn clothing with well-known labels, many from Europe. ■ *2352 W 41st; 266-2885; map:C4; every day.*

MacGillycuddy's for Little People A consignment store for children, selling clothing, footwear, furniture, and some hand-knits. ■ *4881 Mackenzie St; 263-5313; map:C4; Mon–Sat.*

Turnabout Collections Ltd. High-quality consignment, carrying some designers. In any case, you'll get top fashion for your dollar. The W Broadway store is casual, fun, and funky for men and women. At South Granville it's prestige labels, labels, and more labels for women. ■ *3121 Granville St; 732-8115; map:D3* ■ *3060 W Broadway; 731-7762; map:C3; every day.*

▼

▲

COOKWARE

Basic Stock Cookware Enter this store and feel like a chef. There is rack after rack of shining pots and pans of every size and description, and gadgets, gadgets, gadgets. A selection of coffees and teas, and everything you need to make them in, is also offered. ■ *2294 W 4th Ave (and branches); 736-1412; map:N7; every day.*

The Cookshop When we say the Cookshop in City Square has a comprehensive selection of kitchenware basics, name brands, and gadgets, we are not exaggerating. In the 372-square-metre (4,000-square-foot) space, the friendly and knowledgeable staff has assembled anything you'd need or want to furnish your kitchen the right way—from Finnish El-Rod stainless steel cookware to butcher blocks and prep tables, and from John Boos to German Bosch kitchen machines. Cooking classes, offered in a separate kitchen, feature local chefs. There's also a branch in Coquitlam. ■ *3-555 W 12th Ave; 873-5683; map:D3; every day* ■ *1300-2929 Barnet Hwy, Coquitlam; 464-6266; map:K2; every day.*

Ming Wo Since 1917, Ming Wo has maintained the highest standards of quality in the cookware and kitchenware it carries. A large stock of hard-to-find items and a reputation for value have kept Vancouverites loyal to the store. You'll find Ming Wo in suburban shopping centres and several Vancouver locations, but the shop on Pender is the original. ■ *23 E Pender St (and branches); 683-7268; map:U4; every day.*

Tools & Techniques It concentrates on domestic and imported pots, pans, cooking aids, food processors, and cookbooks, but this West Van neighbourhood kitchen store also offers specialty food items. Classes and book signings by respected Vancouver cooks happen in the well-equipped demonstration kitchen. ■ *250-16th St; 925-1835; map:E3; every day.*

CRYSTAL AND CHINA

Atkinson's Recently relocated in a brand-new building at W Sixth Avenue and Granville, Atkinson's now has two floors for its patrons to pore over. Just visiting this store is a luxurious experience, and the lure of the European crystal, silver, and china can charm the credit card right out of your pocket. Splurge on Lalique, Baccarat, Christofle, and Limoges, or treat yourself to bed, table, and bath linen imported from Pratesi of Italy, and double damask Irish table linens. ■ *1501 W 6th Ave; 736-3378; map:P7; Tues–Sat.*

Presents of Mind Hand-crafted dinnerware and accessories for your table—and much more. ■ *3153 Granville St; 1736-6463; map:D3; Mon–Sat.*

DELICATESSENS

J, N & Z Deli This place smells wonderful, with its smoky hams, bacon, and sausages hanging neatly from a rack over the counter. The Polish kielbasas, Berliner ham, and smoked pork chops are legendary, and the locals' secret love is the incomparable red pepper and eggplant spread. ■ *1729 Commercial Dr; 251-4144; map:Z7; Tues–Sat.*

Jackson Meats Jackson's is best-known for its Turkey Royale: a turkey that is boned, then layered with sausage meat, ground ham, boneless chicken, and pheasant breasts. The drumsticks are stuffed with pork tenderloin. There's also a spectacular crown roast of lamb and smoked hams. Connoisseurs of finocchio sausage say Jackson's combination of pork, fennel, spices, cilantro, and Parmesan cheese is the best. There are other sausages worth trying, plus a good selection of—believe it or not—prime buffalo meat. ■ *2214 W 4th Ave; 733-9165; map:N7* ■ *2717 Granville St; 738-6328; map:D3; every day.*

RB's Gourmet Butchers Popular with locals, the English butcher at the Robson Public Market stocks rabbit, ris de veau (veal sweetbreads, once discarded and now an expensive delicacy), and perfectly aged beef. ■ *1610 Robson St; 685-6328; map:R2; every day.*

DEPARTMENT STORES

Army and Navy Even loyal aficionados are unusually closed mouthed about the "A & N Boutique"; the locales and the decor are strictly proletarian. But their semi-annual shoe sales have instigated manic mobs of matronly mavens; their designer sales cause complete breakdowns of social niceties. If you know your stuff you can find bargains in other departments, too. ■ *27 W Hastings St; 682-6644; map:U4* ■ *502 Columbia St, New Westminster; 526-4661; map:I5; every day.*

The Bay The Hudson's Bay Company has a long and romantic past, having served Canadians in one capacity or another for more than 300 years. Although the downtown store hasn't been around that long, it is a handsome heritage building. The times have caught up with The Bay gracefully; when the Granville SkyTrain Station was planted practically in its basement, the owners transformed the Lower Level into a series of bright and attractive boutiques. The other floors in the store have also received renovations to keep them up to date. The Bay is the only store in town to carry authentic Hudson's Bay blankets, with their distinctive coloured stripes on a cream background, and the jackets made from them. The store is connected to the Pacific Centre. ■ *Georgia and Granville St (and branches); 681-6211; map:T4; every day.*

Eaton's The history of this store, though not as long as The Bay's, is just as illustrious. The founder, Timothy Eaton, started it all back in Toronto, and today his descendants still own and operate the chain, which now reaches across Canada. Eaton's still holds a warm and sentimental spot in many rural regions, where the Eaton's catalogue—now discontinued—was the source for everything families put on, cooked on, or sat on. The downtown store, connected to the Pacific Centre, carries on the tradition with a large and varied selection, and a brand-name bargain centre on the seventh floor. ■ *701 Granville St (and branches); 685-7112; map:S4; every day.*

Holt Renfrew This prestigious national chain is one of Vancouver's most fashionable department stores. Designer fashion labels abound in large and tasteful selections for men, women, and children. There are even branches of Tiffany and Hermes within the store. The sales staff is very helpful, and you can get in on a few very nice sales during the year—but don't expect great bargains. However, quality is paramount throughout the store. ■ *633 Granville St; 681-3121; map:S4; every day.*

La Casa Gelato If you are seeking a slightly different taste, be sure to visit this ice cream emporium. It has 88 flavours of ice cream, many of which (we guarantee) you have never tried. How about ginger-garlic? Or wasabi, wild berries with jalapeño, cranberry with rosemary, or lemon tarragon? Luckily, they'll let you taste as many as you want before you buy. ■ *1033 Venables St (and branches); 251-3211; map:Y5; every day.*

Lesley Stowe Fine Foods *(see Specialty Foods)*

Sweet Obsession Lorne Williams and Steve Greenham turn out some of the best-tasting, most addictive desserts in town. Try their triple chocolate mousse and creamy fruit cheesecakes and you'll understand why they supply the finest Vancouver restaurants with finales. Sweet Obsession is also known for homemade lemon curd, biscotti, and hazelnut sponge with Frangelico and chocolate hazelnut cream. Everything is made from scratch with the finest ingredients, which helps make this eat-in or take-out the shop of the moment. ■ *2611 W 16th Ave; 739-0555; map:C3; Tues–Sun.*

True Confections These dessert outlets sell 20 kinds of grand cheesecakes, mile-high chocolate cakes, Belgian mousse tortes, pies, and more than 70 other desserts. ■ *866 Denman St; 682-1292; map:Q2* ■ *3701 W Broadway; 222-8489; map:B3; every day.*

▼

Fabrics

▲

FABRICS

Chintz & Company Floor-to-ceiling racks of fabrics and all the notions you'll need to whip up terrific-looking home decoration projects. The store also carries exotic and intriguing-looking wooden tables and accessories, racks of tassels, and piles of carved wooden fruit. Custom work is a specialty. ■ *950 Homer St; 689-2022; map:S5; every day.*

The Cloth Shop Just strolling into this store makes your fingers itch to create. You'll discover great quilting fabrics and supplies and lots of ideas for homey crafts, plus specialty fabrics and accessories for creating "heirloom bears." The shop runs its own classes on a variety of fabric crafts. ■ *4415 W 10th Ave; 224-1325; map:B3; every day.*

Dressew Supply Ltd. The weeks before Halloween find this store jammed with home sewers looking for the perfect fabric and notions to create a costume. Miles of aisles on two floors are lined with bolts of fabric, thread, buttons, trims, patterns, and craft supplies. ■ *337 W Hastings St; 682-6196 (phone lines are open 9-10am only); map:U4; Mon–Sat.*

Mr. Jax Fashion Fabrics Even if you can't sew a stitch, it's worth picking up some of this great-quality fabric to take along to your favourite dressmaker. You'll also find notions and (im)perfectly lovely "seconds" from the Jax line. ■ *316 W Cordova St; 684-7004; map:U3; every day.*

Ragfinders Decorators can often be found in this Kerrisdale store, chatting with the knowledgeable sales staff and comparing swatches. Good-quality manufacturers and the latest decorator fabrics are represented here. ■ *2045 W 41st Ave; 266-3611; map:C4; every day.*

FLORISTS AND GARDEN SHOPS

The Avant Gardener This is a great store for the serious gardener or the confirmed browser (and what gardener isn't both?). Gardening stock and patio furniture sit alongside decorator accents and designer T-shirts. ■ *1460 Marine Dr, West Vancouver; 926-8784* ■ *2235 W 4th Ave; 736-0404; map:O7; every day.*

Dig This This is a faux-ivy-covered cottage on Granville Island offering supplies for indoor and outdoor gardening as well as decorator accents. A large stock of garden and outdoor furniture can be found. ■ *1551 Johnston St, Granville Island; 688-2929; map:Q6; every day.*

Garden Rooms If your idea of backyard furniture is restricted to beach chairs and tire swings, here's your chance to redecorate the out-of-doors. Garden Rooms' furniture, accents, and handy gadgets make outdoor living gracious living. ■ *2083 Alma St; 224-8900; map:B2; every day.*

Gloriosa Fine Flowers Inc. A bright and budding addition to Yaletown, this shop is gaining fans and a blooming reputation for its arrangements, particularly for special occasions. ■ *1033 Cambie St; 687-3435; map:T5; Mon–Fri, Sat by appointment.*

Hillary Miles Flowers Hillary Miles has been collaborating with designers for more than 20 years, and she brings her sense of style to set decoration, weddings, special events, and this colourful shop. ■ *1-1854 W 1st Ave; 737-2782; map:O6; Mon–Sat.*

Southlands Nursery Now under the skillful guidance of renowned local gardener and florist Thomas Hobbs, the nursery offers indoor and outdoor plants—plus the perfect containers in which to display them. Hobbs is known for his expertise with (and fondness for) orchids, so expect a good selection. ■ *6550 Balaclava St; 261-6411; map:C4; every day.*

Thomas Hobbs Florist by Maureen Sullivan Though under the new ownership of Maureen and Jim Sullivan, this remains one of the finest florists—and certainly the best-known one—in the Vancouver area. Tasteful and creative arrangements are presented in handsome containers. ▪ *2127 W 41st Ave; 263-2601 or (800) 663-2601; map:C4; every day.*

GIFTS AND JEWELLERY

Birks When Henry Birks opened his doors in the beginning of the last century, he could hardly have known that one day his empire would stretch from sea to sea. Birks stores are found in every major Canadian city. For generations, brides have received their engagement rings from Birks, have registered with Birks, and have received their subsequent anniversary presents from Birks—all in that distinctive blue box, which carries a cachet as exciting as the gift it holds. The Vancouver branch has recently relocated to a heritage building, which means locals have had to re-set their compasses for Hastings Street when they meet "under the Birks clock." ▪ *698 Hastings St (and branches); 669-3333; map:T3; every day.*

Catbalue Designer and goldsmith Mary Ann Buis creates dazzling custom jewellery in her on-site workshop/gallery. ▪ *1832 W 1st Ave; 734-3259; map:O7; Tues–Sat.*

Chachkas Whether you're looking for the perfect little gift for a friend or a selfish little treat for yourself, you'll find plenty to choose from at this shop, which carries a large selection of jewellery, decorative items, prints, and imports. ▪ *1075 Robson St; 688-6417; map:R3; every day.*

Georg Jensen Jensen's classic turn-of-the-century designs—all executed in silver—vie for attention with modern styles. This store is part of the international chain founded by the Danish designer and features high-quality jewellery, crystal, and decor items. ▪ *Pacific Centre; 688-3116; map:T4; every day.*

Karl Stittgen Goldsmiths Another local favourite with far-reaching repute, designer Karl Stittgen creates fabulous handmade jewellery of gold and gems. Singularly handsome pieces are often one-of-a-kind. ▪ *2203 Granville St; 737-0029; map:P7; Tues–Sat.*

Lightheart & Co. Whoever said it is better to give than to receive probably had this store in mind. It has the most divine ready-made gift baskets: not only are the baskets themselves charmingly textural and funky, but the contents include everything you could imagine to ensure perfect party (or tête-à-tête) chemistry. (In one basket, designed for a romantic evening, are candles for atmosphere, chocolate truffles for dessert, and a cassette of classical music to help set the mood.) Sherri Lightheart is a human dynamo with taste, which is probably why her shops have picked up such a devoted clientele. She's a Murchie

▼

Gifts and Jewellery

▲

by birth, the coffee family name that in Vancouver is synonymous with "high standards." Her staff will prepare custom baskets if you give it enough notice. Brides flock here for the terrific registry service, which includes a special discount for the bride, free gift wrapping and delivery, and a fabulous selection of crystal, china, decorative items, and linen. ■ *535 Howe St; 684-4711 or (800) 474-4711; map:T3* ■ *375 Water St; 685-8255; map:U3; every day.*

Martha Sturdy A local star with international impact, Martha Sturdy creates simple, charming jewellery designs. Although her artistic renderings change to reflect current fashions, her jewellery remains a classic collectible. ■ *3039 Granville St; 737-0037;map:D3* ■ *775 Burrard St; 685-7751; map:S3; every day.*

Moulé As well as attracting unique pieces from local artists and artisans, the owners of Moulé have scoured the globe and returned with treasures. Giftware, uncommon locally designed ladies' fashions, and a bridal registry service. ■ *1994 W 4th Ave; 732-4066; map:O7* ■ *Park Royal South, West Vancouver; 925-3679; map:D1; every day.*

▼
Gifts and Jewellery
▲

The Museum Co. Inc. This unique and clever store features reproductions from museums around the world. The jewellery, statuary, stained glass, decorative pieces, and stationery are faithful copies of items made in other times, in many other places. You'll find the startlingly realistic paintings of the Canadian-made Artagraph series, which reproduces each brushstroke of the original masterpiece. There's also a great section of artful games and toys for kids—and their parents. ■ *Pacific Centre; 688-1502; map:T4; every day.*

Susan Clark Gallery of Gem Art Inc. The artful use of carved and facetted gemstones combined with yellow and white gold is what makes these unique pieces so sought after. Designer and gemmologist Susan Clark oversees production of each unique bijou at her on-site workshop. ■ *Penthouse, 555 W Georgia St; 688-3553; map:T4; Tues–Sat.*

Tiffany The first name in jewellery can be found at Holt Renfrew in the Pacific Centre. Conscious of Vancouver's loyalty to Birks jewellers, sales staff members point out that they are "the other blue box." You can expect to find classic Tiffany items, watches, Paloma Picasso-designed jewellery, and Elsa Peretti jewellery. ■ *Holt Renfrew in the Pacific Centre; 681-3121; map:T3; every day.*

Toni Cavelti Toni Cavelti is an award-winning goldsmith and jeweller and a Vancouver tradition. His store on Georgia Street is a gemlike setting for his art—please check out the magnificent mural on the east side of the building. It is a magnet for the rich, the powerful, and the beautiful. But we can all afford to gaze into his shop windows. ■ *565 W Georgia St; 681-3481; map:T4; Mon–Sat.*

HARDWARE

Hewer Home Hardware One of those neighbourhood hardware stores where you're just as likely to pick up a toaster as a power tool or a can of paint. Serves the Point Grey area. ■ *4459 W 10th Ave; 224-4934; map:B3; Mon–Sat.*

Lumberland At first, this chain of stores looks just like any other building supply outlet. The differences are subtle but telling. This local, privately owned chain buys almost all its stock from local suppliers, ensuring that stock on hand is current and complete. And because they're not paying for transport and storage, prices are usually lower than the competition's. Even contractors buy here. ■ *2889 E 12th Ave (and branches); 254-1614; map:F3; every day.*

Paine Hardware Limited This hardware-cum-general store has been around since 1908—and it looks it. You can get a fishing licence or outfit your RV, and you'll find everything from penny nails to lawn mowers to explosives. ■ *90 Lonsdale Ave, North Vancouver; 987-2241; map:E1; every day.*

Steveston Marine & Hardware This is the place to find those great-looking brass fittings to add that nautical look to your home. The shop's fabulous antique brass stock varies, giving you an excuse to drop by to see what's on hand or to stock up on power tools, hoses, or marine paint. ■ *3560 Moncton St, Richmond; 277-7031; map:C7; every day.*

▼

Health Food and Products

▲

HEALTH FOOD AND PRODUCTS

Alive Health Centre This chain of stores, found in many of the city's major shopping centres, exudes health and goodwill. There are shelves upon shelves of herbs and vitamins, a good selection of cosmetics, and every yogurt maker and juicer imaginable. A great selection of books to teach you how to get healthy and stay that way. Seniors' discount. ■ *Oakridge Centre (and branches); 263-3235; map:D4; every day.*

Capers Long the private haunt of the health-conscious in West Vancouver, Capers moved to Kitsilano and is jammed. These are the largest "whole foods" markets (and restaurants) in the Lower Mainland, with some 557 square metres (6,000 square feet) in West Vancouver and even larger premises in Kits, devoted to bringing healthier foodstuffs our way. At press time, a Capers has opened on Robson Street as well. Milk is sold in glass bottles, the eggs are free range, and the fresh meat is organic. ■ *2490 Marine Dr, West Vancouver (and branches); 925-3316; every day.*

Choices Market This friendly, family-run grocery makes it easy to shop for allergen-sensitive diets. Its lists of a variety of wheat-free, yeast-free, and dairy-free products comply with dietary rules (and they provide enough selection and flavor for the most discriminating palate). Organic beef and free-run chicken are available, as are all manner of natural foods. ■ *2627 W 16th Ave; 736-0009; map:P3; every day.*

Finlandia Pharmacy When the subject of healthy lifestyle comes up (as it inevitably does in Vancouver), the name Finlandia Pharmacy is often quoted as the "only" place for vitamins, herbal products, and herbal teas; yet inside this spacious and scrupulously clean store there is much, much more. You'll find energy boosters, wellness books, natural sponges and bath brushes, homeopathic allergy remedies, and the full line of BWC (Beauty Without Cruelty) cosmetics. ■ *1964 W Broadway; 733-5323; map:O7; every day.*

Gaia Garden Herbal Apothecary The walls here are lined with oak apothecary cabinets filled with large jars of familiar and exotic herbs. Herbalist Chanchal Cabrera takes appointments for private consultation and also leads "wildcrafting" workshops for the uninitiated. If you're seeking a healthy diet plan or cleansing regimen, this is the place. ■ *2672 W Broadway; 734-4372; map:C3; Mon–Sat.*

The Vitamin Experts Bulk up with bulk vitamins. This chain has some discounts on larger sizes. It also offers personalized service and advice, and it carries lots of new and used books if you want to look it up yourself. Mail-order service. ■ *Pacific Centre (and branches); 685-8487; map:T4; every day.*

HOME FURNISHINGS

Bali Bali Galleria A favourite importer of the exotic and the exciting; a delightful source of handicrafts and objets d'art from the fabled East, including Bali, Java, India, and Tibet. ■ *4462 W 10th Ave; 224-2347; map:B3; every day.*

Bernstein & Gold Everything in this lifestyle store is keyed to the cream and gold decor—for a luxe appeal. Overstuffed and slipcovered pieces are made in BC, accessories are imported from Europe. Beds and bedding abound. ■ *1168 Hamilton St; 687-1535; map:T5; every day.*

Chintz & Company *(See Fabrics)*

Country Furniture If anything is going to convince you of the beauty and simplicity of pioneer life, it's a visit to this store. Okay, so the pioneers may not have had these brilliant designs and whimsical decorative accents, but they should have. ■ *3097 Granville St; 738-6411; map:D3; every day.*

Form & Function Furniture, simply designed, simply beautiful. Much of the stock is made by the store's craftspeople. Custom furniture is also available. ■ *4357 W 10th Ave; 222-1317; map:B3; Tues–Sat.*

Freedom An eclectic mix of home furnishings and accessories are selected by the owners during their extensive travels and combined with pieces from local artists; they're then arrayed in themed displays (the Garden of Eden, Morocco, etc.) in this Yaletown store. A constant, however, is the 2-metre (7-foot) working fountain complete with cherub. ■ *1150 Hamilton St; 688-3163; map:T5; every day.*

Hobbs Veteran florist and gardener extraordinaire Thomas Hobbs owns this store, and he has filled it with chic imported accessories for interior/exterior design accents. ■ *2129 W 41st Ave; 261-5998; map:C4; every day.*

Industrial Revolution This store manages to make high-tech look romantic, and it has lots of those handy little accessories you didn't know you needed—till you fell in love with them here. ■ *2306 Granville St; 734-4395; map:Q7; every day.*

Kaya Kaya Is it a furniture store? A gift shop? A clothing boutique? Who cares? Beautiful Japanese imports with something for everyone. ■ *2039 W 4th Ave; 732-1816; map:O7; closed Sunday (except during July, August, and December).*

Knock Knock Designs Locally made wooden furniture and imported accessories mix with upholstered pieces for the "West Coast" look. A design consultant is on hand to help you with your selection. ■ *1045 Marine Dr, North Vancouver; 988-1675; map:E1* ■ *1091 Hamilton St; 687-0233; map:T4; every day.*

Living Space Interiors Whether you're redoing the whole house or just need the perfect knickknack for a corner, you'll find fascinating items from Europe and the guidance to put it all together. ■ *1550 Marine Dr, North Vancouver; 987-2253; map:E1* ■ *1100 Mainland; 683-1116; map:S5; Mon–Sat.*

Mōtiv There is a lot of cleverly wrought wrought iron here—and ceramic plates and bowls, primitive-looking baskets, and throws. This is a sister store to Ming Wo (see Cookware). ■ *2064 W 4th Ave; 737-8116; map:O7; every day.*

N. Bonaparte Designs Hand-picked, handmade furniture and home accessories are imported and brought here in a casual mix. If you need a little help putting it all together, that's here, too. ■ *1102 Homer St; 688-8555; map:S5; every day.*

Sofas à la Carte This furniture phenomenon is built on the maxim, "give the people what they want, and the world will beat a path to your door." Follow that path to this spacious store and select a style from the various sofas and chairs on display. Then choose a fabric from the huge selection of really big swatches lining the walls. Voilà, you can have your custom-built sofa delivered in as few as 16 working days, due to the modern miracle of a local factory. ■ *909 W Broadway; 731-9020; map:S7; every day.*

Sun Gallery Patio furniture for alfresco decorating. ■ *2572 Arbutus St; 736-6461; map:C3; every day.*

LINGERIE

Diane's Lingerie and Loungewear You'll receive kid-glove treatment from the helpful staff when choosing a gift. The store offers a large selection of underpinnings in all sizes from well-known manufacturers as well as sleepwear, ranging from prosaic jammies to sexy negligees. It also enjoys the distinction of having the largest selection of brassieres in Western Canada. ■ *2950 Granville St; 738-5121; map:D3; Mon–Sat.*

La Jolie Madame Ultra-feminine lingerie in a wide range of sizes. Much of the stock is imported. Friendly, knowledgeable staff. ■ *Pacific Centre; 669-1831; map:T4; every day.*

Monaliza's Clientele of the former Vanity store can rest easy: the reliable staff and outstanding selection have relocated to this Kerrisdale store. Favourite makers include the French Lejaby and Chantelle as well as robes and gowns by Linda. There's a satisfying choice of 100 percent cotton as well. ■ *2283 W 41st Ave; 266-4598; map:C4; Mon–Sat.*

NATIVE ART AND CRAFTS

Hill's Indian Crafts Located in Gastown, Hill's carries a wide selection of aboriginal art and handiwork, spread over three floors. Art ranges from original paintings and limited editions to carved gold and silver jewellery (the design is carved into the metal, not cast). Each is signed. Hill's is also the best-known source for beautiful, durable Cowichan sweaters. ■ *165 Water St; 685-4249; map:U3; every day.*

Leona Lattimer This small gallery features aboriginal art of extremely high calibre. Many items are purchased for collection. You'll find carvings, jewellery, prints, ceremonial masks, and drums and totems—all created by Native artists in the traditional motifs of the Northwest Coast aboriginal peoples. ■ *1590 W 2nd Ave; 732-4556; map:P7; every day.*

The Museum of Anthropology In addition to a fine selection of Northwest Coast Native art and books, the museum shop features Inuit prints, soapstone sculpture, and other handmade craftwork. ■ *UBC, 6393 NW Marine Dr; 822-5087; map:A2; every day.*

ONE-OF-A-KIND SHOPS

The Drivers Den Tucked away in Yaletown, this store is as close as you can get to the automotive experience without getting grease under your nails. From the remarkable vehicle displayed in the back of the store to the gift cards beside the till, everything centres around the worship of the car. You'll find models, hats, and much more—perfect gifts to rev someone's engine. ▪ *1007 Hamilton St; 687-2818; map:S5; every day.*

The Flag Shop Fly your colours. This is the place to find flags for the country, the province, and the city—as well as a surprising number of nonflag items like pins, crests, decals, and even wind socks. The shop will take orders by phone. ▪ *1755 W 4th Ave; 736-8161; map:P7; Mon–Sat.*

Golden Age Collectables It's hard to say which age these folks consider golden, but they do have a fine selection of movie posters, baseball and other sport cards—some bearing autographs—and other flotsam of youth. There are also lots of comic books and posters, and T-shirts with comic and comical designs. ▪ *830 Granville St; 683-2819; map:S4; every day.*

The Umbrella Shop Given Vancouver weather, it's easy to believe that this shop has been in business for over 50 years. You'll find a veritable deluge of bumbershoots in all sizes, shapes, and fabrics. Many of the umbrellas are constructed on the premises, will last for years, and can be repaired at the shop. ▪ *534 W Pender; 669-9444; map:T3; Mon–Sat.*

Wally's Folly The lamps, mirrors, and picture frames in this shop are not so much accessories as they are brilliant bijous. Writer, singer, and artist Judy Walchuk designs exuberant lamp shades under her J. Ginn label and executes them in beads and fabric. Bring in a treasured lamp for a custom-made crowning glory, or choose from the 300 she has in the store. The shop also features the charmingly eccentric mirrors, picture frames, and jewel boxes of local artist Linda Varro, each a unique and completely captivating objet d'art. ▪ *2255 W Broadway; 736-5848; map:N7; Thur, Fri and Sat afternoons or by appointment.*

Yerushalem Imports You can expect to find Hebrew greeting cards and seasonal items for Jewish holidays, but this shop also contains a treasure trove of gift ideas for recipients of every age and religious persuasion—all imported from the Holy Land. ▪ *2375 W 41st Ave; 266-0662; map:C4; every day.*

▼

Recordings, Tapes, CDs, Instruments

▲

RECORDINGS, TAPES, CDS, INSTRUMENTS

A & B Sound You can't always get what you want, but chances are you'll leave satisfied. Immediately identifiable by their orange buildings, these stores boast a large stock of records, tapes, and CDs at great prices as well as a good selection of electronics and even a small bookstore with good discounts. Their biannual sales draw lineups several blocks long. ▪ *556 Seymour St; 687-5837; map:T3; every day.*

Black Swan If you're tired of browsing your local chain store hoping for some international jazz or world music, check out Black Swan, which specializes in these plus folk and blues. The store carries some rare recordings and many hard-to-find numbers. Mail order is available. ▪ *3209 W Broadway; 734-2828; map:C3; every day.*

D & G Collectors Records Ltd. You'll find original discs from the '50s and '60s, including many "classics" of that era, and CD re-issues of discs from the 1920s and beyond. Mail-order service and special orders, too. ▪ *3580 E Hastings St; 294-5737; map:F2; every day.*

Highlife Records and Music This shop carries music from around the world, specializing in Latin, African, and Caribbean, as well as a selection of vintage instruments. ▪ *1317 Commercial Dr; 251-6964; map:Z6; every day.*

The Magic Flute Predictably, this store carries an extensive selection of classical and jazz music. It's a great gathering place for true classics fanatics, and it contains a good selection of CDs and videos. ▪ *2203 W 4th Ave; 736-2727; map:N7; every day.*

Neptoon Records An eclectic mix of just about everything, especially rare and out-of-print vinyl. You'll find lots of music-related memorabilia, including some hard-to-find concert posters from as far back as the '60s. ▪ *5750 Fraser St; 324-1229; map:E4; every day.*

Odyssey Imports Don't look for folk songs here. This is alternative, dance, and house music territory, with imports from the UK, France, Belgium, and Germany. T-shirts, posters, and magazines are also sold. ▪ *534 Seymour St; 669-6644; map:T3; every day.*

Sam the Record Man Sam is the godfather of retail music in Canada. Sam's doesn't look like a night club, and it doesn't constantly play the Top 40, but this family-run business claims knowledgeable employees and a real feel for musicalia. The five-storey downtown location also has a good stock of VHS and laser disc movies for sale. ▪ *568 Seymour St (and branches); 684-3722; map:T3; every day.*

Sikora's Classical Records In this huge store you can expect to find the usual stock of classics and some unusual recordings too. The staff is helpful. ▪ *432 W Hastings St; 685-0625; map:T3; every day.*

Tom Lee Music Just because the Arthur Murray Dance Studio is to be found in the same building as the downtown store doesn't mean you'll get a song and dance from these people! Tom Lee Music has the largest selection of musical instruments in the Lower Mainland and several floors from which to choose. It is the exclusive dealer for Bosendorfer pianos in the city, and also carries Yamaha, Petrof, and Steinway. ■ *929 Granville St (and branches); 685-8471; map:S4; every day.*

Virgin Megastore On the site of the old Vancouver Library, you'll find the first Virgin Megastore in Canada. Occupying three levels, Virgin carries the largest selection of music and entertainment in the country: more than 125,000 music titles on CDs and cassettes; 20,000 movie and music titles on video and laserdisc; the largest selection of entertainment multimedia software for IBM and MAC. There's an in-store deejay booth; 140 listening stations at which customers may sample music; and 20 video/laser viewing stations. This place rocks. ■ *788 Burrard St; 669-2289; map:S3; every day.*

West Indies Records and Tapes If your taste runs to reggae and calypso, this is the place for you. A good selection of Caribbean music. ■ *1855 Commercial Dr; 254-4232; map:Z7; every day.*

Zulu Records New wave, punk, folk, grunge, hip-hop, reggae, rap, and other modern sounds. The store also carries its own label of independent recordings. ■ *1869 W 4th Ave; 738-3232; map:O7; every day.*

▼

Seafood

▲

SEAFOOD

Jet Set Sam Once a storefront operation, Jet Set Sam's is now strictly mail order, specializing in packaging fine BC salmon for travel. They'll mail corporate gifts—in special cedar presentation boxes with personalized engraving—anywhere in the world. Among the varieties of seafood are several species of salmon (smoked, of course), Indian candy (salmon cured in brown sugar, then cooked and smoked), salmon jerky, canned smoked salmon, many varieties of crab, fresh whole salmon, salmon steaks and roasts, salmon pâtés and salmon butter, pickled smoked salmon, shrimp, prawns, and scallops. ■ *653 Gerard Ave, Coquitlam; 279-9521 (fax, 936-1529); map:K3; every day.*

The Lobster Man Buy your lobsters while they're still kicking. In addition to live lobsters, the Lobster Man sells a wide variety of seafood-related gift items (utensils, accessories, and spices, among other things) for those hard-to-please friends. They'll even pack your crustaceans at no extra charge for travel or shipping. ■ *1807 Mast Tower Rd, Granville Island, Maritime Market; 687-4531; map:Q6; every day.*

Longliner Sea Foods The Longliner is one of the best fish markets on Granville Island. Expect to find Vancouver's professional cooks eyeing the goods along with you. Pristine scallops, giant prawns, squid, and whole fish shine alongside less common fishy fare. The staff is generous with cooking advice. ■ *1689 Johnston St, Granville Island; 681-9016; map:Q6; every day (closed Monday in winter).*

The Salmon Shop Once upon a time, the Salmon Shop ran its own fishing boats, but alas, no more, and the prices reflect that change. Still, if you want premium quality, it's here for the taking. Stock includes mahi-mahi and swordfish as well as the best of the local catch, such as octopus, lingcod, and salmon. The smoked salmon is wonderful. ■ *1610 Robson St, Robson Public Market (and branches); 688-FISH (3474); map:Q2; every day.*

SHOES

Bentall Centre Shoe Repair If your sole needs a little TLC, this little shop can help you out in its downtown location and make repairs while you wait. ■ *Bentall Centre, Lower Level, Dunsmuir St at Burrard St; 688-0538; map:T3; Mon–Fri.*

▼

Seafood

▲

John Fluevog Yes, Virginia, there really is a John Fluevog, and he is alive and creating great footwear right here in Vancouver. Indescribably funky shoes. Doc Martens too. ■ *837 Granville St; 688-2828; map:S4; every day.*

Lexy Shoes Fashionable footwear for milady, including names like Nine-West, Evan Picone, Bandolino, and Unisa. ■ *Oakridge Centre; 266-5401; map:D4; every day.*

Melonari Custom Made Shoes Husband and wife Gildo and Livia Melonari started out cobbling exquisite custom-made shoes in the basement of their home. Eventually they moved to their garage, then to a shop, finally to their present location, two blocks west of Clark near Venables. Along the way, they collected a loyal following of shoe fanciers, and they keep them very happy with their very high quality. As well as custom shoes, they stock standard sizes of fine women's footwear, all made right there in their shop. ■ *1165 William St; 255-4459; map:Y5; Mon–Sat.*

Rainbow Shoes Kids' shoes, cute and comfortable. There's a healthy stock of Keds, Nike, Reebok, and so on, and they're always on the look out for innovative footwear. They'll also donate your kids' old shoes to children's charity and give you a 5-percent discount to boot. ■ *4535 Dunbar St; 222-8448; map:B3; every day.*

Salvatore Ferragamo High-quality Italian shoes for men and women from this world-famous maker. Choose a classic style and, with care, you'll still be wearing these shoes years from now. ■ *918 Robson St; 669-4495; map:S3; Mon–Sat.*

Silvano's Shoe Renew Cobbler sevices while you wait. ■ *520 Robson St; 685-5413; map:S4; Mon–Fri.*

Simard & Voyer Shoes Fashion- and quality-conscious men and women enjoy these stylish shoes. Well-made imports are a specialty. ■ *1049 Robson St; 689-2536; map:R3* ■ *Oakridge Centre; 263-1080; map:D4; every day.*

Stephane de Raucourt Locals are fanatical about footwear from this retailer. Fashionable, high-quality women's shoes from Italy, fitted by an especially helpful staff. ■ *1067 Robson St; 681-8814; map:R3* ■ *Oakridge Shopping Centre; 261-7419; map:D4; every day.*

Western Town Boots Serious wranglers—and wrangler wannabes—come here for boots from Tony Lama, Lucchese, and Boulet. Assorted real Western duds as well. ■ *2490 Main St; 879-1914; map:V7; every day.*

SKIN AND HAIR CARE

Aveda Comfort and joy for body and soul with a full line of aromatherapy skin and hair products. All products are made from essential oils from plants and flowers with special properties to calm or rejuvenate. The Chakra line of perfumes works on the seven energy centres in the body. Diffuser oils, rings for your lamps, mists to use in your car, and sterling silver decanters of essential oils to wear around your neck are offered, and Aveda also offers aromatherapy massages, makeup consultation, and eclectic monthly clinics (explore reflexology, blending essential oils, or tapping into your personal energy centres). ■ *1228 Robson St; 688-6727; map:R3; every day.*

Avenir Beauty Consultants The owner, Roger (pronounced Roget, like the thesaurus), has gathered a staff offering complete wedding and makeover services with hair stylists, aestheticians, and the best makeup artist in Vancouver. ■ *2355 Spruce St; 731-1798; map:R7; Tues–Sat.*

Bianches Health & Beauty Clinic Ltd. The 90-minute facial is a mini-vacation. Manicures, pedicures, eyelash tints, and aromatherapy massage are also available. ■ *2741 Granville St; 732-7265; map:D3; every day.*

The Body Shop Anita Roddick's concern for health and the environment is reflected in the selection of beauty and body products at her shops. A large selection of items and minimally packaged products that do the body (and the soul) good. There are tons of locations. ■ *Oakridge Centre (and branches); 261-3381; map:D4; every day.*

Crabtree & Evelyn Choose a gift for a friend and one for yourself at this English shop, which is world famous for its most delightful old-fashioned scented soaps and bath accessories. The shop also sells some of the best teas, jams, and biscuits this side of the Thames. ▪ *Pacific Centre (and branches); 662-7211; map:T4; every day.*

La Raffinage Pampering the body, mind, and soul is the specialty of this full-service spa, which offers regular hair and aesthetic services as well as many New Age therapies, such as energy massage, Reiki, reflexology, aromatherapy, spiritual readings, and more. The spa's gallery-styled reception displays inspiring works of art as well as home care products for the physical, mental, and spiritual body. Ask about the workshop and lecture series. ▪ *501 W Georgia St; 681-9933; map:T4; every day.*

London Drugs *(See Cameras)*

Lush The word on these shops selling "bath basics" has spread like wildfire in just a few years. Lush carries skin care and bath products that pamper and please, and all are made locally. Their "must try" is the Bath Bomb, a richly scented concoction that makes the most mundane ablution a wickedly wonderful experience. ▪ *1118 Denman St; 608-1810; map:P2* ▪ *3084 Granville St; 730-0332; map:D3; every day.*

▼

**Skin and
Hair Care**

▲

Optaderm This skin care shop, and the skin care products and cosmetics of the same name, have garnered a fanatical following over the past decade. Drop by for one of the shop's luxurious European facials and pick up some fabulous lotions and potions: they're happy to supply samples. All products are made locally. ▪ *355-2184 W Broadway; 737-2026; map:N7; Tues–Sat.*

Patina Salon Clients tell us this salon is "divine," pampering them with facials, manicures, pedicures, and makeup application. The salon features two skin care lines from France: Duino and Yon Ka. ▪ *1512 W 11th Ave; 737-7060; map:D3; Mon–Sat.*

Robert Andrew Salon and Spa Relocated in the newly renovated Hotel Vancouver, this total body care salon will indulge you head to toe seven days a week with its own skin care line and treatments from Karin Herzog of New York. Also on offer are full hair care services plus massage and hydrotherapy. Get ready to be spoiled! ▪ *900 W Georgia St; 687-7133; map:S3; every day.*

Suki's Suki's has long been an established name in Vancouver for exceptional hair cuts and care. Here you are assured the best cut and the best head massage (called a shampoo) at any one of its three locations. The state-of-the-art South Granville shop was designed by noted local architect Arthur Erickson;

that's where you'll find haircutter extraordinaire Suki, who is also a nail technician and aesthetician. The salons are open seven days a week and some evenings for busy clients. ■ *3157 Granville St (and branches); 738-7713; map:D3; every day.*

Tech 1 Hair Design The comfort of the clientele is all-important at this salon. From the sophistication of the slate and granite floors in the elegant bathroom to the genteel touch of tea served in china cups, everywhere you'll find a relaxing ambience. As well as offering the best haircolouring from two resident colour technicians, Julian and John, a full-service aesthetician offers manicures and macquillage. ■ *1057 Cambie St; 682-1202; map:T5; every day.*

Versailles Spa This European "water-based" spa is attracting ladies—and gentlemen—to its large facilities at 1st and Burrard. The spa specializes in body care, including massages, wraps, peels, aromatherapy, and eucalyptus steam rooms. Indulge yourself, or each other, with these special treatments. ■ *1838 W 1st Ave; 732-7865; map:O6; every day.*

SPECIALTY FOODS

A. Bosa & Co. Ltd. This is truly a one-stop shop for a culinary expedition to Italy. Here you will find a fine selection of cookware, including pasta-making paraphernalia and equipment for creating specialty dishes. The store also stocks fine European foods, restaurant and delicatessen supplies, and California grapes for winemaking. In short, everything you need for Italian cooking—including the finest extra virgin olive oil. ■ *562 Victoria Dr; 253-5578; map:F3; Mon–Sat.*

All India Foods Here in the heart of bustling "Little India," around Main Street and 53rd Avenue, you'll find unlimited choices of specialty foods and seasonings at this supermarket-size Indian food emporium. The narrow aisles are crowded with more stock than you can imagine. Choose from a vast array of chutneys, curry powders, cardamom seed, saffron, chilies, and other items in more varieties, sizes, and forms than you'll find anywhere else in town. There are also bulk foods, fresh produce, and some of the cheapest milk prices around. Next door, All India Sweets offers confections and a warm and hospitable sit-down cafe. ■ *6517 Main St; 324-1686; map:E4; every day.*

Epicure's Cupboard This attractive gift shop features nonperishable food items exclusively from Canada and the United States—primarily from Canada's West Coast. A great many gleaming jars and pots from small "cottage" suppliers sit on the shelves, so you'll find lots of one-of-a-kind items. Make up your own bag, box, or basket, or have the helpful staff select for you. ■ *5633 W Blvd; 264-8200; map:C4; every day.*

Famous Foods The key to Famous Foods' bargain prices is its repackaging of bulk quantities into small packages, reducing the time spent measuring and weighing. The savings are passed along to the customer. Unlike bulk food outlets, there's no worry about bin contamination; and constant turnover ensures that grains, pasta, and spices are fresh. Added to its superior stock of spices are special deals on bulk peanut butter, honey, and grains as well as an impressive assortment of cheeses. ▪ *1595 Kingsway; 872-3019; map:E3; every day.*

The First Ravioli Store A change of name has not changed Vancouver's oldest and most popular Italian supermarket. It presents an impressive array of fresh pasta and sauces. People crowd the aisles on weekends in pursuit of unusual canned items, olive oils, imported pasta, marinated vegetables, and deli meats. ▪ *1900 Commercial Dr; 255-8844; map:Z7; every day.*

Forster's Fine Cheeses Steve Forster stocks more than 200 types of cheese, cheese spreads, and biscuits. He'll be happy to tell you anything and everything he knows about cheese, while convincing you to try his fresh and aged chèvres from Canada and France. Meat, fish pâté, and Italian pickled onions in balsamic vinegar are available as well. ▪ *2104 W 41st Ave; 261-5813; map:C4; Mon–Sat.*

Fujiya These stores are the best source for Japanese foods and pearl rice in town. They also have weekly specials and carry a wide variety of inexpensive kitchenware, including steamers, woks, and kitchen tools. You'll find some of the best buys in sushi supplies here, such as those hard-to-find bamboo mats for rolling rice in nori. Take-out sashimi available. ▪ *912 Clark Dr (and branches); 251-3711; map:Z4; every day.*

Galloway's The combination of herbs, spices, Indian chutneys, curry pastes, and dried fruit makes this place an aromatic spot for leisurely shopping. This is also the place to find that elusive Mexican vanilla and crunchy Indian snacks such as roast green peas, pumpkin seeds, and nuts. ▪ *904 Davie St (and branches); 685-7927; map:R4; Mon–Sat.*

La Fromagerie This little treasure of a cheese counter is located in Lesley Stowe Fine Foods. Unpasteurized goat cheeses, English Stiltons, and Canadian cheeses coupled with the staff's knowledge make it a treat to explore and experiment here. ▪ *1780 West 3rd Ave (in Lesley Stowe Fine Foods); 731-3663; map:O7; every day.*

La Grotta Del Formaggio Here is where you find the city's largest variety of Italian cheeses. The store also stocks tarragon-flavoured balsamic vinegar, imported tinned fish, olive oils, Italian cookies, panettone, and fresh yeast for the bread baker. ▪ *1791 Commercial Dr; 255-3911; map:Z7; every day.*

Lesley Stowe Fine Foods When Buy and Lie is the best revenge, head to this top-notch take-out (or eat-in) and catering establishment. The shop is brimming with myriad starters, main courses, desserts, breads, specialty foods, and fine cheeses, and you'll soon have a slew of requests for recipes. Stowe has those too, with a stock of fine food magazines and best-selling cookbooks. Special Christmas baskets include "The Antipasto Planter" (terra-cotta planter filled with goodies); "The Nutcracker Sweet"; "The Office Party"; and "The Pantry"—the perfect hostess assortment. Lesley Stowe is also the only retail source for Valrhona chocolate. ▪ *1780 West 3rd Ave; 731-3663; map:P7; every day.*

Meinhardt Fine Foods There's a good selection of gourmet and imported goodies, and a very nice deli with take-out in this South Granville supermarket. True to its health-food roots, it doesn't sell cigarettes, but you can pick up quality housewares and health care items, and a canvas bag to carry it home. (See *Meinhardt Fine Foods* in the Restaurants chapter.) ▪ *3002 Granville St; 732-4405; map:D3; every day.*

Minerva's Mediterranean Deli If you don't feel like cooking up a Grecian feast from the imported foods available, just visit the deli section and pick up something tasty. For do-it-yourself types, olives, olive oils, cheeses, and other necessities are all here. You can also linger on the heated deck outside and sip a cappucino or savour an ice cream. ▪ *3207 W Broadway; 733-3956; map:C3; every day.*

Parthenon Wholesale & Retail Food It's not a Greek island, but on a rainy day it's great to make believe while nibbling such delicacies as taramasalata, baklava, dolmades, Greek olives, and feta. Signs in Hellenic-style lettering add to the ethnic shopping experience. ▪ *2968 W Broadway; 733-4191; map:C3; every day.*

Que Pasa Mexican Foods Que Pasa is Vancouver's best source for the elusive spices and ingredients needed for Central American cooking. This small shop carries a variety of Mexican deli items and fresh vegetables for Mexican cooking: tomatillos, chiles, cactus, and jicama. There are many brands of salsa, including the store's own chunky style (in hot, medium, and mild) as well as its superlative tortilla chips. We've also discovered piñatas, Mexican candles, margarita glasses, and candleholders featuring green glass cactus-shaped bases. Que Pasa also sells a practical *molcajete*—a kind of mortar and pestle for grinding rice into flour—and has a good stock of Mexican cookbooks. ▪ *3315 Cambie St; 874-0064; map:D3; every day.*

South China Seas Trading Co. It's easy to see why people flock to South China Seas Trading Co. on Granville Island: co-owner Kay Leong is familiar with every item and is always ready with advice. The shop stocks an incredible variety of spices, fresh herbs, condiments, sauces, noodles, and prepared ethnic items from Asia, Southeast Asia, Africa, and the Caribbean. Fresh herbs are flown in direct from the country of origin. ▪ *1689 Johnston St, Granville Island; 681-5402; map:Q6; every day (closed Monday in winter).*

The Stock Market Owners Georges and Joanne LeFebvre used to delight guests with their culinary expertise at their restaurant "Le Chef et sa Femme." Now they help you delight your guests with the complete selection of stocks, sauces, dressings, and marinades available at their Granville Island Shop. Everything is fresh and made with no preservatives, so selection depends on the season, but you can depend on finding and enjoying their soups made every day with fresh ingredients. ▪ *1689 Johnston St, Granville Island; 687-2433; map:Q6; summer, every day; winter, Tues–Sun.*

Yaohan Supermarket and Shopping Centre Where can you find more than 20 varieties of Japanese soya sauce, fresh wasabe root, matsutake mushrooms, or squid with smelt roe? Try the Yaohan Supermarket at the new Yaohan Centre—the first Canadian branch of one of the largest department store chains in Asia. Here you can also find ready-for-the-pot precut sukiyaki beef; sushi-grade salmon, tuna, and geoduck; and ready-for-the-pot precut black cod, snapper, pomfret, mackerel, mushrooms, and napa cabbage. This may be the largest supermarket fish department in the Lower Mainland. Across the concourse, in the food court, 15 outlets provide a smorgasbord of Asian fast foods, such as Buddhist vegetarian dishes, Singapore/Malaysian specialties, Vietnamese pho, Northern Chinese dim sum, Chiu Chow stir-fries, Hong Kong coffee shop food, and a Japanese yakitori bar. The centre also features retail shops on the second level as well as a games arcade, a medical centre, and the largest Japanese bookstore in Vancouver. ▪ *3700 No 3 Rd, Richmond; 276-8808; map:D6; every day.*

SPORTS EQUIPMENT AND SPORTSWEAR

Cheapskates This cluster of sporting-good consignment shops (Cheapskates Too, 3, and 19) saves locals many bucks when shopping for bikes, skates, ski equipment, etc. Used gear is priced to clear, with prices dropping the longer unsold merchandise stays in the store. ▪ *3644 W 16th Ave (and branches); 222-1125; map:B3; every day.*

Coast Mountain Sports Affordable camping, hiking, climbing, and travel gear. Boots, sleeping bags, water purifiers, and high-tech items such as freeze-dried food and satellite tracking systems. Knowledgeable staff. ▪ *1828 W 4th Ave; 731-6181; map:O7; every day.*

Cyclone Taylor Sporting Goods This shop is known as THE place for skating gear. You can suit up a hockey team (ice or in-line), get your figure skates hollow-ground, or find safety-equipment for a whole family of Rollerbladers. A second location has opened in the Richmond Ice Centre. ▪ *6575 Oak St; 266-3316; map:D4* ▪ *14140 Triangle Rd (Richmond Ice Centre), Richmond; map:F7; every day.*

The Diving Locker Equipment sales, rentals, and instructions. Diving Locker has been in business more than 20 years. ▪ *2745 W 4th Ave; 736-2681; map:C2; every day.*

Doug Hepburn's Gym Equipment Setting up a home gym? Get your serious weight-training equipment here. ▪ *38 E 4th Ave; 873-3684; map:V7; every day.*

Eddie Bauer Outdoor Outfitters If you want the look of the great outdoors, this is your store. High-quality casual duds for those who brave the elements or like to look as though they do. This is the same store as the North American chain devoted solely to "sportswear," clothes, shoes, and accessories. ▪ *Pacific Centre (and branches); 683-4711; map:T4; every day.*

Hanson's Fishing Outfitters Everything you need to outwit the wiliest fish. Clothing, books, equipment, and a knowledgeable staff. Charters can be booked at the store. ▪ *580 Hornby St; 684-8988; map:S3; Mon–Sat.*

Limbers If you're a dancer (or flexible enough to pass for one) you'll find everything you need right here. Shoes for all kinds of dance are available, as are sizes for all kinds and ages of dancers. ▪ *5635 W Boulevard (and branches); 264-0009; map:C4; every day.*

Mountain Equipment Co-op Join for a few dollars, then shop to your heart's content amid racks of all the gear you'll need to enjoy the great outdoors. The store has recently moved to new and huge premises, reflecting the enormous popularity of the province's scenic parks. There's a good cycling section, helpful staff, and a large selection of clothing. ▪ *130 W Broadway; 872-7858; map:U7; every day.*

Recreation Rentals Are you ready to roll but don't have the wherewithal? Do you want to try a sport but don't want to purchase the regalia? Whatever your sporting needs, these three shops will rent you what you need. From camping and hiking to skating and biking, from water skis to snow skis, even to golf clubs and baseball sets. ▪ *2560 Arbutus St (and branches); 733-7368; map:C3; every day.*

Ruddick's Fly Shop The first—and many say the best—fly-fishing shop in Western Canada. It's the exclusive licensed retail outlet for Orvis rods, clothing, and accessories. The shop also sells custom-tied flies and offers classes in fly tying and fly casting as well as group expeditions to famous fishing locations. ■ *3726 Canada Way, Burnaby; 434-2420; map:G3; Mon–Sat.*

Superstar ■ Lady Superstar Sportswear, footwear, hats, and accessories for a variety of sports. All the top athletic footwear makers like Nike, Reebok, Adidas, etc. Good selection of active wear and lots of matching outfits by top names. ■ *Pacific Centre (and branches); 668-9611; 668-9612; map:T4; every day.*

Taiga This local manufacturer with an international reputation sells high-quality tents, sleeping bags, and sportswear. It also has a great range of fashions in Gore-Tex and Polartec. ■ *390 W 8th Ave; 875-6644; map:T7; Mon–Sat.*

Three Vets One of the oldest and most respected outfitters in the area, Three Vets is famous for its low prices. You'll find good-quality basic equipment for entry-level campers and hikers. Check out the store's small collection of Native art. ■ *2200 Yukon St; 872-5475; map:T7; Mon–Sat.*

Westbeach This is where the boardheads hang out. Skate-and-snow boarders go for the oversized sweats, flannels, and fleeces with their distinctive logos. The brand in which to be seen. ■ *1766 West 4th Ave; 731-6449; map:P7; every day.*

▼

**Sports
Equipment
and
Sportswear**

▲

STATIONERY AND ART SUPPLIES

Behnsen Graphic Supplies Ltd. This is a store for serious graphic artists and designers, but rank amateurs will find a wealth of inspiring colours and supplies. Behnsen sponsors free seminars on how to get the most out of its merchandise. Computer graphic artists will appreciate the store's hardware and software offerings. ■ *1016 Richards St; 681-7351; map:S5; Mon–Sat.*

Opus Framing and Art Supplies Opus is ideally situated on Granville Island across the street from the Emily Carr Institute of Art & Design. A discount art supply and "do-it-yourself" framing shop, Opus offers the lowest prices in the city and has an unparalleled source of art and framing supplies—more than 8,000 in-stock items. Most of the knowledgeable staff have art or design degrees. Don't overlook the Starving Artists' Table for samples and damaged goods at rock-bottom prices. Other locations are in Victoria and Kelowna, and there's a mail-order number: (800) 663-6953. ■ *1360 Johnston St, Granville Island; 736-7028; map:Q6; every day.*

Paper-Ya Try your hand at creating your own art paper. You'll find a terrific selection of paper from around the world as well as papermaking kits for fledgling artists. ■ *1666 Johnston St, Granville Island; 684-2531; map:Q6; every day.*

Return to Sender A tasteful and not-so-tasteful selection of greeting cards, gift wrap, notepaper, magnets, stickers, and party supplies for every occasion, gay or straight. ▪ *1070 Davie St; 683-6363; map:Q4; every day.*

The Vancouver Pen Shop The giant pen in the window is your first clue to the giant selection of pens offered here: Sheaffer, Montblanc, Cross, Waterman, and Dupont pens as well as inks and cartridges. The shop also stocks sketching tools and lower-priced pens. ▪ *512 W Hastings St; 681-1612; map:T3; Mon–Sat.*

Winton's Social Stationery Be spontaneous in your celebrations! These helpful people can supply your personal invitations in a matter of days, or you can choose from their extensive selection. They also sell blank greeting cards that are extremely laser-printer friendly. Guest books, picture frames, and other related gifts. ▪ *2529 W Broadway; 731-3949; map:C3; every day.*

The Write Place Custom stationery, hilarious cards, writing implements, and gifts. ▪ *2843 Granville St; 732-7777; map:D3; every day.*

TOYS

Kaboodles This is the perfect store for stocking goody bags for kids' parties, but there's much, much more than a great selection of low-cost crowd-pleasers. Check out the umbrellas, the backpacks, and the colourful stuffed toys. Cards and wrap too. ▪ *4449 W 10th Ave; 224-5311; map:B3; every day.*

▼

Wine and Beer

▲

Kids Only Market Not *just* toys, of course. The market features more than 20 specialty shops and services, including clothing, art supplies, and more. It's where you'll find the best kite shop in the city, and kids just love to visit. ▪ *1496 Cartwright St, Granville Island; 689-8447; map:Q6; every day.*

Moyer's for Parents and Teachers Guilt-free indulgence for all! Not just toys and games, but *educational* toys and games plus teacher resources. Although the target age group for most merchandise is children from birth through 10 years, parents and grandparents can enjoy most of the games (and maybe win a few). ▪ *Coquitlam Centre, Coquitlam (and branches); 941-5737; map:L2; every day.*

The Toybox High-quality toys and lots of them. Some of the merchandise is upmarket (read expensive), but lots of lower-priced items will please. Games galore. ▪ *3002 W Broadway; 738-4322; map:C3; every day.*

WINE AND BEER

Visitors used to buying their beer and wine day or night at a corner store will no doubt be perplexed by the peculiarities of

BC liquor laws. The distribution and sale of alcohol, be it wine, beer, or spirits, is under the complete control of the **British Columbia Liquor Distribution Branch (BCLDB)** or, as the locals call it, "the monopoly."

Except for a handful of private wine shops and local beer and wine stores attached to neighbourhood pubs, the only place you can buy alcohol is a BCLDB store. The hours of operation vary from store to store, but none operate on Sundays and most close in the early evening. Keep in mind that all posted prices in BCLDB stores include a series of substantial taxes. There are no case discounts and credit cards are not accepted, although most stores are now equipped to take direct-debit bank cards. Cash is the currency of choice at the monopoly. BC law prohibits the sales of alcohol to persons under the age of 19. If you don't look old enough, be prepared to produce a valid ID, a driver's licence with photograph, a passport, or a BC identification card.

On the positive side, it is possible to find just about any alcohol-based product made in the world at one of the many provincial liquor stores. The best stocked venues are the BCLDB **specialty stores** scattered throughout the city. The flagship store is at the corner of 39th and Cambie Streets in South Vancouver (5555 Cambie St; map:D4), about a 15-minute drive from the downtown core. It contains well over 2,500 products, including wine, beer, cider, coolers, and spirits that will pique the interests of most serious collectors. Other stores of note, with slightly less inventory, are the **downtown** specialty store at (1120 Alberni St; map:R3), the **Park Royal** store (570 Park Royal North; map:D1), and the **West Vancouver** store (Park Royal Shopping Centre; map:D1).

For up-to-the-minute advice about products or store locations, you can speak directly with specialty store products consultants by dialling the **BCLDB wine line**. In Vancouver, dial **660-WINE (9463)**, or from outside Greater Vancouver dial **(800)667-WINE (9463)**.

Adventurous wine drinkers may want to visit one of several private wine shops throughout the city and suburbs. In downtown Vancouver, **Marquis Wine Cellars** (1034 Davie St; map:Q4) offers an eclectic selection of hard-to-find labels, as do the **Broadway International Wine Shop** (2752 W Broadway, map:C3) and **Liberty Wine Merchants** (4583 W 10th; map:C3). North Shore travellers will also find a Liberty store at **Park and Tilford** (560-333 Brooksbank, North Vancouver; map:F1). The private shops are open extended hours on weekdays as well as weekends, take credit cards, and sell prechilled wine; but they are prohibited from selling beer, spirits, or food.

LODGINGS

Lodgings

DOWNTOWN

Buchan Hotel ★★ This three-storey 1930s apartment-hotel adjacent to Stanley Park sits on a lovely tree-lined cul de sac in the residential heart of the West End. The 61 small rooms are clean, comfortable, and pleasant enough, especially for the price. The brightest rooms overlook a small city park to the east. There are few amenities (no individual telephones), but the staff is friendly and helpful and downstairs is the new Samson's restaurant. The biggest hassle is finding a parking spot. Bring your walking shoes; Stanley Park is only steps away, and the centre of downtown is a 15-minute stroll along fashionable Robson Street. Weekly rates are available; there is a laundry room. ■ *1906 Haro St; 685-5354; map:P2; $; AE, DC, MC, V; no cheques.*

Coast Plaza at Stanley Park ★★ Situated just off the main artery through the vibrant West End, this former apartment tower offers 267 large rooms, including 170 suites, a dozen with two bedrooms. All have balconies, and more than two-thirds of the rooms have complete kitchens, making this a great place for vacationing families and Hollywood film crews working in Vancouver (the stars stay elsewhere). Amenities include 24-hour room service, a minibar, and a small fridge. But the hotel's strongest point is its proximity to Stanley Park. Request a room with a park view. Guests are welcome at the adjoining health club (popular with local singles). ■ *1733 Comox St; 688-7711 or (800) 663-1144; map:P2; $$$; AE, DC, E, MC, V; cheques OK.*

The Four Seasons ★★★★ The upscale chain of Four Seasons hotels is well known for pampering guests, and the Vancouver hotel only enhances that reputation. Arrival is awkward, however, since guests must enter from a small driveway wedged between concrete pillars and then go up a floor to the lobby, which is also connected to the Pacific Centre shopping mall. Once the hurdle of check-in has been overcome, however, guests wallow in luxury. Although the hotel is located smack-dab in the centre of high-rise downtown, many of the guest rooms offer surprising views of the city. Amenities include bathrobes, hair dryers, VCRs, a complimentary shoeshine, 24-hour valet and room service, a year-round indoor-outdoor pool, complimentary use of health club facilities, and a rooftop garden. Kids are welcomed with complimentary milk and cookie on arrival. Business travellers will appreciate phones with voice mail in English, French, or Japanese, and modular phones are available for computer hookup. Chartwell (see Restaurants chapter) is one of the best dining rooms in the city. The Garden Terrace, just off the lobby, is a place to see and be seen. ■ *791 W Georgia St; 689-9333 or (800) 332-3442, from the U.S. only; map:T4; $$$; AE, DC, JCB, MC, V; no cheques.*

Georgian Court Hotel ★★★ Compared with the other pricey hotels in the city, there's good value to be enjoyed at this intimate and luxurious 180-room European-style hotel situated across from BC Place Stadium and the Queen Elizabeth Theatre. All rooms feature desks, minibars, three telephones, nightly turn-down service on request, and (at last) good reading lamps. Among Vancouverites, the Georgian Court Hotel is best known as the home of the William Tell Restaurant (see Restaurants chapter), where for years flamboyant owner Erwin Doebeli has set the standard for fine dining in Vancouver. The hotel's strong point is value for dollars in a luxury hotel, but a guest, or any visitor to the city, would be remiss not to dine in the William Tell. ■ *773 Beatty St; 682-5555 or (800) 663-1155; map:T5; $$; AE, DC, DIS, E, JCB, MC, V; Canadian cheques OK.*

Hotel Georgia ★ This attractive 12-storey stone hotel, built in 1927, offers old-fashioned charm with its small oak-panelled lobby, elaborate brass elevators, and comfortable rooms furnished with contemporary oak furniture. Yet it has the feel of a hotel for travelling salespeople and bus tours. The rooms with the best views face south to the Vancouver Art Gallery, but they are on a busy, noisy street. Executive rooms have a seating area that is useful for conducting business. The hotel's location couldn't be more central. The Georgia has two bars that are popular with locals. ■ *801 W Georgia St; 682-5566 or (800) 663-1111; map:S3; $$$; AE, DC, JCB, MC, V; no cheques.*

Hotel Vancouver ★★★ One of the grand French chateau-style hotels owned by the Canadian Pacific Railway, the Hotel Vancouver dates back to 1887. The original building was destroyed in a fire, however, and was rebuilt in 1939. The green, steeply pitched copper roof dominated the city's skyline for decades but is a less-obvious landmark today. A complete renovation began in 1989, and the final phase, a $12.7-million refit of the main lobby and lower shopping arcade, recently wrapped up. Stone arches, friezes, and other design elements hidden by earlier renovations have been restored or re-created. A new Lobby Bar and the "elegantly casual" 900 West restaurant (see Restaurants chapter) replace the main floor lobby and Timber Club, but the Roof Restaurant is being turned into meeting space. The new shopping arcade includes a Canadian Pacific Store, featuring private-label goods reminiscent of the early days of Canadian travel. The 508-room hotel is popular for conventions and tour groups; nonetheless, service remains quite good and includes complimentary coffee and newspapers in the morning. An executive floor called Entrée Gold has premium rooms with a dedicated reception desk and concierge, continental breakfast and canapés, and secretarial services. There is a health club with a sky-lit lap pool. Try for a room high above the street noise. ■ *900 W Georgia St; 684-3131 or (800) 441-1414; map:S3; $$$; AE, DC, DIS, E, JCB, MC, V; cheques OK.*

Hyatt Regency ★★ No surprises here. This is a good Hyatt Regency, like all the others around the world. It's popular with conventions and tour groups yet continues to offer personalized service. Good views of the harbour and mountains are available from north-facing upper floors. Try for a corner room with a balcony. A Regency Club floor, with special keyed access, has its own concierge, complimentary breakfast, midday cookies, and late afternoon hors d'oeuvres. Complimentary use of health club and pool for all guests. Standard rooms (which are among the largest standards in the city) start at $180. ■ *655 Burrard St; 683-1234 or (800) 233-1234; map:S3; $$$; AE, DC, DIS, E, JCB, MC, V; cheques OK.*

Metropolitan Hotel ★★★ Mandarin International built this richly appointed, 197-room hotel in time for Expo 86. Delta Hotels operated it for a few years, going through a patch of bad feng shui when the marble Chinese lions guarding the discreet Howe Street entrance were erroneously placed so they stared away from the front door. In 1995, Metropolitan Hotels purchased this gem, quickly bringing back the Mandarin sparkle through attention to detail and renovation. The elegant little hotel has just been accepted as one of 107 independent luxury hotels in 23 countries that form the exclusive Preferred Hotels & Resorts Worldwide. Located in the heart of downtown's business and financial district, it offers outstanding concierge service, private Jaguar limousine service, nightly turn-down service on request, 24-hour room service, a full-scale business centre, and one of the finest hotel health clubs in the city. (You can even watch CNN in the sauna.) There are 18 palatial suites; all other rooms are deluxe with balconies and peekaboo views of the city, elegant contemporary appointments, European duvets, and Frette bathrobes. Technologically enhanced business guest rooms include laser-quality printers and in-room faxes that deliver the latest breaking news from the *Wall Street Journal* and Japan's *Yomiuri Report*. Diva at the Met is the hotel's newest streetfront bar and 116-seat restaurant, and it has some of Vancouver's top chefs rockin' on the pans, a logo inspired by Picasso, and dessert plates inspired by Kandinsky (see Restaurants chapter). It's hip, happening, and hot with Vancouverites (a chilled tomato martini is part of the dinner menu). Lovers head for the intimate fourth tier beyond the open kitchen; theatregoers (an easy walk) return for dessert. **[KIDS] [FREE]** Ask about special winter packages. ■ *645 Howe St; 687-1122 or (800) 667-2300; map:T3; $$$; AE, DC, MC, V; no cheques.*

Pacific Palisades ★★★ The internationally celebrated Shangri-La chain purchased the Pacific Palisades in 1991 and promptly began a complete renovation of what was already a good hotel. The 233 rooms, most of which are one-bedroom suites, have long been popular with the many movie production crews that visit Vancouver. Part of the appeal comes from the hotel's personal attention to guests' needs, but the major draw is spacious rooms, all with a minikitchen that includes a fridge, microwave, and coffee-maker. There's a health club and one of the largest hotel swimming pools in the city. The location on Robson Street is tough to beat if you want to be where the action is. Check out the Monterey Lounge and Grill (see Restaurants chapter). ■ *1277 Robson St; 688-0461 or (800) 663-1815; map:R3; $$$; AE, DC, E, JCB, MC, V; no cheques.*

Pan Pacific Hotel ★★★ No hotel in Vancouver has a more stunning location, a better health club, or a more remarkable architectural presence. As part of Canada Place, the Pan Pacific juts out into Vancouver's inner harbour with its five giant white signature sails. The building, which is also the embarkation point for the thriving summertime Alaska cruise ship market, hasn't achieved the fame of Sydney's Opera House, but it was meant to. The first four floors of the building comprise the World Trade Centre Vancouver, but up on the eighth, where the guest rooms begin, things become more diminutive. Standard guest rooms (high season rates start at $315) are among the smallest of Vancouver's luxury hotels, and the decor is all a bit disappointing after such a grand facade. Nonetheless, perhaps the spectacular views make up for any shortcomings. The best views face west, but you can't beat a corner room (with views from your tub). A complete range of guest services is offered. Cafe Pacifica is open for breakfast, lunch, and dinner, and the fine-dining restaurant, the Five Sails, has achieved a fair bit of attention for its exquisite Pacific Rim cuisine (see Restaurants chapter). The Cascades Lounge, just off the lobby, is a must if you want to watch ships sail into the sunset while seaplanes land beneath you against the backdrop of the North Shore mountains. ■ *300-999 Canada Pl Way; 662-8111, or (800) 663-1515 from Canada, (800) 937-1515 from the U.S.; map:T2; $$$; AE, DC, E, JCB, MC, V; no cheques.*

The Sutton Place Hotel (formerly Le Meridien) ★★★★ Le Meridien may have changed its name, but little else has changed at Vancouver's most elegant hotel. All 397 soundproofed rooms in this sumptuous residential-style hotel look and feel like part of a beautiful home. The beds are king-sized; the furnishings are reproductions of European antiques. (There are plenty of spectacular original pieces throughout the hotel's public spaces.) Maids faithfully appear twice a day with all the amenities one could wish for—including fresh flowers, umbrellas, and complimentary shoeshines. There are 11 no-smoking floors and the fastest elevators in town. The lobby recalls a European manor and posts a concierge service. Bellhops snap to attention whether you arrive wearing blue jeans in a beat-up truck or in black tie and a limo. Sutton Place's restaurants and lounges have been popular with locals since the day they opened, with the richly panelled Gerard Lounge ranking as one of the best watering holes in the Northwest (see Nightlife chapter). Le Spa offers a swimming pool, fitness room, and beauty salons. Room rates in season range from $245 for a standard double to $1,500 for the Presidential Suite; however, special getaway weekend packages are available.

The best rental condominiums in the city are located in a separate building connected to the hotel. (See Condominiums in this chapter.) ■ *845 Burrard St; 682-5511 or (800) 543-4300; map:S4; $$$; AE, DC, DIS, E, JCB, MC, V; no cheques.*

Sylvia Hotel ★★ A favourite for price and location. This ivy-covered eight-storey historic brick hotel is a landmark adjacent to English Bay, Vancouver's most popular beach and strutting grounds. Try for a south-facing room. A low-rise addition was built to compensate for the busy summer season, when you might just need to settle for *any* room. Doubles begin at $65, and reservations are required well in advance. All 119 rooms (some quite small) have baths. Families or small groups should request the one-bedroom suites which can sleep four and which come equipped with kitchen and living room ($100 to $150). Covered parking is extra. The hotel also offers room service, a restaurant, and a lounge—reportedly the first cocktail bar in Vancouver (opened in 1954), and on some winter afternoons it looks as though the original clientele is still there. ■ *1154 Gilford St; 681-9321; map:P2 $; AE, DC, MC, V; cheques OK with credit card.*

Wall Centre Garden Hotel ★★ This stunning 35-storey glass tower houses a wonderful addition to Vancouver's already rich luxury lodging scene. What distinguishes this hotel from the competition is its very stylish decor. The lobby area features furnishings in playful primary colours set amid dramatic marble. Standard double rooms are small, although expansive views from the higher floors make them feel larger. Check into a one-bedroom corner suite with a two-vista view; floor-to-ceiling windows face north up Burrard Street, with Grouse Mountain in the distance, and west to English Bay and the Coast Mountains beyond. Most suites feature deep soaking tubs in the marble bathrooms along with a wet bar and microwave. There's a full health club with 15-metre (50-foot) lap pool and beauty salon in the complex. Complimentary morning newspapers and turn-down service. All in all, this is a wonderful place to stay. ■ *1088 Burrard; 331-1000 or (800) 663-9255; map:R4; $$$; AE, DC, JCB, MC, V; no cheques.*

Waterfront Centre Hotel ★★★ The tasteful rooms in the newish 23-storey Waterfront Centre are among the best in the city. Their size and rich appointments clearly outclass those of the Pan Pacific Hotel, just across the street on Vancouver's inner harbour. Underground passageways connect the Waterfront Centre to Canada Place and the Trade and Convention Centre. Expect wonderful surprises, such as third-floor guest rooms with private terraces and herb gardens that supply Herons restaurant (see Restaurants chapter). Two club floors called Entrée Gold cater to every whim, offering a private concierge, continental breakfast, nightly hors d'oeuvres, and private conference room. Of the 489 guest rooms, 29 are suites and one is fit for royalty. Operated by Canadian Pacific, the Waterfront Centre was named one of the world's top ten business hotels by *Report on Business Magazine*, and, as new as it is, it has the most Canadian feel to it of any of the city's hotels. There is an excellent health club, complete with outdoor pool (a view-and-a-half), nightly turn-down service, no-smoking floors, and rooms designed for people with disabilities. All harbourside rooms have amenities, such as data ports, for business travellers. The works of Canadian artists are prominently displayed throughout the hotel's public spaces and guest rooms. Sunday brunch at Herons features music by members of the Vancouver Symphony. ■ *900 Canada Pl Way; 691-1991 or (800) 441-1414; map:T2; $$$; AE, DC, DIS, E, JCB, MC, V; no cheques.*

The Wedgewood Hotel ★★★ Owner and manager Eleni Skalbania takes great pride in the Wedgewood Hotel. And Ms. Skalbania has much to be proud of. This is a hotel you will want to return to time and time again. Ideally located in the heart of Vancouver's finest shopping district, and across the street from the art gallery, the gardens of Robson Square, and the courthouse built of glass, the Wedgewood offers Old World charm and scrupulous attention to every detail of hospitality. From the potted flowers flourishing on the balcony of every room to the renowned Bacchus Ristorante (see Restaurants chapter), this 93-room hotel is all that a small urban luxury hotel should be. This is the only luxury hotel in the city where you'll hardly ever find tour buses unloading swarms of visitors. The finely appointed rooms, which are surprisingly large and are decorated with vibrant colours and genuine English antiques, have the feel of a grand home. Nightly turn-down service, a bare-essentials fitness room, and 24-hour room service are offered. This is the place to spend your honeymoon (and many do), but any weekend at the Wedgewood is a weekend to savour. ■ *845 Hornby St; 689-7777 or (800) 663-0666; map:S4; $$$; AE, DC, DIS, E, JCB, MC, V; no cheques.*

Westin Bayshore Hotel ★★ The Bayshore sits on the southern shore of Coal Harbour next to the main entrance to Stanley Park. Set back from busy Georgia Street, this is the only downtown hotel that resembles a resort (children love it here). Rooms look out over a large outdoor pool, with Coal Harbour's colourful marina as a backdrop and the North Shore mountains beyond. At a kiosk near the indoor pool you can rent bicycles, and if you're up for a one-hour ride, you can't beat the scenery along the connecting Stanley Park seawall. The marina has moorage for visiting boaters and charter vessels for those who want to get even closer to the water. Amenities include all that you'd expect from a Westin. Guest rooms in the tower all have balconies and will have been totally renovated by March '97. There's also a full, newly upgraded health club. A currency exchange is on-site, and the major business and shopping areas of downtown are a pleasant 15-minute walk away. ■ *1601 W Georgia St; 682-3377 or (800) 228-3000; map:Q2; $$$; AE, DC, DIS, E, JCB, MC, V; cheques OK.*

AIRPORT

Delta Pacific Resort ★★ Formerly called the Delta Airport Inn, this is one of two Delta hotels in the vicinity of Vancouver International Airport. Both are well-run and offer a wealth of recreational facilities. This 4-hectare (10-acre) resort includes three swimming pools (one indoor), an indoor waterslide, year-round tennis courts under a bubble, a play centre with spring break and summer camp for kids (ages 5 to 12), exercise classes, volleyball nets, and a golf practice net. There are meeting rooms and a restaurant, cafe, and bar. Special rooms for business travellers, with amenities like private faxes, are available for $15 over the normal rate. The free shuttle service goes to and from the airport as well as to major nearby shopping centres. If you're driving, ask for directions from the freeway. ■ *10251 St Edwards Dr, Richmond; 278-9611 or (800) 268-1133; map:E5; $$$; AE, DC, DIS, E, JCB, MC, V; no cheques.*

Delta Vancouver Airport Hotel and Marina ★★ This is the closest hotel to Vancouver International Airport, and it spreads along the banks of the Fraser River. There is an outdoor pool, bar, and barbecue as well as bicycle and running trails. Not a bad place for a layover. East-side rooms face the river and marina. Downtown is 30 minutes away. The 415 guest rooms and the dozen or so meeting rooms are popular for conventions and with corporate travellers. "Business Zone" rooms are available for an extra $15. There's a small fitness centre on the top floor, or guests are welcome to take the shuttle to the more extensive facilities at the Delta Pacific Resort nearby. Kids under six eat free in the hotel's dining facilities. ■ *3500 Cessna Dr; 278-1241; map:D6; $$$; AE, DC, DIS, E, JCB, MC, V; no cheques.*

Radisson President Hotel and Suites ★★ We knew we were in for a treat at Richmond's President Hotel and Suites when we received impeccable directions to the hotel over the phone and gracious assistance with some rather unusual park-and-fly arrangements. This new airport hotel is a class act, offering everything from Cantonese cuisine in the President Chinese Restaurant (see Restaurants chapter), to meeting and conference room space, to shopping at the adjoining President Plaza. Staff handled even the most obscure requests with ease: customer service here is prompt and friendly. Rooms are spacious and well-appointed (you can actually open the windows), and business-class accommodations cover small needs and large— from a free morning newspaper to data port hookups for your laptop. Complimentary shuttle service to the airport is available every half hour. The atmosphere in Gustos Bistro is bright and funky (we liked the colour scheme and the cheery round coffeepots), but breakfast prices are expense-account high. The appealing Mediterranean-style lunch and dinner menu created for the Bistro by executive chef Rod Klockow offers a much better value. ■ *8181 Cambie Rd, Richmond; 276-8181 or (800) 333-3333; map:D6; $$$; AE, DC, DIS, E, JCB, MC, V; no cheques.*

GREATER VANCOUVER: NORTH SHORE

Lonsdale Quay Hotel ★ Few visitors take the time to explore the North Shore, which has what are perhaps the best wilderness areas of any major North American city. The pleasant Lonsdale Quay Hotel, located inside the enjoyable Lonsdale Quay market and across the harbour from downtown Vancouver (yet only 15 minutes away via the SeaBus), gives you a comfortable place to stay (as long as you don't need to be pampered). French doors on south-facing rooms open up to the Vancouver skyline, a dazzling sight at night, when the lights reflect off the water. ■ *123 Carrie Cates Ct, North Vancouver; 986-6111 or (800) 836-6111; map:E1; $$$; AE, DC, DIS, E, JCB, MC, V; no cheques.*

Park Royal Hotel ★★ The Park Royal Hotel is a study in contradictions. It's nestled into its own little forest of mature greenery just yards away from one of Vancouver's busiest freeways, but traffic noise never seems to intrude into your surroundings. Some of the rooms are beautifully appointed with custom woodwork and bathrooms full of marble and brass, but a few are still stuck in the '70s. A complete renovation, however, is slated for 1997. The cosiness and romantic setting make it a popular place for weddings. We've seen the human ingredient at work here in some really touching ways. If you arrive at the right time of day, you just might catch the crack kitchen team of toqued and tender-hearted chefs feeding their loyal coterie of alley cats! (People are fed well too, from the revitalized menus in the lounge and dining room.) We like the genuinely friendly housekeeping staff, and the legendary hospitality of Mario Corsi is, well, legendary. When he's around, things and people get looked after in a special way. ■ *540 Clyde Ave, West Vancouver; 926-5511; map:D1; $$; AE, DC, E, MC, V; no cheques.*

INNS AND BED AND BREAKFASTS

English Bay Inn ★★★★ Owner Bob Chapin devotes meticulous attention to his romantic five-room English Bay Inn. Down comforters rest atop Louis Phillipe sleigh beds beneath alabaster lighting fixtures. The pièce de résistance is a two-level suite on the top floor with a fireplace in the bedroom. Extras include terrycloth robes, evening port or sherry, and phones in each guest room. All rooms have a private bath, and two back rooms open onto a small garden. A fabulous breakfast is served in a formal dining room complete with gothic dining suite, crackling (albeit gas) fire, and ticking grandfather clock. Stanley Park and English Bay are just minutes away by foot. ■ *1968 Comox St; 683-8002; map:P2; $$$; AE, MC, V; cheques OK.*

The French Quarter ★★★ C'est magnifique! Ginette Bertrand's French country-style home nestled in the historic, exclusive First Shaughnessy district has a delightful, cosy, well-appointed room in the main house or a private poolside cottage with all the amenities: a queen-size bed, large closet and bathroom, fireplace, TV/VCR, refrigerator, and complimentary sherry. The open kitchen, dining room, pool deck, and living room are spacious and offer privacy. A gourmet sweet or savoury breakfast menu topped off with fresh fruit is served from 8:30am to 10:30am. Access to a well-equipped fitness room is included. Ideal for a romantic getaway, though families with children eight and up are welcome. Some small pets allowed. Minimum two-day stay during summer peak season. One night reservation deposit required. ■ *2051 W 19th Ave; 737-0973; map:D3; $$$; MC, V; traveller's cheques OK.*

The Johnson House ★★★ To say that owners Ron and Sandy Johnson are quite fond of antiques would be an understatement. They have restored a 1920s Craftsman-style home on a quiet street in the city's Kerrisdale neighbourhood and turned it into one of Vancouver's most intriguing bed and breakfasts. Everywhere you turn in the three-storey house there are relics from the past: coffee grinders, gramophones, even carousel horses in the largest of the five guest rooms. Above the front door is a genuine old Vancouver street lamp acting as the porch light. The rooms on the top floor and in the basement are cosy; the Carousel Suite, with its adjoining mermaid-themed en suite bath, is the grandest. A separate guest telephone line, plus a guidebook and map to Vancouver in every room, contribute to the friendly atmosphere. Breakfast is served 8:15am to 9:30am in a bright, airy cottage-style room on the main floor. Suitable for families with children 12 and over. No pets. ■ *2278 W 34th Ave; 266-4175; map:D3; $$; no credit cards; cheques OK.*

Kingston Hotel ★★ Guests often comment that this centrally located inn reminds them of a European bed and breakfast, especially its facade of cut granite and heavy wood and its Tudor style windows. Rooms with private baths have colour TVs, others share bath and TV facilities. All rooms have phones. A continental breakfast is served in the small lounge downstairs. Facilities include a sauna and a coin-op laundry. A neighbourhood pub, the Rose and Thorn, is on the main floor. This three-storey bed and breakfast continues to be a great downtown value, and it even offers seniors' discounts. ■ *757 Richards St; 684-9024; map:T4; $; AE, MC, V; no cheques.*

Laburnum Cottage Bed and Breakfast ★★ This elegant country home is set off by an award-winning English garden that has been tended with care over the past four decades by innkeeper Delphine Masterton, who raised five children here before opening the home to lodgers. The main house, furnished with antiques and collectibles, features four light and airy guest rooms with private baths and garden views. Two of these have a queen bed plus a single. The Summerhouse Cottage—situated in the midst of the garden and accessed by a foot-bridge that crosses a small creek—is a Rosamund Pilcher novel come to life, perfect for honeymooning couples. A larger cottage, with private entrance, kitchen, fireplace, and children's loft, sleeps five. Delphine's gift for being welcoming, and her ability to weave strangers into friends over the cheerful breakfast table, make a stay here all it should be. Geraldo the cat is still in residence. ■ *1388 Terrace Ave, North Vancouver; 988-4877; map:D1; $$; E, MC, V; cheques OK.*

Penny Farthing Inn ★★ This 1912 Edwardian home is a historic treasure in Vancouver's trendy westside Kitsilano district. Try for the attic room overlooking the pretty English garden backdropped by the North Shore mountains. Owner Lyn Hainstock is a professional innkeeper with a wealth of information about Vancouver. Breakfast is a gourmet's feast served on the brick patio. Frolicking cats entertain. ■ *2855 W 6th Ave; 739-9002; map:C3; $$; no credit cards; cheques OK.*

River Run Cottages ★★ River Run Cottages is a jewel on the Fraser River. Located in historic Ladner, 30 minutes south of downtown Vancouver and quite near the ferries to Victoria, the cottages are set among a community of houseboats and offer closeness to nature. Ducks, swans, leaping salmon, and bald eagles all put on a show while you look from your deck at the North Shore mountains and Vancouver Island. Bikes and a two-person kayak are available for exploring. The complex features one floating cottage and three on shore, each with deck, private bath, wood-burning stove, wet bar, mini-fridge, and microwave. A hot gourmet breakfast is delivered. No pets. ■ *4551 River Rd W, Ladner; 946-7778; $$; MC, V; cheques OK.*

Two Cedars Bed and Breakfast Suite ★★ Tourism and hospitality industry veterans Tracey Lott and Peter Burrow have a bright, airy suite for bed-and-breakfast guests in their renovated 1918 Kits Point district home. Two Cedars' prime location, only 2 ½ blocks from the recreation amenities of Kitsilano Beach, is also within walking distance from downtown and Granville Island. The guest suite has its own terraced garden entrance at the rear and a reserved parking spot to boot. The suite accommodates up to four adults. Kids are welcome. Special treats include continental breakfast served in bed and afternoon wine tastings. ■ *1423 Walnut St; 731-0785; map:O6; $$; V; cheques OK.*

West End Guest House ★★ Don't be put off by the blazing pink exterior of this early-1900s Victorian home, which is located on a residential street close to Stanley Park and just a block off Robson Street. Owner Evan Penner runs a fine eight-room inn (each room with private bath), and during summer a vacancy is rare. Rooms are generally small but nicely furnished, and there are antiques throughout the house. The staff members have all worked in major hotels and know what hospitality is. Sherry or iced tea is served in the afternoons. Nightly turn-down service, feather and lambskin mattress covers, robes, and telephones are provided in every room. Breakfast

▼

Inns and
Bed and
Breakfasts

▲

is a bountiful cooked meal served family style or delivered to your room. There is guest parking (a rarity in the West End). Families with children are accepted, but just be careful with the antiques. ■ *1362 Haro St; 681-2889; map:R3; $$$; AE, DIS, MC, V; cheques OK.*

CONDOMINIUMS

Barclay Mansions ★ This is a typical bland 1960s-style West End apartment building, with furnished suites available weekly or monthly. The furnishings are modern-motel, but the rooms are clean, the building is well-run, and the location is convenient—just off Burrard Street (next to the YMCA), two blocks south of Robson Street in downtown Vancouver. Most of the 40 suites are one-bedrooms with full kitchens ($475 weekly; $1,400 monthly). The mostly corporate clientele receives twice-a-week maid service and free parking. ■ *1040 Barclay St; 683-8931; map:S3; $; AE, MC, V; no cheques.*

Capilano RV Park ★ If you take your condominium with you, this is the place to stay. Nicely sited on the Capilano River, just across the Lions Gate Bridge from downtown, this private campground features a pool, playground, and Jacuzzi. Tenting sites are $22, partial hookup sites are $27, and full hookup sites are $32. Reservations are a must in summer for the RV sites, but there are no reservations for the tenting sites. Prices quoted are for two people; extra charges for more people or for pets. ■ *295 Tomahawk Ave, North Vancouver; 987-4722; map:D1; $; MC, V; no cheques.*

La Grande Résidence ★★★★ La Grande Résidence, owned by the Sutton Place Hotel, provides all the amenities of a luxury hotel in 162 spiffy one- and two-bedroom apartments with kitchens and balconies (it is, in fact, attached to Sutton Place). Valet parking, concierge, and secretarial, maid, laundry, and room services are all available. A state-of-the-art security system ensures privacy. Telephone calls and visiting guests are received by the hotel's front desk. The minimum stay is seven nights (starting at $185 per night). ■ *845 Burrard St; 682-5511 or (800) 543-4300; map:R4; $$$; AE, DC, DIS, E, JCB, MC, V; no cheques.*

ALTERNATIVES

Simon Fraser University Residences Simon Fraser is located on top of Burnaby Mountain about half an hour from downtown. The campus is an architectural showpiece designed by Arthur Erickson, and in summer the residence offers budget accommodations. Single rooms are $31.05 if you want bedding and towels or $19 if you supply your own. Twin rooms come with linen service for under $50, and families can stay in townhouse units with four bedrooms, two baths, kitchen, and living room for a little more than $100. The campus is self-contained, with cafeterias, pub, and even fine dining. ■ *Room 212, McTaggart-Cowan Hall, Burnaby; 291-4503; map:I2; $; MC, V; cheques OK.*

University of BC Residences You could probably spend a whole vacation just exploring UBC's beautiful campus: the Museum of Anthropology, the Botanical Gardens, sports facilities, walking trails, and more. From May through August the university opens its student residences to travellers at bargain rates. Dormitory rooms, with two beds and bath down the hall, are as low as $20. Single travellers who want to meet people like the six-bedroom units that share a bathroom, fridge, and living room. There are also studios with bath and kitchenette or, all year round, one-bedroom apartments that sleep four. Parking is free in the summer months, and the main location, Walter Gage Residence, is easily accessible by bus. The other two, Totem Park and Vanier, are a bit of a hike. Lots of dining facilities on campus and in University Village nearby. E-mail address is reservation@brock.housing.ubc.ca. ■ *Walter Gage Residence, 5961 Student Union Blvd; 822-1010; map:B2; MC, V; no cheques.*

YWCA Hotel/Residence ★★ Weary business travellers arriving late at the new YWCA Hotel/Residence on Beatty Street may be somewhat flummoxed by the institutional-style security (separate keys for the parkade, for the elevator, for your room, and for the hall baths; no direct elevator access to the parkade; and front-door entry only via intercom after 11pm), but the hotel was built with safety and security in mind. The rooms are functional, immaculately clean, and reasonably priced for a downtown location. All rooms have sinks; baths are private, shared, or "down the hall." The residence is also remarkably quiet, and although it may not be quite the thing for those accustomed to amenities (no tissues, clocks, televisions, or coffeemakers here), it does provide meeting rooms, kitchen and laundry facilities, and communal lounges. Close to theatres and sporting venues. ■ *733 Beatty St; 895-5830 or (800) 663-1424 from BC and Alberta; map:T5; $; MC, V; cheques OK for deposit only.*

OUTINGS

Outings

BOWEN ISLAND

There's a festive feeling when the ferry pulls into **Snug Cove**, where pleasure boats are docked at the new **Union Steamship Company Marina** and welcoming flags fly from the cheery green wooden **Doc Morgan's Inn**. Vancouver senior citizens fondly remember the moonlight cruises to the Happy Isle back in the 1930s and 1940s. For $1 on a Wednesday or Saturday night, you could dance across Howe Sound on board luxury steamships like the *Lady Alexandra*, follow the orchestra up the fragrant rose-arboured path to the Dance Pavilion (the largest in BC), and then sail back again.

More than 100 cottages, built by the Union Steamship Company and the Hotel Monaco (later Bowen Inn), catered to summer pleasure seekers, but these are largely gone. So is the company. But the 52-square-kilometre (20-square-mile) island of 3,000 people is undergoing a resurgence as a new generation discovers the year-round pleasures of living on—or visiting—an island only 20 minutes away.

Commuting baby boomers, who have moved their families from the mainland to Bowen (it has the highest ratio of schoolchildren under 10 in BC), have created a market for more upscale stores on the main drag (the only drag) in Snug Cove, once the site of the shake dwellings and smokehouses of the Squamish people who hunted and fished the area.

From Horseshoe Bay, it's a pleasant ferry ride to Bowen aboard one of BC's newest ferries (usually the *Queen of Capilano)*, which departs almost hourly until 9:25pm (669-1211, from Vancouver; (250)386-3431, from Bowen Island), carrying

85 cars. Once on Bowen, how you spend your day on the 6-kilometre-wide (3.7-mile-wide) by 14-kilometre-long (8.7-mile-long) island depends on whether you're travelling by car, bike, or foot (you can park in Horseshoe Bay or ride the blue Horseshoe Bay bus right from downtown Vancouver, on Georgia at Granville). When you disembark onto Government Road, you'll confront virtually every service on Bowen, from the **Oven Door Bakery** (pizza after 4pm) and **The Snug Coffee House** (good soups; best lunch) to the Chevron gas station, so this is your chance to pick up information, directions, fuel, food, and copies of *Undercurrent* and *The Breeze*, Bowen's local papers.

Check out **Dunfield & Daughter Whole Food** (Government Rd, 947-2907) mini-grocery and the **Dunfield's Deli** upstairs, which has an impressive range of take-out meals and makings. **Books on Bowen** features local writers like Nick Bantock, author of *Griffin & Sabine*, and Paul Grescoe, who created private eye Dan Rudnicki. Above the bookstore, Bowen's hip new clothing store, **Out of the Blue**, has West Van women shopping by ferry. **Crafty People** (Bowen Berries, Snug Cove, 947-0892) do picnics or backpacks to go and will meet you at the ferry. Also worth investigating is the **Bowen Cafe**'s Saturday night schedule of "visiting" chefs and appropriate entertainment, from jazz to sitar (Government Rd, 947-2209). Owner Victor Chan is a particle physicist and author of the highly praised *Tibetan Handbook*, the guide for walkers. Day trippers can still get the last 9:45pm ferry back to West Vancouver.

The big red building closest to the ferry landing is the renovated **Union Steamship Company General Store**, now a post office and recreation centre. **[KIDS][FREE]** Don't miss the original orchard (just past Dunfield & Daughter) and two restored classic 1920s Bowen cottages. One is a museum, furnished with Bowen bits of the era; the other houses the seasonal tourist information centre (odd hours, so phone 947-0822), where you can pick up the excellent free brochure entitled *Happy Isle Historic Walking Tour*. (Tip: If you can time your visit with the annual July two-day **Bowen Island People, Plants and Places** tour, don't miss it. It regularly sells out, so do call 947-2256 for dates and tickets.) Old photos are keyed to the numbered stops along the 2.5-kilometre (1.5-mile) easy route, which follows roads and trails through **Crippen Regional Park**. Today the park encompasses much of the Union Steamship Company's former resort. Two other options: walk to the historic United Church near the Collins Farm (ask any island resident for directions), or go past the fish ladders (check to see if coho or cutthroat are running in October and November) to **Killarney Lake**, which is warm enough for summer swimming. If you'd like congenial company, sign on with **Rockwood Adventures** (926-7705) for a trip by ferry from Vancouver, followed by a guided rain forest walk on Bowen.

Guide and Culinary Olympics chef Manfred Scholermann prepares your gourmet picnic lunch before a floatplane flight to Vancouver.

Drivers and cyclists can't circumnavigate Bowen because there are only three main roads, all branching out from Snug Cove. Nonetheless, a number of artists, such as Sam Black, open their studios to the public, and this can make for a pleasant tour. You can drive or bike to Killarney Lake to swim, canoe, or kayak, but the 75-minute trail *around* the lake is strictly for hikers. There are plenty of benches and a boardwalk that crosses a marsh at one end of the lake. Look for mink, grouse, ravens, eagles, herons, cormorants, and deer (a sore point with local gardeners). At 760 metres (250 feet), **Mount Gardiner** is Bowen's highest point, and the views of surrounding islands and the Lions peaks are well worth the all-day hike. **Bowen Island Sea Kayaking**'s three-hour starlight Night Paddle is a bargain at $39. There are also lessons and tours (two hours to five days; all levels) available of the 37 kilometres (23 miles) of coastline and nearby islands. Or opt for the do-it-yourself rentals (947-9266 or (800) 60-KAYAK). [KIDS][FREE]Swimmers should head for **Bowen Bay's public beach** (Grafton Road to Bowen Bay Road). With the increase in u-brews, die-hard zymurgists will want to check out how the pros do it at **Bowen Island Brewing Co.** (947-0822 for touring times). A happy thought: registered massage therapist Judith Mallett, who once coordinated the Pan Pacific Hotel's massage service, now takes day trippers' bodies in hand at her Bowen home, aka Cottage Retreat (947-0422). The holistically minded may want to stay overnight and zone out. Mallett will even move out if you want to rent the whole house.

The flagship of Bowen's marina resort (including docks, renovated cottages, a chandlery/gift shop, and boardwalks) is **Doc Morgan's** cosy marine pub/restaurant. The owners are enthusiastic, the menu extensive, and the patios are tempting, despite the overpowering canned music. High point so far: a fireside schooner of Bowen Ale. From April to September, Harbour Air offers Fly & Dine at Doc's packages (seaplane one way; limo and ferry the other) for $124 with dinner (688-1277). Bowen could use a truly great dinner spot, but in the meantime **Bushwacker Pizza** (947-2782) will deliver to your boat or home.

If you can't get enough of the Happy Isle in one day, there are more than a dozen B&Bs plus **Doc's Snug Cove rental cottages** (from $65), which are a slice of renovated Union Steamship history, each with cheery woodstove and kitchen. The classic old boathouse is basic but nifty if you can live with all the smells of dock life and don't mind being on display to passersby. Summer weekends are booked up as much as a year in advance (947-0808).

Someone no doubt will tell you about Bowen's newest

upscale lodging, **The Vineyard at Bowen Island** (687 Cates Lane, 947-0028), but we were more entranced by **The Lodge at the Old Dorm** (460 Melmore Rd, 947-0947). The four-minute stroll from the ferry terminal to the Lodge may be one of the world's loveliest little promenades, and hosts Dan Parkin and Julia McLaughlin have restored the historic Lodge to perfection. Parkin and McLaughlin have also added a twist to the typical weekend lodge retreat: arts classes. By teaming up with a Bowen organization called ISLE (Island-Stay Learning Experiences), brainchild of writer-residents Paul and Audrey Grescoe, the Lodge is able to offer house weekend courses in areas such as romance writing, film appreciation, printmaking, and portrait painting. Another bonus: Dan, a fine cook, whumps up dinner, too. (For course information, call 947-9183.)

Angela McCulloch's heritage **Rosebank Cottage B&B** is another charming spot on the island (Millers Landing, 947-9737), with English tea, dahlias, and a nearby beach. **Salty Towers** (947-2779) is right on Bowen Bay, with spacious deck views, Persian carpets on hardwood floors, and easy access to the island's best swimming. Relaxed hosts Ghemia and John Frith cook breakfast for guests in two of their rooms; ingredients are provided to those in the self-catered, spacious four-room Sybil suite.

FRASER VALLEY AND HARRISON HOT SPRINGS

To drive through rural Fraser Valley farmland east of Vancouver is to slip into a slower time, when neighbours didn't lock their doors and you knew where your eggs came from. It's a full day's drive to Harrison Hot Springs if you meander through the wonderfully peaceful countryside, taking advantage of the many interesting stops along the slower backroads (without stops, 2 1/2 hours from Vancouver). It's not New England, but, come fall, the changing red, yellow, and orange leaves are impressive.

You have a choice of two highways out to Mission: the Trans-Canada (Hwy 1) or the Lougheed (Hwy 7), which is more scenic but can be grim getting out of Vancouver. From there, travel in a long, easterly loop, which begins on the north side of the Fraser River, crosses south of Agassiz, and returns along the south side.

To get a jump on the day, drive east on the Trans-Canada for 70 kilometres (43.5 miles) to the Highway 11 turnoff and head north through Abbotsford. Keep an eye out for **Clayburn Road** on your right. Be sure to take this short detour down to the old, little-known **Clayburn Village**. You'll think you've missed it as you head through a new suburb of massive houses, but keep going and you'll suddenly round a bend onto a street of small brick bungalows facing the village green.

[FREE] Clayburn is not a tourist village but, rather, a real community of people determined to save what was once the employees' town for one of Canada's largest brick mills. Few people know that it was designed by BC's noted Arts and Crafts architect Samuel McClure. Stop at the **Clayburn Village Store** (Clayburn Rd, 853-4020) for tea, coffee, scones, or pastries, imported British sweets, and local history. During Clayburn Heritage Day (usually the third weekend in July) a number of private homes and the church are open to the public, tea is served, and a visiting historian provides intriguing background. Ask for directions back to Highway 11 without retracing your route for the 10-minute drive to Mission.

Mission, the rhododendron capital of BC, has a small-town friendliness and an artful coffeehouse in **Glass Bean Espresso Gallery** (33128 1st Ave, 826-2766). Here you'll find peaceful music, '50s red Naugahyde and chrome stools, and, in back, the work of some 10 local artists. Cheerful owner George Jaeckel is happy to give you tips about more off-the-beaten-track spots in the valley. Ask directions (this town of railway tracks and one-way streets can be confusing) to the locally popular Mexican **Locomotive Club Cafe**, operated by an ebullient Italian-Polish Canadian (end of Glasgow Rd, 826-7759; closed Mondays, dinner only Sundays).

▼

Day Trips

*Fraser-
Harrison*

▲

[FREE] The hilltop setting of **Westminster Abbey Seminary of Christ the King**, Canada's smallest arts university, is splendid. The seminary has some 40 students training for the priesthood and was built over a period of 28 years by and for members of the Benedictine order. The founders of the site dropped to their knees in praise when they saw the vistas and rolling hills beyond. St. Benedict's Holy Rule 53: *All visitors who call are to be welcomed as if they were Christ, for he will say, "I was a stranger and you took me in."* You're free to wander the peaceful woodland trails—where PAX is carved into a stump—anytime, but if you want to see the inside of the impressive contemporary cathedral, with its massive sculptures and 64 stained-glass windows, you may do so from 1:30pm to 4:30pm Mondays to Saturdays, and from 2pm to 4pm Sundays, or come for public worship; dress modestly. Bells are rung Sundays at 9:45am and 4:15pm. Couples, single men, or two or more women seeking solitude may arrange with the guest-master (826-8975) to stay overnight.

[KIDS][FREE] If you're looking for a picnic spot, head back to Highway 7 and drive five minutes to Sylvester Road. Turn left, drive 20 minutes (when the road forks, stay right), park at the **Cascade Falls** sign, and walk down the trail. Back on Highway 7, continue east on the prettiest section of the winding road (between Dewdney and Deroche) to signs for **Kilby General Store Museum**.

[KIDS] This is one historic site—showing a once-bustling community that was bypassed—that shouldn't be missed. The

General Store was in operation until the 1970s. It was built on pilings because this area was a floodplain, and the view is splendid. The Tearoom has tasty light lunches and an intriguing selection of gifts, including colourful replicas of early canned salmon tins. Generally open May to September; weekends only October and November, but hours may expand (call 796-9576).

From here, depending on how much time you have, you could drive the 15 minutes north on Highway 9 to **Harrison Hot Springs** for a quick look at a classic old-time lakefront resort, now home to the [KIDS] **World Championship Sand Sculpture Competition** each September (796-3425, Info Line). Stop for a cold one or a snack at the **Old Settler** log pub on the way up to the springs (outside seating overlooks the water lilies and willows of the Miami River). Cross the Fraser River south of Agassiz.

This will put you on the more rural **Yale Road** through Chilliwack, where cars still angle-park, before reconnecting with the Trans-Canada. Boot it back to Highway 11, where you first turned north, and turn north again, passing Clayburn Road to turn left (west) at Harris Road, which will lead you along a delightful stretch past communities like Mount Lehman and **Bradner** (with fields of daffodils, gladioli, and tulips and lots of seasonal roadside produce stalls). Eventually you'll feed back onto the Trans-Canada, which will take you to Vancouver.

GIBSONS

[KIDS][FREE] One of BC's best—and shortest—ferry trips is the delightful 40-minute trip up Howe Sound from West Vancouver's Horseshoe Bay Terminal to **Langdale**. Note: Ferry ticket sales are now cut off five minutes before sailing for vehicles; 10 minutes for foot passengers (277-0277 for recorded info; 669-1211 for a ferry agent). A 5-kilometre (3-mile) drive from Langdale lands you in front of the familiar "Welcome Back" sign on **Molly's Reach**, which presumes you have been here before, if only via television. This simple seaside village is known to television viewers in 40 countries as the setting for 19 seasons of *The Beachcombers*. (Stephen King movie fans will also see Gibsons in *Needful Things*.) The cafe setting is only a facade, but there's enough in the marina, shops, restaurants, and nearby hiking trails and beaches to assuage visitors' initial disappointment.

The stairs just below Molly's Reach lead down to the marina and government wharf. You can follow **Gibsons Sea Walk** to either the left (glance up at vintage waterfront residences above) or to the right past **Smitty's Marina** and marine enterprises, servicing the active fishing and recreational port. The walk takes one detour up to the road, just below the **Elphinstone Pioneer Museum**, before continuing along to the **Mariners' Locker** general store, a good place to get really functional boating, fishing, and weather gear. Signs in the marina advertise fishing charters and kayak and boat rentals if you cannot resist the lure of the sea. The Elphinstone museum recreates the turn-of-the-century office, bedroom, and kitchen of early settlers and includes photos of old Gibsons streetscapes, a Native dugout canoe, a double-ender fishing boat, and equipment from early commercial ventures in logging, fishing, and the W. M. Malkin cooperative jam cannery. Open Monday and Tuesday 1pm to 5pm; Wednesday to Sunday 9am to 5pm.

At **Gibsons Fish Market** the crisp, battered fish and chips are always freshly cooked. Farther down the road, **Truffles** offers up heavenly baked goods, hearty soups and sandwiches, quiche, cappuccino, and decadent Belgian truffles. For a seaside beer, head for **Grandma's Pub** by the government wharf.

A number of small galleries show the work of local artists and artisans, but at **Quay Works Gallery and Shop** (across the street from Truffles and downstairs), you have a chance to talk to artists as they work. **Molly's Lane Market**, between Gower Point Road and Molly's Reach, is worth a browse for the chance to pick up antiques, old books, and local crafts.

There's a spectacular overview of the town and surroundings, best reached by car, since the road is steep. Drive up School Road to reach **Soames Hill Park Trail** (via North Rd west, turning right onto Chamberlin Rd, then left on Bridgeman). Park here and get ready for a steep (but rewarding) half-hour climb up to the Knob (local name for the summit).

[FREE] Gibsons is surrounded by a well-marked network of hiking trails called the **South Elphinstone Heritage and Recreation Trails**, entwined with the roads and camps from the early logging trade (expect to see the remains of old Japanese and Chinese labour camps and the Drew-Battle 1903 steam-powered sawmill at First Camp). [KIDS] The most popular family beach destination is **Chaster Provincial Park**, 5 kilometres (3 miles) past Gibsons.

The **Bonniebrook Lodge**, across the street from the park (886-2188), is now run by the former chef of Vancouver's Le Gavroche, Philippe Lacoste, and his wife, Karen. They have transformed this seaside lodge into a first-class retreat, with four Edwardian-style bed-and-breakfast rooms available. Downstairs, **Chez Philippe Restaurant** has become the newest spot on the Sunshine Coast for fine dining. Remember: the last ferry sails at 8:20pm!

It is possible to visit Gibsons without taking your car on the ferry (to avoid the irritating weekend lineups). Bus service starts right at the ferry dock, and funky taxicabs in town can get you out to Chaster Park. Or you can do the whole excursion easily by bicycle. Any time of the year is a delight on the Sunshine Coast. If you do have your car, you can also drive on to the much larger village of Sechelt. (See Sunshine Coast in the Excursions section of this chapter for details.)

LADNER

Slip back in time and enjoy the sensory delights of this farming community tucked against the reaches, sloughs, and marshes at the mouth of the mighty Fraser River. It's an ideal starting point for side trips to the **George C. Reifel Migratory Bird Sanctuary** on **Westham Island** and the less-known **Deas Island Regional Park**.

Take the River Road exit off Highway 99 (the first exit immediately south of the George Massey Tunnel, also known as the Deas Tunnel). You'll soon be driving down a road where fat ponies graze next to old wooden houses with graceful verandas and hollyhocks. **[KIDS][FREE]** Cross a wooden bridge past pretty sloops and fish boats to **Ladner Harbour Park** and its trails through the cottonwoods. Swenson Walk, a lovely tree-lined trail, leads from the park to Ladner Marsh, a freshwater tidal marsh that is home to many species of waterfowl, such as cinnamon teal ducks, great blue herons, and marsh wrens.

Just before the bridge, you will have passed Ferry Road. If you're looking for a snack, follow it north for about 1.6 kilometres (1 mile) to a small parking lot. To the east is the Captain's Cove Marina (public) and, more important, **Captain's Cove Pub** (6100 Ferry Rd, 946-2727), with a panoramic view of the Fraser and the west end of Deas Island plus a menu that includes seafood and homemade soup.

[KIDS][FREE] A stroll along Ladner's "old village," centred on Delta Street and 48th Avenue, should include a visit to the delightful **Delta Museum & Archives** (4858 Delta St, 946-9322) housed in the 1912 Tudor-style former municipal hall and jail. The six furnished Victorian rooms are fun, but quirkier and more local are exhibits on early Ladner, including True Haviland Oliver—"renowned Canada Goose hunter—and his trusty bicycle." You'll find some good, affordable Native art in the gift shop. Next door, at **Uncle Herbert's Fish & Chip Shop** (946-8222), you have to be from Yorkshire to appreciate "true mushy peas" but not to relish the fine fish and chips; and the separate themed rooms are exhibits in themselves. Across the street, **Stillwater Sports** (4849 Delta St, 946-9933) has a cougar in the window and enough decoys to fill a punt. Ladner locals like the friendly style and riverside patio of **Sharkey's Seafood Bar & Grill**. You can't miss this bright blue building (4953 Chisholm St, 946-7793).

Head down River Road West, past the fruit stands to the sign at the bridge directing you to turn right to Westham Island. Drive on another 15 metres (50 feet) and stop at the **Canoe Pass Village** sign. Clamber up the dyke bank for a jaw-dropping gander at mega-float homes, some complete with kayak davits. If you have a bike, you might want to cycle down one of the farm roads, inhaling the earthy smells as you go.

[KIDS] The **George C. Reifel Migratory Bird Sanctuary** (946-6980), 9.5 kilometres (6 miles) west, is a rural remnant of the once-vast Fraser estuary marshes, now home to thousands of migratory birds on their ages-old path along North America's Pacific flyway. More than 250 species can be sighted throughout the year, from the Canada goose to the uncommon black-crowned night heron and the extremely rare Temminck's stint. In winter don't miss the unforgettable sight of thousands of snow geese rising up as one on their journey to California from their Arctic breeding grounds off Siberia. (See the Recreation chapter for details.) Early risers should start with Reifel, returning to Ladner for lunch or tea. In season, look for pick-your-own berries on Westham.

Back in town, stop in the 5000 block of 48th Avenue for a look at an old church (now a Montessori school), the restored **Bridgeport School**, and Heritage House Interiors.

[KIDS][FREE] Peaceful **Deas Island Regional Park** is technically located right above the George Massey Tunnel. It's also one of the finest river parks on the lower Fraser, the world's largest salmon river. (En route, you can't miss the area's Tourist Information office housed in a reproduction Victorian once you leave Highway 99.) Here you can enjoy the river's breeze or cast your line toward salmon-loaded gillnetters or freighters carrying cars from Japan. Wander to the viewing tower for a dreamy view of river traffic and wildlife, and cast a thought to poor Billy Deas, the black tinsmith who built a cannery here and made tins by hand, ultimately dying of Tinsmith's Disease attributed to lead soldering. There are three historic buildings, dating from 1894–1906, relocated on Deas Island. Burvilla, once home to the Burr family, opens to the public during the summer, selling antiques and country collectibles. People picnic here year round, but the big family event is **Fraser Fest**, held every June (call 946-4232 for specific date).

If you plan to be near Ladner around dinnertime, make reservations for a leisurely if pricey dinner at **La Belle Auberge** (4856 48th Ave, 946-7717).

Day Trips

Pitt Polder and Widgeon Marsh Reserve

PITT POLDER AND WIDGEON MARSH RESERVE

[KIDS][FREE] Coquitlam's turquoise Pitt Lake, about a 35-minute drive from Vancouver, is the largest freshwater tidal lake in North America, but the true attractions in this spectacular rugged valley are Pitt Polder, a marshy area south of Pitt Lake, and the Widgeon Marsh Reserve (432-6350). The latter—the Greater Vancouver Regional District Parks' newest acquisition—is already well known to birders. Views of the jagged peaks of Golden Ears Provincial Park and the Coast Mountains are spectacular.

You can walk or cycle the series of dykes ringing nearby **Pitt Polder** (polder was a term used by early Dutch homesteaders to describe a low-lying area behind dykes). Holland's Queen Juliana, who stayed in Canada during the Second World War, provided the funds to employ returning servicemen to build these dykes. Allow two hours around the bottom; three around the top, taking into account bird-watching towers en route.

A better way to get close to the wildlife and appreciate the calming beauty of these pristine wetlands is to rent a canoe at **Ayla Canoes** (941-2822) from March through October ($30 a day). Owner Gordon Williams knows the area well and can tell you about the 44,000 salmon that return to spawn and the bird species found here. At present, boats are the only way in to **Widgeon Marsh Reserve** (it's closed to the walking public), which was purchased in 1992 as a park reserve for the future.

Follow the Lougheed Highway (Hwy 7) to Port Coquitlam. Cross the Pitt River Bridge into Pitt Meadows and turn left onto Dewdney Trunk Road. Follow it for 6.2 kilometres (3.8 miles) and turn left onto Neaves/208th Street, which becomes Rannie Road and finally ends at the parking lot by the public boat launch at the mouth of Pitt Lake. (The lake can become dangerous when a wind comes up.) Cross Pitt River to Widgeon Creek on the west side. Instead of the direct 10-minute crossing, you can take the more leisurely route around Siwash Island. Along the way watch for herons, ospreys, and eagles atop the mooring posts that tether log booms.

Head north up the narrow channel between **Siwash Island** and the western riverbank, where marsh marigolds bloom in spring. Drifting silently with the current, you may slip past red-tailed hawks, widgeons, trumpeter swans, and rare Sandhill cranes, whose nesting areas in the polder are closed to dyke-walking visitors from April through June. The paddle up Widgeon Creek to a covered picnic area with campsites takes about one hour. Look for the lime-green garbage cans, which are easier to spot than the white-and-brown sign reading "Widgeon Creek BC Forest Service Recreational Site." Pull up on the beach for a picnic and swim. You can leave your canoe here and follow well-marked Forest Service trails upstream for a view of the impressive **Widgeon Falls**, a delightful three-hour round trip. Tip from the foresters: If you're hiking in the fall or winter, take the drier road for the first three kilometres if there's been a lot of rain. It will merge back into the trail. A signed fork on the trail directs you to Widgeon Falls or Widgeon Lake. Only those in good shape should tackle the steep, nine-hour round-trip to Widgeon Lake. It is spectacular, and the trout fishing is great at this emerald in the sky.

▼
Day Trips

Pitt Polder and Widgeon Marsh Reserve

▲

[KIDS][FREE] Fourteen times larger than Stanley Park, the Seymour Demonstration Forest remains one of the best-kept secrets on Vancouver's North Shore, despite the 350,000 annual visitors (many are school kids). Originally a closed watershed, the forest opened to visitors in 1987 as one of Greater Vancouver Regional District's 22 "natural state" parks. Now the 5,600-hectare (13,837-acre) Seymour Demonstration Forest (north end of Lillooet Rd, 432-6286) attracts enthusiastic regular hikers, cyclists, and in-line skaters drawn by the 50 kilometres (31 miles) of paved and gravel logging roads and trails as well as by access to the Seymour River.

The idea is to help people understand that logging can work if the forest is managed well. Because of the controversy in BC about clearcut logging and the bad press that the province has received, people want to learn more—and are surprised to discover that many of the big western red cedar, western hemlock, Douglas fir, amabilis fir, and Sitka spruce are only 75 years old. Visitors will also learn what makes sap rise in a tree and how to spot stumps left from logging in the 1900s.

Follow Lillooet Road north past Capilano College and the cemetery. A gravel road will take you to the parking area and information centre, where friendly staff are happy to point you to the best routes for your ability. For families with children, there is the pleasant **Forest Ecology Loop Trail** around pretty **Rice Lake**. It's one of the few freshwater lakes on the North Shore, and you can fish for trout from the small docks (or on the Seymour River), provided you have a provincial fishing licence (available from any tackle shop).

The big draw is the 22-kilometre (13.7-mile) round-trip trek on the "mainline" to **Seymour Dam**, which includes a broad, spectacular vista from **Mid Valley Viewpoint**. Walking is easy, although on weekends most people seem to be on wheels (bikes and in-line skates), enjoying the broad paved road. Note: You can't wheel whenever you want. (See restrictions at end of this section.)

The prettier trail beside the river takes almost double the time of the road. [KIDS][FREE] There are many **free guided tours** (phone 432-6286 weekdays or pick up a list when you arrive), and one of these could pay big dividends some day: "Lost in the Woods" offers survival skills for kids 4 to 10 years old (with an adult escort). Sunday bus tours, guided by volunteer foresters, run from June to October, 9:30am to 12:30pm and 1:30pm to 4:30pm. It's best to reserve a seat (drop-in only if space available).

If you've packed a picnic, there are swimming holes between the main gate and Mid Valley, and the water is warm compared with the better-known but chilly Lynn Creek (but keep an eye out for bears). Or plan to eat at the base of the

▼

Day Trips

*Seymour
Demonstra-
tion Forest*

▲

massive dam, whose dramatic concrete architecture would have fit right into Terry Gilliam's movie *Brazil*. It's worth the short climb up to overlook the lake. Don't miss the five-minute trail to the nearby [KIDS][FREE] **Seymour Salmonid Society Fish Hatchery**. Note: The hatchery gate is open 8am to 3:30pm daily. Aside from fish-rearing ponds (you can see young salmon even closer in the troughs) and adult coho spawning in the fall, it's a great picnic site and the only close source of drinking water. Check for Open House hatchery dates in spring and fall. A shuttle bus runs all day to the hatchery.

No dogs are allowed in the forest at any time; bikes and in-line skates are permitted on the paved road to Seymour Dam only after 5pm (year-round) and weekends. Public hours are not steadfast, but generally the walking public is welcome 7am to 9pm in summer, 8am to 5pm in winter. Access for canoeing and kayaking is by special-use permit only (987-1273).

North Shore Option: Few tourists ever see Indian Arm, a spectacular forested fjord carved out by the last ice age. Now there's a way: Peter Loppe's **Lotus Land Tours** (684-4922) runs four-hour (return) kayak trips up Indian Arm to Twin Island for a barbecued salmon lunch. Outfit offers hotel pickups.

STEVESTON

Steveston, once the biggest fishing port in the world (with more than 50 canneries) hasn't a single operating cannery left. It is still Canada's largest port, though, with more than 1,000 vessels, most of which are commercial fishing boats. It's a colourful place that still smells of the sea and history—a place where you can often buy fresh prawns, salmon, snapper, sole, and crab right off the boats.

Drive south from Vancouver along Highway 99 to the Steveston Highway turnoff, or take the 406 or 407 bus from downtown Vancouver. Park or get off the bus at **Steveston Park**, which pays tribute to the Japanese-Canadians who helped build Steveston and were later evacuated to the Interior during the Second World War. The nearby **Martial Arts Centre** is the first dojo house ever built outside Japan. This house, built specifically for martial arts, has two halls—one with hardwood floors for kendo and karate, the other with tatami mats for karate.

Old-timers may grumble about the incursion of walkers, joggers, and cyclists on the new bike trails and the upscale **Steveston Landing** retail complex (3800 Bayview St), but these developments have saved the wetlands (the salt marshes of Sturgeon Bank are Canada's largest wintering spot for ducks) from being turned into oil tanker docks.

Plan to spend the morning wandering through the historic fishing village centred on Bayview, Moncton, and Chatham Streets. Pick up fish and chips from the take-out window at

Dave's Fish and Chips (3460 Moncton St, 271-7555) or **Jake's on the Pier** (3866 Bayview St, 275-7811) on the waterfront. Or spoon up some chowder at **Pajo's**, a boat restaurant anchored at the dock (summer only).

Danny's Rainbow Charters, a converted deep-sea, Dutch-built, diesel-powered lifeboat, leaves on demand from the dock at the foot of Second Avenue for a 30-minute narrated harbour tour past boats, eagles, great blue herons, and sea lions. Or see the harbour by land via the dykes that wrap around the southwestern edge of Steveston (a leisurely walk could take up to 2½ hours).

Try the famous Spanish paella or crab served on the outside patio at **Casa Sleighs** (3711 Bayview St, 275-5188), newly risen from the ashes of Sleigh's, destroyed by arson. **Steveston Seafood House** (3951 Moncton St, 271-5252) is also something of an institution; the decor is no-surprises nautical, but the wine list is surprisingly good.

Moncton Street is a mix of new boutiques and authentic fishing gear stores located in one-storey false-fronted buildings. The **Steveston Museum** (3811 Moncton St, 271-6868, Mon–Sat) was erected as a prefab bank and built in four-foot sections in 1905. It now doubles as a post office. Some visitors claim to feel "definite vibrations" of ghosts.

[KIDS][FREE] Most of what you'll want to see lies to the west, eventually ending where ocean and river meet at **Garry Point Park**. Here the Musqueam people camped for over a thousand years when following the salmon runs. The small Japanese garden is a gift of Wakayama, Japan, a sister city. Ten kilometres of dyke paths head out from here. **Britannia Heritage Shipyard**, the oldest building on the waterfront, is a huge timbered dry dock that began life as a cannery. Old-timers have revived the art of wooden shipbuilding and repair. With any luck, you'll catch them working on an old wooden gillnetter.

The cedar plank pathway was once Steveston's main street, when the town was a heady Saturday night boomtown with more than 10,000 people strolling the boardwalks between hotels, saloons, and houses of prostitution. Nearby, drop in for a piece of Judy's deep-dish pie at the **Steveston Cannery Cafe** (3711 Moncton St, 272-1222), a turn-of-the-century cookhouse.

[KIDS][FREE] Don't miss the former **Gulf of Georgia Cannery**, another landmark at the foot of Third Street newly opened by Parks Canada as a National Historic Site. The 40-seat Boiler House Theatre uses multimedia to tell the story of the "Monster Cannery." In summer, you'll also have a chance to shop at the many roadside fruit and vegetable stands in this prime farming area or to join in on the July 1 (Canada Day) Salmon Festival, Canada's largest one-day community festival.

Detour: most people miss **London Farm Heritage Site** (276-4107), just east of Steveston. Follow Steveston Highway to

Number Three Road in Richmond. Turn south to Dyke Road, drive west to parking at the foot of Gilbert Road. Charles London built a farmhouse and wharf here in the 1880s, which soon became the prime stop (more accessible than Steveston's Phoenix Cannery Wharf) for boats carrying people, farm products, and supplies to and from Victoria. Eventually it was to become the London Post Office. Nearby sandy **Gilbert Beach** is great for beachcombing, bar fishing, or picnicking.

VICTORIA
See also Victoria in Excursions section of this chapter.

By ferry or air, getting there is half the fun, which makes British Columbia's capital city on Vancouver Island doable in a day. The ferry ride through Active Pass and the southern Gulf Islands takes 1 hour and 35 minutes, but allow at least 3 hours travel time downtown to downtown. **Pacific Coach Lines** (662-8074) offers frequent reliable service between the two downtown areas from Vancouver's bus terminal at 1150 Station Street. If you prefer to drive yourself, call **BC Ferries** (669-1211 or (888) 223-3779 in BC only) for sailing times (recorded information, 277-0277). Summer and holidays, arrive at least half an hour to 1 hour before sailing.

Helijet Airways (455 Waterfront Rd, 273-1414) and **West Coast Air**'s floatplane service (Tradewinds Marina, west of Canada Place, (800) 347-2222) are pricier, but they offer 35-minute harbour-to-harbour service. (Helijet also links downtown Victoria direct with Vancouver International Airport.) The two best times to travel to Victoria are on a crisp, clear day in early December when the sea is calm, and in the summer months, despite the many tourists. Here's why. In December, the **Empress Hotel** is decorated for Christmas. So too is [KIDS] **Craigdarroch Castle** (1050 Joan Cres, (250) 592-5323), and the gift shop of the **Art Gallery of Greater Victoria** (1040 Moss St, (250) 384-4101) has wonderful glass ornaments.

But first, settle back into an earlier, gentler time in the **Bengal Lounge** of the Empress, where a buffet of assorted curries is served up for a warming tiffin. After lunch, check the Empress archives on the lower level for the days when a suite cost $15, the William F. Tickle Orchestra played, and wartime menus urged: "All persons in ordering their food ought to consider the needs of Great Britain and her Allies and their Armies for wheat, beef, bacon and fats." Afternoon tea is served in, of course, the Tea Lobby, but $22 is hefty and the six-course tradition is more than a meal. Another option is tea and "just scones, please," in the Bengal Lounge.

In summer, there isn't a more heavenly place to spend the afternoon than in the gardens of **Point Ellice House** (2616 Pleasant St, (250) 387-4697). Walk a few blocks first to local eatery **C'est Bon** (Bastion Square, (250) 381-1461), notable for its homemade soup, breads, and croissants as well as a new view to the harbour since the city removed a wall. Vegetarians head for cheery **Re-bar Modern Foods** in the same square ((250) 361-9223). Lemon risotto pancakes to die for; you could die *from* "Pharoah's Sneakers" wheatgrass juice.

[KIDS] From the Inner Harbour, board the mini **Victoria Harbour Ferry** for the 10-minute ride up the Gorge to the Point Ellice House, where you step up onto the landing dock and back into the 19th century. (Tip: *Do* arrive by sea, not by land. The neighbouring auto repair garages spoil the mood for those arriving by car.) Until 1977, Point Ellice was the home of the gardening-besotted O'Reilly family, whose slip into genteel poverty meant subsequent generations never replaced the original Victorian furnishings. Sir John A. Macdonald, Canada's first prime minister, once dined here

Afternoon tea is still served on the croquet lawn 1pm to 4pm Thursday to Sunday (summers only; reservations suggested); in June, the dreamy garden, still being carefully renovated, is heady with the scent of old-fashioned damask roses. Sundays are best (and quietest) for, sadly, Point Ellice is the last bastion of peace on the now quite noisy Pleasant Street.

Victoria's charm lies in its comfortable human scale, which you can enjoy year-round as you stroll up Government Street. Few buildings in the heart of the city are over seven storeys. Being on foot makes sense here, since 90 percent of what most visitors want to see is within two blocks of the waterfront.

[KIDS] In under an hour you can walk across town or stroll most of the waterfront past sailboats and floatplanes and then go on to Bastion Square, where the less well known but fascinating **Maritime Museum** houses *Trekka*, a 6-metre (20-foot) ketch that sailed solo around the world in the 1950s, and *Tilikum*, a converted 11.5-metre (38-foot) Native dugout canoe that made an equally impressive two-year passage to England at the turn of the century. Aviation buffs will enjoy **The Aviator** in Bastion Square, where pilots, from the First World War to the Gulf War, sign in. Nearby is **Dig This**, a great gardener's shop.

The return trip down the very English Government Street takes you past the gleaming mahogany and stained-glass interiors of heritage buildings like the century-old tobacco shop **E. A. Morris** ((250) 382-4811), which ships tobacco throughout the world but also stocks nifty shaving gear, seltzer bottles, and walking sticks. You will also pass **Munro's** ((250) 382-2464), which *Maclean's* columnist Allan Fotheringham calls the best bookstore in Canada, and **Rogers' Chocolates** ((250) 384-7021), whose near-hockey-puck-size Victoria creams wrapped in waxy, pink-gingham paper have been shipped to Buckingham Palace.

British Woollens specializes in good-quality women's

clothes; **Sasquatch Trading Company Ltd.** and the **Indian Craft Shop** both stock some of the best Cowichan sweaters available. Two quick side excursions off Government Street are worth taking. First, dip into the Eaton Centre for a gander at **British Importers**, whose present store, complete with Italian leather floor tiles and handmade lighting fixtures, won a national design award. Its exclusive products go beyond English brollies and Bally shoes to Armani and Valentino designs. Then, turn up from Government Street to 606 Trounce Alley, where the **Nushin Boutique**, one of Victoria's elite women's clothing stores, brings together many European designers. Some, less well known, offer surprisingly good value.

For a not-so-British take on shopping, head for Canada's oldest and perhaps smallest Chinatown, down **Fisgard Street** and **Fan Tan Alley**, Canada's narrowest byway. Call **Les Chan** ((250) 383-7317) to see if he's running one of his popular tours of tea shops, temples, herbalists, and the dim sum lunch at Kwong Tung. **Eastern Interiors**, a former Buddhist temple, has museum-quality pieces.

Check the funky shops along **Johnson Street** and in historic **Market Square** (where, back in 1887, 23 factories produced 90,000 pounds of opium for Canada's legal trade of the narcotic). Artist Bill Blair and partner Shelora Sheldan have filled tiny, colourful **Hoi Polloi** (fronting on Pandora St, (250) 480-7822) with weird and wonderful goodies, from his birchbark lamp shades with *Rosemarie*-era Mounties to Mexican "Festival of the Dead" skull-headed figures and an artful selection of postcards.

There are some intriguing home design, furnishings, and surplus stores just beyond Chinatown on **Herald Street** (Surplus City) and **Store Street** (North Park Design, Capital Iron, and Chintz & Co.). Serious antique hunters head for **Antique Row** in the 800 to 1000 blocks of Fort Street.

Hunger pangs while shopping? Do what the locals do and hang out in coffee bars like the **Sally Cafe** (714 Cormorant St, (250) 381-1431), or **Demitasse Coffee Bar** (1320 Blanshard St, (250) 386-4442), or totally retro **Bohematea** on lower Yates (515 Yates St, (250) 383-2329)—all good sources of quick meals and even of art. Or relax with the crossover crowd of Victorians at **Dilettante's Cafe** (787 Fort St, (250) 381-3327) over oven-roasted chicken, stir-fries and polenta, and over-the-top desserts.

Someone invariably recommends the **Royal British Columbia Museum** as one of the best in the country, with dramatic dioramas of natural BC landscapes and full-scale reconstructions of Victorian storefronts. It's definitely a must-see. Of particular interest: the Northwest Coast First Nations exhibit, rich with spiritual and cultural artifacts. Open every day, Belleville and Government St ((250) 387-3701). Only two blocks away is another museum, one considered quite "timeless": With 300 wax figures, **The Royal London Wax Museum** is worth a visit—and a chuckle (470 Belleville St, (250) 388-4461).

It's a fairly short walk from there to 75-hectare (184-acre) Beacon Hill Park, with its splendid ocean views and the hand-holding couples who stroll the walkways and give retirement a good name. A lovely spot to get away from the shopping mania downtown.

Even better, hop the #2 Oak Bay bus from downtown and explore the charming village of Oak Bay, where the Tweed Curtain truly begins. Skip the overrated Blethering Place tea spot, reboard, and stop instead at the park-side **Windsor House Tea Room** (2540 Windsor Rd, (250) 595-3135) that's also a "scone's throw from the beach." Along the way, you'll pass historic **Oak Bay Beach Hotel** (1175 Beach Dr, (250) 598-4556), where lunch on their pub's seaside patio is a summer treat. Exploring Victoria by bus really is a breeze. You can buy Scratch 'n' Ride Day Passes at many outlets (not sold on the bus), and *Explore Victoria by Bus* spells out exactly how to get to every attraction, neighbourhood, park—and back.

Although Victorians do weary of being touted as a little bit of old Blighty, let's face it: an early Victorian man-about-town once shared a mistress with the Prince of Wales (later Edward VII), the Empress Hotel still pours 1.6 million cups of afternoon tea a year, and horse-drawn vehicles have been clopping along the Inner Harbour since the city started sightseeing tours in 1903. And where else can you step back in time to visit Anne Hathaway's thatched cottage (albeit a full-size replica of the home where William Shakespeare's wife was born) and see Queen Victoria in wax, alongside replicas of the crown jewels, without crossing the Atlantic?

EXCURSIONS

BARKLEY SOUND

[KIDS] Say "Lady Rose" to British Columbians who travel their own province and you'll see faces light up. Year-round, the stout, Scottish-built, 1937 packet freighter MV *Lady Rose*, and its newer companion, the MV *Frances Barkley*, carry mail and supplies from Port Alberni to remote communities along the Alberni Inlet and on the distant islands of Barkley Sound, all the way out to the west coast of Vancouver Island. Both working freight vessels also carry passengers (100 and 200 respectively), for whom the cargo calls make a scenic diversion. Our favourite destination is Bamfield. Whether you prefer to fish, hike, dive, beachcomb, bird-watch, or curl up with a book, you can do it here.

There are two routes by sea. The year-round scheduled run to **Bamfield** operates every Tuesday, Thursday, and

Saturday ($38). Come summer, on Monday, Wednesday, and Friday, additional summer sailings serve the beautiful Broken Group Islands (popular with kayakers) before heading on to **Ucluelet** (also easily reached by Pacific Rim Highway). Isolated Bamfield (population 270) holds more charm than the larger Ucluelet. From October to May, the Bamfield run stops at the Broken Group Islands if canoeists or kayakers make an advance request. From early July through Labour Day, a special Sunday sailing stops here. Try for that sailing, but call to confirm ((800) 663-7192 or (250) 723-8313) or write Alberni Marine Transportation, PO Box 188, Port Alberni, BC V9Y 7L6. They also rent kayaks and canoes.

The boat stops to drop supplies at some 20 tiny floating fishing and logging camps and ice at fish farms. Sometimes it just stops to sell a candy bar to a fisherman with a sweet tooth or to deliver a newspaper. Once in a while the cargo is more unusual—like a piano or a horse. You can also drive to Bamfield over a gravel road from Port Alberni in an hour and a half or charter a floatplane, but we recommend the leisurely float down the inlet. If you miss the big boats, you can hire the speedy Bamfield Express Water Taxi, (250) 728-3001, which takes one-third the time of the longer trip.

The *Lady Rose*'s happy band of 100 passengers ranges from loggers, anglers, and scientists to kayakers, hikers, and tourists along for the 9-to-10-hour return trip ($32 to $36; kids under seven are free). It can be breezy even in summer. Take warm clothes, a camera, extra film, and binoculars. Besides being a better way to reach Bamfield than travelling over a rough road filled with logging trucks, the 4 1/2-hour cruise down Alberni Inlet is breathtaking.

Given the 8am departure time from the Alberni Harbour Quay, you'll probably have to overnight in **Port Alberni**. This working town is worth a look, especially in spring when the cherry blossom-lined streets are oddly juxtaposed with the mill's hulking profile. **The Curious Coho** (4841 Johnston Rd, aka Hwy 4 as you enter town, (250) 724-2141) is a great bookstore, and the staff will tip you off to good local eateries. **Swale's Rock** (5328 Argyle, (250) 723-0777) is good for lunch; try the dynamite Fisherman's Bread. [KIDS][FREE] Given BC's checkered logging reputation, the Alberni Forestry Information Centre, at the nearby new wharf development, hopes to offer adults some insight into the relationship between forestry and the environment and give kids some fun stuff to explore. The nearby Doughnut Shop touts "the best doughnuts on Vancouver Island." **Coast Hospitality Inn** (3835 Redford St, (250) 723-8111) is Port Alberni's best commercial bet; **Alberni Valley Visitor Info Centre** (you can't miss it driving into town) has a list of bed and breakfasts ((250) 724-6535). Some are 15 minutes from town on beautiful Sproat Lake, where morning dips are encouraged. Some hosts will drive you to the *Lady Rose* and store your car.

Breakfast and lunch are served in the *Lady Rose* galley; or you can take along a loaf of cheese bread from Port Alberni's **Flour Shop** ((250) 723-1105). Start with coffee at the **Blue Door**, a diner down by the docks.

Bamfield spans the inlet, which acts as the main street of the town. A local water taxi joins west and east Bamfield. [KIDS][FREE] The tiny fishing village is heavily populated by marine biologists from the nearby Marine Research Station (half-hour visits are available summer weekends at 1:30pm to coincide with the boat arrivals, but it's a good idea to call ahead at (250) 728-3301).

In Bamfield you might want to stay at **Imperial Eagle Lodge** ((250) 728-2334), where Jim and Karen Levis's charming country-style main lodge and small, rustic "fisherman's cabin" are ideal for romantic couples or travellers who appreciate the attention to detail, not to mention the harbour view from the deck, star view from the hot tub, and excellent meals of locally harvested seafood. American plan or bed and breakfast for boat charters.**Woods End Landing** ((250) 728-3383) has truly superb self-contained log cottages in a woodland and formal garden setting. Owners Susan and Terry Giddens suggest exploring Bamfield Inlet by canoe or paddling a kayak to the Deer Group Islands. Fishing enthusiasts and families are happy at **McKay Bay Lodge** ((250) 728-3323), where rooms upstairs and out front are best. **Bamfield Lodge** dates from the '50s, but it's our choice as the hottest harbour-side cappuccino bar.

[FREE] Take a short walk to **Brady's Beach** or hike farther along to **Cape Beale Lighthouse** and the wild beaches just beyond. The stretch of coastline from here south to Port Renfrew is one of the most rugged and unforgiving shores in the world. With one shipwreck for every 1.6 kilometres (1 mile) of coastline, it became known as the Graveyard of the Pacific and spurred the building of the original West Coast lifesaving trail, part of which is now the hikers' celebrated West Coast Trail. If time allows, hike to the northern end of the trail at **Pachena Bay**, just 5 kilometres (3 miles) from Bamfield. (This is the prettier end of the 77-kilometre (48-mile) trail: some hikers just take the short route to **Nitinat Narrows** and retrace their steps.)

Getting there: from Nanaimo, take the Island Highway to Parksville, then Highway 4 to Port Alberni. [KIDS][FREE] Natural wonders along the way worth checking out: **Englishman River Falls**, a provincial park with pretty hiking trails, and Cathedral Grove, a truly wondrous slice of old-growth forest straddling the highway 11 kilometres (6.8 miles) west of Coombs (yes, that is a goat on the grass roof of Coombs Old

Country Market). Be sure to park and walk in. Within a few steps you'll see sights unseen from the road. Some of the giant old-growth Douglas fir, western red cedar, and western hemlock were growing here when King John signed the Magna Carta in 1215.

COAST MOUNTAIN LOOP

BC's West Coast rain forest is beautiful but so is the dry cattle country of the Interior. This circle route takes you past mountains, glaciers, canyons, and Chilcotin wilderness and, best of all, into the Cariboo. The section of Highway 99 (still called **Duffey Lake Road**) that links Whistler to BC's cattle country has long been familiar to four-wheel-drive owners. Thanks to the recent paving of the old logging road, this spectacular drive has opened to the rest of us. Any BC Tourist InfoCentre can provide a brochure and map detailing the Coast Mountain Circle Tour, which takes you north from the year-round resort of Whistler (see Whistler section in this chapter) through near-desert Lillooet to the high plateau country of Cache Creek and Ashcroft, where grass was once as high as a horse's belly and smart men found real money raising cattle for hungry gold miners.

From there, you'll circle south to Vancouver on the Trans-Canada (Hwy 1) through the dramatic Fraser Canyon, past the rafting capital of Lytton (which routinely records Canada's highest summer temperatures), and then to Hope before turning west through the farmlands and distant mountains of the Fraser Valley (see Fraser Valley in Day Trips section of this chapter) to the coast.

Driving time from **Whistler** to Cache Creek is about 3 1/2 hours. If you're just looking for a scenic drive with a few stops along the way, you can certainly do the whole circuit in two days, but it's a pity not to spend three or four exploring this fascinating route, which follows much of the historic gold rush trail built in the late 1850s and early 1860s. In summer, with any luck, this can be a hot, sunny drive, so load up the cooler with cold drinks and picnic goodies.

[KIDS][FREE] **The Lillooet Museum and InfoCentre** (Main St, (250) 256-4308 in summer, (250) 256-4556 off-season), set in a disused Anglican church that was packed in piece by piece on the backs of miners, is a reminder of the gold rush days, when, with 15,000 people, Lillooet was the second-largest city north of San Francisco. Another whole section is devoted to one of BC's best-known newspaper women, feisty Ma Murray. The nearby **Hanging Tree** (the key limb has rotted off) is a reminder of the stern days of "Hanging Judge" Matthew Begbie, when killers were hung.

From Lillooet, the Coast Circle route normally heads south on Highway 12 to Lytton. Instead, drive Highway 99 to

Highway 97 and the newly opened **Moondance Guest Ranch** at the base of the Marble Mountains ((250) 459-7775). Owners Pete and Sherry Boeda owe their good fortune to a highly successful coffee shop, **Bean Around the World**, which they opened in West Vancouver in 1990. Pete's no city slicker, having worked on guest ranches in Ontario and Alberta. Now they raise Herefords and foam BC's best cappuccinos for guests staying in four comfortable cabins, each with quilts, antiques, and private bathroom. Sherry's gourmet meals and books by the fire are served up in the lodge; pool and cards in the "saloon." After a day riding the high country on good saddlehorses, it's back to the barn and the wood-burning sauna. On crisp, clear winter days and moonlit nights a team of Belgian horses pulls a sleigh.

[KIDS][FREE] **Pavilion Lake** is a great spot for a swim after the drive across the peaceful big-sky plateau country, where every breath smells of sagebrush and pine. **Historic Hat Creek Ranch** (north of Cache Creek, junction of Hwy 97 and Hwy 12, (250) 457-9722) is a must. You can take a guided wagon or trail ride around the last remaining intact Cariboo Wagon roadhouse and its buildings (well-trained, fat 'n' sassy retired ranch horses match your level as a rider, giving as good as they get). Admission by donation.

Carry on through Cache Creek (mostly gas stations and motels at this highway crossroads) past the benchlands to nearby **Ashcroft** for a fine meal or afternoon tea in the shade of leafy acacia trees at the delightful **Ashcroft Manor** (Hwy 1, take turnoff to Ashcroft, (250) 453-9983), a former stopping house that now operates its own museum and arts and crafts house.

Come July, country fans find it hard to resist detouring east to Merritt, once known only as the midway point on the Coquihalla Highway. The **Merritt Mountain Music Festival** is the place to be for country music, and recent years have featured the likes of Johnny Cash, the Carter Family, and Prairie Oyster.

For a delightful (and reasonable) night's stay and an excellent dinner, drive south 43 kilometres (27 miles) to **Spences Bridge** and the renovated historic (1890s) **Steelhead Inn**, now operated by the Ryans, with Scottish chef Ian McKay doing a nice turn in the kitchen ((250) 458-2398). The Ryans do rafting trips too. Curiously, there are few notable places to stay along the Coast Mountain route (there are plenty of motels). One alternative is to take a detour west from Pemberton or Lillooet to the $3-million newly hewn log **Tyax Mountain Lake Resort** ((250) 238-2221), which is open year-round and whose broad range of activities in the Chilcotin wilderness—helieverything, hiking, fishing, canoeing, and horseback riding in summer and skiing, snowmobiling, tobogganing, and skating in winter—draws families and guests from Europe and Japan. Some find it a bit overwhelming.

[KIDS] There's good fall steelhead fishing at Spences Bridge, and most whitewater rafting happens on the stretch of the Thompson River between here and **Lytton** (named for Sir Edward Bulwer-Lytton, British civil servant and novelist who penned the immortal line: "It was a dark and stormy night...."). It's an unforgettable experience. Rafting operators **Kumsheen Raft Adventures** claim to have pioneered both paddle- and power-rafting on the Thompson ((800) 663-6667). They've certainly got the most handsome rafting centre, 6 kilometres (4 miles) northeast of Lytton. Inspired by early ranch houses, the big-roofed building sits high on a Ponderosa pine flat with a spectacular view of the Thompson. New in 1996: their large safari-style cabin tent accommodation with patio, lockable doors, duvets—all cheerily lit by the warm glow of a propane lantern ($69 for four people).

[KIDS][FREE] Along the road, keep an eye out for two small provincial parks: **Goldpan** (beside the river) and, even better, the lesser-known **Skihist** (above the highway), a very special near-desert location with prickly pear cactus and the occasional Pacific rattlesnake. Here you'll also see impressive river panoramas and, if you're lucky, a Rocky Mountain bighorn sheep. If you don't go rafting, **Hell's Gate Airtram** (south of Boston Bar) will give you a 153-metre (502-foot) trip across the turbulent river. It draws a lot of tourists daily during the mid-April to mid-October season (there's even a Christmas shop at the bottom of the tram), but the trip across the river is worth doing at least once to see the fish ladders or to sample the salmon chowder at the Salmon House Restaurant. To make your travels along the old wagon trail through **Boston Bar** and **Yale** more interesting and educational, pick up material on gold rush history at any of the information centres along the way.

Many people blast through **Hope** (junction for the Fraser Canyon or the Hope-Princeton route east), but do stop to see the site of the 1965 **Hope Slide** (Hwy 3, 15 minutes east of Hope), where two of the four people killed in a massive avalanche remain entombed; a related mud slide filled the valley to a depth of 61 metres (200 feet). The **Othello Tunnels**, off Highway 5, are less well known to tourists and even to British Columbians, although Sylvester Stallone fans will recognize the dramatic setting from *First Blood*. Ask at the **Info-Centre** (919 Water Ave, 869-2021) for directions to the five tunnels that were carved out of rock to link the Kootenays and that were used by the Kettle Valley Railway until 1961. The tunnels drip, and they're closed in winter, but they're fascinating to walk through, with views of the Coquihalla River roaring by in the 100-metre-high (328-foot-high) gorge.

*See Day Trips section in this chapter for
information on getting to Victoria.*

Forty minutes north of Victoria and one hour south of Nanaimo lie the winding roads, rolling hills, green pastures, and fresh streams of **Cowichan**. The name means "land warmed by the sun," which may explain the deserved success of the many small vineyards that are now open to visitors. Cowichan Valley includes Mill Bay, Shawnigan Lake, Cowichan Bay, Duncan, Chemainus, Ladysmith, Yellow Point, Cobble Hill, and Lake Cowichan. Too many people see it only as the stretch they have to drive between Victoria and Nanaimo. They're missing a lot.

At Duncan's lauded **Native Heritage Centre** (200 Cowichan Way, (250) 746-8119) you can try traditional food, watch carvers at work, view *Great Deeds* (a multimedia theatre presentation), or shop for the real version of the much-copied Cowichan sweater, hand-knit in one piece. If you're near Duncan at dinner, the **Quamichan Inn** (just east of Duncan; 1478 Maple Bay Rd, (250) 746-7028) may be offering Indian curry, roast prime rib and Yorkshire pudding, or Fanny Bay oysters. Take your after-dinner coffee in the garden among fragrant wisteria and colourful dahlias. Faced with the shutdown of its mill in 1981, **Chemainus** became "the little town that could" when citizens bucked up and hired artists to paint the story of the town—all over everything. The artwork is far more enticing than you might think, and the little town is peppered with tearooms, funky cafes, and antique shops. For the finest dining for the thinnest dollar in this neck of the woods, you can't beat the **Waterford Inn & Restaurant** (5 minutes north of downtown Chemainus at 9875 Maple St, (250) 246-1046). If you long to leave it all behind, park your car in Chemainus and walk on to the ferry to Thetis Island, one of the smallest islands and an ideal day trip.

Keepers of inns and bed and breakfasts take pains with food. So, happily, do some vintners. Visits to tiny **Venturi-Schulze** (4235 Trans-Canada Hwy, Cobble Hill, (250) 743-5630) winery (one of BC's finest) are by appointment only. Make one! Better yet, book one of their four-hour winemaker dinners ($75 all inclusive) hosted by Giordano Venturi, as good a storyteller as a vintner, and wife/partner Marilyn Schulze. Two guest rooms.

Other vineyards to visit: **Vigneti Zenatta Winery** (5039 Marshall Rd, Duncan, (250) 748-4981) serves Italian food with a West Coast influence; **Cherry Point Vineyards** (840 Cherry Point Rd, Cobble Hill, (250) 743-1272) is also a bed and breakfast, where your stay includes a wine-tasting evening; **Blue Grouse Vineyard** (4365 Blue Grouse Rd, Duncan, (250) 743-3834), run by ex-veterinarian Hans Kiltz, offers a great view in lieu of food; and Al Piggot's **Merridale Cider Works** (1230

Merridale Rd, Cobble Hill, (250) 743-4293) makes cider in the French and English tradition (strong scrumpy!).

You can sample local wines at **Sahtlam Lodge and Cabins** (River Bottom Rd W, along the Cowichan River, (250) 748-7738), the only licensed dining room linked to a B&B operation in the valley. Or you can drink-and-ride with Brian Storen (maître d' at the original Sooke Harbour House) and wife Linda Collier, who run quaint **Hummingbird Cottage** ((250) 743-4004) in Shawnigan Lake. They've partnered with Cobble Hill Corral to offer guests a five-hour round-trip horseback ride to Blue Grouse Vineyard, with gourmet picnic. Bring a suit for a quick dip in Bamberton Quarry en route. **Marifield Manor** ((250) 743-9930), on the other hand, is eminently civilized, from linen under bone china teacups to owner Cathy Basskin's occasional salon events. Over at **Fairburn Farm Country Manor B&B** ((250) 746-4637), Anthea Archer raises her own nitrite-free bacon and shops in Duncan's Saturday morning farmers market.

HORNBY ISLAND

This funky, laid-back, northern Gulf Island is seldom described in detail in guidebooks or even in government publications, despite some of the warmest swimming and one of the finest white sandy beaches in BC. The 1,600 locals like it that way. For one, it's a five-hour, three-ferry journey from Vancouver. Take the Horseshoe Bay ferry to Nanaimo, then allow two hours for the 80-kilometre (50-mile) drive north on Vancouver Island to **Buckley Bay**. From there, take the 10-minute ferry ride to the pastoral and artistic sister island of Denman, cross it, and then catch the next ferry for the short crossing to Hornby. Ferries are timed so you can make it easily, but check times for the last Mainland to Denman ferry that connects to Hornby (as early as 6pm).

Hornby is another world—no cash machines, no liquor store, and relatively few restaurants or places to stay other than campgrounds or private cabins; however, for people happy to schlep around in old shorts and thongs, Hornby is heaven. The tiny bucolic island is filled with characters: longhairs from the '60s; barefoot earth mothers (who weren't even born in the '60s); permanent artists like potter Wayne Ngan; and longtime summer families of architects, musicians, and such painters as Jack Shadbolt and Robert Bateman. You can kayak around the island in a long day or cycle the few roads in a couple of hours.

There are three social hubs to Hornby. The first is the local **recycling depot**—a sort of communal Dogpatch, complete with **Free Store**. The second is the local hobbit-house-like **community centre/theatre**, where movies like *Nixon* alternate with subtitled films like China's *Jou-Dou*. The third is the **Hornby Island Cooperative**, a grocery/hardware/video store ((250) 335-1121) that makes it unnecessary to pack in your own Asiago cheese, basmati rice, and the like. Also here are some artists' stores and two tiny food stands: **VORIZO** (Hornby's postal code) for cappuccino and quesadilla addicts, and **Jan's Cafe** with indoòr tables for carnivores and vegans alike.

A bike trip around the occasionally hilly island (rent at the **Hornby Island Off-Road Bike Shop**, ((250) 335-0444) is a pleasant blur of artisans' studios and produce gardens (don't miss the small sign for dreamy **Gordon's Garden** just before Ford's Cove Art Gallery, a good spot for local jewellery, crafts, and art supplies), punctuated by stops for a cold draft at the **Thatch** by the ferry or inland at the island's only bakery, the **Cardboard House Bakery and Cafe** (Central Rd, (250) 335-0733).

If you've never tried ocean kayaking, call Brad Fraser at **Hornby Ocean Kayaks** ((250) 335-2726), which rents kayaks and runs guided trips for novices. Brad's happy to tell you about prevailing winds, tides, best beaches, and chances for seeing mink, seals, eagles, and, perhaps, an orca. Best view from a kayak: hugging the coastline stretch between Tribune Bay and Whaling Station Bay, where cormorants hang off the sandstone cliffs of Helliwell Park. Detour to Flora Island, where curious sea lions bob off the most easterly point. Divers should know Hornby is one of the few places in the world where six-gill sharks can be seen. They can grow up to six metres (20-feet) and tend to run two to four metres (6 to 12 feet), but everything looks bigger through a mask.

Don't like to get your face wet? **Inter-Island Charters** at Seabreeze Lodge ((250) 335-2321) runs glass bottom boat tours and fishing charters. Topside, simply stroll along the dramatic grassy tops of the seaside cliffs. Best white sand beaches: Whaling Station Bay and Tribune Bay, aka Big Trib (Little Trib, around the next bay, is a nude beach). Tip: Tribune's warm when the wind blows onto shore; and when Trib's cold, Whaling Station is warm.

Hornby's newest bed and breakfast is a delight. The owner's of **Saltspray Landing B&B** are artists, fine hosts, and gourmet cooks. Each large waterfront bedroom has a fireplace and private bath, and you can watch cruise ships sailing by from the windows. A bountiful breakfast is served, and guests are welcome to use the barbecue (or meals can be arranged). Safe beach nearby; children welcome ((250) 335-2945). If waterfront isn't essential, check the bucolic setting of **Outer Island B&B**. It's a block from the beach, with a small pool, tennis, three rooms, and one housekeeping cabin (4785 dePape Rd, (250) 335-2379). Juanita can suggest other options through the free bed and breakfast reservations service ((250) 335-0506) and Magic Island Realty can help you find a private cabin to rent ((250) 335-0423). Campers are tempted by Tribune Bay Campsite's easy walk to Tribune Beach, but it can be noisy ((250) 335-2359). **Bradsdadsland Waterfront Camping** ((250) 335-0757) is superior in every way, especially if you like peace and quiet, family style, no music, and "whispers after 11 pm."

Dinner choices on the island are simple: the **Thatch** by the ferry for pub-style meals and summer barbecues, and the **Sea Breeze Lodge** ((250) 335-2321) at Tralee Point, which takes reservations for nonguests. The 13 cottages—unpretentious but comfortable—overlook the ocean, and the newest have fireplaces. Simplest of all, ask which nights the **Pizza Galore** people will be at the bakery cranking out great pizza. Plan to eat at the bakery's orchard picnic tables or phone ahead for take-out.

Summer brings the **Hornby Island Bike Fest**, a weekend of amazing feats when hammerheads climb sandstone formations on Tribune Bay Beach or pound the gruelling cross-country race up Mount Geoffrey (call the Hornby Island Off-Road Bike Shop for dates). The less energetic connect summer with the **Hornby Island Festival** in August, a rustic fest that began with the elegant Purcell String Quartet and still celebrates music, theatre, dance, and film in style.

If you've still got time to kill, plan a day of cycling or driving on neighbouring Denman, touring the studios of weavers, potters, painters, and other artisans, especially **Beardsley Pottery** (4920 Lacon Rd, (250) 335-0308), which is always open.

Heading back on Vancouver Island, you'll go through Qualicum and Parksville, beach towns with a difference. Both have broad sweeping beaches. **[KIDS] Parksville** is rather more commercial, but its sandier beaches are great for kids and are the site of the **International Sandcastle Competition** every July ((250) 954-3999). Much more low-key is **Qualicum**. British royalty have stayed with friends in the area. They apparently didn't know about the romantic, airy rooms at **Grauer's Getaway** (395 Burnham Rd, (250) 752-5851). Stephen and Brenda Grauer's home, Peppercorn Cottage, was built in 1929 on an acre of bluff property with spectacular views of Georgia Strait and its islands. Now guests are encouraged to use it as a mini-resort, sharing the pool, tennis court, fragrant rose gardens, and the private pathway to the beach below. Two-day spring packages include steelhead fishing and a round of golf.

Detour: a couple of islands off Nanaimo are worth a tour—Newcastle and Gabriola. The 10-minute ferry ride to **Newcastle** for foot passengers and cyclists leaves on the hour from behind the Nanaimo Civic Arena and lands you at a provincial marine park with many lovely trails and beaches. You can walk the entire island. Call (250) 753-5141 for sailings, and Tourism Nanaimo, (250) 754-8474, to see if there's a special event, such as a big band dance. There's a small concession, but if you're camping, take your own supplies.

Gabriola Island is a bedroom community for Nanaimo, so close it seems you could spit across to this literary island immortalized by Malcolm Lowry in his book *October Ferry to Gabriola*. Ironically, his protagonists never reached their destination. If you do, explore **Raspberries**, a substantial bookstore useful for hunting down information on any community events as well as books by local writers. Also check out **Fogo Studio** (3065 Commodore Way), where former Saskatchewan farmers Dee and Bob Lauder create hilarious life-size folk art figures that double as furniture (leave an appropriate seat impression and they'll do a custom chair for you). Don't miss the sea-shaped sandstone formation known as **Malaspina Galleries**, a natural wonder that Spanish captain Dionisio Galiano sketched in his 1792 journal.

MV UCHUK III *AND MV* AURORA EXPLORER

[KIDS] Forget cruise ships to Alaska. These two working boats and a new BC Ferries route will give you a whole other view of British Columbia's coast. More northerly, remote, and historic than the *Lady Rose* is the MV *Uchuk III* operated by Nootka Sound Service Ltd. (for reservations call (250) 283-2325). To board it, drive west from Campbell River to Gold River on the west coast of Vancouver Island. The 41-metre (135-foot) converted American minesweeper built in 1943 carries passengers, mail, and cargo year-round from Gold River to Tahsis and Kyoquot Sound. The $45 Tahsis day trip operates year-round, leaving Gold River at 9am, returning at 6pm. Come summer, the boat adds a $38 Nootka Sound day trip that leaves every Wednesday at 10:30am. You could overnight in **Campbell River** and drive 1 1/2 hours to Gold River in the morning.

This six-hour round-trip trip via fjordlike inlets to historic **Nootka Sound** includes a one-hour stop at Yuquot or **Friendly Cove** (Captain James Cook's first known landing place on the west coast in 1772 triggered the sea otter fur trade). Britain and Spain also vied for power here (in the 18th century, *Nootka Incident* played in a theatre in London's West End, yet most British Columbians today couldn't place Nootka on a map). The $7 landing fee includes a guided tour by local Native people. The stained-glass windows in the small Roman Catholic church commemorating the early explorers are a recent gift from Spain. Walking on a spongy trail under the tall spruce trees, cast a thought back to Cook's men, who once brewed spruce beer here.

Year round, the two-day cruise to **Kyoquot**, a secluded fishing village on a small sheltered bay, departs every Thursday. The price of $165/$270 double (free for kids under 12) includes accommodation—a bed-and-breakfast arrangement whereby you cook your own breakfast with supplies that are provided. On both trips, stops are made as required at logging camps and settlements in the area to deliver supplies and passengers. Expect to see seals, clearcuts, salmon, passing trollers, and south polar skuas on their flight to colder climes. If you long to stay longer, Nootka Sound Service can arrange a flight out with Air Nootka or side trips to visit off-lying islands (parts of these trips are in open waters—not for the queasy).

The 27-metre (90-foot) landing craft MV *Aurora Explorer* (Marine LinkTours, (250) 286-8847) is a working freight boat with accommodation for paying passengers (basic twin-occupancy bunk-bed style with shared washrooms). Up to nine passengers join the crew of five, travelling the sheltered waterways of coastal BC, past such places as Bute Inlet, Hernando Island, Hole-in-the-Wall, Hakai Pass, and Kingcome Inlet. Dolphins often play in front of the vessel's bow; bald eagles, otters, killer whales, sea lions, and black bears are part of the passing scene. During the day, there's the vibration and noise associated with vessel operation and freight activities. But, oh, the solitude and peace of a night at anchor in a quiet cove.

"Explorers Wanted" reads BC Ferries' pamphlet for its newest route, **The Discovery Coast Passage**. You've never been on a ferry ride like this before—and neither has anyone else in BC. Officially known as Route 40, it serves mid-coast communities (tourists will make the route pay) between Port Hardy on northern Vancouver Island and Bella Coola, where your wheels hit the road again if you've travelled by car. (Only 300 passengers, 33 cars, and 45 "overheights," so you do need reservations, (800) 663-7600.) From here, you can make a circle tour through the Chilcotin and down the coast to northern Vancouver Island or out to Williams Lake and through the Cariboo to Vancouver.

En route, the ferry stops at Finn Bay, Namu (archaeological sites), Shearwater (historic Graveyard Island), Bella Bella (marine tour), Klemtu, Ocean Falls (historic mill and dam), and Bella Coola. You can stop and explore for a few days along the way. Okay, it's not the *Crystal Harmony*, but it's a bargain at $94/person, $209/car, not including passenger (both one-way), and the refitted 1978-vintage *Queen of Chilliwack* is offering packages that include transportation, accommodation, and shore excursions. You can even fish over the side with tackle rented from BC Ferries! Informal entertainment may include Native people from the area talking about their culture or a sea-shanty-singing third mate. Crew are encouraged to mix with passengers; barbecues on deck, weather permitting. The only drawback: some trips leave Port Hardy at 10pm, with passengers sleeping their way to Namu in airplane-style reclinable seats (7:30am departure arrives in Bella Coola at 9pm). There are no cabins on board, but sleeping bags on the floor or freestanding tents on outside decks are okay. Do it soon. Tourism

BC estimates 50 percent of passengers will be German, Swiss, and French once the word hits Europe.

OKANAGAN WINERY TOUR

It has been less than a decade since the British Columbia wine industry instituted a comprehensive program of revitalization, but already the results are encouraging. From the dozen or so wineries that launched the VQA (Vintner Quality Alliance) program back in 1989, the numbers have tripled, with many more expected to come into the fold before the end of the century.

As a result, touring British Columbia wine country has become a passion not only for locals but also for visitors. Notwithstanding the exciting developments on Vancouver Island, the pulse of the BC wine industry is in the Okanagan Valley, approximately 350 kilometres (217.5 miles) inland from Vancouver.

Getting there from Vancouver entails a comfortable four-hour drive via the Trans-Canada Highway (Hwy 1) to Hope, then along the scenic Coquihalla Highway (Hwy 5) into Merritt, and from there along the Coquihalla Connector (Hwy 97) into the Okanagan Valley. (The Coquihalla Highway is a toll road, so plan on an extra $10 (or so) one way, depending on the size of your vehicle.)

The valley itself runs north-south, wrapping around Okanagan Lake from Vernon to Penticton, and then spreading south to the U.S. border. More than three dozen wineries operate in the region, including four large commercial concerns, numerous boutique or estate winery producers, and an eclectic handful of tiny, farmgate wineries.

Almost every winery is open to visitors: all that is required is a map and a sense of curiosity. Specific information about touring British Columbia wineries is available at most tourist information kiosks between Vancouver and the Okanagan. If you want to meet the winemaker and tour the facility beyond the tasting room, be sure to call ahead for an appointment. The **British Columbia Wine Institute** (BCWI) produces a highly recommended brochure outlining most of the province's wineries, including maps and information on visiting hours. You can contact them from anywhere in the country at (800) 661-2294 or in Vancouver at 986-0440.

The following is a brief look at some of the region's leading properties, beginning some 20 minutes north of Kelowna at Winfield.

Just west of Winfield, over the hills on Camp Road, is **Gray Monk Estate Winery** (1051 Camp Rd, (250) 766-3168), etched perilously into the slopes above Okanagan Lake. Owners George and Trudy Heiss, two of the Okanagan's finest ambassadors, now count more than 20 years in the business. There is no finer way to pass a warm summer's day than by sitting on their sun-drenched balcony overlooking the lake and

▼

Excursions

*Okanagan
Winery
Tour*

▲

sipping on a Gray Monk Rotberger, pinot gris, or kerner.

From Gray Monk, head back south along Highway 97 to downtown Kelowna. Look for the signs at Lakeshore Road that point you south along the eastern edge of the lake to pictur-esque **CedarCreek Estate Winery** (5445 Lakeshore Rd, (250) 764-8866). Tucked neatly into the hillside, high above the shores of Okanagan Lake, CedarCreek offers guided tours, out-standing views, and much-welcomed picnic tables nestled among its steep-sloping vineyards. Best bets here include an award-winning merlot and a refreshing gewürztraminer.

On the way back to Kelowna, not far from CedarCreek, is **Summerhill Estate Winery** (4870 Chute Lake Rd, (250) 764-8000), the region's first commercial sparkling wine producer. The winery operated for several years in temporary premises, but in the spring of 1996 a new winery and visitor centre opened. Summerhill's unique method of aging wines under a pyramid attracts thousands of visitors annually. Best bets here are the cipes brut, pinot blanc, and a legendary ice wine.

Upon your return to Kelowna, head downtown to the Okanagan's finest restaurant, **de Montreuil's** (368B Bernard Ave, (250) 860-5508). Chef/owner Grant de Montreuil is a ded-icated pioneer in his use of local, seasonal, and organic produce and meats. Signature dishes include Vegetarian Wellington, the Ultimate Tomato Salad (featuring at least five different va-rieties and colours of organic tomatoes), and BC venison chops. The wine list is small but well chosen, with a good se-lection of local sparkling, red, white, and dessert wines. To con-tinue your tour, cross the floating bridge west and follow Highway 97 as it winds its way south to Penticton. First up on your left is Westbank, home to **Quails' Gate Estate** (3303 Boucherie Rd, (250) 769-4451). Owner Ben Stewart and wine-maker Jeff Martin offer a wide range of superb varietals, avail-able for tasting at the historic stone cottage that houses the winery tasting room. Just up the road **Mission Hill Winery** (1730 Mission Hill Rd, (250) 768-7611) has a 360-degree view of the Okanagan Valley and makes the region's most famous chardonnay. Winery tours and an expansive wine shop are all part of the package at Mission Hill.

Continuing south on Highway 97, next up is Peachland and **Hainle Estate Vineyards** (5355 Trepanier Bench Rd, (250) 767-2525). Newly renovated visitor facilities make its el-evated tasting room one of the valley's best for sipping, snack-ing, and enjoying the surrounding vistas. Hainle was the first winery in the province to obtain a licence allowing it to serve visitors light lunches featuring local, seasonal, and organic in-gredients and wines by the glass. Although known as British Columbia's first producer of ice wine, proprietors Tilman and Sandra Hainle also produce a tight range of ultra-dry table wines that are certified organic from the vineyard to the bottle.

Farther south, on the northern edge of Summerland, is the hilltop estate winery of **Sumac Ridge** (Hwy 97, (250) 494-0451). Owner Harry McWatters is a walking encyclopaedia of Okanagan wine history and a fine producer of pinot blanc, gewürztraminer, and *mèthode champenoise* sparkling wine. At press time, sommelier/restaurateur Mark Taylor, from Whistler's Opossum Cafe, had been engaged to operate Sumac's new on-site bistro. The menu (lunch only) features fresh seasonal Okanagan foodstuffs.

Penticton is the next stop and the perfect base from which to explore the wineries of the south Okanagan. Plan to stay overnight at **The Clarion Lakeside Resort** ((250) 493-8221) at the lake's southern end. Nearby Naramata is home to several farmgate wineries, all of which present fun tasting opportunities. Best bets here include Lang Vineyards (2493 Gammon Rd, (250) 496-5987), Lake Breeze (Sammet Rd, (250) 496-5659), and Nichol Vineyard (1285 Smethurst Rd, (250) 496-5962). It's a good idea to call ahead with these small producers. Twenty minutes farther south you come upon Okanagan Falls, where there are two wineries you'll want to visit: Blue Mountain Vineyard and LeComte Estate.

Call ahead to make an appointment to tour the **Blue Mountain Vineyard** (Oliver Ranch Rd, (250) 497-8224). It is one of BC's newer estate wineries, although owners Ian and Jane Mavety have actively grown grapes on the site for many years. Nestled in a canyonlike setting at the northern end of Vaseaux Lake, Blue Mountain is making some of the country's best varietal wine. Best bets here include the pinot gris, pinot blanc, and pinot noir.

Across the valley on the western slopes of Hawthorn Mountain sits **LeComte Estate** on Green Lake Rd, (250) 497-8073. The arrival of winemaker Eric von Krosigk has brought instant respectability to LeComte. A new tasting room that looks down on a shimmering Skaha Lake is a magical place to stop and taste wine. Best bets include a crisp gewürztraminer and sumptuous pinot meunier.

Continuing south, past the town of Oliver, one last visit should be made at **Gehringer Brothers Estate Winery** (Hwy 97 and Rd 8, (250) 498-3537). Walter Gehringer has been producing fine German-style varietals here for years, and riesling fans must make a stop. The lineup runs from ice wine to dry riesling, with some wonderful, floral, fruity pinot auxerrois and ehrenfelser thrown in for good measure.

QUADRA AND CORTES ISLANDS

When General Norman Schwarzkopf wanted bigger fish to fry, he headed for **April Point Lodge** on **Quadra Island** (April Point Rd, (250) 285-2222), possibly the toniest fishing resort in the Pacific Northwest. BC is world famous for salmon fishing, and Vancouver Island's Campbell River, home of the mighty tyee (chinook weighing more than 14 kilograms or 30 pounds), helped put it on the map. Take the 10-minute ferry ride from **Campbell River** to tiny Quadra Island, where longtime lodge owners the Peterson family have drawn such serious anglers as John Wayne, Julie Andrews, and Kevin Costner. You'll be hooked too.

There are some 35 professional fishing guides to help you land that 60-pounder (27 kilograms). Boston whalers take two guests out or you can opt for the big boats (with a head) that carry four—usually for a minimum of four hours. The price includes boat, fuel, tackle, bait, rain gear, and guide. You can fly-fish for northern coho, troll or mooch for chinook, or row for the tyee (the best time to catch one is from July to September).

The one- to six-bedroom guesthouses facing west are expensive but spacious, beautifully furnished, and graced with large fireplaces. North-facing thin-walled cabins overlook the marina; you could be kept awake by late-drinking or early-rising fishermen in adjoining rooms. There are also suites and single rooms in the sunny and cheerful main lodge. The food—from fresh Dungeness crab to Gulf Island lamb—is always good, thanks to chef Dory Ford. Your catch is expertly cleaned, frozen, and packaged in coolers for travel. You can also have it smoked, canned, or made into lox. Instead of having the Big One mounted, ask April Point's guide Eiji Umemura to make a gyotaku, a Japanese "fish print" suitable for framing.

If you're not there to fish—really fish—you may sense a good-natured (more likely slightly puzzled) fish-or-cut-bait attitude from guests who come to do only that. But there is another reason people travel to the island: to attend the April Point Cooking School during the spring and fall, when talented chefs like Tojo Hidekazu, of Tojo's in Vancouver, cook up a storm on holiday long weekends.

Quadra Island has lots to offer. About 8 kilometres (5 miles) in either direction are exceptionally lovely beach walks. To the south, you can walk along the shore to **Cape Mudge**'s lighthouse. To the east lies the **Rebecca Spit Provincial Park**, where a shallow bay offers surprisingly warm swimming.

Or if you've caught your limit, head for the **Kwagiulth Museum and Cultural Centre** ((250) 285-3733), one of BC's best small museums, which has an outstanding historical collection of Northwest Coast Native art, thanks to the return of goods confiscated by the government when potlatches were banned. Ask where you can see petroglyphs across the street. Summer workshops open to the public include rubbings of these ancient carved "drawings" in stone.

The same Cape Mudge Band opened the **Tsa-Kwa-Luten Lodge** (Lighthouse Rd, (800) 665-7745), the only Canadian resort owned and operated by Native people that features authentic Native culture. There's good seafood, but the contemporary lodge, built in the architectural spirit of a longhouse, somehow seems bare; the polyester napkins don't take advantage of a unique culture.

All islands are good. Second islands are better. No one "passes through" **Cortes** (40 minutes from Quadra by a second ferry). They come because they're coming. What they're coming to is a 23-kilometre-long (14-mile-long), 13-kilometre-wide (8-mile-wide) forested cork in the mouth of Desolation Sound—that dreamy mix of tightly packed inlets, islands, mountains, warm water, and secure anchorages that sailors have revered since the first Spaniards cruised by in 1792. Many of the island's 800 residents earn their keep by farming and exporting oysters and clams around the world. In fact, it's worth your life to eat an oyster on Cortes. Your best bet is to sign on for a weekend or week-long getaway at oceanside **Hollyhock Seminar Centre**, Canada's leading holistic learning centre, where the soul is free to expand and the body to wander the blowsy garden or sandy beach. Packages ((800) 933-6339) include room (from tents and dorms to private rooms or cottages), meals (gourmet vegetarian and a seafood feast), massage, optional morning yoga, afternoon tea, nature walks, biking, evening entertainment, and a pre-breakfast nature row out to the tiny islet of Long Tom for hot coffee and warm zucchini muffins in the 10-oared lifeboat *Harlequin*, with naturalist Bill Ophoff at the helm. Cortes, smack in the middle of the Pacific flyway, is home (however briefly) to more than 240 bird species.

If you'd rather do it yourself, book into **The Blue Heron B&B**, the peaceful waterfront home at the sunny end of the island, where the Danish Hansens understand real coffee and serve pancakes with homemade blackberry sauce. Their patio and living room is literally yours. The en suite ocean-view room in a separate guest wing is a bargain at $70 ((250) 935-6584). Nearby Sutil Point or Smelt Bay are great spots to watch the sun set.

Make reservations for fresh prawns and beer at the excellent **Old Floathouse Restaurant**, transplanted from Kingcombe Inlet and now landlocked at the Gorge Marina Resort on Hunt Road ((250) 935-6631), where you can rent scooters or boats. **T'ai Li**, a marine-adventure lodge in a spectacular walk-in setting, offers one of BC's best-run introductory kayaking sessions in ideal waters ((250) 935-6749). Rent or take your own boat. Several simple, cosy rooms are in the owners' home, but the safari-style tented platforms (with hot shower and outhouse) are irresistible in decent weather.

[KIDS] On your way home from Cortes and Quadra, try a final cast from Campbell River's 180-metre-long (590-foot-long) wooden **Discovery Pier**, the first built in Canada specifically as a saltwater fishing pier. As you head for Nanaimo, keep an eye out for Fanny Bay, where you can buy direct from **Mac's Oysters** ((250) 335-2233). Farther on, **Dot's Cafe** (5921 North Island Hwy, (250) 390-3331) is famous for Lemon Meringue Mile High Pie. For a final thrill, drive 25 minutes south of Nanaimo to tie a line to yourself at Nanaimo's **Bungee Zone** ((250) 753-5867), North America's only legal bridge jump. Yes, you can jump buck naked over the "scenic Nanaimo River gorge." Stormin' Norman didn't bungee jump, but back at April Point, he did use a skip fly—an extremely difficult and esoteric method—to land a 11.5-kilogram (25 1/2-pound) spring salmon.

SALT SPRING AND SOUTHERN GULF ISLANDS

All you need know about the Gulf Islands is that they have the best climate in Canada. Of the three groups collectively referred to as the Gulf Islands, the best known and most populous are the southern ones—Gabriola, Galiano, Mayne, Salt Spring, Saturna, and Pender—tucked along Vancouver Island's shore between Victoria and Nanaimo. In fact there are around 200 southern Gulf Islands, but BC Ferries only serves the eight largest. Happily, they offer the widest choice of inns, eateries, and other goodies. We'll give you an overview of Salt Spring here and a brief introduction to Galiano, Mayne, and Pender.

The Canadian Gulf Islands B&B Reservation Service ((250) 539-5390) can book you into one of more than 100 B&Bs and refer you to agencies that rent cottages. Five tips: Fill your gas tank; BYOB (few gas stations, fewer liquor stores); take cash as well as plastic; don't think you can cook the toxicity out of shellfish in red tide "closed" areas (paralysis and death can follow); and don't try to rocket from island to island. Island time is part of the appeal.

Named for the unusually cold and briny springs on the north end of the island, **Salt Spring** is the largest and most populous of the Gulf Islands chain. (Residents of smaller islands pooh–pooh it as the "West Vancouver" of the Gulf Islands.) Its population has been growing steadily since the first permanent settlers (black Americans) arrived in the 1800s. The last influx consisted of burned-out urbanites clutching copies of *The Electronic Cottage*. The island even has two nine-hole golf courses: public Blackburn Meadows ((250) 537-1707), where tee times are still not required, and semi-private Salt Spring Golf and Country Club, where the public is also welcome ((250) 537-2121). Like the other islands, it's generally drier and warmer than Vancouver and has the bark-shedding arbutus tree to prove it.

Salt Spring is **accessible by three ferries**: from Tsawwassen (to Long Harbour, 1 1/2 hours); from Crofton, near Duncan on Vancouver Island (to Vesuvius, 20 minutes); or from Swartz Bay (32 kilometres (20 miles) from Victoria) on the

Saanich Peninsula (to Fulford Harbour, 30 minutes). Crofton is the best route from Vancouver, via Horseshoe Bay. **Island Spoke Folk** ((250) 537-4664) will deliver bikes to foot passengers arriving at any ferry. Locals caught in a Fulford lineup, knowing that the ferry has only machine-dispensed snacks and drinks, pass the time at nearby **Rodrigo's** restaurant and ice cream window.

All roads lead to **Ganges**, as the natives are fond of saying. Ganges, the largest town in the Gulf Islands, has a colourful Saturday morning **[FREE] Farmers Market** (early morning to 2pm) with high-quality crafts, as well as a growing number of pleasant cafes and restaurants, a condominium complex overlooking the harbour, and a flurry of new retail development. Just when your nostrils catch the whiff of yuppification, you stumble onto **Mouat's** department store, an island mainstay since 1907 and still owned by the same family ((250) 537-5551).

For light meals and snacks (vegetarian too) try **Boardwalk Cafe** (Mouat's Mall, (250) 537-1436), which has indoor and outdoor seating (check out the adjoining mini-garden shop, **Boardwalk Greens**), the **Bouzouki Restaurant** (waterfront in the Grace Point complex), or **Glad's Ice Cream** (across from Mouat's, (250) 537-4211). For a relaxing dinner, the tiny blue-and-white Scandinavian **House Piccolo** (108 Hereford Ave, (250) 537-1844) is charming and the local lamb yummy; the upper deck of **Alfresco's** (3106 Grace Point Sq, (250) 537-5979) overlooks boats bobbing in the Ganges harbour. For a more casual night, head for a veranda table at the lively, rebuilt **Vesuvius Inn** (180 Vesuvius Bay Rd, (250) 537-2312) for decent burgers and cold draft; only the overly loud music detracts from the bobbing seals and the sunset. However, it is **Hastings House** (160 Upper Ganges Rd, (250) 537-2362) that put Salt Spring Island on the international map. Just minutes from Ganges, nestled among trees overlooking a rolling lawn and the sea, this splendid resort is undeniably luxe, and the dining room is quite wonderful. Prices, as you might suspect, are stiff.

If your idea of comfort begins with a breakfast of crème fraîche and strawberries, a sorrel and asparagus soufflé, and freshly baked cinnamon buns, head for the **Old Farmhouse Bed & Breakfast** (1077 Northend Rd, (250) 537-4113). Like Hastings House, it is minutes from Ganges, the Vesuvius ferry, and the community centre that doubles as a movie theatre. It is a newly restored 100-year-old heritage farmhouse (complete with the benign, hatted ghost of a former eccentric owner) with a separate guest wing (all rooms with private bath and balcony or patio). Hosts Karl and Gerti Fuss (she trained in European hotel school and managed Vancouver's Il Giardino restaurant) have combined solid wood doors, gemlike stained-glass windows, antique pedestal sinks, pine floors, and cheerful, crisp

▼

Excursions

*Salt Spring
and
Southern
Gulf
Islands*

▲

contemporary chintzes. Some rooms seem less soundproof than others. You might ask about this when booking.

Another lesser-known romantic spot, the tiny **Windmill** ((250) 653-4386), is ideal for a twosome with a mind to be tucked into the well-kitted-out base of a windmill in Fulford Harbour. At night, barbecue over the firepit and watch the ferries roll by. Ocean-front, adult-oriented **Beddis House B&B** (131 Miles Ave, (250) 537-1028) is a turn-of-the-century farmhouse with clawfoot tubs and afternoon tea. **Anne's Ocean-front Hideaway** ((250) 537-0851), with fireplaces, hot tub, and fitness room, is just that, and it is totally wheelchair accessible.

There are also **camping facilities** at St. Mary Lake, Ruckle Park, and Mouat Provincial Park on the southeastern tip of the island, where you'll find a spectacular mixture of virgin forest, rock and clamshell beach, and rugged headlands.

Any of the island's 90-plus bed and breakfasts and hotels can provide you with a map of Salt Spring. If it's Sunday, drive around the island armed with the **Sunday artists' studio tour** map. Summer visitors can see most work represented in the summer-long **Artcraft** show in Mahon Hall—convenient, but not nearly as interesting as the tour.

[KIDS][FREE] Sandy beaches aren't common on this island, but there is a pretty little beach at the end of **Churchill Road** (near Ganges) and a beautiful shell and sand beach at the end of **Beddis Road** (eastern side of the island). Drive to Ruckle Park to stroll the paths and explore the rock pools left by the receding tide. Some members of the Ruckle family still reside in the farmhouses you see scattered throughout under a tenancy-for-life agreement made after they donated the land as a park in 1973. The park warden's home, built in 1938 for Norman Ruckle's bride-to-be, was never lived in because the wedding failed to take place. Instead, it was used to store potatoes! Be sure to stop at the nearby **Everlasting Summer Dried Flower & Herb Farm** (194 McLennan Dr) to wander the formal herb and rose gardens and gape at the ceilings full of drying flowers.

For an astounding view of the archipelago from Salt Spring to the American mainland, pick a clear day and drive up Cranberry Road to the top of **Mount Maxwell**. **Salt Spring Island Guided Rides** ((250) 537-5761) will take you over island trails on horseback.

Despite being the first stop off the Tsawwassen ferry and a common day trip for Vancouver cyclists, **Galiano** retains an undeveloped, secluded character. This is thanks to residents who've worked to protect the wildflower meadows and forested areas like **Bluffs Park**. Its sweeping dress-circle views overlook Active Pass, where ferries routinely pass in the tight channel. [KIDS][FREE] **Montague Harbour Marine Park** is the largest park in the Gulf Islands, and BC Parks run free interpretive programs here in the summer. Shell Beach is a good swimming spot but it can be noisy. **Elderhostel** ((250) 529-2127) and **Gulf Islands Institute for Environmental Studies** ((250) 539-2930) also run programs interpreting the environment throughout the year. Those who want to check out the surroundings firsthand should call **Ben's Gulf Island Sea Kayaking** ((250) 539-2442), which will send someone to meet you at the ferry for lessons, rentals, or tours. Local spots for quick grub: the former Chez Ferrie, now **Max and Moritz**, which serves up German and Indonesian food in a green-and-yellow caravan at Sturdies Bay; and **Hummingbird Pub**, the local hangout (menu is 15 pages long), which in July and August runs an hourly red-and-white converted school bus shuttle between the boat harbour at Montague and the pub, complete with Chuck Berry rockin' on the sound system. A regular bus has begun service on the island, too. October's **Blackberry Festival** is a sea of pies, jam, and themed ethnic entertainment (call (250) 539-2233 for Galiano Visitors Information).

Woodstone Country Inn (Georgeson Bay Rd, (250) 539-2022) is elegant and formal. Guest rooms are spacious and bright (most have fireplaces; some have lovely views of green pastures); the dining room gave Galiano its first taste of haute cuisine. Other options we like: upscale **Galiano Lodge** (134 Madrona Dr, (250) 539-3388) by the ferry, with a choice of 10 deluxe rooms with fireplaces or seven modest rooms in the original beachside building; **The Laidlaws'** (Ganner Dr, (250) 539-5341), where Sally and Joe deliver breakfast to two charming stone cottages on their woodsy 10 acres; and **Sutil Lodge** (Montague Harbour, (250) 539-2930), a thriving 1920s resort restored by Tom and Ann Hennessy, who offer memorable sailing trips on their 14-metre (46-foot) catamaran, *Great White Cloud*. Best local souvenir: a birch-handled knife by master knife maker and 1960s Berkeley post-graduate Matthew Schoenfeld (who also runs the Galiano bicycle shop, (250) 539-2806).

Rolling orchards and warm rock-strewn beaches abound on rustic **Mayne Island**. By ferry, Mayne is usually the second stop from Tsawwassen (1 1/2 hours). The 13-square-kilometre (8-square-mile) island is small enough for a day trip but pretty enough for a lifetime. It's hard to believe Mayne was once a booming stopover point in 1858 for thousands of would-be gold miners bound for the Cariboo. Residents today are happy to lie low; wonderful older home with flower-strewn verandas line Georgina Point Road. At Miners Bay dock, a "coronation bench" encircles the copper beech planted to commemorate the coronation of George VI. Sink your teeth into a burger or savour a Caesar salad at the comfortably dilapidated **Springwater Lodge** (400 Fernhill Dr, (250) 539-5521), drop by the lighthouse, visit tiny St. Mary Magdalene Anglican Church (consecrated in 1898 with a unique 160-kilogram (352-pound)

▼

Excursions

*Salt Spring
and
Southern
Gulf
Islands*

▲

sandstone baptismal font), or stroll up to the top of Mayne's Mount Parke for a view of the Strait of Georgia and you'll begin to discover what Mayne's all about. Easiest of all, check into **Oceanwood Country Inn** (630 Dinner Bay Rd, (250) 539-5074). Jonathan and Marilyn Chilvers retired early from city life to open a small, perfect inn, which is exactly what they did. They provide seven lovely suites with casually elegant country furniture (all with private baths), a convivial atmosphere, and endless suggestions of what to do on Mayne, from guided naturalist walks to a do-it-yourself list. Their "630 Dinner Bay Road" address leads to one of the Gulf Islands' best restaurants, with an award-winning 100-wine list, all the entries of which hail from North America's West Coast.

Green, rural **North and South Pender Islands** are separated by a canal and united by a bridge. The population is decidedly residential; don't expect many restaurants, lodgings, or shops. Beaches abound, however, including **Mortimer Spit** and **Gowland Point Beach**, both on South Pender. **Pender Island Golf and Country Club** ((250) 629-6659) has a challenging nine-hole golf course laid out by the local Auchterlonie family, reputed to have played the famous St. Andrews. Hike up **Mount Norman**, one of three provincial parks, for spectacular views. Come summer, you can ogle the hundreds of cruising boats that pass through Bedwell harbour, location of Canadian customs. South Pender's gentle topography is especially inviting to bikers. Rent bikes at **Otter Bay Marina** ((250) 629-6659) on North Pender or a kayak from **Mouat Point Kayaks** ((250) 629-6767) next door. The ferry stops at the dock at Otter Bay, where the **Stand** ((250) 629-3292)—an unprepossessing trailer—grills the best oyster burgers around. At Hope Bay, the **Hope Bay Heritage Store**, dating from 1912, is where residents still gather for cappuccino, gossip, and classical or folk music. For dessert, ask the way to **Old Orchard Farm**, recently restored to its Victorian glory (when it was known as Sunny Side Ranch). More than 50 varieties of apples, plums, and pears, many now rare, are sold here in season from the stand at the gate. On Saturday mornings, the **Driftwood Centre** adds a farmers market to its mix of shops and **Libby's Village Bakery**. Don't be put off by **Corbett House B&B**'s nonseaside setting (phone for directions; (250) 629-6305). This lovely heritage home has brave decor (the Yellow, Red, and Blue Rooms are all equally cosy), and hosts John Eckfeldt and Linda Wolfe know how to run a fine bed and breakfast in a beautiful pastoral setting.

SOOKE

Like more northerly Long Beach, Sooke sits on the west coast of Vancouver Island. But Sooke is just a 45-minute drive "around the corner" from Victoria. Thanks to the protective (and scenic) curve of Washington's mountainous Olympic Peninsula, which hooks up around the southern tip of Vancouver Island, much of the Sooke area is protected from the heavy surf, rain, and strong winds associated with the open Pacific a few miles farther north. The small communities of **Sooke**, **Jordan River**, and **Port Renfrew** contain excellent parks and dozens of trails, some of which do lead down to surf-flung beaches. Ask at the **Sooke Museum/Information Centre** housed at the Sooke Region Museum just off Highway 14 on Phillips Road (look for the flashing lighthouse light!) for directions to **French Beach Provincial Park**, **Sandcut Beach** (it's easy to miss the sign), **China Beach Provincial Park** (which has a 15-minute trail to a secluded sandy beach with a hidden waterfall at the west end), and **Mystic Beach** (a rugged 20-minute trail takes you there). Be careful about incoming tides.

Where you stay depends on your budget, mood, and desire to cook in or eat out. Again, the excellent Sooke Information Centre has photographs of local bed and breakfasts, some of which almost straddle the **Galloping Goose Trail**, 60 kilometres (35 miles) of former rail line between Victoria and Leechtown, just north of Sooke, past some of BC's finest scenery. You can, as they say, "Walk the Goose, cycle the Goose, or ride the Goose on horseback." The stretch along Sooke Basin is the only waterfront section. While in Sooke you can rent a bike from **Sooke Cycle** ((250) 642-3123), an employee of which will take you to the trail. A good section of the trail is Sooke Potholes (diving pools and grottoes) en route to Leechtown, past the abandoned but still spectacular Deer Trails Conference Centre. The **Sooke Region Museum** itself ((250) 642-6351) is well worth a stop, especially if you arrive in time for the 20-minute dramatized tours of pioneer Moss Cottage at 10am and 4pm. Step over the threshold and you're welcomed into the year 1902.

New to the area: Tudor-style **Markham House** bed and breakfast (1853 Connie Rd, (250) 642-7542), run lovingly by innkeepers Sally and Lyle Markham, the latter having retired early from a career in four-star hotels. Outside there are sloping lawns, a small river, a trout pond, tall trees, and, from mid-May to mid-June, glorious iris gardens (3,500 rhizomes: 110 species with wonderful names like Pacific Mist and Warm Embrace). Feather beds, charming rooms, and country hospitality (from afternoon tea and scones on arrival to fireside port or tea in a green pot before bed) are offered indoors. Note: Markham House is *not* the Tudor-style house you see to the right on Highway 14.

The oceanfront **Sooke Harbour House** (1528 Whiffen Spit Rd, (250) 642-3421), under the stewardship of Frederica and Sinclair Philip, has gained international attention for a kitchen dedicated to the freshest natural local ingredients;

dinner may begin with a chowder of smoked golden delicious apple and butter clams. One letter, framed in the lobby of the 1931 white-clapboard house, misaddressed to "Owner, Suke House, Whiffenpoof, Victoria Island," was duly delivered. You can see future racks of lamb grazing across the inlet. It's worth stopping, even if you're not staying, just to stroll the herb gardens and sniff the mix of sea, brown fennel, and rosemary. Each four-star room is a singular treat, with a name that inspired the decor—among them are The Seagull Room (our favourite), The Ichthyologist's Study, and The Underwater Orchard. Views, decks, fresh flowers, and decanters of port are a given; Dutch Babies—soufflé pancakes don't begin to describe them—are reason enough to wake to the tap on your door. Rates include full breakfast and lunch (ask for a picnic if you're leaving). "What we give people is the gift to do nothing," says Sinclair. A happy thought, but some guests report they would also appreciate the gift of friendlier phone manners and more consistent service.

French Beach Retreats ((250) 646-2154) relies largely on word of mouth for its two private oceanfront getaways. While filming on location, Sharon Stone rented the 167-square-metre (1,798-square-foot) contemporary home, complete with antiques, woods, trails, and a vegetable garden for the use of guests (there are a sandbox and swings for little guests). The smaller octagonal Ocean Tree House is ideal for twosomes who prefer to eat out. Within Sooke, **Good Life Bookstore and Cafe** (2113 Otter Point Rd, (250) 642-6821) invites you to read while you eat in this old house, where the former living room is the dining room. A couple of bedrooms are now a bookstore (an ideal teatime table is tucked around one corner). **Country Cupboard Cafe** (402 Sheringham Pt, (250) 646-2323) also offers up excellent down-home food. Diner-style **Mom's Cafe** (Sooke Rd at Shields, (250) 642-3314) reputedly has great halibut and chips, but we couldn't get past the heavy pall of cigarette smoke. **Margison House** (6605 Sooke Rd, (250) 642-3620), an elegant cottage on pretty grounds just off the highway, serves up the best afternoon tea as well as light lunches, but it has closed for a sabbatical of undetermined length. Worth checking for its return.

[FREE] Consider a detour from Sooke into **Lester B. Pearson College of the Pacific** on Pedder Bay. Open since 1974 and offering a two-year program to foster international understanding, Pearson is one of only seven United World Colleges, and the setting and architecture by well-known West Coast architect Ron Thom are worth seeing (self-guided tours anytime; for occasional guided tours, call (250) 478-5591).

Twenty-four kilometres (15 miles) west of Sooke, **Point No Point Resort** draws a faithful following of travellers who can live without TV and telephones in 20 cabins set above 1.6

kilometres (1 mile) of beach and among 16 hectares (40 acres) of wooded trails. Some of the older cabins are rustic and quite dark, but four new cabins hang right over the water, where you sleep lulled by rolling swells. Firewood is supplied, but pick up food en route. Afternoon tea, light lunches, and now dinners are served in a small, convivial dining room with a big view.

The paved but twisty road continues, for about half an hour; to **Port Renfrew**, where it ends. **[KIDS][FREE]** Time your drive to coincide with the low tides at **Botanical Beach** just south of Port Renfrew. Here exceptionally low tides in early summer expose kilometres of sea life seldom seen so high in the intertidal zone. Check with the local gas station about conditions on the deeply grooved road leading to the beach (the Park Information Office is open only from June through September). Remember, this is black bear country. Take time to read the bear brochure (available at the Sooke Museum/Information Centre). Tip: Botanical Beach is a twisty hour and a half from Sooke, and if anyone's prone to car sickness, opt for a similar experience at French Beach or even in front of Sooke Harbour House.

Once in Port Renfrew, you can take an optional slow loop via the 55-kilometre (34-mile) gravel logging road from Port Renfrew through the forest and past woodland lakes to Lake Cowichan. A paved highway connects you back to Duncan and Highway 1, leading to Nanaimo or Victoria.

Port Renfrew is probably best known as one end of the famous **West Coast Trail**, one of the greatest (and most demanding) coastal hikes in the Northwest. Average hiking time to Bamfield is five to six days one way; but reservations are required and hikers pay a $100 fee (May to August, stop at the Trail Information Centre in Port Renfrew; or call (250) 391-2300). The great new news is the **Juan de Fuca Marine Trail**, a just-completed 73-kilometre (45-mile) hike between Port Renfrew and China Beach, which passes bathtub-size tide pools and seal-birthing caves as yet almost unknown. Designed for all levels of hiking ability, the trail and its 30 bridges can be hiked in three days, or day trippers can step in at different access points to do day sections as short as four hours (one bouncy suspension bridge over Loss Creek is not for those with vertigo). Unlike the very busy West Coast Trail, no reservations are required. Part of the trail goes through large clearcuts—an eye-opener. Park officials suggest August and September as the driest months to hike through the rain forest, but it's berry season and bears like berries. Don't count on signs to Sombio Beach, a great surfing spot halfway along the trail. Surfers and longtime residents have been known to rip it down. Any visitor information centre will have a brochure, or contact BC Parks ((250) 391-2300).

Hikers looking for secluded beaches, sea lion caves, waterfalls, and virgin trails through old-growth forests rarely seen

▼

▲

should call **Freedom Guiding** ((250) 642-7702) run by Michel Jansen-Reynaud, who has found solitude exploring this area over the last 20 years. Each five-hour trip is geared to the ability of a maximum of four people and includes a splendid West Coast picnic.

On the other extreme, make your own way to popular East Sooke Regional Park, whose 1,422 hectares (3,512 acres) of natural and protected coastal landscape are big enough to absorb everyone. **East Sooke's Coast Trail** is one of Canada's premier day hikes, a 10-kilometre (6-mile) trip, challenging even for experienced hikers. Aylard Farm is the starting point here for easy, brief excursions out to the petroglyphs.

Tip: **All Sooke Day**, held the third Saturday in July, is the longest running logger sports event in Canada, attracting about 10,000 visitors.

SUNSHINE COAST

Curiously, this coast is part of the mainland but, like an island, is accessible only by boat or small plane. BC Ferries (669-1211) is the link from Vancouver. And Vancouverites have caught on. Not only is there more to see and do on the Sechelt Peninsula (aka the Sunshine Coast) than on many of the Gulf Islands, the ferry travel time is shorter and often half the price. And what rain forest denizen could resist the promise of a sunshine coast, even if Environment Canada's records suggest that the popular name is a bit misleading?

Lack of direct road access has probably saved this beautiful peninsula from rapid development. But each year lineups are longer for the pleasant 40-minute ferry ride from **Horseshoe Bay** to Langdale and for the spectacular ride through the fjordlike waters of Jervis Inlet between **Saltery Bay** and **Earls Cove** at the north end of the peninsula. If you can, travel midweek to avoid lines, or at least leave Vancouver early Friday afternoon or late Saturday morning and return early on Monday. (The gift shop on the spiffy Langdale ferry has a rich selection of regional books and magazines.)

Strung along the main road running south to north between the two ferry terminals are two main pockets of population—Gibsons and Sechelt—and a series of delightful getaways: Roberts Creek, Redroofs, Smugglers Cove, Secret Cove, Pender Harbour, Garden Bay, Irvines Landing, and Egmont. Amazingly, the entire drive nonstop is only one hour and 25 minutes, but you can easily spend a week here.

[KIDS] Drive into **Gibsons** for at least a quick look at the town where *The Beachcombers* television series was once shot. Molly's Reach may just be a prop, but the marina is very real. If you were smart enough to stay in the gift shop rather than the restaurant on the ferry, this is a good place to eat (see Gibsons in Day Trips section of this chapter).

If you take the upper road (North Rd) off the ferry, you will bypass Lower Gibsons and meet up later with Highway 101. Northbound, the **Roberts Creek Road**, just past the public **Sunshine Coast Golf and Country Club**, leads to "the Creek," an intimate spot to be waylaid, have an ice cream at the funky General Store on Flume Road, read the newsy bulletin board, walk the long pebble beach, or indulge in a sumptuous European-style dinner at the **Creekhouse Restaurant**, long considered the best on the Sunshine Coast (885-9321). At the **Country Cottage Bed & Breakfast** (near Roberts Creek Rd and Cedar Grove Rd), guests now have the option of either the new Adirondack-style minilodge, complete with rock fireplace, or the cottage (about half the size). Welcoming owners Philip and Loragene Gaulin cook boundless breakfasts for guests on their 1927 wood cookstove. Additional treat: afternoon tea at 4pm (885-7448). The nine-hole **Sunshine Coast Golf and Country Club** near Roberts Creek is open to the public. Hikers stroll through **Cliff Gilker Park** adjacent to the course. Divers are drawn by the HMCS *Chaudire*, sunk to form **BC's first artificial reef**. Porpoise Bay Charters, 885-5950, or Seasport Scuba, 885-9830, will bring you back from the deep.

There are few sandy beaches on the Sunshine Coast, and of those the best is at **Davis Bay**, which explodes into view after a sharp bend in the highway just before Sechelt, 30 minutes from the ferry. As you arrive in **Sechelt**, the massive, unappealing structure on the left is the **House of Hewhiwus** (House of Chiefs), administrative centre of the Sechelt Indian Government District, which in 1988 became Canada's first self-governing Indian band (behind the building stands a commanding circle of totem poles commemorating this event). Do stop. The complex has a good Tourist InfoCentre, a small but interesting museum of local history and Native artifacts, the Tsain-Ko Gift Shop (which sells Native arts, crafts, clothes, and jewellery as well as books on Native culture), and the **Raven's Cry Theatre** (call 885-4597 for a schedule of live performances and movies).

Sechelt's **Blue Heron** (885-3847) gets raves for its outstanding meals and its equally outstanding view of the inlet. For lighter meals and small shops, cruise Cowrie Street: the **Family Bulk Food and Delicatessen** (885-7767) does excellent packed lunches; **Kafe Kitago** (885-7606) and **Mother Earth Cafe** (885-7626) are good spots for cappuccino, tasty soups, quiche, and mouth-watering desserts; and in the summer the artsy outdoor **Shadow Baux Cappuccino and Dessert Bar** (885-7606) tucked behind Stepping Stones offers entertainment Friday and Saturday evenings.

Across the street, **Tzoonie Outdoor Adventures** (885-9802) offers great ecotourism trips including sweat lodges, moored houseboats, kayaking, scuba diving, bird-watching, and crabbing. The **Sechelt Farmers Market** (Saturday, Trail Bay Mall, Hwy 101) runs from spring to Thanksgiving weekend.

Tickets sell out in spring for readings by the biggest names in Canadian literature and journalism at Sechelt's annual August **Festival of the Written Arts**, held at the woodsy Rockwood Centre. Plan ahead by calling 885-9631.

Redroofs Road, 6 kilometres (3.8 miles) north of Sechelt, leads to a unique getaway that, alone, is worth the trip. Heavenly **Halfmoon Bay Cabin** (bookings a must, 688-5058) is a rustic yet luxurious 120-square-metre (1,292-square-foot) waterfront cabin, with a massive stone fireplace, skylights throughout, and all the perfect touches, from magazines to linens. Surrounded by an English country garden and huge sundeck (with a private outdoor shower and gas barbecue), it sits on a hill overlooking its own beach, complete with cabana. Steps or driveway to the beach (wheelchair accessible). Midweek off-season rates are a bargain.

The scenery gets wilder as you continue north, offering great **hiking options**, such as the Saturday morning excursions with Friends of Caren (883-2807) to see Canada's oldest forest, the newly discovered nesting ground of the rare marbled murrelet. The 1.6-kilometre (1-mile) round-trip hike around **Smugglers Cove Marine Park**, 2 kilometres (1.2 miles) west of Halfmoon Bay, is an easy and wonderful way to experience it firsthand. At **Secret Cove**, 2 kilometres (1.2 miles) farther north, settle onto the restaurant decks of either the **Jolly Roger Inn** (885-7860) or **Lord Jim's Resort Hotel** (885-7038), both great spots for a lingering drink and a bird's-eye view of Thormanby Island beyond. **Blackberry Bed and Breakfast** (885-3567) provides a two-bedroom house with a breathtaking view from the deck (breakfast fixings are supplied, right down to the homemade blackberry jam and plates decorated with blackberries, but you do the cooking).

[KIDS] At **Madeira Park**, locals gather at **Frances' Hamburger Takeout**, where the best hamburgers, milkshakes, and fries on the Sunshine Coast are miraculously produced out of a small trailer. Head for the quieter picnic area in front of the Harbour Gallery for your first beautiful view of the indented waterway known as **Pender Harbour**. Wind along Highway 101 past Madeira Park to Garden Bay Road, which gets you to the other side of the harbour.

Garden Bay and nearby **Irvines Landing** have recently added chic to faultless natural beauty and abundant recreational choices. Check out **John Henry's General Store and Post Office**, an ice cream, local gossip, and booze outlet with info on chartering almost anything that floats, plus the scoop on local dinner cruises. The **Garden Bay Hotel Restaurant** includes fine dining, a pub, and a deck (883-2674) and overlooks the Royal Vancouver Yacht Club outport, which attracts the well-heeled. The landmark **Sundowner Inn and Restaurant** (883-9676), overlooking Hospital Bay and renovated under new owners, is worth visiting if only for the fact that meals are served in what was the women's ward of this converted hospital.

At Irvines Landing, reserve at the **Seaside Bed & Breakfast** (883-9929). There's a 180-degree view of the sea (hot tub, TV, and fridge are included as well as a deluxe breakfast served on your own private deck). It's a short walk from here to the area's primo fish and chips at **Irvine's Landing Pub**.

Climb **Pender Hill** for a view of the whole harbour or hike up cone-shaped **Mount Daniel**, spurred on by the knowledge that Sechelt Native women once hiked up daily to bring food to girls who were isolated on the mountaintop for four months during their puberty rites. The **Pender Harbour Golf Club**, carved out of the rain forest north of the Garden Bay Road turnoff, is worth a few lost balls in exchange for the challenge and the scenery.

One of BC's greatest natural sites, **Skookumchuck Rapids** near Egmont, lies at the northern tip of the peninsula. To get there it's an easy 8-kilometre (5-mile) round-trip hike to see the largest saltwater rapids on the West Coast. Tide changes trigger iridescent turquoise cascades in this bottleneck, resulting in whirlpools that are 18 metres (59 feet) across and 2.5 metres (8 feet) high. Daredevils actually fly across these in kamikaze speedboat joyrides. Lie safely on the smooth rocks on shore and feel the vibration. Timing is everything. Check local newspapers, *Coast News* (885-3930) and the *Press* (885-5121), for the best viewing time or call **Bathgate's Store and Marina** in Egmont (883-2222). Greatest tidal range is in early June. Nonhiking option: take the cruise up the inlet from Porpoise Bay. Call **Tzoonie Outdoor Adventures** in Sechelt (885-9802) or **Cruise Tours** in Garden Bay (883-2280), which also runs tours up to beautiful Princess Louisa Inlet and organizes winter diving. Later, hit Egmont's **Back Eddy Pub** for great burgers, cold beer, and yet another postcard view.

From here take the quaint 50-minute ferry trip from **Earls Cove** through the fjords of Jervis Inlet to **Saltery Bay**. Once there, take the road through Powell River that ends 54 kilometres (33.5 miles) later in the tiny fishing village of **Lund**. Along the road in Powell River, stylish **Jitterbug Cafe** is a wonderful stop; or order a Dos Equis in **La Casita** and you could be in Puerto Vallarta.

Lund is the gateway to Desolation Sound and the end of Highway 101, which starts 24,000 kilometres away in Chile (Lund, of course, considers itself the "start" of 101). You can't drive any farther on BC's coast. Check out historic **Lund Hotel** (483-3187). It's also the grocery store, antique store, laundromat, and marina as well as the coffee shop, dining room, pub, and post office. Sit in the coffee shop for a day and you'll see the entire Lund population. Wander the docks and ponder a boat charter. Powell River is a hot spot for scuba diving, with more than 100 dive sites: wolf eels, sea lions, and record-size octopi abound. Call the **Sliammon Indian Band** (483-4111) about its guided tours of a chum salmon enhancement facility. Eagles gather in the hundreds at salmon spawning creeks October to December (InfoCentre, 485-4701).

Detours: **Fiddlehead Farm**, 20 kilometres (12 miles) north up Powell Lake by private boat, is a bit like Shangri-la—not easy to get to, but you know when you've been there. Fiddlehead, run by Linda Schreiber and family, is no ordinary hostel, it's an experience (483-3018 is a radiophone; let it ring at least 10 times). For $22 plus two hours of farm chores (collecting eggs, weeding, milking Sally, pressing apples for cider, chopping wood, baking bread), you can stay at this former back-to-the-land '70s commune, now part of Hostelling International, which draws all ages. It is a six-room guesthouse, simply but attractively furnished.

Savary Island is a land of enchantment, with tropical white sand and warm aqua water, no electricity, and only a few cars. No wonder lucky Vancouver families settle in for the summer, leaving the dads to commute on Harbour Air's "Daddy" plane each weekend (278-3478). From Lund, pedestrians can take the scheduled water taxi. There are no campsites. A warm welcome awaits at **Rosemary Primrose B&B** (483-4789) and **Savary Island Summer House B&B** (925-3536 or 483-4727). Juanita Chase drives the island taxi and handles cottage rentals (483-4314).

TOFINO AND LONG BEACH

Winter winds can hit 100 kilometres per hour here on the wild west coast of Vancouver Island, where the next stop across the Pacific is Japan. Dense as Lyle Lovett's hair, scrubby shorepine are permanently bent back, proof they know which way the prevailing wind blows. Curiously, the waves come directly from the Antarctic or, after mid-October, Alaska. It's the long Antarctic swells, 15 seconds apart, that make this the surfing capital of Canada. Local entrepreneurs are pitching to make it the winter storm-watching capital as well, just as Oregon's coast is.

But most of the 600,000 people who find their way to Vancouver Island's **Pacific Rim National Park** every year still come between April and October. Commonly known as Long Beach, the three-part Pacific Rim National Park actually encompasses the Broken Group Islands and the West Coast Trail as well.

The entire trip along Highway 4 from the Parksville bypass north of Nanaimo to **Tofino** (where the road abruptly ends) is only 166 kilometres (103 miles). There's a lot to see along this winding route, so allow at least two hours, six hours from Vancouver. (See Barkley Sound in this section for details.) Major bus lines from Victoria and Vancouver service Tofino. North Vancouver Air ((800) 228-6608), a small but great private airline with a swish departure lounge in Vancouver, can fly you from Vancouver or Victoria. Note: There is no public transport in Tofino and only one taxi.

[KIDS][FREE] Travelling west, at the **Port Alberni** junction—the logging town that survived the 1964 tsunami from the Alaska earthquake—you'll pass by a number of Native reserves belonging to the 14-band West Coast Natives, now referred to as the Nuu-Chah-Nulth (pronounced *ne shaw nulth*). For a unique picnic spot, turn in at **Sproat Lake Provincial Park**. Chances are good that you will see the lake's fabled mirror reflections, and you may catch the Martin Flying Tanks, the world's largest water bombers, scooping up 27 tonnes (30 tons) of water in 22 seconds for forest-fire fighting (West Coast Rangers, (250) 723-2952).

The small towns of Ucluelet and Tofino bracket Pacific Rim National Park, and both celebrate the **Pacific Rim Whale Festival** from mid-March to mid-April, when some 20,000 Pacific grey whales—virtually the world's population—pass by on their migration from Baja, Mexico, to the Arctic Ocean. **Ucluelet** (BC's third-largest port for landed fish catch), at the south end, is closer to Highway 4 and claims to be the whale-watching capital of the world, but you can do that from Tofino too, and the latter has infinitely more charm.

Tofino is also the gateway to Clayoquot Sound, the largest intact ancient temperate rain forest left on Vancouver Island. Its future is hotly disputed by environmentalists and forest companies. Stop at the **Pacific Rim Park InfoCentre** ((250) 726-4212) just five minutes after turning north to Tofino from the Highway 4 junction. Anyone parking within the park must buy a $5 day pass from dispensers by Visa or cash, so you may want to choose a full day to explore the park. (Except for camping at Green Point, all accommodation lies outside park boundaries.) [KIDS][FREE] Inside the park, don't miss the self-guided boardwalk loop through the weird woods on **Shorepine Bog Trail**, where stubby, broccoli-like trees are centuries old. Outside the park, Willowbrae and Half Moon Bay trails trace part of the route villagers trudged before roads linked Tofino and Ucluelet.

Best beaches? Long Beach, all 19 sandy kilometres (11 miles) of it; Cox and Chesterman for breakers; MacKenzie for relative warmth; Templar for peace in miniature. **Florencia Bay**, aka Wreck Bay, former home to hippy squatters, is a local favourite—no crowds, good tidal pools.

The stretch of surf-swept sand that is **Long Beach** is best explored by hiking the beaches, headlands, and woodland trails, so pick up a free *Hiker's Guide* or, better yet, buy the new

▼

Excursions

Tofino and Long Beach

▲

Official Guide/Pacific Rim National Park Reserve or Bruce Obee's excellent *The Pacific Rim Explorer*, which is loaded with history, practical tips, and even the nitty-gritty on how whales do it. Ask for tips on whale watching and where to see the permanent colonies of basking sea lions. [KIDS][FREE] There are also daily evening interpretive lectures at Green Point Theatre and occasional guided storm walks.

[KIDS][FREE] The biggest news (and most confusing) for visitors to Tofino and Long Beach is **Wickaninnish Inn** ((800) 333-4604), a splendid new $8.5-million oceanfront inn built on Chesterman Beach, the longest beach outside the park, just five kilometres (three miles) south of Tofino. The original inn, once a haven to world travellers, was located on Long Beach until 1977, when the Pacific Rim National Park was created. Longtime resident Dr. Howard McDiarmid was behind the park's creation, and now he, his sons, and investors are behind the new inn with the beloved old name. The new inn is selling bad weather, offering a roaring fire when it's howling outside; a 100-seat restaurant (The Pointe) and bar (On-the-Rocks) built out over the rocks so the surf pounds in all around; and 46 extra large rooms, each with an ocean view, gas fireplace, soaker tub for two, and private balcony. Chef Rodney Butters brings a new level of West Coast cuisine to the Tofino area (reservations are a must). Rates will drop by $100 come winter, and packages with North Vancouver Air's twin engine turbo-prop are a deal.

The confusion arises because, although the old inn was basically torn down, the timbers, rafters, and stone hearth were built into the **Wickaninnish Interpretive Centre** on the original picturesque point at the end of Long Beach Road. This centre also includes a restaurant still referred to as Wickaninnish, but, sadly, it's more remarkable for the view than the food.

The Interpretive Centre itself is well worth a stop. Operated by Parks Canada (closed winters), the centre's exhibits have recently been completely redone. Check out the telescopes on the observation decks. Beach fires are allowed, but you'll need to gather firewood while it's still daylight if you plan to picnic here.

The best guest lounge (but much smaller guest rooms) is minutes away at the delightful ocean-front **Middle Beach Lodge** ((250) 725-2900), where guests disappear into down-filled easy chairs and ottomans by the great rock fireplace or snooze in broad-armed wooden Adirondack chairs on the deck. Ralph Lauren would be happy here. If you want the pounding roar of open ocean, you won't find it here; instead, gentle waves on tiny Templar Beach lull you to sleep. Nearby, Middle Beach's new year-round Headlands Lodge has more family-oriented suites (up to sixplexes) and self-contained cabins five nights a week (Middle Beach and Headlands alternate serving meals); off-season guests can dine Saturday nights at Head-lines. Otherwise you forage at local restaurants. Until Wick-aninnish's The Pointe opened, **Orca Lodge** (1254 Pacific Rim Hwy, (250) 725-2323) had the best food (albeit no view), start-ing with the bread salad appetizer. Tip: Don't waste the chef's skills on basic cracked Dungeness crab; for that head for the Crab Bar (601 Campbell, (250) 725-3733).

There are lots of campsites, motels, and cabins available. Our favourite is the well-run **Pacific Sands Beach Resort** on Cox Beach ((800) 565-BEACH), with a choice of nine basic cab-ins or two blocks of apartmentlike suites with fireplaces and TVs.

Walkable Tofino (population 1,103) is a relaxed town and a popular reprovisioning spot for sailors circumnavigating Van-couver Island. You'll find locals at the **Common Loaf Bake Shop** behind the bank (it has wonderful cheese buns, and, come summer nights, bread dough becomes pizza dough) and at the organic pink-and-turquoise **Alley Way Cafe** (also behind the bank), where everything, right down to the mayonnaise on the clam burgers, is made in-house.

Be sure to visit well-known Native artist Roy Henry Vick-ers's **Eagle Aerie Gallery** and experience the remarkable calm of the adzed cedar interior inspired by the traditional form of a West Coast longhouse ((250) 725-3235). **[KIDS][FREE]** For a unique tour, drop by the **Coast Guard Rescue Station** ((250) 725-3231) during the daily informal open house, 10am to 2pm, and imagine turning turtle in the self-righting rescue vessel. Right next door, you can rent a kayak (or take lessons) at **Tofino Sea Kayaking** (320 Main, (250) 725-4222) or sip a cap-puccino at the tiny seaside espresso bar. **[KIDS][FREE]** Sunday nights, the Legion hosts Java Jam (entertainers and kids free).

Once you arrive at Tofino's only traffic light in town, hang a right, drive down to the dock, and know you've arrived at the Pacific terminus of the Trans-Canada Highway. The best view in Tofino is right across from you in the **House of Himwitsa** building, home to the First Nations–run **Sea Shanty** restaurant and **Himwitsa Lodge** ((800) 899-1947). Charleton Heston stayed here while filming *Alaska*. The Nuu-chah-nulth people are moving into tourism; if you're looking for off-the-beaten-path, you can't do better than one of their guided tours to Meares and Flores Islands ("Walk on the Wild Side"). Ask at Tourist Information or House of Himwitsa Hotel to see if they're operating.

Another must is sailing, cruising, or flying to **Hot Springs Cove**, which has an unforgettable forest hike into the 43°C (109°F) waterfalls and pools, shared by tourists, shampooing boaters, and anglers. Bring a bathing suit. If you can't bear to leave, you can book into one of the six self-contained units in tiny **Hot Springs Lodge** ((250) 724-8570). You take in your own supplies and do your own cooking, but, oh, the peace of it all!

Spring is best for whale watching, but some companies—there are many—guarantee sightings into October. Check with **Tofino's Information Centre** (380 Campbell St, (250) 725-3414). Tour guide "Pipot'" at **Remote Passages Zodiac Adventures** ((800) 666-9833) is particularly good with kids. Tip: 12-passenger rubber zodiacs offer a more thrilling encounter, but the bounce can be tough on back problems.

VICTORIA AND BEYOND
See Day Trips section in this chapter for
transportation to Victoria information.

Although Victoria was ranked by *Condé Nast Traveler* magazine readers as one of the top 10 cities to visit in the world, and as number one in the world for ambience and environment, its greatest charms may be its close proximity to delightful places that lie just outside BC's small capital city on southern Vancouver Island. Victoria's "backyard" includes a variety of landscapes, from nearby Saxe Point naval base to the wild west coast just around the southern tip of Vancouver Island (see Sooke in this chapter).

Best day trips: the so-called Western Communities of **Colwood** and **Metchosin**, one of the oldest settled communities in British Columbia. If you'd rather look than drive, hop a bus in Victoria (check the excellent *Explore Victoria by Bus* free booklet, available from Victoria's Tourism Information across from the Empress). The #50 Goldstream bus takes you to the Western Exchange; from there it's a scenic hike to fascinating **Fort Rodd Hill National Historic Park** (603 Fort Rodd Hill Rd, (250) 380-4662), where soldiers manned the guns from 1878 to 1956, and to **Fisgard Lighthouse**, the oldest lighthouse on the coast. Drive along Ocean Boulevard Spit, where navy spouses wave tearful good-byes alongside the bird sanctuary to manoeuvres-bound destroyers. Nearby, golfers weep over a missed putt on **Royal Colwood Golf Course** (off Sooke Rd), ranked as BC's best.

The Metchosin area is loaded with great parks, including **Witty's Lagoon** nature park and beaches, which are an afternoon in themselves (the Nature House, on the lagoon trail, is open weekends year round). Along the way you can see **Chosin Pottery** (Canadian award-winning ceramics), roadside "honour" boxes for vegetable and egg stands, and, in spring, wild orchids on the grounds of **St. Catherine's Church** in Metchosin. Tailgate-style **Metchosin Market** operates behind Metchosin Firehall Sundays from 11am to 2pm.

For sustenance, pick up unusual picnic goodies at **Rebecca's** (1127 Wharf St in Victoria, (250) 380-6999) from the seven metres (20 feet) of take-out. The chefs cook different dishes every day, but look for Dungeness crab, samosas, burritos, 10 different salads, and 10 homemade desserts, including chocolate espresso torte. Eat on the grounds at Ford Rodd (military concerts are held on summer Sunday afternoons). Or stop for a draft at **Spinnakers** brewpub (308 Catherine St, (250) 386-2739) and for halibut fish and chips (yeast for the batter is supplied by the on-site brewery).

Back in Victoria, **Victoria Marine Adventure Centre** (950 Wharf St, (800) 575-6700) offers one-stop shopping for adrenaline junkies. They'll rent boats and bikes or book a kayaking or scuba diving tour; custom plan your adventure from rock climbing to nature walks; or serve up an authentic taste of the West Coast at their Blackfish Cafe. Locals will urge you to visit the (award-winning) **Royal British Columbia Museum** (Belleville St and Government St, (250) 387-3701). It's a great stop (even antsy kids love it), but for a more active afternoon why not sign on for one of the museum's own truly excellent Eco-Tours; they are designed to take the museum back into the real world. The museum offers day trips (Spelunking the Horne Lake Caves; Sail Away to Race Rocks; Cowichan Bay Marine Ecology Station; Salmon Belly Tours; and If the Trees Could Talk) and Overnighters (from bird-watching in Clayoquot Sound to grizzly bears in the **Khutzehmateen Valley**). The experts are there with you as amiable resource people ((250) 386-3311 for reservations).

[KIDS] Make time to visit **Craigdarroch Castle** (1050 Joan Cres, (250) 592-5323), built by coal baron Robert Dunsmuir to induce his Scottish wife to live in distant Victoria; and the **Art Gallery of Greater Victoria** (1040 Moss St, (250) 384-4101), complete with the only Shinto shrine outside Japan, a fine gift shop housed in a modern building, and an Edwardian house.

[KIDS] The Old Cemeteries Society now offers Lantern Tours of the Old Burying Ground—"fun for the whole family!"—every night at 9:30pm in July and August, starting from Cherry Bank Hotel, 825 Burdett Street. Year round the society runs walking tours of Victoria's many cemeteries on Sundays (and on Tuesday and Thursday evenings in summer), but the majority of tours go to **Ross Bay Cemetery**, with good cause. It's a veritable who's who of Victoria, including coal magnate Robert Dunsmuir and artist Emily Carr (Fairfield Rd at Memorial Dr, (250) 384-0045). You can also buy a booklet at Munro's bookstore and do a self-guided tour anytime. The annual **Ghost Walk** takes place on October 31. Call (250) 384-0045 for meeting locations.

Come spring, with new life in mind, head by car or bus to Fairfield neighbourhood's Trutch Street, one of the city's oldest enclaves of Arts-and-Crafts-style houses. Every April, Yoshina cherry trees, planted in the 1930s, are heavy with pink blossoms. That's another great thing about Victoria. Its many neighbourhoods are distinctive but easily reached in five to 15 minutes at the most.

You cannot fail to rest your head happily in such splendid small inns as **Abigail's** (906 McClure St, (250) 388-5363), where the halls smell of good coffee and delicate perfume, or **Holland House Inn** (595 Michigan St, (250) 384-6644), all artful bliss and duvets. And there are bed and breakfasts like **Prior House**, a gracious 1912 mansion hidden deep in residential Rockland, a swank neighbourhood of leafy streets and roomy rock-walled estates on Victoria's east side (620 St. Charles St, (250) 592-8847). Once home to a lieutenant governor, Prior House's Lieutenant Governor's Suite now has a ballroom-size bathroom with crystal chandelier. Before Candice Cooperrider fixes breakfast in bed (or dining room), tea from the terrace trolley, or sherry by the parlour fire, stroll over to the splendid perennial and rose gardens of 100-room Government House. Regulars at the award-winning heritage **Beaconsfield Inn** (998 Humboldt St, (250) 384-4044)—all gleaming Edwardian mahogany and deep leather couches— will be happy to hear the inn now also books for the new romantic "Beach Cottage," 10 minutes away on Cadboro Bay, with two in mind for the country pine sleigh bed, rock fireplace, and outdoor hot tub. But **The Brass Bell Floating B&B** ((250) 480-0958) takes the prize for a unique Victoria experience. This is not shared accommodation, but a private, romantic B&B, and in this case B&B means "boat" (vintage 1931 wooden motor yacht lovingly restored) and "breakfast" (at nearby restaurants).

Downtown, the guest rooms of **Swans Hotel & Pub** are more basic, but the location is ideal for shoppers and walkers (506 Pandora Ave, (250) 361-3310). (Wherever you stay, do stroll the 2.7-kilometre (1.67 mile) waterfront walk along Songhees Westsong Way that leads to curving beaches and boardwalks.) Swans' public rooms are a treat, thanks to Victoria's best public display of a private art collection. Owner Michael Williams, art enthusiast and former Shropshire shepherd, transformed this award-winning complex from an ugly duckling warehouse—he also brews excellent beer.

When the lights go down low, head for **Belfry Theatre** in Fernwood village. It's a wonderful converted heritage church at 1219 Gladstone Avenue ((250) 385-6815), whose productions draw Vancouverites across the Gulf. Victorians reserve at nearby **Soho Village Bistro** (1307 Gladstone Ave, (250) 384-3344) for a memorable dinner in low light and gentle jazz and the chance to return for dessert after the performance. Tiny, quirky, 50-seat **Theatre Inconnu** in Market Square ((250) 280-1284) likes to take risks with new playwrights, occasional nudity, and Shakespeare. The lead actor may also take your (under $10) ticket and serve coffee at intermission. **Vic Theatre** (at 808 Douglas St, around the corner from the Empress) now runs higher-brow and alternative movies.

Still married? Pack your marriage licence between

November 1 and January 1 and you can check into the handsomely renovated **Empress Hotel** (721 Government St, (250) 384-8111)—where Bob Hope once hit golf balls off the front lawn—paying only the year in which you married as room rate (maximum of three nights). If you married in 1958, you pay only $58 a night—such a deal! Afternoon tea in the main Tea Lobby is lovely but very pricey at $25, and the endless courses of fruit, scones, sandwiches, and cakes leave you too stuffed for dinner. Arrive instead for the 12 noon "tea" sitting in lieu of lunch. Those without reservations or proper attire may still find tea in the Bengal Lounge. (Sadly, a newly relaxed "Smart Casual" dress code at the Empress now includes jeans, but mercifully not running shoes, short shorts, or tank tops.) The dining room has expanded to take in the former Empress Lounge, which means harbourside window tables for the first time. From October to May be sure to ask for reservations at the best room rate (harbour views are wonderful); there are often unadvertised specials. For the best view of the Empress or the illuminated Parliament Buildings, ride the tiny ferry across the Inner Harbour to the newly opened **Ocean Pointe Resort** ((250) 360-2999). Some find the interior decor in the public areas a bit too international/modern/I-could-be-in-any-major-city, but the fine dining **Victorian Room** is charming and popular for dinner.

Dinner recommendations include the excellent high-energy **Herald Street Caffe** (546 Herald St, (250) 381-1441); the **Il Terrazzo** (555 Johnson St, (250) 386-4747), which was the Grand Central Cafe, now named for its cozy brick-walled patio; and sister restaurants **Villa Rosa** (1015 Fort St, (250) 384-5337), which is more Italian, and San Remo (2709 Quadra St, (250) 384-5255), which is more Greek. *CityFood* magazine notes that Patrick Bevington, formerly of the Met Bistro, has joined forces with three young women at **Dilettante's Cafe** (787 Ford St, (250) 381-3327), which draws a crossover crowd from "opera goers to the hip young in black." Seafood fans (and game lovers) need look no further than the harbour view and Maritimes-born chef David McQuinn of **Blue Crab Bar and Grill** (146 Kingston St, (250) 480-1999). Farther afield and much pricier is the elegant **Chez Daniel** (2524 Estevan Ave, (250) 592-7424).

Best-kept secret: Victoria Harbour Ferry's bargain $8 minimoonlight cruise of the harbour aboard a miniferry. Show up at the Inner Harbour or reserve at the Tourism Victoria InfoCentre on the Inner Harbour. Daytime cruises up the Gorge or over to Ocean Pointe are a pleasant diversion, too.

WHISTLER

Highway 99, running north from Vancouver to Whistler's four-season resort, is an adventure in itself. Allow two hours on the aptly named Sea to Sky Highway, whose curves hug fir-covered mountains that tumble sharply into Howe Sound. On a clear day, look for the spectacular **Tantalus Range** turnoff north of Squamish. As an alternative, take Maverick Coach Lines, or the scenic 7am BC Rail train trip from North Vancouver, or fly via North Vancouver Air ((800) 228-6608; 278-1608 in Vancouver) from Vancouver International Airport. For details, call Whistler Activity and Information Centre at the Conference Centre (932-2394; from Vancouver, 985-6107, ext. 161).

Along the way: just north of Lions Bay, golfers should check out the spectacular Robert Muir Graves-designed **Furry Creek Golf & Country Club** (896-2216), which opened in mid-1993 after it was built where everyone said it was impossible to build. The course is partially open to public play until all memberships have been sold. [KIDS] Stop at Britannia Beach (once the largest processor of copper in the British Empire) for seasonal underground mining museum tours and sustenance: **Mountain Woman's** for great burgers and fries; **Twin Gables Tearoom** (896-2265) for home-baked goods, breakfast, lunch, and tea; **Jane's Coffee House** (896-2245) for cappuccino, cinnamon buns, textiles, and collectibles; or the **99er** (896-2497) for quick, cheap coffee to go. South of Squamish, 61 kilometres (38 miles) from Vancouver, watch rock climbers from around the world scaling Smoke Bluffs (lobbying to be the first Canadian National Park designated for climbers) or the imposing 650-metre (2,133-foot) granite mass that is **Stawamus Chief.** You can also view the climbers from inside the **Howe Sound Inn and Brewing Company**, where wonderful, handcrafted ales are served in both a charming brewpub and a restaurant (unrated at press time), which focuses on Northwest regional foods. There are 20 guest rooms and meeting services as well. [KIDS] Kids of all ages will want to make the detour (turn west on Centennial Way, approximately 3 kilometres (2 miles) north of McDonald's on Highway 99 in Squamish) to the newly opened **West Coast Railway Heritage Park** (898-9336). The 5-hectare (12-acre) park houses Canada's second-largest collection of railway rolling stock with 58 vintage railway cars and locomotives, all in a beautiful natural setting. Admission is $4.50 adults; $12 family, with a $1 surcharge to ride the miniature railway.

Rated North America's number-one ski resort by *Ski, Snow Country*, and *Skiing* magazines, **Whistler Resort** has gained a reputation as a world-class year-round resort. (1996 was the first year all three magazines were unanimous in their choice of the top ski destination.) In ski season, you'll hear plenty of Southern U.S., European, and Japanese accents in the chair lift lineups along with those of the many Aussie lifties. If you haven't been there in a year, you'll hardly know your way around. The huge European-style resort is actually two communities: pedestrian-only **Whistler Village** and **Upper Village** (also known as **Blackcomb** Resort). (A third village (where cars can park), **Village North**, is home to Market Place, which in turn is home to shops, cafes, post office, and liquor store.) The two communities, however, are now owned by the same company. At this writing, Intrawest Corporation, the owner of Blackcomb, and Whistler Mountain Holdings, Inc., the company that manages Whistler, have combined forces under the Intrawest name. More than $35 million in enhancements is planned for Whistler; Intrawest has announced that it plans to retain the distinct personalities of each mountain. Currently, the newest development in Village North is the Town Plaza, between Whistler Village and Market Place. A smaller, less expensive "base" a few miles closer to Vancouver is the **Whistler Creek** area (down at Whistler's original south side).

In the heart of Whistler Village, check out the complex that houses Hot Rock Cafe (Madonna's first gold LP is on display; Joplin, Hendrix, and Elvis are on the ceiling), Helly Hansen, Starbucks coffee bar, Mongolie Grill, and health-minded Grassroots restaurant.

Accommodation outside the Village and Blackcomb is cheaper, but you'll need a car or taxi if you're not on the bus route. Reservations are recommended far in advance. Call **Central Reservations** for info on hotels, lodges, condos (some of the best among North American ski resorts and a popular choice with locals), and pensions: (932-4222; from Vancouver, dial 664-5625; United States and Canada, (800) 944-7853). Many lodgings now require 30 days' cancellation notice with a three-day minimum stay in peak season. The $75-million **Chateau Whistler** (938-8000—ask for special packages) is a peaceful resort in itself (Robin Leach proclaimed the Mallard Bar "the premier address at Whistler"), where the staff's goal is a happy guest. Don't miss the art-filled lobby, brunch at Wildflower, or the shops below. The best Whistler has to offer in a traditional alpine country inn is the **Durlacher Hof** (932-1924), located 1.6 kilometres (1 mile) north of Whistler Village. Once you're inside, Erika and Peter's hospitality takes over with the wonderful smells of Austrian baking and the prospect of putting your feet up après-ski (in the pair of Austrian hut slippers provided) around the *kachelofen*, an old-fashioned farmhouse fireplace oven. The eight guest rooms have private baths, balconies, and views of Whistler, Blackcomb, or Wedge Mountain. At press time, Whistler's first boutique hotel, **The Pinnacle Resort**, (938-3218), has opened on Main Street in the new village center. With 84 suites (all with jacuzzi tubs for two, fireplaces, and mountain views), the Pinnacle promises to be a bright addition to Whistler's lodging. In addition, it is the setting for a Mediterranean-style restaurant, **Quattro**, which has already garnered critical praise.

The **Whistler-Blackcomb ski area** has two mountains, with the largest high-speed lift system in North America. The friendly rivalry benefits the skier, as each mountain jockeys for the best runs, grooming, restaurants, and service. Knowing how to take advantage of North America's longest vertical—given the 200-plus runs, 3 glaciers, and 12 massive, high-alpine bowls—is a challenge.

The best way for first-time visitors to discover the two mountains is to sign on for the fun-filled three- and four-day **Ski Esprit** packages (932-3400) for a guided introduction and instruction by friendly local instructors.

[FREE] It is also a good idea to attend the Thursday or Sunday night welcome and orientation at the Conference Centre. If you want to ski two mountains in one day, ski Blackcomb first. At noon, ski to Whistler's gondola base, have lunch in the village, and then take the 15-minute gondola ride to the top. Summit to summit is 40 minutes. Nonskiers are welcome to go topside for the view and lunch (many resorts don't allow this).

Biggest thrill for intermediates: riding up Whistler's steep Peak Chair knowing there is an easy way down the backside as well as an unforgettable view over the back of bowls, glaciers, and Black Tusk. Blackcomb's double black diamond (Canada's first) Couloir Extreme is still a badge-of-courage gulper. Advanced and expert Vancouver skiers regularly sign up for adult camps (moguls, masters, women only) (938-7720). The best ski tuning: **First Tracks** in the Delta Hotel; best boot refitting: George McConkey at **McCoo's** (reserve ahead). In winter it pays to reserve at older favourite restaurants such as romantic **Rim Rock Cafe** (932-5565), the popular Araxi Ristaurante (932-4540), and Umberto's **Il Caminetto** (932-4442), which some Vancouver skiers prebook for the season. Après-ski at the base of Blackcomb: enjoy leisurely patio viewing from **Monk's Grill** or the Chateau's Mallard Bar (great pasta snacks), or lively beer drinking at **Merlin's**. In the Village, head for the **Garibaldi Lift Co.** and **Longhorn**. Later try **Buffalo Bill's**, which usually has good and sometimes great live bands; **Savage Beagle** and **Tommy Africa's** attract younger crowds.

If you haven't tried **paragliding**, **snow-boarding**, or **heli-skiing**, do. Call Whistler Activity and Information Centre and ask about **snowshoeing**, **snowmobiling**, and **sleigh rides** as well. When the lights go down low and the snow begins to fall, cross-country ski in the moonlight on the peaceful track-set trails (rentals in the Village).

Whistler has done a lot to develop year-round recreation and is definitely worth checking out even when there's no snow on the ground. Again, the Whistler Activity and Information Centre is a useful clearinghouse. In summer, you can go glacier skiing on Blackcomb mid-June to early August. Hikers can take chairlifts to a network of alpine trails; and mountain bikers can load their cycles onto Blackcomb's express chairs or Whistler's gondola for the ultimate guided mountain descent. Many consider the Whistler-Pemberton area the best mountain-biking terrain in the world (pick up *Sea to Sky Mountain Bike Guide*). New to trail riding? Try the mostly paved, mostly flat Valley Trail, which links up to Lost Lake's 25 kilometres of connecting trails.

In-line skating is hot, and **Blackcomb Ski & Sport** (938-7788) offers bargain instruction packages. **The Escape Route's** professional guides can introduce you to Whistler's backcountry (day hikes to expeditions), 932-3338. **Whistler Outdoor Experience Company** (932-3389) is the best adventure source. Do-it-yourselfers need only Paul Adam's excellent *Whistler and Region: Outdoors* as a starting point. It describes such odds and ends as Highway 99's Tantalus Viewpoint, the Duffey Lake circuit, and Taseko Lake's 90-minute floatplane tour (split five ways, $125 each).

Something less rigorous? Tiny **Armchair Books** has a remarkable selection. But an absolute must is the idyllic paddle down the River of Golden Dreams. This is genuine Wind-in-the-Willows country. Rent a canoe or kayak through Whistler Outdoor Experience (932-3389) or Whistler Sailing and Water Sports (932-7245) and ask for directions regarding where to drift along the meandering river.

Eating out is a major activity at Whistler, with more than 90 restaurants scattered through the Village. When the Village sushi bars are packed, head to Upper Village's **Thai One On** (932-4822), where even the black rise dessert is divine. Nearby, **La Rúa** (in Le Chamois Hotel, 932-5011) has comfortably elegant, eclectic dining with great appetizers. In Village North, local favourites (they like to escape the Village) include **Caramba!** (Village North, 938-1879) and **Gaitors Bar and Grill** (on the highway above the Shoestring Lodge, 938-5777).

Local hangouts: **South Side Deli** (Whistler Creek) for rock 'n' roll breakfasts and great cheap food in a diner-like atmosphere; **The Cookie Company** for lattes. Condo-cooking tourists shop at the **Grocery Store** in the Village; locals shop at **Nester's** on the highway. Hit **Ingrid's** in the Village for dynamic veggie burgers.

Watersports are hot on all five local lakes (windsurfing began on Alta Lake in Canada). Golfers have their pick of three championship courses: the Arnold Palmer-designed **Whistler Golf Course** (932-3280)—his first Canadian course; the rugged links-style **Chateau Whistler Golf Course** (938-8000) by Robert Trent Jones Jr.; and the newest, **Nicklaus North Golf Course** (938-9898) by Jack Nicklaus, which opened in 1995 to raves.

Performers entertain almost daily on the Village stage from June to September, and the resort hosts Labour Day,

Canada Day (July 1), and Octoberfest celebrations as well as the Roots Festival (mid-July), a classical music fest with a mountaintop concert by the Vancouver Symphony Orchestra (mid-August), and an alpine wine festival and jazz festival (September). The **Farmers Market** is open Sundays at the base of Blackcomb throughout the summer.

Keep on driving north of Whistler to dreamy, mountain-ringed Pemberton Valley (where much of the produce used in Whistler restaurants is grown) for great cheap golf at **Big Sky Golf and Country Club** ((800) 668-7900) and great horseback riding and organic food at Pony Espresso (894-5700). The regular crowd likes **Willy G's Cafe** (894-6411) for big helpings of Greek food and big views of Mount Currie. Spawning salmon run on the Gates and Birkenhead Rivers come September. This is the traditional home of the Lil'wat people. Don't miss **Spirit Circle Art, Craft and Tea Company** (on Hwy 99 (Portage Road), 894-6336), which incorporates some 100-year-old timbers from the Mount Currie elders' lodge formerly on this site. It's a welcoming place with relaxed, home-cooked meals and cappuccino as well as bannock and intriguing local Salish herbal teas and artwork (894-6336). [KIDS][FREE] The long hike up into the glorious **ancient cedar grove** between Whistler and Pemberton (ask directions at the Whistler Activity Centre) is well worth it; you can smell the grove before you see it. For a much flatter stroll, take the pleasant half-hour walk into dramatic **Nairn Falls**, 32 kilometres (20 miles) north of Whistler. Access is on the right-hand side of the highway as you drive from Whistler toward Pemberton.

RECREATION

Recreation

BICYCLING

Vancouver's superb recreational cycling trails offer expansive views of the sea and mountains as they wind through stands of fir, cedar, and hemlock and follow the shoreline of numerous bays and inlets. Not all of the treasures are 100 percent natural: along the way there are plenty of places to stop for cappuccino, pizza by the slice, fish and chips, and frozen yogurt. Cyclists with more time can explore the Sunshine Coast and Gulf Islands with the help of the largest ferry system in the world. A full water bottle is a good idea, and, as of August 1996, all bicyclists are required by law to wear a helmet—failure to don one may result in a fine if you're spotted. Also, bring a shackle-style U-lock if you plan to stop and shop or walk around. It's against the law to cycle while wearing a headset, so keep it in the daypack. The best one-stop source for bicycling information is the resource library of **Cycling British Columbia** (1367 W Broadway Ave, 737-3034). You'll find maps, bike routes, guidebooks, and a competition calendar. Racers should note that time-trials and criteriums are held each week throughout the summer at UBC. Call the Cycling BC event hotline at 737-3165 for more details.

Here are some of the best rides around the city. For further information, refer to Mountain Biking in this chapter.

Gulf Islands From March to October, cyclists use the BC Ferries dock at Tsawwassen as a departure point for exploring the southern Gulf Islands. Salt Spring, Galiano, Mayne, North and South Pender, and Saturna are the most popular. Accommodation ranges from provincial park campgrounds to a variety of bed and breakfasts. Swimming coves, pubs, and shady arbutus trees give welcome relief from the occasional hill. You can take BC Ferries from Tsawwassen or Horseshoe Bay near Vancouver, bearing in mind that schedules change seasonally. If you're taking a motor vehicle, be prepared for lengthy line-ups during the summer months. Vehicle reservations can be made on the Tsawwassen routes (669-1211). Call the BC Ferries recorded information line (277-0277) for sailing times.

River Road to Steveston [KIDS] A fun, flat, 36-kilometre (22.5-mile) loop in the suburb of Richmond. Families often do just a portion of this circuit, parking their cars at the RV park on the west side of the Dunsmuir Bridge. Cycle along the gravel dyke path to the fishing village of Steveston to buy an ice cream or the catch of the day. The finely pebbled route is level but twisting in spots. There is no finer place to watch the sun go down than Garry Point Park, just west of Steveston.

Seaside Bicycle Route A terrific 15-kilometre (9.4-mile) route linking the seawall with other waterfront pathways around False Creek, Vanier Park, Kitsilano Beach, Jericho Beach, and ending below UBC at Spanish Banks. A less-crowded alternative to the seawall, this route offers more rest-stop options: a cappuccino on Cornwall Avenue, swimming at Kits Pool or Jericho Beach, and kite flying in Vanier Park. Parts of this route follow city streets; look for the green and white bike-route signs. Maps can be picked up at several info kiosks along the way. **Recreation Rentals** (2560 Arbutus St, 733-7368) rents hybrid bikes suitable for bike paths and urban riding, as well as mountain bikes rugged enough to go anywhere.

Stanley Park Seawall No cycle visit to Vancouver is complete without a spin around the 10.5-kilometre (6.5-mile) seawall. Watch seaplanes taking off and landing in Burrard Inlet, stop and smell the rose gardens, brace yourself for the Nine O'Clock Gun from Hallelujah Point, and gulp great breaths of cedar-scented air while trying not to disturb nesting Canada geese around Lost Lagoon. To escape the crowds, venture off the pavement onto other dirt-packed trails inside the park's core. There are many bike-rental shops near Stanley Park; the best known is **Spokes Bicycle Rental and Espresso Bar** (1798 W Georgia St, 688-5141 or 681-5581), which combines cycling and coffee, the favourite passions of many Vancouverites.

CANOEING AND KAYAKING

British Columbia doesn't have a canoe on its coat of arms, but it could. More than 50,000 residents of the province are regular canoeists or kayakers, and paddlers can take their pick of thousands of lakes and rivers as well as explore more than 6,500 offshore islands.

On any day of the year, marine enthusiasts carry on the

Northwest Coast Native tradition by paddling modern versions of the baidarka, or sea kayak. The sea kayak is longer and sleeker than its whitewater cousin, and some boats are specially constructed for tandem paddlers. Most of the bays and inlets around Vancouver are perfect for even novice paddlers, but taking an introductory course offered by the **Ecomarine Ocean Kayak Centre** (689-7575) on Granville Island is a good idea. Learn the basic paddle strokes and self-rescue techniques, then rent single- or two-person kayaks at Jericho Beach or False Creek. The waters of English Bay toward Stanley Park and by Kits Beach and Spanish Banks offer a mix of benign and moderately challenging conditions. Watch for unpredictable winds and tides around Spanish Banks and around Lighthouse Park in West Vancouver. Sea kayakers are prohibited from using the busy harbour area between the Lions Gate and Second Narrows Bridges. **Indian Arm** is a finger-shaped fjord that bends northward for 30 kilometres (18.8 miles) deep into the heart of the Coast Range Mountains. See impenetrable forests growing on impossibly steep hillsides, rising from the bowline for hundreds of vertical metres. You can rent boats at the **Deep Cove Canoe and Kayak Centre** (929-2268) and paddle across 1.6-kilometre-wide (1-mile-wide) Indian Arm to Jug Island, Combe Park, or Belcarra Park. A paddle south leads to Cates Park, where Malcolm Lowry wrote *Under the Volcano*. It takes about four hours (one way) to reach the head of this glorious fjord. Inexperienced paddlers should beware of wake-swells from larger yachts, speedboats, and sailboats.

Betty Pratt-Johnson is the grande dame of whitewater trips in the province. A number of her books cover kayaking and canoeing across British Columbia. John Ince and Hedi Kottner's *Sea Kayaking Canada's West Coast* is an indispensable guide to exploring the province's 27,000 kilometres (16,875 miles) of coastline. Marine charts and tide tables are available from most Vancouver marine stores and from the Canadian Hydrographic Service, Department of Fisheries and Oceans, Institute of Ocean Sciences, 9860 W Saanich Rd, Box 6000, Sidney, BC V8L 4B2; (250) 356-6358.

Sea kayaking is the best way of getting a cormorant's-eye view of the **Gulf Islands**. The paddling here is done in safe, scenic waters. Tiny pebble-beach coves shaded by rust-barked arbutus trees beckon the weary paddler. **SaltSpring Kayaking**, (250) 653-4222, offers guided outings. If you have your own boat, just get on the ferry and follow your maps. Although this area is one of the sunniest and most temperate in the province, the water is frigid, even in summer. Less experienced kayakers should stay close to shore, where an easy swim leads to safety in case of a spill.

The **Powell River Canoe Circuit**, located on the Sunshine Coast, takes in more than 57 kilometres (35.6 miles) of canoeing and 8 kilometres (5 miles) of portages. There are eight lakes in the loop, but easy access to various parts of the route via logging roads makes day trips popular. The entire circuit takes a week to complete and rewards paddlers with good views of coastal rain forest and glimpses of inaccessible, seldom-visited mountain peaks. This route is best paddled between April and November, since the higher lakes are frozen during the winter months and roads become inaccessible. Call Sunshine Coast Forest District Office at 485-0700 for maps and directions.

The Canoeing Association, the Whitewater Kayaking Association, and the Sea Kayaking Association of British Columbia are useful sources of information about paddle sports in the province. They can be contacted through the Outdoor Recreation Council of British Columbia at 737-3058.

CLIMBING AND MOUNTAINEERING

The Coast Mountains stretch northward from the 49th parallel, the largest portion of a massive cordillera extending from the Mexican border to Alaska. Within its huge geographical boundaries, hundreds of unclimbed summits and cross-country traverses remain to be tackled. Virtually every kind of mountaineering challenge can be found within a day's drive of downtown Vancouver, from frozen-waterfall climbing in Lillooet to rock climbing the sun-baked granite of the Smoke Bluffs near Squamish. Spectacular glacier ascents can be made in Garibaldi Provincial Park and on the peaks surrounding the Joffre Lakes Recreation Area east of Pemberton.

Some of the best views of the city can be seen from the summit of several prominent peaks that dwarf the city skyline. Most of these peaks are accessible by well-maintained hiking trails. Fog, rain, wind, and freezing temperatures can turn even the least-technical climb into an ordeal, so always carry extra food and clothing, even for a day trip.

With its gondola towers and lighted ski runs visible from many parts of the Lower Mainland, **Grouse Mountain** (1,128 metres or 3,700 feet) is one of Vancouver's best-known natural landmarks. Purists can walk up the Grouse Grind Trail adjacent to the Skyride to the Grouse Nest restaurant and follow the ski run to the top; the less energetic can take the tramway up. Trail maps are available at the guest services booth at the Grouse Mountain Skyride ticket office.

Mount Seymour Provincial Park is a 30-minute drive from downtown. Hiking to the top of the three rounded summits, each slightly higher than the last, provides a surprisingly authentic wilderness experience if you go there midweek or in the winter on snowshoes. Your reward is an unparallelled view north into the heart of the Coast Range, south beyond the urban sprawl to the Gulf and San Juan Islands, east to Mount

Baker and the Cascades, and west toward Vancouver Island. The 8-kilometre (5-mile) return trip takes about four hours.

[KIDS] Black Mountain in **Cypress Provincial Park** can be climbed on foot or reached by chairlift. Nearby Cabin Lake is on the Baden-Powell Trail and is a good spot for a refreshing midsummer dip. The two-hour Black Mountain Loop Trail is perfect for introducing the family to the joys of hiking in the mountains. **Garibaldi Provincial Park** is accessible from several points along Highway 99 en route to Whistler. Diamond Head, the Black Tusk Meadows, Singing Pass, and Wedgemount Lake provide varying degrees of challenge and are suitable for day trips or overnight expeditions. Perhaps the most outstanding landmark is the volcanic plug of the 2,315-metre (7,595-foot) **Black Tusk**. The trail to its base starts at Taylor Campground. Because of crumbling rock and high exposure, climbing the tusk itself is for experienced hikers only. Contact **BC Parks** at 898-3678 for trail and weather reports.

Many local rock climbers learn their craft indoors at the **Edge Climbing Centre** (984-9080) in North Vancouver. This is the rock climber's version of an indoor jungle-gym, and the carved holds and textured surfaces present a stunningly realistic simulation of routes and situational problems found on the real crags. All of the routes are rated, with varying degrees of difficulty. Even if you get vertigo standing too close to a guardrail, it's a fun place to go and watch human spiders in action. You can take courses, rent shoes and harnesses, and play until 11pm, seven days a week. The **Cliffhanger** (874-2400) and **Rock House** (276-0012) are two other popular climbing gyms.

For a taste of the real thing, drive 60 kilometres (37.5 miles) north to Squamish. The **Stawamus Chief** is the second-largest freestanding granite outcropping in the world, next to the Rock of Gibraltar. There are more than 280 climbing routes on its various walls, faces, and slabs. The dramatic University Wall climb, ending on the Dance Platform, is rated the hardest rock climb in Canada. The vehicle pullout north of Shannon Falls provides an excellent vantage point from which to see climbers in action. Less dramatic (but equally challenging) climbs can be found in **Murrin Provincial Park** and on the **Smoke Bluffs**. Novice climbers will like the grippy granite and easy moves on Banana Peel, Diedre, Cat Crack, and Sugarloaf.

There are so many hiking and mountaineering organizations in the Lower Mainland that they have their own umbrella group, the **Federation of Mountain Clubs of British Columbia** (737-3053). Trail building, safety and education, wilderness preservation, and public awareness of mountain recreation issues are all part of their mandate. Courses run by the Federation's Canada West Mountain School offer the best introduction to the wilderness currently available.

Outdoor Sports

Climbing and Mountaineering

DIVING

The clean, cold, and clear waters between Vancouver Island and the Lower Mainland are home to some 450 fish species, 600 plant species, 4,000 invertebrates, and the ghosts of countless sunken vessels. The best time to dive is in the winter, since plankton growth in the summer months often obscures visibility. Betty Pratt-Johnson's *141 Dives in the Protected Waters of Washington State and British Columbia* is essential reading for divers. Wreck-divers should pick up a copy of Fred Rogers's *Shipwrecks of British Columbia*. Get air, tanks, and the latest news on what's hot from **Diver's World** (732-1344) at the corner of Fourth Avenue and Burrard Street.

Whytecliff Park in West Vancouver is a fine undersea park close to the city. It contains a variety of marine life in its protected cove and nearby waters. Copper Cove, Telegraph Cove, and Cates Park in Deep Cove are also local favourites. Be sure to check local regulations before harvesting edibles like crabs or sea cucumbers. With more than 100 dives mapped by local enthusiasts, **Powell River**, at the top of the Sechelt Peninsula on the Sunshine Coast, is officially the scuba diving capital of Canada. Charters, rentals, air, and guides are all available through **Beach Gardens Resort** (485-6267). Wreck-diving is the attraction here. Look for the remains of the *Shamrock* off Vivian Island. Rare red coral thrives in these waters, as do octopus and wolf eels. Many divers seek out the underwater mermaid, a sunken statue that resides near the BC Ferries dock at Saltery Bay.

FISHING (FRESHWATER AND SALTWATER)

BC's scenic coastline and unspoiled wilderness are a magnificent backdrop for fishing and make up for the rare occasion when anglers get skunked. Freshwater anglers can catch trout, char, and salmon. Saltwater anglers can try for five species of salmon (including the fabled chinook), rockfish, lingcod, and halibut.

Two government agencies administer sport fishing. The **Federal Department of Fisheries and Oceans** (666-6331) regulates saltwater fishing and the provincial **Ministry of Environment, Lands, and Parks** (582-5200) regulates freshwater fishing. Licences are required for both. You can purchase these at tackle shops throughout the Lower Mainland (also great sources of information about where the fish are biting). Shops and tourist information centres also have copies of the Provincial Sport Fishing Regulations. The section on catch-and-release streams and lakes is particularly important for the freshwater angler.

Fishing in the creeks and rivers off the Coquihalla Highway, north of Hope, is usually rewarding, especially after spring runoff. The feeder creeks and tributaries of the Fraser and

Thompson Rivers number in the thousands and yield coho salmon, rainbow trout, and the much-prized steelhead.

Horseshoe Bay/Hole in the Wall Howe Sound, the 40-kilometre-long (25-mile-long) inlet that starts at Horseshoe Bay, is perfect for saltwater fishing. Whether you're out to hook the fish of your dreams or just want a relaxing few hours on the saltchuck, **Sewell's Marina** (921-3474) offers a fleet of 60 rental boats as well as a regularly scheduled group fishing tour. Rock cod and salmon can be caught at the legendary Hole in the Wall, several kilometres north of the marina.

Rice Lake This lake is in the Seymour Demonstration Forest. To get there, take the Mount Seymour Parkway exit from Highway 1 and follow Lillooet Road past Capilano College to the road's end. The lake is wheelchair-accessible. The Seymour River provides excellent angling opportunities as well.

Salmon Lake Resort Set high in the rolling grasslands of the Nicola Plateau on the Douglas Lake Ranch (Canada's largest cattle ranch), Salmon Lake Resort offers superior fly-fishing and the thrill of stalking trophy-size Kamloops rainbow trout. The resort's number is (800) 663-4838; it is a 3 1/2-hour drive northeast of Vancouver via the Coquihalla Highway.

Spences Bridge Spanning the emerald-green waters of the Thompson River, Spences Bridge is the place to go for steelhead fishing. It's a 4-hour drive north of Vancouver on Highway 1.

GOLFING

The popular lotus-land image of going skiing in the morning and golfing in the afternoon is not as far-fetched as you might think. Although courses aren't exactly in prime condition in December or January, by the time April rolls around many of the Lower Mainland links are in midsummer shape. Golf has been the fastest-growing activity for some time now, and new courses are being built as quickly as developers can acquire land. North of the city, four brand-new courses take advantage of the spectacular mountain scenery. The **Furry Creek Golf and Country Club** just past Porteau Cove is carved from a mountainside and hugs the shoreline of Horseshoe Bay in several places. The breathtaking Robert Trent-Jones-designed **Chateau Whistler Golf and Country Club** complements the decade-old Arnold Palmer-designed **Whistler Golf and Country Club**. Two new challengers are sure to become just as popular; the **Nicklaus North Golf Course** at Green Lake and the **Big Sky Golf and Country Club** in Pemberton. All of the Whistler tracks are true tests of a golfer's talent, but the scenery makes those bogeys more bearable. For a more small-town ambience, the **Squamish Golf and Country Club** boasts a mature layout with several holes straddling the Mamquam River. Watch for bald eagles soaring overhead.

The City of Vancouver operates several municipal golf courses, and some privately owned courses are open to the public as well. Here's a sampling of the best:

Fraserview Golf Course On some days it seems that every golfer in Canada has descended onto the fairways of this south Vancouver course, which overlooks the Fraser River. Featuring wide-open fairways for most of its 6,346-yard length, Fraserview is a pleasant course—and the busiest in the province. ■ *7800 Vivian Ave at 54th St; 280-8633; map:F4.*

Mayfair Lakes Golf Course "Water, water, everywhere" might be the unofficial motto of this very attractive course in the suburb of Richmond. Not as tree-lined as some of the more established tracks, but definitely a must-play in terms of challenge and design. Par 72, 6,641 yards. Watch for salmon jumping in some of the water hazards. ■ *5460 No. 7 Rd, Richmond; 276-0505; map:F6.*

Peace Portal Golf Course Glance to the right on Highway 99 as you enter Canada and you'll see one of the Lower Mainland's oldest courses, Peace Portal Golf Course, named after the international boundary monument that straddles the border. Established in 1928, this mature course is open year-round and is a local favourite. ■ *16900-4th Ave, Surrey; 538-4818.*

Queen Elizabeth Pitch and Putt Serious golfers might scoff at the inclusion of a lowly pitch-and-putt, but this course offers some of the most breathtaking views of the city from its vantage point atop Little Mountain. Nongolfers can stroll the adjacent grounds of Queen Elizabeth Park or visit the Bloedel Conservatory. ■ *Cambie St at 33rd Ave; 874-8336; map:D3.*

University Golf Club A gorgeous course, well-maintained and a treat to play in almost any condition. You don't need any connection with the university to play here, and many people attend classes under the tutelage of seven certified CPGA pros. ■ *5185 University Blvd; 224-1818; map:B3.*

HIKING

A tell-tale sign of the popularity of hiking in Vancouver is that David and Mary Macaree's *103 Hikes in Southwestern British Columbia* is now into its fourth edition. A companion volume, *109 Walks in the Lower Mainland*, is almost as popular. The Macarees know their terrain well, and distances and estimated hiking times are not based on the dawdler. Several of the most popular hikes are listed in the Climbing and Mountaineering section; what follows is a more diverse selection.

Garibaldi Provincial Park This park is the jewel of West Coast mountain parks, with more than 60 kilometres (37.5 miles) of developed hiking trails. The trails near Singing Pass can be reached by taking the Whistler Gondola Express and following a well-defined trail over the Musical Bumps. This is particularly beautiful in August, when the meadows are filled with blooming lupines, Indian paintbrush, and saxifrage. Cheakamus Lake, Diamond Head, and Black Tusk meadows are all worthwhile day trips. If you're going to Black Tusk, avoid the crowds and mind-numbing boredom of the infamous Barrier Switchbacks by using the alternative Helm Creek Trail (same access as the Cheakamus Lake turnoff). ▪ *898-3678.*

Golden Ears Provincial Park Although many hikers like the rugged trails of Garibaldi Park and the North Shore, Golden Ears (east of the city) provides some spectacular views of seldom-visited glaciers and mountains. The best part about climbing Golden Ears is that, although it looks incredibly steep from its precipitous west face, the route up the east side, calling for some use of hands on the way, is little more than an exerting hike. Fit hikers can tackle the 1,706-metre (5,597-foot) North Ear, but an early start is necessary as the trailhead is almost at sea level. Once on top you can marvel at Pitt and Alouette Lakes, two large bodies of water nearby. The latter is suitable for swimming after you descend. This is not a short day trip and should be attempted only after the upper meadows are free of snow. ▪ *463-3513.*

Howe Sound Crest Trail Strong day hikers might want to tackle the Howe Sound Crest Trail, a 30-kilometre (18.8-mile) (one way) trek across several summits, including Black Mountain, Mount Harvey, Mount Brunswick, and Deeks Peak, and ending in Porteau Cove. Portions of this trail can be reached at various points along Highway 99 north of Horseshoe Bay, but to do the whole trip you need to park one car at Cypress Bowl and another at Deeks Creek. There are stiff hills and slippery descents en route, and weather can change very quickly. Still, this trail has some awesome views of Howe Sound and the Strait of Georgia. ▪ *924-2200.*

Lighthouse Park On the bluffs above West Vancouver's Point Atkinson, **Lighthouse Park** features one of the few remaining stands of old-growth Douglas fir trees. Next to the California redwood, Douglas fir is the tallest tree species found in North America. This park is fun to walk in regardless of the weather. Crowds are most easily avoided during the misty, moody winter months. The smooth igneous rock surrounding the lighthouse provides an ideal spot to rest and enjoy a picnic. Eagles' nests, rust-red arbutus trees, and the red and white lighthouse casting its beam across the water complete this very beautiful West Coast postcard. ▪ *925-7200.*

Manning Provincial Park [KIDS] A three-hour drive east on the Trans-Canada Highway and Highway 3 (take the Hope-Princeton route at the Hope interchange), Manning Park is especially spectacular when in bloom. In June, stop at the

Rhododendron Flats pullout near the highway; in August, see the brilliant carpet of alpine wildflowers at higher elevations. Trained park naturalists are on duty during periods of peak bloom, and the trail to the alpine meadows is ideal for children as well. If they're restless, have them smell the fragrant sitka valerian, a white wildflower known for its mild calming effect. ■ *(250) 840-8836.*

Pitt River Dykes The Pitt is a major tributary of the Fraser and a walk along its dykes can be enjoyed at any time of the year. You can drive directly to Pitt Lake and take in the breathtaking view of the Coast Range to the north, then work your way south along the river's edge, past Chatham Reach and on toward the Pitt's confluence with the Fraser. If you go on different days and wonder where all of the water has gone, your eyes will not have deceived you. The Pitt is subject to changing river levels due to tidal activity. There's great bird-watching here, too. ■ *Pitt Meadows Municipal Hall, 465-5454.*

HORSEBACK RIDING

Cowboys roam the ranges on the Ponderosa-size ranches of the Cariboo and Chilcotin, but city slickers can don hats and boots for horseback riding in the Fraser Valley.

Campbell Valley Regional Park This nature park features equestrian trails, cross-country jumps, picnicking, and nature study areas. Hop off your horse and pick a handful of blackberries at summer's end. ■ *From Hwy 1 take the Langley 200 St exit southbound. Travel 14.5 km (9 miles) and turn east on 16th Ave for the North Valley entrance; 530-4983.*

Golden Ears Provincial Park A great place for both urban cowboys and the saddle-savvy to trail-ride. Commercial stables in Maple Ridge organize summer day rides to Alouette Lake. Hitch your horses, swim in the lake, then head 'em home. Golden Ears Riding Stable is 48 kilometres (30 miles) east of Vancouver on Highway 7. ■ *13175-232 Ave, Maple Ridge; 463-8761.*

Manning Provincial Park This park, which is less than three hours east of Vancouver in the Cascade Mountains, is a spectacular place to ride horseback. Several hundred kilometres of horse trails crisscross the park. Bring your own horse or rent one through the Manning Park Corral. ■ *Manning Park Resort; (250) 840-8844.*

HOT-AIR BALLOONING

Fraser Valley Langley Airport serves as the base for **Fantasy Balloon Charters**. They specialize in dawn or dusk champagne flights, taking wing once the air is cooler and less susceptible to turbulent currents. It's the most relaxing way to get an eagle's-eye view of Mount Baker, Golden Ears, and the

patchwork quilt of rich farmland bordering the Fraser River.
■ *Langley Airport, Unit 209, 5333-216 St, Langley; 530-1974.*

ICE-SKATING

Unlike Canadian cities with below-zero temperatures, Vancouver has a mild winter climate less conducive to traditional winter recreation like tobogganing and ice-skating. Nevertheless, several recreation facilities are open to skaters, and some outdoor ponds are suitable for a quick pirouette or double-axel when an infrequent cold snap hits.

Karen Magnussen Recreation Centre [KIDS] Named after an ex-Olympic medallist who grew up in the neighbourhood, this North Vancouver facility is the premier skating rink on the North Shore. ■ *2300 Kirkstone Rd, North Vancouver; 987-7529; map:G1.*

Kerrisdale Cyclone Taylor Arena [KIDS] This west side arena holds special parties to commemorate events like St. Patrick's Day. Open fall and winter; call ahead for a public skating schedule. ■ *5670 East Blvd; 257-8121; map:C4.*

Kitsilano Community Centre Year-round public skating is available at this popular west side recreation centre. The arena is closed every few years in April and May for maintenance. ■ *2690 Larch St; 257-6983; map:B3.*

Lost Lagoon, Stanley Park, and Other City Parks [KIDS] [FREE] When arctic air comes pouring out of the north, many of the ponds in Vancouver parks freeze over. The Parks Board cordons off part of Lost Lagoon in Stanley Park for free public skating until rising temperatures and precipitation make ice levels unsafe (map:C1). Other ponds are located in Queen Elizabeth Park, along the south shore of False Creek, and on Como Lake in Coquitlam. ■ *257-8400.*

Robson Square Join power-lunching businesspeople whirling around the outdoor rink on the lower level of Robson Square from November until early March. Rentals are not available, so bring your own skates. ■ *Map:S4.*

▼
**Outdoor
Sports**

*In-Line
Skating*

▲

IN-LINE SKATING

A decade after the introduction of in-line skates, it's apparent that they are here to stay and will not be the hulahoop of the 1990s. Vancouver's rather hilly geography means that you should have your braking techniques mastered, especially if you're going to be out chasing traffic on city streets.

Kerrisdale Cyclone Taylor Arena Like many other Vancouver ice-skating arenas, when the ice comes out in the spring, Kerrisdale becomes a popular in-line skating centre, and it even has an energetic street hockey league for boys and girls. ■ *5670 East Blvd; 257-8121; map:C4.*

Stanley Park Seawall Bladers can travel on parts of the 10.5-kilometre (6.5-mile) seawall, taking in the spectacular viewpoints. This is a busy pedestrian and cycling area, so etiquette prevails. Mostly flat. ▪ *Map:P1-Q1.*

University of British Columbia Skaters can share an undulating cycle path that loops along 16th Avenue through Pacific Spirit Park and back along Chancellor Boulevard into University Village. The paved shoulder of Marine Drive from 16th Avenue to 49th Avenue is also prime skating territory. The closest rental store is **Recreation Rentals** at 2560 Arbutus Street; 733-7368. ▪ *Map:A2-A3.*

KITE FLYING

When the winds blow whitecaps on the waters of English Bay, it's time to unravel the kite strings and join other fliers at one of the seaside parks.

Vanier Park Vanier Park on Kits Point is a frequent-flyer spot, where many enthusiasts fly high-performance combat kites that engage in exciting dogfights. ▪ *Map:P5.*

Garry Point Park The windswept meadows at the mouth of the Fraser River in Steveston are flat and very exposed to south and westerly winds. This park isn't visited often by Vancouverites, but it's well worth the trip. If the wind dies, you can always enjoy a beach bonfire. ▪ *Drive south across the Oak Street Bridge (Hwy 99) to the Steveston Hwy turnoff, then west (right) along Steveston Hwy to the end and turn south (left) to the park; Map:B7.*

▼

Outdoor Sports

In-Line Skating

▲

MOUNTAIN BIKING

Although many recreation-oriented towns claim to be mountain-biking meccas, there is a good case for making Vancouver the fat-tire capital of North America. Every possible accessory and kind of bike is available in area specialty stores, and some of the finest frames and components are built right in Vancouver. Designers test their prototypes on some of the most technically difficult trails to be found anywhere.

Pacific Spirit Regional Park This large tract of land was one of the earliest places to be discovered by mountain bikers, and it remains popular despite trail closures in some areas. Wardens patrol the park and have the authority to fine those who stray. Trails are especially muddy (and uncrowded) after a few days of rain. ▪ *Map:B3.*

The Secret Trails Society In most mountain communities in North America, hikers and mountain bikers have shared, at best, an uneasy coexistence. Ross Kirkwood is a local enthusiast who took matters (and a chainsaw) into his own hands by fashioning the most challenging riding (and environmental-impact-resistant) trails in North America in places where hikers seldom wander. These trails are so "secret" that a comprehensive trail guide and map to the area does not exist. General areas in which you can pick up the trails are below Cypress Bowl, behind Grouse Mountain, and in the Seymour Demonstration Forest. Local **bike shops** like Mountain & Beach at 163 W Broadway (876-2683) and the Deep Cove Bike Shop (929-1918) can provide details. Bicycle Sports Pacific (988-1800) on Mountain Highway at Lynn Valley Road is the closest shop to the largest network of easily accessible trails. This terrain is not suitable for novice riders and should never be cycled alone. Frequent riders are asked to help maintain the trails and obey proper etiquette when encountering other users.

Whistler Area Once the snow melts and Whistlerites have retired their skis and snowboards for the season, the toys of summer come out. Whistler offers as much variety for mountain bikers as it does for skiers—from wide-open cross-country ski trails, to old logging roads leading to magnificent stands of old-growth red cedar, to some of the gnarliest and most technically difficult riding imaginable. Not all of the trails are easy to find, so pick up the *Sea-to-Sky Mountain Bike Guide* or the *Whistler Off Road Cycling Guide* by Grant Lamont and Charlie Doyle. The Cheakamus Challenge, the largest mountain bike event in Canada, is held on the last weekend in September each year. The 63-kilometre (32-mile) course features gear-grinding ascents, white-knuckle descents, and a great post-race party. Novices will enjoy the Lost Lake Loop (stop for a refreshing dip either at the public beach on the south side of the lake or at a clothing-optional dock on the east side). For greater challenge and a bit more solitude, Brandywine Falls and Cheakamus Lake are ideal trips, often scheduled by one of the **local guiding companies** like Backroads Bicycle Tours (932-3111), Whistler Outdoor Experience Company (932-3389), and Mountain Trail Leisure (938-3018). Hard-core riders will head straight for legendary trails like the Emerald Forest, A River Runs Through It, Northwest Passage, and the Rebob Trail.

NATURE OBSERVATION

Although the intrusion of civilization has had a devastating effect on the habitat of indigenous flora and fauna, many areas still exist where one can observe the rhythms and life cycles of the natural world. Birds, whales, fish, and mammals are constantly foraging for food in the same places where Native people hunted them centuries ago. Other locations, like the Fraser River Delta, are favourite stopping points for migrating flocks of snow geese, brants, and terns. Many clubs and associations provide detailed information on nature observation in the province. Some of the local natural history societies sponsor field trips and can give you information about tour operators who specialize in wildlife viewing. The umbrella organization for the province is the **Federation of BC Naturalists** (737-3057), which can provide details of area clubs.

Bird-Watching [KIDS] Naturalists come from all over the world to the **George C. Reifel Migratory Bird Sanctuary** on Westham Island at the mouth of the Fraser River, 9.6 kilometres (6 miles) west of Ladner. More than 250 species of birds can be sighted; the peak viewing season is between October and April. This wetlands environment is especially attractive to shorebirds like herons, geese, and ducks. Occasionally, migratory birds from Asian countries lose their way and end up here, drawing crowds of ornithologists seeking to cross another exotic bird off their "life lists." Kids love to feed seeds to the the quacking hordes of ducks looking for a free handout. Take a picnic, sneak into a bird blind, or climb up a viewing tower, particularly in November during the **Snow Goose Festival** (946-6980).

Eighty kilometres (50 miles) north of Vancouver on Highway 99, the small community of **Brackendale** calls itself the Bald Eagle Capital of Canada. During January hundreds of these majestic birds flock to the banks of the Squamish River to feed on the spawned-out carcasses of a late-fall salmon run. The best place for viewing is an area called Eagle Run, behind the Sunwolf Outdoor Centre. During the early winter, this area has the highest eagle count in North America next to the Chilkat River in Alaska. For special photography courses, tours, and information on the annual eagle count each January, call the Brackendale Art Gallery and Cafe at 898-3333. During the winter, guided river-rafting trips down the Squamish are operated through Rivers and Oceans Expeditions at (800) 360-RAFT.

Farm Animals and Zoos [KIDS] The **Zoological Centre** in Aldergrove is open year-round. Its well-treed, parklike 48 hectares (120 acres) are home to 126 species of animals, including tigers, wolves, zebras, rhinoceroses, bears, elephants, parrots, flamingoes, ostriches, bison, and many others—all roaming freely. You can walk, cycle, or drive through the farm, a favourite with kids. ■ *48 kilometres (29.8 miles) east of Vancouver off the Trans-Canada Highway at the 264th St exit; 856-6825.*

[KIDS] Teeming with domestic animals, North Vancouver's municipal park farm, **Maplewood Farm**, is a great hit with kids. Its "Rabbitat" and "Goathill" are particularly popular petting areas. Visitors to the 2-hectare (4.9-acre) municipal park farm can also take part in daily hand-milking demonstrations. Watch for special family events like the Sheep Fair in May, the Farm Fair in September, and Christmas Caroling in December. ■ *From Vancouver via the Second Narrows Bridge exit 23-B (Deep Cove/Mt Seymour exit), turn left at the second traffic light to 405 Seymour River Pl, North Vancouver; 929-5610; map:G1.*

[KIDS] [FREE] **Richmond Nature Park** offers everything you always wanted to know about bogs. Interpretative trails and Nature House, complete with salamanders and snakes, make this a hidden gem in the suburban sprawl. ■ *11851 West-minster Hwy, Richmond; 273-7015; map:D6.*

Salmon Spawning [KIDS] [FREE] **Capilano Salmon Hatch-ery**, a federal government fish hatchery set on the Capilano River among majestic red cedars and lush huckleberry bushes, is a family favourite. Meander through the self-guiding facility where information panels describe the life cycles of Pacific salmon. Then watch juvenile fish in the ponds and returning salmon jumping up a series of chutes (from July to December). This park also boasts some of the tallest trees still standing on the Lower Mainland—the Giant Fir is more than 500 years old and 61 metres (200 feet) tall. Open daily. ■ *Drive up Capilano Rd in North Vancouver, take the first left past the Suspension Bridge onto Capilano Park Rd. Proceed about 1.5 km (.9 mile) to the hatchery; 666-1790.*

[KIDS] Every four years (1994, 1998, 2002), it's worth tak-ing the six-hour drive to the **Adams River** for the fall sockeye run. This is one of the great life-cycle stories in nature, where salmon that have spent their entire lives on the Pacific Ocean return up the Fraser and Thompson Rivers to spawn and die. ■ *Head west from Salmon Arm on Hwy 1 to Squilix, then north-east on the paved highway for 3.8 km (2.4 miles) to the junction just after the Adams River Bridge. Contact BC Parks, Thompson River district; (250) 828-4494.*

Whale Watching For grey whales, the best lookout locations are on the west coast of Vancouver Island, a five-hour drive from Vancouver (including ferry). Migrating grey whales can be seen beginning in late November but are more often seen in March and April as they travel between their Arctic breeding grounds and Mexican calving lagoons. Many whale-watching boat charters operate out of the west coast communities of Tofino, Bamfield, and Ucluelet. There are good land viewpoints in the Long Beach area, all of which have telescopes and are accessible by car. The **Wickaninnish Centre** at Wickaninnish Beach is a prime viewing spot.

Although it's BC's second-largest city, Victoria is one of the best places in the province for spotting killer whales. In fact, you may even see a pod from the ferry on the way over to the island. **SeaCoast Expeditions** in Victoria, (250) 383-2254, offers guaranteed sightings of killer whales on its three-hour trips, available by special arrangement June 1 through September 15. Listen to orcas chatting on the hydrophone. SeaCoast also makes two-hour excursions to Race Rocks Ecological Reserve and Lighthouse to view California and Steller's sea lions, har-bour seals, porpoises, cormorant colonies, and bald eagle nests.

RIVER RAFTING

For a sheer adrenaline rush, it's hard to beat a day's rafting on one of the province's many stretches of white water, interspersed with a lazy drift through calm patches. Watch for deer nibbling on shoots and leaves near the water's edge, bald eagles whirling on air currents overhead, or even grizzled prospectors panning for gold. River rafting is regulated provincially (for safety reasons) under the Commercial River Rafting Safety Act.

Chilliwack River   Located 96 kilometres (60 miles) from Vancouver, this river is very popular just after spring runoff (roughly early May to mid-July) for one-day rafting trips. Chilliwack River is also popular with whitewater kayakers. ▪ *Hyak Wilderness Adventures; 734-8622.*

Fraser River   Most one-day Fraser River excursions are offered from May to the end of August. Customers travel in motorized rafts downriver from Boston Bar to Yale. Raft Scuzzy Rock, China Bar, and Hell's Gate with experienced operators. ▪ *Kumsheen Raft Adventures; (800) 663-6667.*

Nahatlatch River   The Nahatlatch River, a four-hour drive north of Vancouver, seethes with boiling chutes of white water from May to mid-August. Join the Nahatlatch experts' **REO Rafting Adventures** for a wild ride through ominous-sounding rapids like the Meat Grinder, Lose Your Lunch, and the Big Chill. Free overnight camping is available at REO's private campsite. ▪ *684-4438.*

Thompson River   The emerald-green waters of the Thompson River provide a pleasant mix of casual floating and stomach-churning white water. Rafters follow the Thompson from Spences Bridge to the take-out point at Lytton, where the clear Thompson joins the murky, silt-laden Fraser. The trip includes thrilling rapids like the Devil's Kitchen and the Jaws of Death. ▪ *Hyak Wilderness Adventures; 734-8622.*

Whistler Area Rivers   The stunning Coast Range Mountains provide the scenic backdrop for rafting on several rivers in the Whistler area. Trips range from white-knuckle excitement on the Green and Elaho Rivers to placid float-trips down the Squamish and Lillooet. ▪ *Whistler River Adventures, 932-3532, and Wedge Rafting, 932-7171, operate trips daily from late spring to the end of September.*

RUNNING AND WALKING

Especially at peak periods like lunch hour and after work, there are so many runners on the municipal pathways that visitors to Vancouver might be forgiven for asking, "Is there some kind of race happening today?" Once you include the in-line skaters, mountain bikers, triathletes, and race-walkers it seems as though the entire city is clad in Lycra tights and carrying water-bottles. Exposure to fitness starts early, with jogging moms pushing their infants in specially constructed strollers, and continues into the golden years, with local Masters racers routinely running faster than men and women half their age. More than 30,000 runners participate annually in the Sun Run, a 10-kilometre (6.2-mile) race for elite athletes and joggers alike, which is held each April. A complete list of running events may be found in the running calendar of *Coast*, the outdoor recreation magazine.

Ambleside Park, West Vancouver As the name implies, this is a great place for a beachside amble or jog. Watch cruise ships, freighters, barges, and even the odd battleship passing underneath the Lion's Gate Bridge into Burrard Inlet. Start at the east end of the park, where the Capilano River enters the ocean, and follow the seawall west. Great views across the First Narrows to Stanley Park. ▪ *Map:C1*.

Central Park The wooded trails of Central Park begin at the boundary between Vancouver and Burnaby, just off Kingsway. Track athletes regularly use Swangard Stadium for interval workouts. For runners who wish for more diversity, a fitness circuit featuring a variety of exercise options is available nearby. ▪ *Map:F4*.

Kits Beach/Vanier Park A 5-kilometre (3.1-mile) network of flat asphalt and dirt paths skirts Vanier Park on the Kitsilano side of the Burrard Street Bridge. The paths follow the water around Kits Point and past the Vancouver Museum, the Pacific Space Centre, the Maritime Museum, and Kits Beach. In the summer, Kits Beach is Vancouver's home of the bronzed and muscle-bound, and there's always a game of beach volleyball or street basketball happening. ▪ *Map:P5–N6*.

Lost Lagoon, Stanley Park [KIDS] The 1.6-kilometre (1-mile) trail that encircles Lost Lagoon is an easy stroll and a great spot for watching nesting Canada geese in the springtime. At intervals, the fountain in the centre of the lagoon emits a fine spray. ▪ *Map:C1*.

Pacific Spirit Regional Park Surrounding the University of British Columbia, this park contains 50 kilometres (31.1 miles) of walking and jogging trails through deciduous and coniferous forests, including Camosun Bog. Trails vary in length; you can enjoy a short stroll or you can take a more vigorous walk all the way from the Fraser River Estuary to Spanish Banks. The Visitor Centre is located on the north side of 16th Avenue, just west of Cleveland Trail. ▪ *Map:B3*.

Stanley Park Seawall The longest seawall in Canada (10.5 kilometres or 6.5 miles) is a great place to jog or walk. Plaques set in the wall at half-kilometre intervals detail the wall's history. Runners and walkers can also detour into the park. The seawall is a brisk, nonstop, two-hour walk. ▪ *Map:C1-D1*.

SAILING

Perhaps no sport quite defines the West Coast lifestyle like sailing. From two-person high-speed catamarans to double-masted schooners, virtually every kind of sailboat can be found in the waters around Vancouver. Some of the best cruising is in the Strait of Georgia, where the land mass of Vancouver Island shelters many tiny bays and inlets that make perfect anchorages. Sailors wishing to charter boats for self-sufficient expeditions must pass tests administered by the Canadian Yachting Association. **Sea Wing Sailing School and Yacht Charters** (669-0840) on Granville Island offers combination learn-to-sail cruises and classroom lectures to develop navigation and other nautical skills.

English Bay During the summer **Cooper Boating Centre** on Granville Island (687-4110) will take you on three-hour cruises in English Bay on 6- to 12-metre (19.7- to 39.4-foot) yachts. Cruising in English Bay can also consist of a leisurely sail into spectacular Howe Sound, where salmon, killer whales, and dolphins are often seen.

Gulf Islands Several sailing schools offer five-day cruise-and-learn trips around the Gulf Islands. Alternatively, you can rent a yacht, with or without a skipper, and cruise the islands to discover the solitude of arbutus-lined coves, the charm of neighbourhood pubs and restaurants, and the thrill of watching marine life like harbour seals, whales, porpoises, and sea otters.

Princess Louisa Inlet Princess Louisa Inlet is a saltwater bay carved deep into the Coast Mountains wilderness. Located on the Sunshine Coast north of Sechelt, its calm waters and cascading waterfalls make it an ideal sailing destination. Farther north, the Desolation Sound Marine Park is also a favourite summertime objective.

SKIING: CROSS-COUNTRY

The moist, mild climate of the south coast means that skiers take their chances on conditions when skiing locally. In Vancouver, cross-country skiing can either be as casual as a trip around a golf course or city park during one of the city's infrequent snowfalls or as extreme as a multi-day expedition into the heart of the Coast Range. Cross-country skiers generally divide along two lines: aerobic-sports enthusiasts, who prefer striding or skating along specially manicured machine-grooved tracks, and backcountry skiers, who blaze their own trails into the wilderness. The former can take classes in everything from skate skiing, waxing, and racing strategy, while the latter will be interested in telemarking, backcountry navigation, avalanche awareness, and winter camping. Both types of skiers should be aware that local weather conditions can change rapidly, and extra food and clothing should always be brought in a day pack.

Cypress Bowl [KIDS] The groomed trails closest to Vancouver are at Cypress Bowl on the North Shore. You'll find 16 kilometres (10 miles) of groomed, track-set trails radiating from historic Hollyburn Lodge. Five kilometres (3.1 miles) of trail are lit for night skiing. A backcountry trail to the top of Hollyburn Mountain is also navigable, but it is quite steep in places and not suitable for children or inexperienced skiers. Nevertheless, the view over the city and into the Coast Range is unforgettable. Because Cypress is the closest place where Vancouver parents can take their kids for an authentic "winter experience," it's not really a place to get away from it all. Rentals and lessons are available. **Cypress Mountain Sports** (878-9229) in West Vancouver's Park Royal Mall is the closest full-service cross-country shop to the trails. ■ *926-6007 for weather and trail information.*

Garibaldi Provincial Park The alpine meadows of Singing Pass, Black Tusk, and Diamond Head, which yield an awesome profusion of wildflowers in the summer, are blanketed with several metres of snow each winter. These three areas are prime backcountry skiing territory, with small huts close by for protection from the elements. Backcountry skiers travelling in any areas within Garibaldi Park should be entirely self-sufficient, and everyone should be trained in avalanche safety. Winter backcountry ski courses are taught through the Federation of Mountain Clubs of British Columbia's Canada West Mountain School (737-3053) and through the Alpine Guides Bureau at Whistler (938-3338). If you're short on experience but still want a winter wilderness adventure, certified alpine guides can also be hired there. ■ *898-3678.*

Manning Park Resort [KIDS] Three hours east of Vancouver, Manning Park Resort offers skiers everything they could ask for: cross-country trails especially designed for skating and classic techniques, hundreds of square kilometres of rugged Coast Range ski touring, and even a challenging little downhill area for perfecting telemark turns. Sigge's Sport Villa (731-8818) in Kitsilano organizes bus trips from Vancouver that can include transportation, rentals, and lessons. Manning is a good place to take kids, and the ticket prices won't break the bank, either. Overnight accommodation is available in wonderful log cabins or at the main lodge. ■ *(250) 840-8822.*

Mount Seymour Provincial Park Mount Seymour is another local favourite, especially for those with backcountry skiing aspirations. The skiing between First (Pump) Peak and Second Peak can be excellent, especially after a big snowfall. Outside the downhill ski-area boundary, skiers must stay close to the wanded trail, especially in foggy weather. It's not uncommon for skiers or snowshoers to become lost in this bluffy, confusing terrain. ■ *879-3999 for weather and conditions.*

Whistler/Lost Lake Trails Although Whistler is known primarily as a downhill ski resort, the nordic facility at Lost Lake is worth checking out. There are 22 kilometres (13.7 miles) of machine-groomed cross-country trails set around Lost Lake and the Chateau Whistler golf course, with 5 kilometres (3 miles) lit for night skiing. These trails are easily accessible from the Village; turn left on Blackcomb Way after entering Village Gate Boulevard and follow the signs for parking at the trailhead. Two warming huts and water stations are provided. Rentals are available at the Village Sports Stop (932-5495) and Mile High Sports (938-7736). ■ *See Whistler in Skiing: Downhill and Snowboarding.*

SKIING: DOWNHILL AND SNOWBOARDING

With the possible exception of Salt Lake City, no city in North America boasts such excellent skiing facilities within a two-hour drive from downtown as does Vancouver. The closest areas are on the North Shore. Cypress Bowl, Grouse Mountain, and Mount Seymour have respectable vertical drops and are ideal places to learn the sport. But ninety minutes north lies the resort municipality of Whistler, North America's largest ski destination, which combines two great skiing mountains: Whistler Mountain and Blackcomb. Both are fantastic places to snowboard as well, and both boast fabulous trail networks, starting deep on adjacent sides of the Fitzsimmons Creek valley and rising over a vertical mile in elevation into an alpine wonderland of open bowls, glaciers, and astonishing views. Anchoring both lift complexes is a European-style pedestrian village with an exciting array of restaurants, nightclubs, hotels, and shops. There is simply no other mountain town in Canada like Whistler, and the only caveat for visitors is that it can get crowded during peak times and that, as usual, the best does not come cheap. The first-time skier to Whistler and Blackcomb will find its size so overwhelming that spending one day skiing here will hardly be enough. Each of the two mountains has a distinctive character (despite the fact that both are now owned by one company). Which mountain you and your friends enjoy the most will be the topic of endless après-ski debate.

Blackcomb Mountain This is simply the most modern, best-planned first-class ski resort in North America. Intrawest Development Company, which operates it, has spared no expense in building high-speed lifts, cutting well-designed fall-line runs, pampering skiers with food far above the norm at most ski resorts, and blanketing the trails with artificial snow when Mother Nature does not cooperate. Blackcomb is shaped like an inverted triangle, with trails spreading out in every direction as you gain altitude. Four runs are "can't miss" on any skier's agenda: south-facing Xhiggy's Meadow, on the Seventh Heaven

Express; the fabulous Blackcomb Glacier run, which is one of the longest above-treeline slopes outside Europe; the aptly named Zig-Zag, a winding cruise run that seems to go on forever; and the vertiginous chutes of Rendezvous Bowl, including the heart-stopping Couloir Extreme. Even lunch at the mountaintop Rendezvous or the spectacular new Glacier Creek restaurant is an experience to be savoured. ▪ *For conditions call 687-7507 from Vancouver; in Whistler, 932-4211. For guest services, ski school programs, and general information, call Blackcomb Mountain at 938-7747.*

Cypress Bowl For the advanced skier, Cypress Bowl boasts some excellent mogul skiing, especially the Top Gun run underneath the Sky Chair. Cypress is the largest downhill facility on the North Shore and can be a fantastic place to ski after a big snowstorm. Cars driving the Cypress Bowl road should be equipped with tire chains or good winter tread tires. ▪ *For conditions and weather information, call 926-6007. For ski school programs, call 926-5612.*

Grouse Mountain Closer to Vancouver, the ski runs and lit trails on Grouse are visible from most parts of the Lower Mainland. You can take the bus from downtown right to the base of the mountain, where you're shuttled to the top on the Skyride, an aerial tram that gives a spectacular view of the city and across the Strait of Georgia to Vancouver Island. Although Grouse's slopes are a fraction of the length of those found at Whistler, it's still a great place to go for a quick ski fix. ▪ *Snow report phone number, 986-6262; program information, 980-9311.*

Hemlock Valley Tucked in a side-valley tributary of the Fraser River, Hemlock is one of the least-conspicuous ski areas in the province. Its quaint day lodge and older, slower lifts make it a throwback to the days when even downhill skiing was an adventure sport. But that's a good thing, since powder skiing here often lasts longer than it does at more crowded destination resorts. Some slopeside accommodation is available through privately rented cabins. ▪ *797-4444 for reservations and general information. The Hemlock Valley snow phone is 918-0002. For general information, call also (800) 665-7080.*

Mount Seymour [KIDS] This ski area lies within the provincial park of the same name and is where many Vancouverites are exposed to skiing or snowboarding for the first time. The learn-to-ski programs are inexpensive and are often operated in conjunction with the local schools. Even if you don't ski, there's a great tobogganing area at the south end of the parking lot. Seymour's somewhat irregular terrain also makes it popular with snowboarders. All-season tires or chains are recommended for this road as well. ▪ *879-3999 for weather and conditions, 986-2261 for special events and instruction.*

Whistler Mountain The beauty of skiing Whistler is that its reputation has not been diminished by having such a high-tech, glitzy neighbour to the north. Whistler has an ambience that cannot quite be described; perhaps it can only be experienced by blasting through a snow-choked glade in waist-deep powder without a soul in sight. It's the kind of place you can ski for days on end and not cross the same trail twice, and it only gets better the more you traverse its trails in search of its special charms. The credo of customer-first service starts with the president and goes right down to the parking lot attendant, making Whistler a more intimate, down-home place to ski than is Blackcomb. And we hope that doesn't change: as of this writing, the owner of Blackcomb, Intrawest Corporation, and the two families that have co-owned Whistler for 17 years, the Youngs and the Barkers, announced their intention to combine forces (along with the owners of a resort in Colorado). A $35 million investment is planned for enhancements to Whistler's already spectacular offerings. At present, the pick of Whistler's litter would include Franz's Run, the original high-speed cruiser that starts near the treeline and drops right to the valley floor at the base of Whistler Creek. Harmony Bowl, Symphony Bowl, and the precipitous Glacier Bowl are above-treeline expanses that have cemented the Whistler legend for hard-core thrills, yet even low-skill intermediates can enjoy the bowl skiing on Highway 86 and Burnt Stew Basin. With its banked runs and rocky bluffs, it's also an ideal mountain for **snowboarding**. Snow-phone hotline numbers for Whistler Mountain are 687-6761 in Vancouver, 932-4191 in Whistler. For general information on special events and programs, call 932-3434 or 664-5614 in Vancouver. Winter recreation at Whistler, however, is not just for skiers. There's heli-flightseeing, ice-skating, mountaintop sightseeing, snowshoeing, snowmobiling, and sleigh rides. ■ *All reservations are handled through the Whistler Resort Association. From Vancouver, 664-5625; from Whistler, 932-4222.*

▼

**Outdoor
Sports**

*Skiing:
Downhill
and Snow-
boarding*

▲

SNOWSHOEING

Snowshoeing is a tried-and-true way of getting off piste into the backwoods snowy terrain that is often too uneven for cross-country skiers.

Manning Provincial Park Three hours east of Vancouver, Manning has extensive snowshoeing terrain in its vast backcountry. As with any winter backcountry activity, snowshoeing entails being wary of avalanches and changing weather conditions as well as having mountain navigation skills. ■ *(205) 840-8822 for information.*

Mount Seymour Provincial Park Over the Second Narrows Bridge, 16 kilometres (10 miles) north of Vancouver, Mount Seymour offers snowshoe rentals and instruction. Snowshoers

can skirt some of the winter cross-country trails, including
Goldie Lake Loop, Flower Lake Loop, and Hidden Lake Loop.
Guided snowshoeing tours and rentals are operated through
the Mount Seymour ski school (986-2261). ▪ *879-3999 for
snow conditions.*

SWIMMING

[KIDS] Vancouver's 11 sandy beaches are fine for swimming,
even in slightly brisk temperatures. Lifeguards patrol June,
July, and August. Favourite swimming beaches include English Bay (site of the annual New Year's Day Polar Bear Swim),
Sunset Beach, Kits Beach (especially after a strenuous session
of beach volleyball), Jericho Beach, Locarno Beach, and Spanish Banks (the three latter are popular with cycling and windsurfing crowds).

Kitsilano Pool Kitsilano Beach has a gigantic outdoor saltwater pool adjacent to English Bay. It is heated to 26°C (79°F) and
has a graduated depth, making it ideal for both children and
strong swimmers. ▪ *Open from Victoria Day (late May) to
Labour Day (Sept), every day; 731-0011; map:N6.*

Newton Wave Pool [KIDS] Because the waters of Vancouver
are protected from the ocean swells of the Pacific Coast, surfing is not part of the city's aquatic culture. But in the suburb of
Surrey, a wave-action leisure pool generates 1-metre (3-foot)
waves for bodysurfing. There are also two water slides, a
wading pool, steam room, whirlpool, weight room, and even a
licensed lounge. ▪ *13730 72nd Ave, Surrey; every day; 594-
7873; map:K7.*

Splashdown Waterpark The owners of Splashdown Waterpark have taken advantage of Tsawwassen's sunny location
(less than half the annual rainfall of downtown Vancouver) to
construct a giant 2.8-hectare (7-acre) park featuring 11 water
slides. There's a full range of summertime fun to be enjoyed
here, from volleyball and basketball courts to a mini-golf
course. It's a great place to pack a picnic and is maybe the most
reliable spot in the Lower Mainland for getting a suntan.
▪ *Open from Victoria Day (late May) to Labour Day (Sept),
4799 Nu Lelum Way (near Hwy 17), Tsawwassen; 943-2251.*

University of British Columbia Aquatic Centre UBC has
Olympic-size indoor and outdoor pools with sauna, steam
room, whirlpool, exercise gym, and toddler pool. Open late into
the evening for public swimming. ▪ *822-4521 for pool times;
map:B2.*

Vancouver Aquatic Centre In the West End overlooking Sunset Beach, the Vancouver Aquatic Centre features an Olympic-
size indoor pool, sauna, whirlpool, and toddler pool. ▪ *1050
Beach Ave; every day; 665-3424; map:Q5.*

Farther north along the Stanley Park seawall, the newly refurbished Second Beach outdoor pool is popular with locals and visitors alike during the summer months. ▪ *257-8371; map:O1.*

TENNIS

Keen tennis players can perfect their topspin lob or two-fisted backhand year-round on Vancouver's 180 public courts, even though the outdoor season officially runs from March to October. Most public courts are free and operate on a first-come, first-served basis.

Stanley Park has 21 courts (17 by the Beach Avenue entrance and four by Lost Lagoon at the foot of Robson). From April to September, you can book a Beach Avenue court for a small fee (878-8600). **Queen Elizabeth Park** courts (33rd Ave at Cambie St) are centrally located but can be quite hot when there's no breeze. **Kitsilano Beach Park** has 10 courts near the ocean, with a concession stand nearby for a cool drink or french fries. **Jericho Beach Park**, behind the Jericho Sailing Centre, offers great rugby viewing on the pitch south of the courts while you wait your turn.

WINDSURFING

Although Vancouver is practically surrounded by water and is exposed to breezes from every direction, capricious conditions can test the patience of high-wind sailors looking for waves to jump and steady, consistent winds. But the light winds often found on the beaches of the city's west side are ideal for learning the sport. **Windsure Windsurfing School** (224-0615) operates from the Jericho Sailing Centre. Their specialty is an intensive six-hour course that guarantees results. At Sunset Beach, **English Bay Oceansports** (685-7245) is more convenient for guests staying in downtown hotels. **Pacific Boarder** (734-7245) in Kitsilano sells boardsailing equipment and wetsuits, along with surfboards and body-boards.

For some of the most consistent wind conditions in North America, you need to drive an hour north to the town of Squamish (Squamish is a Native word meaning "place where the wind blows"). The Squamish Spit is a human-made dyke that separates the saltwater bay of Howe Sound from the frigid waters of the Squamish River. Skim out on your board within view of the Stawamus Chief, Shannon Falls, and Howe Sound. Conditions are best from May to August, when afternoon thermals generated by warm air create steady, consistent conditions. The water is very cold, so a thick wetsuit or drysuit is mandatory, especially if you are still developing your jibing and waterstart skills. The **Squamish Windsurfing Society** administers the park, charging a daily fee to pay for rescue boats, washroom maintenance, and liability insurance. ▪ *Turn left at the Cleveland Ave (McDonald's restaurant) intersection, and turn right onto Buckley Ave. Cross the railways tracks onto*

Government Rd, pass the Squamish Feed Suppliers, and turn left onto the first gravel road. Continue 2 km (1.2 miles) along a dusty, potholed road to the spit. For wind conditions, call 926-WIND or 892-2235.

SPECTATOR SPORTS

See also the Calendar chapter for specific sporting events.

BC Lions Football The BC Lions play in the Canadian Football League. A longer, wider field and only three downs to make ten yards means that the passing game rules, making it a far more exciting game than its American counterpart. Action is the name of the game in this league, which is decades older than the NFL. Avid fans enjoy home games downtown in the BC Place Stadium from June through late October, and the season culminates in the Grey Cup championship. ■ *BC Place Stadium tickets through Ticketmaster, 280-4400; general information, 589-7627; map:T5.*

Horse Racing From April to October the thoroughbreds race at Exhibition Park (Hastings and Renfrew Streets). Serious punters study the horses' form in the paddocks, with the North Shore mountains as a backdrop. It's easy to get caught up in the excitement of an afternoon's racing. ■ *Exhibition Park; 254-1631; map:F2.*

Triple A Vancouver Canadians Baseball On a sunny midsummer afternoon, many members of the city's power elite (and their employees) are out, out, out at the old ball game. Although Vancouver doesn't have a team in The Show yet, the Triple A Canadians play at Nat Bailey Stadium on the east side of Queen Elizabeth Park (Ontario and 29th). Believe it or not, the stadium, with its slow, lush field and its beautiful natural setting, probably accounts for the Canadians' continual box-office success. New York Yankee stalwart Roger Maris once called it "the prettiest ballpark I've ever played in." Discount tickets are available through local food chains, but arrive early on sunny days because the 7,000-seat stadium frequently sells out. ■ *Nat Bailey Stadium; 872-5232; map:D3.*

Vancouver 86ers Vancouver's diverse ethnicity has created a ready-made audience for soccer, especially amongst homesick Brits, Portuguese, and Italians. The Vancouver 86ers played their first season during the year of Expo '86 and promptly won four straight Canadian soccer league titles before switching to the A League, a seven-team international circuit. The season starts in early May and winds up in September. Matches are played at Swangard Stadium on the Burnaby/Vancouver boundary, and tickets are available through Ticketmaster or at the gate. ■ *Swangard Stadium, Burnaby; 930-2255; map:G3.*

▼

Spectator Sports

▲

Vancouver Canucks Hockey Although the National Hockey League has been diluted with the addition of too many new teams and a punishing regular season schedule, a well-played hockey game is still the most spine-tingling spectacle in pro sport. You don't need to know anything about the rules to watch; it's all pretty self-explanatory. The hometown Canucks have had some bright, shining moments during their 25-year history, but their inconsistent ways and failure to live up to potential have let a lot of fans down. Still, the faithful have stuck with the team through good times and bad and that makes getting tickets a challenge—especially against popular teams like the Montreal Canadians and Toronto Maple Leafs. Home games are at the spanking new GM Place from September to April. ■ *GM Place; 899-4625; map:U5.*

Vancouver Grizzlies Basketball Basketball ain't just shooting hoops any more, not in the show-biz world of the National Basketball Association. Sometimes diehard roundball fans have to look beyond the fireworks, jugglers, mascots, rock music, and acrobats to see what's going down on the floor. But that's just as well, for the hometown Grizzlies set records for losing and general ineptitude in their 1995–96 inaugural season. (In the off-season, management wheeled and dealed for some new players, so the sophomore season looks more promising.) Mostly, fans were dazzled by GM Place (home for the Grizzlies, the NHL Canucks, and in-line hockey's VooDoo), one of the most luxurious and well-designed sports stadiums in North America. There's simply not a bad seat in the house. Tickets can be difficult to come by for games with popular teams like the Chicago Bulls and Orlando Magic, but walk-up seats are usually available for other games. Season runs from September to April. ■ *GM Place; 899-4667; map:U5.*

▼

Spectator Sports

▲

Vancouver VooDoo Over the past decade, in-line skating has been one of the fastest-growing sports in North America. Using in-line skates to play "road hockey" has become so popular that there's now a professional hockey league. The Vancouver VooDoo play in the Roller Hockey International League against teams from both Canada and the United States. Some differences are apparent from the winter version: teams play with five players instead of six, and the season runs from late May to late August. Games tend to be higher scoring than the on-ice counterpart. The VooDoo are part of the Orca Bay Sports and Entertainment Group, which own the NBA Grizzlies and NHL Canucks. Tickets are available at the door at GM Place stadium. ■ *GM Place; 899-4800; map:U5.*

ESSENTIALS

Essentials

TRANSPORTATION

AIRPLANES: VANCOUVER INTERNATIONAL AIRPORT

Vancouver International Airport (276-6101) is located south of Vancouver in the city of Richmond, approximately a 20-minute drive from downtown Vancouver.

Often referred to by its three-letter international code, **YVR** serves 26 major airlines, including Air BC, Air Canada, Air China, Air New Zealand, Alaska Airlines, American Airlines, America West Airlines, British Airways, Canadian Airlines, Cathay Pacific, Continental Airlines, Delta Airlines, Horizon Air, Japan Airlines, KLM Royal Dutch Airlines, Korean Air, Lufthansa German Airlines, Malaysia Airlines, Mandarin Airlines, Northwest Airlines, Qantas Airways, Reno Air, Singapore Airlines, Swissair, Time Air, and United Airlines.

A new international terminal, control tower, and third runway opened in 1996 as part of a $465-million expansion project. The old terminal, which now handles only flights within Canada, was built for 3.5 million passengers a year but saw 12 million pass through in 1995. The new terminal has 113 check-in counters and 16 gates for travellers bound for international destinations. There is improved customs clearance and there are added services for the disabled and passengers connecting to other flights or cruise ships. **Green Coats**, an army of 150 volunteer ambassadors, are on duty 7am to 10pm daily to assist airport users and answer questions.

To finance the expansion, an airport-improvement departure tax of $5 is charged for passengers of flights within BC and the Yukon Territory; $10 for flights to the rest of Canada, U.S., and Mexico; and $15 for international flights. There are

12 automated teller machines and six full-service Royal Bank branches open all day, 365 days a year, for negotiating travellers' cheques, foreign exchange, Registered Retirement Savings Plans (RRSPs), and loans. A shopping mall contains four Allders Duty Free shops, an officially licensed PGA Tour golf shop, bookstores, clothing boutiques, beauty salons, toy stores, and chocolate shops.

The Oriental Tea Garden, the Elephant and Castle English-style pub, and Starbucks Coffee are among the many **food and beverage** outlets. The Pacific Market is a unique experience, with its West Coast cuisine and casual, market-style dining. The "street pricing" policy enforced by airport management ensures airport customers pay the same prices for goods and services here as they would downtown.

Parking (276-6106) is plentiful at the airport and is offered on an hourly, daily, or weekly basis. Parking rates range from $7 a day in the economy lot to $20 a day in the parkade, a new 2,080-stall complex located near the main entrance. Free shuttle buses run from economy lot to terminal. Valet parking is $2.50 an hour or $10 a day plus an $8 valet fee (276-2575). Off-site parking and 24-hour shuttle-bus service is available at **Air O Lot** (3231 No 3 Rd, Richmond, 244-8599) and **Park 'n Fly** (6380 Miller Rd, Richmond, 270-9476).

Vancouver Tours and Transit's **Airporter** offers luxury bus service between the airport and downtown locations, stopping at most major hotels and the bus depot. One way, $9; round trip, $15. Average **taxi** fare between the airport and downtown is approximately $25, though you can travel in style via **Air Limo** (273-1331) for $29. **BC Transit** provides service to the Vancouver International Airport on the #100 route. Perimeter Transportation (261-5386) offers service from the airport to the Whistler Village ski resort on its **Whistler Express**. One way, $41.80. Car rental companies that operate at YVR include: **Alamo** (1-800-327-9633), **Avis** (606-2847), **Budget** (668-7000), **Hertz** (606-3700), **National-Tilden** (273-3121), and **Thrifty** (606-1666).

AIRPLANES: CHARTER/HELICOPTER/SEAPLANE

Harbour Air Seaplanes (688-1277) offers "harbour-to-harbour" service between Vancouver and Victoria for $65 one way. Flights to the Gulf Islands and Sunshine Coast, and tours of the region are also available. **North Vancouver Air** (278-1608) flies from Vancouver and Victoria to communities along BC's coast. It also provides charter service to anywhere in North America.

Helijet Airways (273-1414) has scheduled service between downtown Vancouver and Victoria ($125 one way; $78 on weekends) and also has service to Victoria from Vancouver International Airport. Flights are aboard spacious 12-passenger Sikorsky S-76 helicopters. **Vancouver Helicopter**

Tours (270-1484) has charter jet-powered flights to suit your schedule and desired destination.

BUSES AND LIGHT RAIL

BC Transit (521-0400) makes it easy to get around Vancouver without a car. Bus stops are clearly marked and often list the route numbers serving the stop. Enter by the front door and leave by the rear. Lift-equipped buses that are easily accessible for wheelchairs are identified by a sign on the bus windshield. Deposit exact cash fare ($1.50, one zone; $2.25, two zones; $3.00, three zones) in the fare box and request a transfer if you plan to continue your journey on a second bus or on the SkyTrain or SeaBus. Transfers are good for 90 minutes of travel in any direction. A DayPass ($4.50) is valid all day weekends and holidays and after 9:30am weekdays. Books of 10 Faresaver tickets start at $13.75 for one zone and are available at many convenience stores. Schedules are available at libraries, community centres, and city hall. Call for special rate information for seniors, children, students, and disabled persons.

HandyDart (540-3400) is a customized service for passengers with a disability restricting movement who are not on an accessible route or who cannot use the lift-equipped buses. Book at least 48 hours in advance. Depending on the number of zones travelled, cost varies from $1.35 to $2.50.

SkyTrain, Vancouver's advanced light rapid transit system, operates on an elevated guideway between the Vancouver waterfront and Surrey. The four downtown stations are underground and are marked at street level. Fast, efficient, and scenic, the red, white, and blue carriages are computer driven but patrolled by roving attendants. Tickets (same price as BC Transit fares) are dispensed from machines in each station and are good for travel on city buses and the SeaBus. Trains run from 5am to 1am.

SeaBus is one of the best services offered by BC Transit ($2.25). Twin-hulled catamarans shuttle up to 400 passengers per sailing between the foot of Lonsdale Avenue on the North Shore and SkyTrain's Waterfront Station at the foot of Granville Street downtown. Every 15 to 30 minutes. For **West Vancouver** bus schedule call 985-7777.

BUSES: OUT OF TOWN AND CHARTER

Vancouver's bus station is at the **Pacific Central Station**, 1150 Station Street. This former western terminal for Canadian National Railways also serves VIA Rail and Amtrak passenger railways. It is a short walk from the Main Street SkyTrain station and services all of the bus lines listed below.

Greyhound Lines of Canada (662-3222 or 1-800-661-8747) travels to points across Canada and North America.

Maverick Coach Lines (669-5200) serves Nanaimo, the Sunshine Coast, Squamish, and Whistler.

Pacific Coach Lines (662-7575) provides scheduled intercity service between downtown Vancouver and downtown Victoria, including scenic Butchart Gardens.

Quick Shuttle Service (244-3744 or 1-800-665-2122) offers regularly scheduled coach service between Vancouver and Sea-Tac Airport near Seattle, $68 round trip. It also serves Bellingham Airport from Vancouver. Buses leave from the Sandman Hotel, 180 W Georgia St.

CRUISE SHIPS

Vancouver is a major port for cruise liners sailing the Alaska tour route. Princess Cruises, Holland America, and several smaller companies depart from **Canada Place** or **Ballantyne Pier** terminals. Vancouver Port Corporation Cruise Ship Info Line, 666-6068.

FERRIES

BC Ferries (277-0277 or (888)223-3779 in BC); schedule information available by fax: call 299-9000, extension 4789) is a provincial government-operated service that offers a minimum of eight sailings daily from Tsawwassen (more than a dozen in summer), about a half-hour drive south of Vancouver, and from Swartz Bay, a similar distance from Victoria. Travel time, city centre to city centre, is about three hours. Car and driver, $33.50 one way during peak season, $28.25 during low season; additional passengers, $6.50 each. Other routes go from Tsawwassen or Horseshoe Bay to Nanaimo, the Gulf Islands, and the Sunshine Coast. The ferries provide a pleasant, stable cruise, with amenities that include dining room, snack bar, news-stand, and promenade decks. **Foot passengers**, $6.50, can either take West Vancouver Blue Buses (985-7777) to the Horseshoe Bay terminal or travel via coach. Pacific Coach Lines (662-7575) goes to Victoria; Maverick Coach Lines (669-5200) goes to Nanaimo. Both depart from Pacific Central Station in downtown Vancouver and have priority boarding ferries.

TAXICABS

Vancouver has several taxicab companies, but four are the primary providers of service to the downtown core and surrounding communities: **Black Top and Checker Cabs** (731-1111), **MacLure's Cabs** (683-6666), **Vancouver Taxi** (871-1111), and **Yellow Cab Company** (681-1111 or 1-800-898-8294). Vancouver Taxi specializes in wheelchair accessible cabs. Fare is $1.21 per kilometre, plus a $2.10 "flag" or service charge.

TRAINS

Amtrak (1-800-872-7245) departs Pacific Central Station for Seattle once a day at 6pm. A return train arrives in Vancouver at 11:40am. One-way fare is $29 or $42 return (U.S. funds). **BC Rail** (1311 W 1st St, North Vancouver, 984-5246 or 1-800-663-8238) operates a spectacular daily round-trip rail journey to Whistler, Lillooet, the Cariboo region, Prince George, and Quesnel. BC Rail also operates the Royal Hudson historic steam-powered train, which runs daily during the summer from North Vancouver to Squamish.

Rocky Mountaineer Railtours (Pacific Central Station, 606-7200 or 1-800-665-7245) operates a sightseeing train from Vancouver to Calgary via the breathtaking Rocky Mountains. **VIA Rail** (Pacific Central Station, 669-3050 or 1-800-561-8630 in Canada; 1-800-561-3949 in the U.S.), Canada's national passenger rail network, operates thrice-weekly full-service trains through the Rockies to major destinations in Central and Eastern Canada.

West Coast Express (683-7245) is a weekday commuter rail service between Mission City in the Fraser Valley and Waterfront Station in downtown Vancouver. Trains are equipped with various amenities, including cappuccino bars. Five morning trains head west beginning at 5:28am. Eastbound service in the afternoon ends with the last departure from Waterfront Station at 6:15pm. Fare is $7 one-way, $13.66 return. Interurban rates, as well as weekly and monthly passes, are also available.

KEYS TO THE CITY

CATERERS

There's nothing lazy about Susan Mendelson, owner of **The Lazy Gourmet** (1595 W 6th Ave, 734-2507), Vancouver's best-known catering operation. Mendelson is the author of seven cookbooks, and her centrally located establishment is open seven days a week serving generous meals, mouth-watering take-aways, and homemade breads and desserts. Other caterers of note include **Culinary Capers** (4075 Main St, 875-0123); **Menu Setters** (3655 W 10th Ave, 732-4218); **Gallery Cafe & Catering** (750 Hornby St, 688-2233); **Lesley Stowe Fine Foods** (1780 W 3rd Ave, 731-3663); and **Major The Gourmet** (102-8828 Heather St, 322-9211). See also Caterers in the Food and Other Features index in the Restaurants chapter.

CHILD CARE

Most major hotels can arrange for baby-sitters if notified in advance. **A Babysitter Every Time** (737-2248) brings adult sitters to your door for $10 per hour. Discounts available for members. Same-day booking.

CITY OF VANCOUVER COMPLAINTS AND QUESTIONS

Vancouver City Hall (453 W 12th Ave, 873-7011) provides information about the city and fields complaints. A switchboard operator will refer you to the department that can best handle the problem. The city's web page http://www.city.vancou-ver.bc.ca contains a wealth of information on civic services.

CONSULATES

There are no embassies in Vancouver, but there are more than 30 consulates. Major consulates include: **Australia** (602-999 Canada Place, 684-1177), **China** (3380 Granville St, 736-3910), **France** (1201-736 Granville St, 681-2301), **Germany** (704-999 Canada Place, 684-8377), **Great Britain** (800-1111 Melville St, 683-4421), **India** (325 Howe St, 662-8811), **Italy** (705-1200 Burrard St, 684-7288), **Japan** (900-1177 W Hastings St, 684-5868), **Mexico** (810-1130 W Pender St, 684-3547), the **Netherlands** (475 Howe St, 684-6448), **New Zealand** (1200-888 Dunsmuir St, 684-7388), **Singapore** (1305-999 W Hastings St, 669-5115), **South Korea** (1066 W Hastings, 681-9581), **Spain** (3736 Parker St, Burnaby, 299-7760), and the **United States** (1095 W Pender St, 685-4311).

DISCRIMINATION

The **BC Council of Human Rights** (406-815 Hornby St, 660-6811) assists people who believe they have been the victims of discrimination due to race, age, sex, religion, marital status, political or sexual orientation, or disability.

DRY CLEANERS AND TAILORS

The Valetor has built a name for itself over the past 50 years and has six locations around Vancouver (5405 W Blvd, 266-7141; Oakridge Centre, 266-4421; 3020 Cambie St, 879-1776; 202-16th St, West Vancouver, 922-2535; 2065 Burrard St, 732-7817; 5309 Headland Dr (Caulfeild Village), West Vancouver, 925-3900). **Scotty's One Hour Cleaners** (834 Thurlow St, 685-7732) offers good service and a professional job.

Wheely Clean (816-8721) will pick up and deliver dry cleaning to your home or downtown/west-side office at reasonable rates. **Woodman's Cleaners** (Bentall I, 505 Burrard St, 684-6622, and Royal Centre, 1055 W Georgia St, 684-3623) offers same-day dry-cleaning or shirt laundry as well as alterations and repairs. **Townline Tailors** (541 Howe St, 684-6105) and **Andrew's Custom Tailors** (666 Burrard St, 669-8616) also provide custom tailoring.

FOREIGN EXCHANGE

You can exchange U.S. dollars at any major Canadian bank; however, it can be difficult to exchange other foreign currencies. There are numerous foreign banks in Vancouver. Many businesses accept U.S. dollars but often give exchange rates below market value. **American Express** (666 Burrard St, 669-2813) is open Monday to Saturday. **Custom House Currency** (375 Water St, 482-6000 or 1-800-350-6001) in Gastown is open late seven nights a week. It also has counters at Book Warehouse (1150 Robson St), the Westin Bayshore (1601 W Georgia

St), and the Canada Place and Ballantyne Pier cruise ship terminals. **International Securities Exchange** (1169 Robson St, 683-9666, and 1036 Robson St, 683-4686) is open seven days a week, including some evenings. **Thomas Cook Foreign Exchange** (1016 W Georgia St, 687-6111, and Pan Pacific Hotel, 130-999 Canada Place, 641-1229) is open Monday to Saturday.

FOREIGN VISITORS

The **Society of Translators and Interpreters of BC** (684-2940) provides names of accredited translators. The **College of Physicians and Surgeons** (733-7758) provides a list of multilingual doctors.

GROCERY DELIVERY

Safeway Food and Drug (643-6950) stores throughout Vancouver offer delivery via a private contractor. Price varies depending on distance.

INFORMATION

Vancouver Tourist InfoCentre (200 Burrard St, 683-2000) offers a wealth of information about Vancouver. The **Vancouver Public Library** (Central Library, 350 W Georgia St, 331-3600) is happy to take your call and refer you to applicable departments within the library.

LEGAL SERVICES

The Canadian Bar Association, BC branch, offers the free **Dial-A-Law** service. Call 687-4680 or 1-800-565-5297 to access a library of recorded messages on various legal topics. The **Lawyer Referral Service** (687-3221) advises people seeking legal representation. The **Law Society of BC** (669-2533), the governing body of lawyers, assists people who have problems with a lawyer. The **Law Students' Legal Advice Program** (822-5791) offers a free consultation service.

LIBRARIES

There are 21 branches of the **Vancouver Public Library** located throughout the city. In addition to books, magazines, and audio and video recordings, they offer author readings and lectures. The **Central Library** (350 W Georgia St, 331-3600) at Library Square is one of Vancouver's newer architectural wonders. Modelled after the Roman Colosseum, the bright, spacious building is open Monday to Wednesday, 10am to 9pm; Thursday to Saturday, 10am to 6pm; and Sunday, 1pm to 5pm (October to May). No phone service on Sundays. The **University of British Columbia** (Point Grey, 822-2077) also operates a multi-branch library system open to the public, though only students, researchers, and teaching staff are able to borrow from its collection. Many municipalities have their own library systems; next to the Vancouver Public Library system, West Vancouver's library system is tops in the province.

LIMOUSINE SERVICES

Star Limousine Service (685-5600) has been around for more than 15 years and has a fleet of more than two dozen limousines. Others that deliver prompt, reliable service include **Classic Limousine** (267-1441) and **Air Limo** (273-1331).

LOST CAR/TOWING

First check to find out if the car was towed. Call **Unitow** (1717 Vernon St, 606-1255) if it was parked on a city street or lane and **Buster's** (685-8181) if it was parked in a private lot. Both of these companies provide 24-hour towing within Vancouver. If neither of these contract towing companies has your wheels, call 911 and report the missing car to the police.

MEDICAL/DENTAL SERVICES

The **College of Physicians and Surgeons of BC** (1807 W 10th Ave, 733-7758) has a list of doctors accepting patients. The **Vancouver Health Department** (1060 W 8th Ave, 736-2033) is also a good source of information on local health care. Walk-in clinics, with no appointment necessary, include **Care Point Medical Centres** (1175 Denman St, 681-5338; 3419 Kingsway, 436-0800; 1623 Commercial Dr, 254-5554); **Maple Medical Clinic** (103-2025 W Broadway, 730-9769); **Medicentre** (Bentall Centre, 1055 Dunsmuir St, 683-8138); and **Royal Centre Medical** (238-1055 W Georgia St, 682-6886). The **College of Dental Surgeons of BC** (1765 W 8th Ave, 736-3621) has a list of dentists accepting patients.

NEWSPAPERS

The *Vancouver Sun* (732-2111) is published every morning except Sunday. A complete entertainment section is published on Thursday and a TV listings magazine on Friday. The *Province* (732-2222), a tabloid whose mandate appears to be flashy, headline-grabbing journalism with an emphasis on sports and entertainment, is published every morning except Saturday. Both are part of the Southam newspapers chain and can be read on the Internet at http://www.southam.com/vancouversun or http://www.southam.com/vancouverprovince.

The *Georgia Straight* (730-7000), a free entertainment weekly that often contains strong features and investigative journalism, is published on Thursday. *Terminal City* (669-6910) is a similar free weekly that caters to an alternative audience. *Sports Only* (482-6500) is an excellent weekly primer on the latest local sports news. *Business In Vancouver* (688-2398) is Vancouver's weekly business authority, and *Vancouver's CityFood* (737-7845) is the insider's guide to cooking and dining. The city also has thriving Chinese-language newspapers. *Ming Pao* (662-8118) and *Sing Tao* (669-8091) offer daily news to Greater Vancouver's large Chinese-Canadian population.

Hugs & Kisses Pet Sitters (731-1948) provides a network of animal lovers who will take pets as temporary guests in their homes. Pick-up and delivery service.

Yuppy Puppy Dog Day-Care offers "surrogate master" services, including walking and massages for your pooch. Longer hours to suit working people and a common play area make this a nontraditional kennel. Daycare fees start at $20 a day (1625 W 3rd Ave, 732-6446).

PHARMACIES (LATE NIGHT)

Shoppers Drug Mart (1125 Davie St, 669-2424) is open 24 hours. Five other locations are open to midnight (1020 Denman St, 681-3411; 4326 Dunbar St, 732-8855; 2947 Granville St, 738-3107; 2302 W 4th Ave, 738-3138). The pharmacy in **Safeway** (2733 W Broadway, 732-5030) is open daily 8am to midnight.

PLACES OF WORSHIP

The five main churches located downtown are recognized as civic heritage buildings. **St. James Anglican Church** (303 E Cordova St, 685-2532) serves the oldest parish in the city and the largest on the downtown east side. **Christ Church Cathedral** (690 Burrard St, 682-3848) is also Anglican and was saved for future generations from the developer's wrecking ball. Its Gothic Revival style and stained-glass windows offer a quiet sanctuary from the busy traffic and skyscrapers in the heart of downtown. **Holy Rosary Cathedral** (646 Richards St, 682-6774) is the city's largest Roman Catholic church and is reminiscent of European cathedrals, with its twin spires and bell tower. **St. Andrew's Wesley United Church** (1012 Nelson St, 683-4574) and **First Baptist Church** (969 Burrard St, 683-8441) are neighbours at the highest point of the downtown peninsula. While downtown is home primarily to Christian places of worship, there are Buddhist (220 Jackson St, 253-7033) and Sikh (1890 Skeena St, 254-2117) temples nearby. There are also major centres for celebrating the traditions of other faiths, such as Judaism (5750 Oak St, 266-1313), Hinduism (3885 Albert St, Burnaby, 299-5922), and Islam (12300 Blundell Rd, Richmond, 270-2522).

PUBLIC RESTROOMS

Most locals simply stop at any major downtown hotel. You'll also find restrooms in shopping malls and at downtown Sky-Train stations.

RADIO AND TV STATIONS

Vancouver has a wide enough variety of AM and FM radio stations to suit any listener's taste. **CKNW** (980 AM, 331-2711) is Western Canada's most-listened-to radio station because of its thorough news and sports programming; **CKWX** (1130 AM,

873-2599) offers news headlines around the clock; **CBC Radio** (690 AM, 662-6000) is part of Canada's public radio network; **CBC Stereo** (105.7 FM, 662-6000) airs classical music by day and jazz and alternative music by night; **99.3 the Fox** (99.3 FM, 684-7221) is Vancouver's favourite contemporary rock station; and **Rock 101** (101.1 FM, 331-2727) is the classic rocker's choice. **Z95.3** (95.3 FM, 241-0953) broadcasts a mix of Top 40 and alternative. **KISS FM** (96.9 FM, 872-2557) has a mix of soft rock favourites, while **JR FM** (93.7 FM, 731-7772) is the place for country music. **The Bridge** (600 AM, 731-6111) has a contemporary Christian music format. **CJVB** (1470 AM, 688-9931) and **CHMB** (1320 AM, 263-1320) are Vancouver's multicultural stations, both of which emphasize Chinese-language programming. **Co-op Radio** (102.7 FM, 684-8494) and **CITR** (101.9 FM, 822-3017) are community-supported and noncommercial.

Four Canadian network-affiliated TV stations broadcast from Vancouver. **CBUT** and **CBUFT** are CBC-TV stations that broadcast in English and French, respectively. **BCTV** is part of the CTV network, while **U.TV** is an affiliate of the CanWest Global System. CBC's programming is all Canadian, while the others offer a smorgasbord of local news along with American network and syndicated shows. Cable subscribers are treated to six Washington State TV stations and several specialty services that air sports, music, arts, news, and lifestyle programming. Cable Channel 2 in most areas lists upcoming, hourly schedules. **TV Week**, available at most news-stands and grocery stores, is Vancouver's most thorough listings magazine.

SENIORS SERVICES

Seniors Resources & Research Society (410-1755 W Broadway, 733-2310) and **Seniors Information and Referral Services** (875-6381) provide information about programs and services available to seniors.

TIPPING

Gratuities are not mandatory for most services rendered, but tips of 10 to 20 percent on the pre-tax amount are encouraged when above-average service is encountered. An easy formula is to double the GST (federal tax) to equal 14 percent. Add a little and you have a decent tip on the pre-tax bill. It is courteous to tip hotel staff $1 to $5 depending on the service provided, such as baggage delivery ($1.50 per bag at top hotels) or room service.

UNIVERSITIES

Simon Fraser University (Burnaby Mountain, 291-3111). Award-winning architecture set in breathtaking scenery. Student guides lead free tours of the main Burnaby Mountain campus, starting at the Administration Building. A satellite campus is situated downtown (Harbour Centre, 291-5000). **University**

of **British Columbia** (Point Grey, 822-2211), Canada's third-largest university, is famous for its scenery and attractions, including botanical and Japanese gardens and the Museum of Anthropology. The campus is surrounded by a 763-hectare (1,885-acre) park with kilometres of hiking trails and ocean shoreline. Free campus tours available May to August. Visitors welcome year-round.

VETERINARIANS: EMERGENCY AND WEEKEND SERVICE

Centrally located, the **Animal Emergency Clinic** (1590 W 4th Ave, 734-5104) is open 24 hours a day.

ALL-NIGHT SERVICES

COURIER

North Shore Taxi's **Express Courier** (987-7171) will pick up and deliver your package anywhere in the Lower Mainland 24 hours a day.

PHARMACIES
(see Keys to the City)

RESTAURANTS

Far from being "greasy spoons," Vancouver's late-night eateries are decent restaurants and cafes located mainly on the west side. The **Naam** (2724 W 4th Ave, 738-7151) was Vancouver's first vegetarian restaurant. The flagship of the **Bread Garden** gourmet bakery-cafe chain (1880 W 1st Ave, 738-6684) spawned a knockoff called **Calhoun's** (3035 W Broadway, 737-7062). **Benny's** (2503 W Broadway, 731-9730) is a chic all-night, candle-lit bagelry. (See also the indexes in the Restaurants chapter.)

SERVICE STATION

The 24-Hour Chevron Station (1698 W Georgia St, 681-0028) is centrally located on a busy, well-lit street between downtown and the West End.

SUPERMARKET

Super Valu (1255 Davie St, 688-0911) is Vancouver's only 24-hour, full-service supermarket. It provides a delivery service Monday to Saturday, 9am to 6pm.

BUSINESS SERVICES

COMPUTER RENTALS

Pacific West Office World Rentals by the day, week, or month; leasing options; rent-to-own; and delivery. IBM compatibles, printers, copiers, office furniture. A complete computer system with printer and necessary software is about $100 a week. Extremely accommodating and friendly service. Central downtown location. ▪ *1134 Homer St, 681-9666.*

Central Computer Source Rent IBM and peripheral systems for about $150 a month. Delivery and set-up service. Fax machines available. ■ *881 Hamilton St, 684-4545.*

Byte Computer Offers Macintosh computer rentals. ■ *2151 Burrard St, 738-2181.*

CONVENTION LOCATIONS

Most major hotels and many restaurants rent meeting rooms. The following is a list of other rental facilities appropriate for business meetings, private parties, and receptions. Both the University of British Columbia (822-3465) and Simon Fraser University (291-3649) offer numerous halls, auditoriums, and meeting rooms. Most private and public museums and art galleries also have space available.

ABC Boat Charters A fleet of nine boats (the largest can carry 90 passengers) is available for luncheons, dinners, or private conferences on the water. Catering and entertainment available. ■ *M100-750 Pacific Blvd S, 682-2070.*

BC Place Stadium The entire 60,000-seat domed stadium is available for concerts, conventions, sporting events, or just about anything else. There are also private suites, banquet rooms, several meeting rooms with various configurations, and a food court. ■ *777 Pacific Blvd S, 661-3403.*

Centennial Theatre Centre The North Vancouver recreation department rents its 718-seat theatre for meetings and presentations. The department provides twin slide projectors and is equipped to handle light catering. ■ *2300 Lonsdale St, North Vancouver, 984-4484.*

General Motors Place (GM Place) The home of the Vancouver Canucks, Grizzlies, and VooDoo is available for groups of 12 to 20,000. ■ *800 Griffiths Way, 899-7400.*

Performance Works Used as a rehearsal space for professional performing arts, this venue is also available to the public, accommodating 500. The airy building provides a parklike setting with natural light. ■ *1218 Cartwright St (Granville Island), 666-8139.*

Robson Square Conference Centre Part of the Robson Square complex—which includes the law courts, art gallery, and food court—the centre offers two theatres, six meeting rooms, an exhibition hall, two smaller boardrooms, and full catering. You can rent all or part of the facilities. ■ *800 Robson St, 482-1800.*

Vancouver Art Gallery Formerly the provincial courthouse, the neoclassical art gallery is available for receptions and meetings after hours. Rent the entire gallery, the main floor, or the historic boardroom of the Supreme Court of British Columbia (available for day use). Ideal space accommodates 50 to 500.

Open to recommended outside caterers. ■ *750 Hornby St, 662-4700.*

Vancouver Aquarium How about a boardroom situated in the killer whale underwater viewing area? Or maybe you'd like the entire aquarium for a standup reception of 1,700 people. From September through June, after business hours until midnight, the Vancouver Aquarium rents its venue for parties, receptions, or formal dinners. Dine with an octopus or sip cocktails in the presence of killer whales. Functions are catered by a number of preselected caterers. A boardroom and theatre are available for day use. Prices are competitive. Definitely a best place. ■ *Stanley Park, 631-2502.*

Vancouver Trade and Convention Centre The centre is housed in a spectacular harbour setting, under the distinctive sails of Canada Place. Three levels and 21 meeting rooms, with one massive ballroom and a lengthy entrance hall. ■ *Canada Place, Burrard St, 641-1987.*

COPY SERVICES

Kinko's Nobody else offers such a wide range of services, including copying, computer rentals, résumé writing, desktop publishing, and passport photos. Open 24 hours a day. ■ *1900 W Broadway, 734-2679.*

If you need fast, competitively priced copying or printing done at a handy downtown location, these are the places: **Copy Time Printing & Copying Service** (427 Granville St, 682-8307) or **Zippy Print** (100-220 Cambie St, 662-8848; 851 Homer St, 669-8833).

MESSENGER AND DELIVERY SERVICES
See also ALL-NIGHT SERVICES: COURIER above

Federal Express (1-800-GO-FEDEX) and UPS (1-800-PICK-UPS) Both offer next-day service to and from anywhere in the world and both have downtown customer service and drop-box locations. No weight limit. Agents can offer advice about customs requirements.

Dwarf Courier (278-1935), PDX Courier (684-3336), VIP Courier (253-7874). Fast, reliable delivery service anywhere within Greater Vancouver.

SECRETARIAL SERVICES

Offices and meeting space with all the required secretarial support and communications services in a professional atmosphere are available at a number of downtown locations. **Total Office** (Park Pl, 1300-666 Burrard St, 688-9276), **HQ** (700-555 W Hastings St, 443-5000), and **Suite 400 Executive Offices and Secretarial Services** (400-850 W Hastings St, 687-5516) all offer short- and long-term rentals. **Mail Boxes Etc.** (125A-1030 Denman St, 689-1243; 242-757 W Hastings St, 688-8848;

101-1001 W Broadway, 732-4147) offers mail box rentals, photocopying, faxing, and postal services.

TELEPHONE NUMBERS

*All numbers listed below use the area code (604),
unless otherwise indicated.*

EMERGENCY

Emergency: police, fire, ambulance	**911**
Directory Assistance	**411**
AIDS Vancouver Helpline	687-2437
Alcoholics Anonymous	434-3933
Animal Emergency Clinic	734-5104
Animal Pound	251-1325
Canadian Coast Guard Emergency	(800) 567-5111
Crisis Centre	872-3311
Customs: Canada	666-0545
Customs: U.S.	(360) 332-5771
Legal Services	687-4680
Passports	775-6250
Planned Parenthood	731-4252
Poison Control Centre	631-5050
Rape Relief	872-8212
Royal Canadian Mounted Police	264-3111
Vancouver City Police	665-3535

TRANSPORTATION/CAR TROUBLE

BCAA (BC Automobile Association)	268-5600
BCAA Emergency Road Service	293-2222
BC Ferry Corporation	277-0277
toll-free in BC	(888) 223-3779
BC Rail	631-3500
BC Transit	521-0400
VIA Rail	(800) 561-8630

TOURISM/EVENTS

Chamber of Commerce	681-2111
City Parks and Recreation Board	257-8400
Consumer and Corporate Affairs	666-5000
Information Services Vancouver	875-6381
Tourism Vancouver	683-2000

GENERAL INFORMATION

Better Business Bureau	682-2711
Citizenship and Immigration	666-2171

City Hall General Switchboard 873-7011
Postal Code Information .... (800) 267-1133
Post Office Information .... (800) 267-1177
Red Cross.................................... 879-6001
Road Conditions .... 299-9000 ext. 7623
Vancouver Health Department 775-1866
Weather 664-9010

SPORTS ORGANIZATIONS
BC Lions (football) 583-7747
Vancouver Canadians (baseball)................ 872-5232
Vancouver Canucks (hockey) 899-4600
Vancouver Grizzlies (basketball) 899-4666
Vancouver VooDoo (roller hockey) 899-4800
Vancouver 86ers (soccer) 299-0086

METRIC SYSTEM

In the late 1970s, Canada adopted the metric measurement system. Though widely used, it is not uncommon to encounter old imperial measurements at grocery stores and other businesses. Here is a handy conversion guide:

	If you know	multiply by	to get/ If you know	multiply by	to get
Length	inches	2.54	centimetres (cm)	0.39	inches
	feet	0.30	metres (m)	3.28	feet
	yards	0.91	metres (m)	1.09	yards
	miles	1.61	kilometres (km)	0.62	miles
Area	square inches	6.45	square centimetres (cm2)	0.15	square inches
	square feet	0.09	square metres (m2)	10.76	square feet
	square yards	0.84	square metres (m2)	1.19	square yards
	square miles	2.59	square kilometres (km2)	0.4	square miles
	acres	0.4	hectares (ha)	2.47	acres
Mass	ounces	28.35	grams (g)	0.035	ounces
	pounds	0.45	kilograms (kg)	2.2	pounds
	tons	0.9	tonnes (t)	1.1	tons
Volume	fluid ounces	28.41	millilitres (ml)	0.03	fluid ounces
	pints	0.57	litres (l)	2.1	pints
	quarts	0.95	litres (l)	1.06	quarts
	gallons	3.79	litres (l)	0.22	gallons
	cubic feet	0.03	cubic metres (m3)	35.31	cubic feet
	cubic yards	0.76	cubic metres (m3)	1.31	cubic yards
Temperature	Fahrenheit (F)	subtract 32, then multiply by $5/9$			Celsius (C)
	Celsius (C)	multiply by $9/5$ then add 32			Fahrenheit (F)

CALENDAR

Calendar

JANUARY

Average daily maximum and minimum temperatures: 5°, 4°C (41°, 39°F). Average rainfall: 201 millimetres (8 inches).

Chinese New Year [FREE] [KIDS] In late January or early February (depending on the lunar calendar), Chinatown greets the Chinese New Year with a fanfare of fireworks, displays, and a lively parade of writhing dragons accompanied by exotically garbed dancers and musicians. Besides the parade there is a bazaar, banquets, and martial arts demonstrations at the Chinese Cultural Centre and the Dr. Sun Yat-Sen Classical Chinese Garden. ▪ *Chinatown; 687-0729; map:V4.*

Pacific International Auto Show They're all there, all gleaming. Even if all you can afford is a Skoda, you can sit behind the wheel of a Hummer and make like you're actually thinking about buying the thing. Who's to know? This late-January cavalcade of cars is the official unveiling of the year's models, and it's fun even if you're not in the market. ▪ *BC Place Stadium; 294-8330; map T5.*

Polar Bear Swim [FREE] [KIDS] Start the new year by plunging into the cold Pacific with several hundred others, urged on by thousands of noisy supporters. ▪ *English Bay; 732-2304; map:N1-O5.*

FEBRUARY

Average daily maximum and minimum temperatures: 8°, 3°C (46°, 37°F). Average rainfall: 161 millimetres (6.3 inches).

BC Great Outdoors Show Ideas galore for the great outdoors, indoors every late February/early March. Where to go and what to take. All the newest gadgets with plenty of time-tested wisdom. ■ *BC Place Stadium; 294-1313; map:T5.*

Spring Home Show If you're looking for contemporary West Coast ideas for decorating, this is the place. The largest home show in Western Canada. ■ *BC Place Stadium; 433-5121; map:T5.*

Women In View Festival During the doldrums of the post-holiday season, there is at least one reason for celebration. The Women In View Festival, whose mandate is to showcase work initiated by women, presents a variety of performances, work-shops, and networking sessions. From solo performers to choirs, from the traditional to the cutting edge, the festival ros-ter highlights the creative achievements of women in music, theatre, dance, storytelling, and other art forms. Performances are held in various venues around Vancouver, attracting a mix of viewers. ■ *685-6684.*

MARCH

Average daily maximum and minimum temperatures: 9°, 4°C (48°, 39°F). Average rainfall: 151 millimetres (6 inches).

Pacific Rim Whale Festival Migrating grey whales can be ob-served during March and April just off the shores of the Long Beach section of Pacific Rim National Park. Numerous charter boats and a seaplane company offer close-up looks at the pods. The actual festival, including dances and education programs, begins the last week in March. ■ *Tofino; (250) 725-3414.*

Vancouver Playhouse International Wine Festival Held in ei-ther March or April, North America's largest and most presti-gious consumer and trade wine event sells more than 10,000 tickets and attracts more than 125 wineries from around the world. Events during this five-day festival include an opening night gala and auction, evening tastings (with more than 600 wines), wine-and-food matching dinners, and public and trade seminars. ■ *Vancouver Trade and Convention Centre and various venues; 872-6622; map:T2.*

Vancouver Storytelling Festival [KIDS] Few events underline Vancouver's ethnic mix as well as the storytelling festival, held for three days each March at various West End locations. More than 20 participants, including First Nations storytellers, spin tales in five different languages (translators come too) and hold audiences spellbound. ■ *876-2272.*

APRIL

Average daily maximum and minimum temperatures: 13°, 6°C (55°, 43°F). Average rainfall: 91 millimetres (3.5 inches).

Bradner Daffodil Festival Here's a chance to see 400 varieties of daffodils as well as geraniums and orchids at an old-fashioned, homegrown flower show. The 70-year-old festival is held the second week in April. The adjacent tearoom features true home cooking. ■ *Community Hall, Bradner; 856-2794.*

Brant Festival The annual Brant Festival celebrates the stopover of the brant (a species of geese) on their migration from Mexico to northern Canada. Staging areas provide fine opportunities to view the geese, once nearly extinct, as they feed. Wildlife art, photography exhibits, and carving competitions too. ■ *Parksville; (250) 248-4117.*

Taste of the Nation Eat and feed others. You'll find samples from 40 or so local restaurants and several wineries at this popular Share Our Strength benefit event, with entertainment and a silent auction too. Proceeds are distributed among selected charities. ■ *Hotel Vancouver; 691-7764; map:S3.*

TerrifVic Dixieland Jazz Festival Twenty Dixieland jazz bands from all over the world shake up the town for five days. Sixty dollars gets you an event badge good for every concert in every location. Shuttle service is available between participating hotels and the eight concert locations. ■ *Victoria; (250) 953-2011.*

Vancouver Canadians Baseball Play ball! See the future superstars of the major leagues at the greatest little ballpark in baseball. The Pacific Coast League Triple-A Canadians play April to September. ■ *Nat Bailey Stadium; 872-5232; map:D4.*

Vancouver Playhouse International Wine Festival (see March)

MAY

Average daily maximum and minimum temperatures: 16°, 9°C (61°, 48°F). Average rainfall: 76 millimetres (3 inches).

Cloverdale Rodeo The Lower Fraser Valley Exhibition Grounds attract competitors from around the world for one of this continent's largest rodeos. ■ *6050-176th St, Cloverdale; 576-9461.*

Hyack Festival The Hyack Anvil Battery, which has fired a "21-gun anvil" salute to the memory of Queen Victoria since 1871, gave today's festival its name. Hyack is a Chinook word meaning "hurry up." Highlights of the nine-day New Westminster festival include the May Day celebration, an international parade, sporting events, and fireworks. ■ *New Westminster; 522-6894.*

Music West One of Canada's biggest new-music events features four days of up-and-coming and internationally known alternative rock, hip-hop, punk, jazz, and folk acts playing at various downtown venues. A music industry convention and international skateboarding event take place at Music West's Plaza of Nations base. ■ *684-9338; map:U5.*

Swiftsure Race Weekend Held the weekend following Victoria Day, this event attracts boats from North America and foreign ports. Three races are held, the longest going west out the Strait of Juan de Fuca to the Pacific and back. Spectators can watch the vessels from Clover Point or Ogden Point. ■ *Royal Victoria Yacht Club, Victoria; (250) 592-2441.*

Vancouver International Children's Festival [KIDS] International theatre, music, dance, storytelling, and comedy for youngsters. Lots of hands-on activities, roving performers, games, arts, and crafts. Big-top tents on the lawns of Vanier Park at the entrance to False Creek. For kids, it's a winner. ■ *Vanier Park; 687-7697; map:O5-P5.*

Vancouver International Marathon An international field of runners sets out from the Plaza of Nations on the first Sunday in May for a 42-kilometre (26.2-mile) race that takes more than 4,000 runners through Stanley Park, across the Lions Gate Bridge, along the North Shore, back across the Second Narrows Bridge, and through East Vancouver to the finish line. A half-marathon and the Health and Fitness Expo take place in conjunction with the main event. ■ *872-2928.*

▼

▲

JUNE

Average daily maximum and minimum temperatures: 19°, 11°C (66°, 52°F). Average rainfall: 63 millimetres (2.5 inches).

Bard on the Beach From June through September, Bard on the Beach presents Shakespeare under a tent at Vanier Park. The company presents 78 performances with renowned actors in two plays each summer. Tickets go on sale in early April. ■ *737-0625; map:O5-P5.*

Brewmasters Festival A two-day celebration of suds, featuring brewers from all over the West. Talk to the brewers and industry reps and educate your palate with tasting, food and beer matching (beer and ice cream!), and food prepared with beer. A fundraiser for BC Sport and Fitness Council for the Disabled, it takes place in late June. ■ *Plaza of Nations; 290-4268; map:U5.*

Canadian International Dragon Boat Festival Vancouver's premier multicultural festival features dragon boat racing, entertainment, and food from around the Pacific Rim. ■ *Plaza of Nations; 688-2382; map:U5.*

du Maurier International Jazz Festival Vancouver Hundreds of jazz and blues artists from five continents perform during the two-week festival, presenting a full spectrum of traditional and contemporary jazz at various locations. ■ *Downtown area; 682-0706 or (888) GET-JAZZ.*

Kitsilano Soap Box Derby [FREE] [KIDS] Kids up to age 12 race hand-built soap box cars down a long Fourth Avenue hill and occasionally into the hay bales that line the course. Local merchants sponsor the cars, and the whole thing has a nice old-fashioned neighbourhood feeling. It takes place during Kits Days, usually the second or third Sunday of June. ■ *4th Ave between Balsam and Stevens; 731-4454; map:C2.*

Salmon Festival British Columbia is famous for its salmon, and Steveston, a traditional fishing village, is famous for its salmon festival. It's worth the 45-minute drive out of town to feast on barbecued salmon, clam chowder, and other treats. The Salmon Festival is the finale of special events held throughout June. ■ *Steveston; 277-6812.*

JULY

Average daily maximum and minimum temperatures: 22°, 13°C (72°, 55°F). Average rainfall: 50 millimetres (2 inches).

Canada Day [KIDS] July 1 is Canada Day and the biggest celebration is at Canada Place on the Coal Harbour waterfront. The family entertainment and activities go on all day and fireworks end the evening with a bang. The event is mostly free, with only a couple of mainstage concerts charging admission. ■ *Canada Place; 666-7200; map:U2.*

Caribbean Day Festival Enjoy a day of island music, food, dancing, and arts and crafts. ■ *Waterfront Park, Lonsdale Quay; 303-1455; map:E1.*

Dancing on the Edge The Firehall Arts Centre plays host to this almost-two-week annual festival of dance shows and workshops. However, free outdoor performances can also be viewed at various venues around the city. ■ *Firehall Arts Centre; 689-0691; map:V3.*

Harrison Festival of the Arts During this nine-day event, more than 35,000 people visit Harrison Hot Springs to celebrate the musical, visual, and performing arts of a different set of countries each year. Theatres, lectures, workshops, and live entertainment give visitors many activities from which to choose. ■ *Harrison Hot Springs; 796-3425.*

Italian Week The Italian community offers pasta, parades, marvelous coffee, games, and many more activities for one week in early July. The city's Italian area is famous for its cosmopolitan flavour and great food. ■ *Commercial Dr; 430-3337; map:Z3-Z7.*

Symphony of Fire [FREE] [KIDS] Pyrotechnicians from around the world compete in an extravaganza of fireworks set off from a barge on English Bay before thousands of people. On four nonconsecutive nights beginning the last Saturday in July. ■ *English Bay; 688-1992; map:N1-O5.*

Theatre under the Stars (TUTS) Amid the towering trees of Stanley Park, community theatre actors perform two Broadway plays each July and August in repertory—rain or shine. ■ *Malkin Bowl; 687-0174; map:Q1.*

Vancouver Chamber Music Festival Leila Getz's tradition of presenting the best of young, budding artists during the summer months has made the Chamber Music Festival one of the hottest tickets in town. In a relaxed, casual setting, concerts are held during the last week of July and the first week of August. Each of the six concerts features a cast of superb soloists, who combine their talents to offer a wonderful menu of chamber music. ■ *Crofton House School for Girls; 3200 W 41st Ave; 602-0363; map:C4.*

Vancouver Early Music Festival Running from mid-July to mid-August, the concert series features music from the Middle Ages to the classical era performed on period instruments. ■ *UBC Recital Hall; 732-1610; map:A2.*

Vancouver Folk Music Festival [KIDS] Travel around the world in 2½ days, aurally. The third weekend in July, the United Nations of the folk music world gathers at Jericho Beach Park, a spectacular setting for a spectacular celebration of music, heritage, and folklore. Over the festival's 16-year history, an amazing diversity of performers has made this event one of the best music festivals anywhere. The heart and soul of the festival are the various themed workshops held on six separate stages throughout the day. Evenings are devoted to music making, with one mainstage holding the limelight. An alcohol-free event, the festival also stages a little-folks' festival that includes water play, face painting, crafts, and great food. Throughout the year, the festival also hosts independent concerts at various venues. ■ *Jericho Beach Park; 602-9798; map:B2.*

Vancouver International Comedy Festival Featuring an eclectic and diverse mixture of comic artists, the festival stretches over nearly two full weeks, from the end of July to early August. Headliners perform at local theatres and comedy clubs, but there's plenty of free entertainment at outdoor stages. ■ *Granville Island; 683-0883; map:Q6.*

Whistler Country and Blues Festival The third weekend in July enjoy the sounds of country, blues, rockabilly, and zydeco onstage at Whistler. Don't miss the Whistler Chili Cook-off! ■ *Whistler; 664-5625.*

Whistler Roots Festival A three-day mosaic of roots music from around the world—bluegrass and banghra, Cajun and Celtic, and more. Roots food cook-offs as well, and a rockin' party. Look for the festival on a weekend in late July. ■ *Whistler Village; 664-5625.*

AUGUST

Average daily maximum and minimum temperatures: 22°, 14°C (72°, 57°F). Average rainfall: 48 millimetres (2 inches).

Abbotsford International Airshow/Airshow Canada Want to see a Stealth bomber up close or watch wing-walkers defy gravity? How about the aerobatics of the U.S. Thunderbirds and the Canadian Snowbirds? Abbotsford's International Airshow has it all and more. Airshow Canada is a trade show that happens in odd-numbered years. ■ *Abbotsford Airport; 857-1142.*

Fine Arts Show Southern Vancouver Island artists display their paintings and sculptures in the largest juried art show and sale in BC. A $6 admission is good for the entire 10-day event. ■ *Sooke Region Museum, Sooke; (250) 642-6351.*

Pacific National Exhibition The second-largest annual summer exhibition in Canada. It features big-name musical entertainment, livestock displays, equestrian events, arts and crafts, and amusement rides. (Will move after 1997.) ■ *Hastings St at Renfrew St; 253-2311; map:F2.*

Powell Street Festival This is one of the city's largest ethnic festivals, held every year in early August. A celebration of Japanese-Canadian history, arts, and culture, the festival provides a fascinating range of events and experiences, including sumo wrestling, exotic foods, martial arts, theatre, and dancers performing traditional dances in delightful costumes. ■ *Oppenheimer Park, Powell St; 682-4335; map:W3.*

Street Fare [FREE] The buskers of the world unite for a three-day festival of eclectic entertainment on the sidewalks surrounding the Vancouver Art Gallery and Robson Square. ■ *685-7811; map:S4.*

Under the Volcano Festival A one-day independent festival of arts and music on the shores of Deep Cove and Burrard Inlet in North Vancouver's Cates Park, which was once home to Malcolm Lowry, author of *Under the Volcano*. Admission by donation. ■ *980-3559; map:H1.*

Average daily maximum and minimum temperatures: 18°, 8°C (64°, 46°F). Average rainfall: 69 millimetres (2.7 inches).

Feast of Fields A mid-September celebration of the harvest featuring some of BC's best chefs, brewers, and vintners. Held at a different Fraser Valley farm each year, Feast of Fields is a benefit for the Farm Folk/City Folk society, a charity that promotes healthy, safe, and sustainable agriculture. ■ *730-0450.*

Fringe Vancouver Theatre Festival An 11-day alternative theatre festival featuring close to 100 productions of original works and classics by local, national, and international artists. ■ *Commercial Drive area; 873-3646; map:Z3-Z7.*

Molson Indy Vancouver For three action-packed days on Labour Day weekend, a world-class field of racing superstars thunders through the streets of Vancouver in wheel-to-wheel combat to decide who is Indy Car's best on the challenging 2.6-kilometre (1.6-mile) circuit. ■ *Concord Pacific Place; 684-4639; map:Q5-V6.*

Terry Fox Run Every September, hundreds of thousands of people around the world walk, run, bike, and blade 1 to 10 kilometres (.62 to 6.2 miles) to raise funds for cancer research in memory of Terry Fox. He began his Marathon of Hope Run across Canada in 1980 but had to stop after cancer spread to his lungs. ■ *Terry Fox Run Foundation; 464-2666.*

Tri-City Children's Festival [KIDS] Musical shows, hands-on activities, storytelling, clowns, and more delight and fascinate children of all ages! The fun begins the second weekend in September and goes for two days. ■ *Town Centre, Lafarge Lake, Coquitlam; 931-8821; map:L3.*

Vancouver Recital Society Internationally celebrated artists perform on various dates throughout the September to May season. ■ *Orpheum Theatre; 602-0363; map:S4.*

Whistler Jazz and Blues Festival The Pacific Northwest's premier jazz and blues acts perform at the mainstage and more intimate venues throughout the Village on a mid-month weekend. ■ *Whistler Village; 664-5625.*

Whistler Street Fest Since 1986, Whistler has hosted the cream of street entertainers on the Labour Day weekend. Musicians, comedians, jugglers, prestidigitators, and those who defy definition cap the summer season with nonstop entertainment. ■ *Whistler Village; 664-5625.*

Word on the Street Word on the Street is the annual one-day celebration of the written word held in and around the Vancouver Public Library's main branch on the final Sunday of September. Publishers and authors display, and even demonstrate, their wares. Similar events happen simultaneously in Toronto and Halifax. ▪ *Library Square; 331-3600 or 323-7148, map:T4.*

World Championship Sand Sculpture Competition On the second weekend in September, thirty master sculptors build 150 sand creations on the Main Beach at Harrison Hot Springs. As many as 25,000 spectators show up to view the masterpieces and see who will win $20,000 worth of prize money. ▪ *Main Beach, Harrison Hot Springs; 796-3425.*

OCTOBER

Average daily maximum and minimum temperatures: 14°, 4°C (57°, 39°F). Average rainfall: 158 millimetres (6 inches).

International Writers and Readers Festival This five-day event during the third week of October brings together more than 50 Canadian and international authors, playwrights, and poets from diverse cultural backgrounds, life experiences, and places of origin, writing in every conceivable genre. Readings, interviews, and a poetry bash are informative, challenging, and entertaining. ▪ *Granville Island; 681-6330; map:Q6.*

Masterpiece Chamber Music A season of romantic masterpieces is presented from October to April. Call for performance dates. ▪ *Vancouver East Cultural Centre; 254-9578; map:E2.*

Vancouver International Film Festival Similar to film fests held in Seattle and Toronto, this event at the beginning of October features more than 250 films from 40 countries. Order tickets beginning in mid-September. ▪ *Downtown area; 685-0260.*

NOVEMBER

Average daily maximum and minimum temperatures: 9°, 2°C (48°, 36°F). Average rainfall: 235 millimetres (9 inches).

Hadassah Bazaar The first Wednesday of November, the Jewish community puts on a giant fund-raising flea market, with gently used and new clothing, books, household items, commercial exhibitors, and Jewish and international foods, as well as a fashion auction, silent auction, and giant auction. ▪ *PNE Food Building (will move after 1997); 257-5160; map:F2.*

Vancouver Cantata Singers The four-concert season offers performance dates from November to March. ▪ *Orpheum; 921-8588; map:S4.*

Average daily maximum and minimum temperatures: 7°, 4°C (45°, 39°F). Average rainfall: 243 millimetres (9.5 inches).

Christmas Carol Ships Parade [FREE] [KIDS] Carollers sail around the harbour on brightly lit boats accompanied by a flotilla of charter vessels carrying holiday revellers. ▪ *Vancouver Harbour; 682-2007; map:S1-Z2.*

Christmas under the Sails [KIDS] For the last three weeks of December, Canada Place gets into the spirit, creating a forest of beautifully decorated trees and an animated world of Christmas behind glass. Admission is by donation, with partial proceeds going to local children's charities. Santa is also on hand for consultation. ▪ *Canada Place; 666-8477; map:T2.*

VanDusen Botanical Garden Festival of Lights [KIDS] At Christmastime the gardens are transformed into a twinkling fairyland by 15,000 lights. There are also holiday events and special displays to help set the seasonal mood. ▪ *37th and Oak St; 878-9274; map:D4.*

▼

Calendar

▲

Index

Satisfaction Guaranteed

We stand by our reviews. Co-publishers Sasquatch Books and Raincoast Books are proud of *Vancouver Best Places*. Our editors and contributors go to great lengths and expense to see that all of the reviews are as accurate, up-to-date, and honest as possible. If we have disappointed you, please accept our apologies; however, if this second edition of *Vancouver Best Places* has seriously misled you, we the publishers would like to refund your purchase price. To receive your refund:

1) Tell us where you purchased your book and return the book and the book-purchase receipt to the appropriate address below.

2) Enclose the original hotel or restaurant receipt from the establishment in question, including date of visit.

3) Write a full explanation of your stay or meal and how *Vancouver Best Places* misled you.

4) Include your name, address, and phone number.

Refund is valid only while this second edition of *Vancouver Best Places* is in print. If the ownership has changed since publication, Sasquatch Books and Raincoast Books cannot be held responsible. Postage and tax on the returned book is your responsibility. Please allow six to eight weeks for processing.

Please address to Satisfaction Guaranteed, *Vancouver Best Places*, and send to the publisher in your country of origin:

SASQUATCH BOOKS

RAINCOAST BOOKS

Vancouver

Sasquatch Books
615 Second Avenue, Suite 260
Seattle, WA 98104
U.S.A.
e-mail: books@sasquatchbooks.com

Raincoast Books
8680 Cambie Street
Vancouver, BC V6P 6M9
Canada
e-mail: info@raincoast.com

Vancouver Best Places
REPORT FORM

Based on my personal experience, I wish to nominate the following restaurant, place of lodging, shop, nightspot, sight, or other as a "Best Place"; or confirm/correct/disagree with the current review.

_____

_____

_____

_____

Please include address and telephone number of establishment, if convenient.

REPORT:

Please describe food, service, style, comfort, value, date of visit, and other aspects of your experience; continue on a separate sheet of paper if necessary.

_____

_____

_____

_____

_____

I am not concerned, directly or indirectly, with the management or ownership of this establishment.

Signed _____

Name (please print) _____

Address _____

_____

_____

Phone Number _____

Date _____

Please address to:
Vancouver Best Places
and send to :

Sasquatch Books
615 Second Avenue, Suite 260
Seattle, WA 98104
U.S.A.
e-mail: books@sasquatchbooks.com